Standard for Auditing Computer Applications

Martin A. Krist

CRC Press
Taylor & Francis Group
Boca Raton London New York

CRC Press is an imprint of the
Taylor & Francis Group, an **informa** business
AN AUERBACH BOOK

CRC Press
Taylor & Francis Group
6000 Broken Sound Parkway NW, Suite 300
Boca Raton, FL 33487-2742

First issued in hardback 2018

© 1999 by Taylor & Francis Group, LLC
CRC Press is an imprint of Taylor & Francis Group, an Informa business

No claim to original U.S. Government works

ISBN 13: 978-1-138-43693-0 (hbk)
ISBN 13: 978-0-8493-9983-1 (pbk)

Visit the Taylor & Francis Web site at
http://www.taylorandfrancis.com

and the CRC Press Web site at
http://www.crcpress.com

Library of Congress Cataloging-in-Publication Data

Catalog record is available from the Library of Congress.

Contents

Contents

Contents

Contents

Contents

Contents

Introduction

Technology is widely perceived as having permanently changed the business environment that we once knew. Yet there is a basic idea that appears immobile against this irresistible technological force: companies that deliver more true value to the customer survive.

The audit function continues to provide assurance services to internal and external customers. External audit fees may continue to fall under competitive press uses, while internal audit staff sizes may continue to shrink in concert with the constant movement toward a leaner organization and increasing shareholder value, but the questions to be answered are not similarly diminished.

If we take a revenue cycle perspective, then we might consider the following questions:

1. Do we enter into agreements or accept orders with adequate margins to meet our ultimate shareholder obligations?
2. Do we effectively acquire or produce goods or deliver services in a timely manner?
3. Do we collect the amounts due to the company in an effective manner?[1]
4. Are the collected amounts booked properly to customer, account, amount, and period?

Technology's impact is in the answers, not the questions. Therefore, we should assert that they continue to be asked and answered on some periodic basis. This guide to evaluating controls in today's AASs is intended to facilitate highly effective reviews of these controls.

The prior main volume of SACA was oriented more toward the general or financial auditor than toward the IT auditor. This volume was built on the assumption that most, if not all, of the potential issues should be raised for discussion.

The need to include the entire audit community is clearly reflected in the continuing growth of the Information Systems Audit and Control Association and in the significant percentage of the Institute of Internal Auditors resources, courses, and column inches devoted to technology issues. These comments are not intended to further the debate over IIA issues ISACA. We are trying to highlight the internal audit reality that almost every review done places some reliance on an application and the hardware that supports it.

The 1998 edition of SACA includes more workpapers dedicated to specific applications and systems, while always returning at least one fully generic workpaper set to facilitate each subscriber's customization requirements. There are even alternative formats for a simple type of workpaper like an audit program. This was done to reflect differences between internal auditors, their situations, their needs, and their preferences.

This volume is divided into five main parts. First is an overview of the issues potentially inherent in any AAS review. Second is a review of the audit planning process. Third is a guide to evaluating the general controls that determine the reliability of the underlying hardware and operating environment. Fourth is an approach for evaluating the process used to develop new AASs, along with the logic for applying that process knowledge to evaluating the basic development process or to the actual development of a single AAS. Last are the procedures for evaluating an AAS that is already in a production environment.

There are also things discussed which the auditor must guard against, whether an IT, financial, operational, or other. Some of those items are listed below:

1. Presuming that automated solutions are always preferable to manual ones
2. Believing that an AAS will process a transaction the same way every time
3. Ever concluding that an AAS's input controls result in the entry of correct data, as automated input controls can only determine validity[2]
4. Building a correlation apparent and actual behavior[3]
5. Concluding that anyone can audit any technical control area; the auditor must recognize the potential to be out of their depth in a particular review, and to call for technical expertise when necessary.

Fully indexed files are included on the enclosed CD so that any item that may be useful can be readily accessed. Where appropriate, logical relationships have been established between the forms, such as audit programs and working papers.

Notes

1. This author uses the term "effective" under the premise that efficient is a necessary, but not sufficient, condition of anything that might be considered effective.
2. The distinction being made here may not seem significant when it is. The auditor must understand that almost every field where data is entered has more than one possible valid value. If there were only one valid value,

why would anyone have to enter it? Data relationships may be established to reduce the number of valid customer-product combinations, for example, although this only increases the probability that the data entered is correct. It never guarantees it.

3. The author was involved in a review with the external auditors, who recommend a new feature for a system to address the potential risk that certain end users responsible for reacting to exception reports were not actually doing so. The external auditors wanted to program a digital sign-off that would require each of these users to "click" that box each day to indicate their review procedure was completed. When they were reminded that the end user could simply click without reviewing anything (at a development cost exceeding $40,000 USD), they insisted that having to click that box would cause them to review the exception reports. Readers are welcome to reach their own conclusion. The author was dubious.

Part I
Overview of Integrated Auditing

Ten years ago, the internal auditor encountered an automated application system in almost every internal control review performed. Today's IT auditors and financial auditors expect to find automation, and are often concerned when they do not. This book is intended to meet the needs of both the technical and general auditor. The auditing models include basic and advanced technical subjects, along with generic and tailored approaches for evaluating IT security and control issues. This volume speaks to the IT auditor, while recognizing that many general auditors are also conducting technical reviews.

AUTOMATED APPLICATION REVIEW OVERVIEW

IT auditors face several challenges when auditing automated applications. First, the IT auditor must understand the environment in which the applications are developed and operated. Stronger environmental controls reduce the potential risk for every application operating within that environment (see Part I). Second, the increasing complexity of automated applications demands that the IT auditor employ an equally effective approach. An effective audit process is almost certain to result in unidentified vulnerabilities.

IT auditors often work with a self-assessment questionnaire to help evaluate the problems faced when auditing automated applications. The self-assessment questionnaire often brings two major benefits. First, it can help to change the environment. The IT manager completes the self-assessment questionnaire, normally identifying potential control risks before the audit even begins. The more capable IT managers can then begin to take corrective action immediately, having performed their own audit. The IT auditor may choose to reward this response by refraining from proposing an unnecessary recommendation whose only purpose is to overstate the auditor's success.

Second, the IT auditor can leverage the IT staff's experience and local knowledge by having them complete a self-assessment questionnaire. The time required to interview the staff to obtain and document environmental information is freed up for substantive procedures to confirm and evaluate that the control structure weaknesses exist; the auditor should look for compensating controls. If there are no compensating controls, the IT auditor may need to expand the audit scope to compensate for those control weaknesses. The IT auditor can also use the self-assessment questionnaire data to determine the staffing requirements for the detailed portion of the review.

Section 1
What Integrated Application Systems Are

The environmental controls that support automated computer applications are collectively referred to as general controls. If the general controls are inadequate, the IT auditor normally cannot rely on application controls, regardless of how effective they may appear to be. This section explains how an IT department should operate and identifies the critical general control factors that form the basis of the self-assessment presented.

PROPER OPERATION OF THE IT DEPARTMENT

The auditor should review two key elements to determine the effectiveness of management control: the organizational structure of the department and IT's position within the overall corporate structure. The IT department should maintain an appropriate level of management independence from the departments or customers that it services, and a level of internal segregation of duties for effective internal controls.

The IT department should also maintain open lines of communication with its customers. The IT manager should ensure that a written organization plan exists that specifically defines the lines of authority and the responsibilities for each position. This plan should facilitate communication, promote operational efficiency, and support the segregation of duties.

IT Organization

The IT department must be an integral part of the overall company structure. IT managers should report to the highest possible level in the company. Ideally, the information technology department should be an independent unit to ensure the proper mix of authority and communication between IT and its customers. A steering committee is normally formed to facilitate that communication (see discussion of IT steering committee later in this chapter).

The board of directors sets policies, and should be familiar with strategic IT department activities; however, they do not need to be technically proficient in IT concepts. Senior management ensures that the board's policies are followed and that the IT department is meeting the needs of the organization. IT management supervises the department's daily activities, which requires a high level of technical proficiency.

Organization Charts

The IT auditor can determine the relationship of the IT department to other departments by reviewing an organization chart. Effective organization charts graphically describe position titles and illustrate the interrelationships and reporting requirements among the various functions. This chart should be distributed to employees to enhance their knowledge of the organization and the lines of communication within it. Responsibility overlaps may become apparent while reviewing the organization charts. Any exceptions such as programmers who are also security officers should be questioned.

Furthermore, small, medium-sized, and large IT departments have inherently different characteristics and their organization charts should reflect these differences. The IT auditor should normally find IT departments that are sized in proportion to the company, but cannot assume this to be the case.

The Small IT Department. Exhibit 1-1 represents the IT department in a small company with an in-house computer. The IT department provides a variety of IT services to other departments in the company, but programming activities are limited. Occasionally, the software vendor provides program updates and corrections. Other possible characteristics include no internal programming function, no IT management function, no formal periodic communication, and no segregation of duties.

The Medium-Sized IT Department. Exhibit 1-2 represents the IT department in a larger organization. In this type of organization, communication is usually more formal due to the increased customer base and the additional coordination required to convey information to senior management and the board of directors. Systems development and programming may be an in-house function, or it may be outsourced, The medium-sized IT department

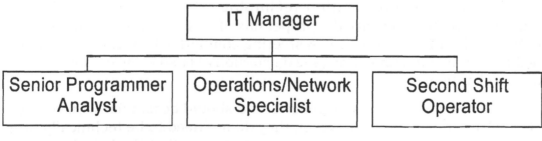

Exhibit 1-1. Organization Chart: Small IT Department

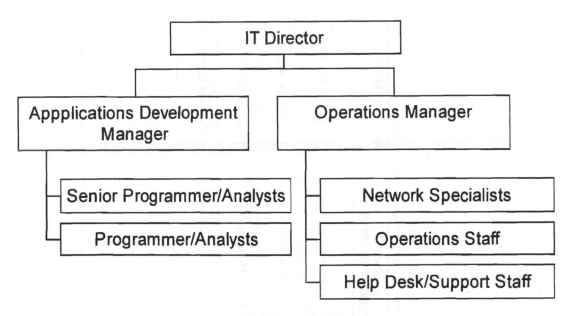

Exhibit 1-2. Organization Chart: Medium IT Department

normally has an increased segregation of duties, although not sufficiently segregated to warrant reliance.

The Large IT Department. Exhibit 1-3 represents IT departments that range from large to the very largest. This department should have detailed organization charts and position descriptions. It also should have specific committees and regularly scheduled management meetings to enhance communication and monitor activities. The segregation of duties should be adequate for the IT auditor to conclude that reliance may be warranted. One interesting feature of large departments is that they often have effective controls in place. If they did not, they would have almost constant problems due to the lack of coordination and structure.

Position Descriptions

Responsibilities should be defined for each IT function. IT management determines what functions are required based on the department's size and complexity, and spreads out responsibilities across the actual functions. One method of defining responsibility is through job descriptions. Written job descriptions communicate areas of responsibility, accountability, and reporting authority. They also provide an objective means of measuring job performance because employees who know what is expected of them can be evaluated against their job description. Job positions, descriptions, and terminology can vary considerably among organizations. Therefore, the following descriptions should be used only as examples when reviewing the positions within an IT department.

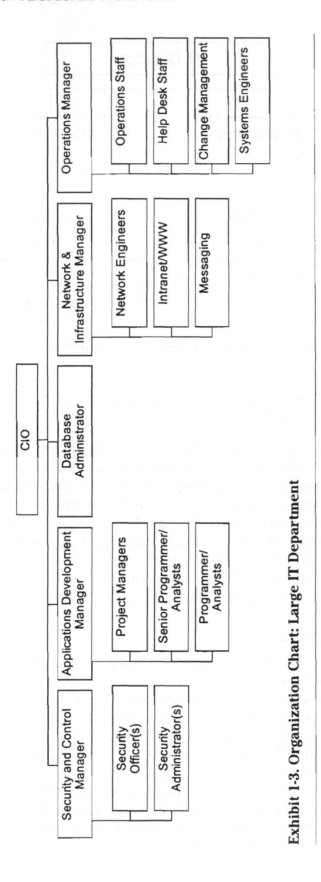

Exhibit 1-3. Organization Chart: Large IT Department

Data Processing Manager. This individual plans, organizes, leads, and controls the overall activities of the IT department, including systems analysis and programming and computer operations; consults, advises, and coordinates between the IT area and customer departments; and reports to senior management on IT plans, projects, performance, and related matters. The IT manager may also choose to have assistant managers who have line rather than staff responsibility. Their functions may be technical or administrative, with each reporting to the manager or another assistant manager.

Operations Manager. This individual coordinates the daily activity of the data center; monitors current production to assure adherence to pre-established schedules; redirects work flow in cases of processing interruptions; and provides for cross-training and rotation of personnel.

Computer Operator. This individual operates hardware according to instructions detailed within the run manual. This person may also support application processing based on similar documentation. Operators should not perform any programming or librarian functions and should only have access to documentation necessary to run a given program, if the department is large enough to support full segregation of duties.

File Librarian. This individual is responsible for the physical control and safekeeping of the data centers online and offline storage of programs and data. This person is responsible for accurate disk inventories, maintains accurate records of library activities, and ensures that any remote backup library contains appropriate files and has appropriate physical access security.

Input Preparation and Output Control Personnel. These once-common positions have largely vanished from today's IT departments. They have been replaced by end users empowered to input data directly, automated data acquisition equipment, etc.

Input Preparation Personnel. The individuals who perform the following tasks:

- The Proof Operator reviews the batch for possible errors and confirms or prepares the appropriate control totals.
- The Data Entry Operator inputs the batch in anticipation of its processing by an application.

Output Control Personnel. The output staff is divided into the following two categories:

- The Reconciliation Staff validates accuracy of transactions, reconciles all output, prepares rejected/nonreader items for reentry, and completes the reconciliation forms.

- The Distribution Staff ensures that output is routed and distributed to assigned destinations and decollates and bursts output in accordance with operating instructions.

Application Development Manager. This individual coordinates overall activities of the programmer/analysts; is responsible for programming and other departmental procedures; and is responsible for administrative tasks that might include measurement of progress relative to predetermined goals.

Application Programmer/Analyst. This individual has two types of responsibility that were commonly separate in the past. First, this individual analyzes requirements for information, evaluates the existing system and designs or revises procedures for accomplishing the activity, and designs program logic, application system flowcharts, and narratives. Once the design is complete, this individual creates and modifies programs and program documentation, tests the new or changed programs, and corrects errors in logic or coding.

Systems Programmer/Analyst. This person is responsible for the same tasks as an Application Programmer/Analyst, except that the System P/A is responsible for developing overhead programs that, although necessary for the computer equipment to function, do not directly perform an application task (e.g., generating sales invoices). This person may also maintain management routines, database systems, and large communication networks, and develop programs that monitor and measure the performance of application programs.

Technical Support Personnel. These individuals act as liaisons with manufacturers, software support personnel (customer engineers), applications programmers, and systems analysts.

Network Services Support Personnel. These individuals act as liaisons with software support and operations personnel to ensure a proper and effective online communications network.

Database Administrator. This individual acts as the coordinator for any requests to change the database structure, to delete data elements, or modify access to the database. This person is also responsible for organization and effectiveness of the logical access security established to protect the data in the databases.

Quality Control and Assurance Personnel. These individuals serve in a review capacity as an adjunct to project development, but do not direct systems development efforts. They are responsible for reviewing the progress of systems development projects to determine conformity to the organization's standards and procedures. These individuals also assist in developing and evaluating the effectiveness of the IT processes and manage most quality control programs.

Planning

The IT planning process should be fully integrated into the company's planning process. The complexity of any formal plan varies significantly, depending on the size of the organization. All plans must, however, meet the organization's needs. The formalized planning process involves developing written plans, having them approved by company management, and distributing them as needed.

It is imperative that IT management include senior management and user management in the planning process. The board of directors, individually and collectively, has legal responsibility for the continuity of the organization's operations. Senior managers ultimately implement all strategic plans and, therefore, must be active participants in the planning. User management either requests changes or is impacted by changes requested by others, which is why they also must participate in regular planning activities.

The plan is likely to consist of short- and long-range elements. Short-range elements span one year or less. Long-range elements usually cover at least one to as many as five years. IT management should perform regular comparisons of budget to actual results, just as senior and end-user management do, because periodic revisions to the plan may be required.

The plans produced by this planning process should always include the following items, along with any others relevant to a particular situation:

- *Applications software*—should focus on the maintenance or changes that will ensure that business requirements are satisfied in an effective manner.
- *System software*—should focus on providing the most efficient environment to reliably support the application software.
- *Hardware*—should focus on acquiring and maintaining the equipment needed to support the software environment consistently and cost-effectively.
- *Personnel*—should focus on acquiring and retaining the individuals to support the in-place hardware and software.
- *Budget*—should focus on accurately portraying the resources required to support the plan. These resources may include, but are not limited to, the potential costs for new applications software, new equipment, and staffing changes.

The IT Steering Committee

Many companies have a management group that is responsible for overseeing IT department activities. This group may bear one of various titles: IT steering committee, IT operations committee, etc. The committee should include corporate senior managers, select end-user managers, and IT managers. The internal audit department should also participate, although only in an advisory capacity.

These managers do not have to be department heads but should be knowledgeable about policies and procedures. They should also have the authority to speak for, and make decisions affecting, the areas they represent. The committee should not become directly involved with daily operations, and the duties and responsibilities of the committee should be clearly defined in a formal charter. Such committees typically:

- Recommend major capital expenditures
- Approve major projects
- Monitor progress against tactical and strategic plans
- Compare budgeted to actual expenditures.

The IT Steering Committee should solicit information from all the areas served by the IT department, including the audit department to effectively monitor IT departmental activities. The committee also works to ensure that expected results are achieved by taking whatever action is necessary. The IT steering committee meetings should be documented in minutes, not only as a record of the proceedings and decisions but to inform management of various IT activities.

Control

The reason that corporate senior management wants IT management to develop and implement effective controls is to ensure that business objectives are met on an accurate, timely, and complete basis. The company needs to be able to rely on the IT department. The following is a discussion of key elements needed to implement effective controls.

Policies and Procedures. Formal written standards and procedures are essential to establishing and maintaining control. Written standards promote uniform policy implementation and support new employees orientation. IT management must provide individual groups within the IT department with operational policies. These policies should give each group the guidelines needed to effectively coordinate and perform their jobs. IT policies and procedures can be established in a variety of areas, including the following:

- Applications development
- Naming conventions
- Special request handling
- Data security
- Physical security
- Use of consultants
- Contingency plan development and testing

These standards and procedures support the segregation of duties, limit physical and electronic access to valuable assets, and provide for the efficient and effective allocation of resources. Procedures should provide audit trails to ensure that independent control is exercised by the user departments.

Internal Controls. The American Institute of Certified Public Accountants has defined these as "the plan of organization and all of the coordinate methods and measures adopted within a business to safeguard its assets, check the accuracy and reliability of its accounting data, promote operational efficiency, and encourage adherence to prescribed managerial policies." In the past, accounting systems were clearly segregated from the daily business cycle. Financial auditors had become accustomed to situations where, once a month, information from sales, accounts receivable, accounts payable, inventory, etc. was posted to the ledger in the form of a summary ledger. This led to the conceptual separation of accounting controls from operational controls.

The continuing integration of these two control groups is evident when today's auditors look at the general ledger and see the details of every sale, every purchase, etc. The following list of six controls represent three former accounting controls and three former operational controls that must be considered together in an integrated environment.

- Authorization
- Numerical sequencing
- Dual control
- Processing efficiency
- Policy compliance
- Asset safeguarding

Statistical Reporting. This is the next logical step in the control process. IT management has numerous opportunities to gather and summarize statistical data that measures overall IT department performance. Reporting can be separated into three areas: data center operations, applications development, and administration. The scope, frequency, and sophistication of such reporting varies greatly depending on the size and nature of the installation. IT personnel should review the raw data that is, or could be, easily generated, looking for elements that could be summarized into useful information.

Automatic logging generally produces data that can be summarized by a job accounting system or an audit retrieval program. The summarized data may be used to produce statistical reports. In addition, project management software may also be used to summarize data for application development activities.

A total list of all possible statistical reports may be lengthy and contain many diverse options, depending on the hardware and software being used. Examples of statistical reports are:

- Reruns per period by application and total runtime
- Incident or failure reports per period
- Overtime hours by functional area
- Missed checkpoints per period
- Programmer/analyst time by development project
- Terminal response time
- Percentage of downtime per period
- Special report runs per period

IT management must decide on the best reports to be used in monitoring data center operations. The reporting period varies with anticipated usage. Although middle management may review weekly or monthly statistics, first-line supervisors may need data daily in many areas. Senior management and the IT steering committee may require monthly or quarterly statistics, reduced to graphic format. Typically, senior management reports compare projections with actual performance and prior periods with current performance. This is as valid for statistical analysis as it is for financial budget vs. actual vs. prior reporting.

Variance Analysis. The next step is to understand significant differences in these reports and respond to them. In this instance, significance should be deferred in both technical and financial terms. Standard cost/benefit analysis should be prepared whenever a meaningful change is considered. Please note that cost in these instances should include the cash expenditures along with the internal opportunity cost of the project. The IT auditor should also always remember that the direct responsibility for IT controls lies with IT management, and ultimate responsibility with company senior management.

Both internal and external IT auditors should perform IT reviews that are independent, measure performance, and provide and assess the adequacy of policies and procedures. This provides management with an impartial evaluation of the IT department's condition. IT audit reports should cite exceptions and recommend corrective action. The IT auditors then must follow up to ensure that corrective action has been taken. In addition, IT and senior management must review and follow up on recommendations made in audit reports.

DEVELOPING AUTOMATED APPLICATIONS

Applications development encompasses numerous tasks and multiple phases that are characterized by the nature of the work and deliverables produced. Over time, IT professionals have concluded that there are a set of basic steps that are common to all development methodologies. These steps are called the Systems Development Life Cycle (SDLC). IT management in each company needs to define and implement an SDLC methodology that is consistent with the organization's needs. The IT auditor should be aware that any effective SDLC methodology will include at least three decision points. At each decision point, the appropriate managers should assess progress and performance and, if necessary, reevaluate, reschedule, or terminate the project.

Decision Points

The SDLC methodology should include at least three phases that are consistently followed for all applications development projects in the company. The three minimum phases are the requirements definition, program development and testing, and implementation. In other sections of this book, these three minimum phases will be broken down into more discrete phases, but these additional phases will not normally apply to all IT departments, while the three-phase approach does.

The standard phasing of key activities provides a structured approach for applications development and a systematic framework for management control. IT management should establish procedures for maintaining projects that are closely aligned with the SDLC methodology. Pertinent information summarizing performance vs. plan along with information that changes or contradicts the overall project plan should be summarized in a written deliverable at the end of each phase. This documentation gives IT management the information needed to make effective decisions. Generally, each phase should be complete, and a formal decision made to proceed before the next phase begins.

CRITICAL INFORMATION TECHNOLOGY CONTROLS

The IT auditor will learn that there are many ways to group general and application controls based on the company, the business the company is in, how technology is employed to do business, etc.

When in doubt, the IT auditor should be able to consider any situation at the most basic level, which only has two groupings.

- What technology is already available in this situation?
- How is that technology being used?

The IT auditors able to answer these two questions will be able to respond to any specific question or issue, either because they will already have the answer or know what has to be done to get the answer. One way to group these control issues follows.

Strategic Plan

Individual IT projects must be planned and carried out consistently with the IT department's strategic plan. A strategic plan should ensure that new and existing applications will meet the company's current and future needs. IT decision makers who have access to high-quality strategic information are likely to make decisions that ensure compatibility between hardware and software, prevent duplication by different systems in collecting and producing information, and clearly define individual projects. The plan can help IT decision makers to resolve difficult choices and provide a framework for assessing and prioritizing the unexpected items that always seem to arise.

Senior management must support the IT strategic plan for it to be successful. The Board of Directors may choose to handle IT directly by forming an IT Steering Committee and delegating its responsibility. The IT manager often oversees the strategic plan development and suggests priorities for the various tactical projects. Senior management then reviews the plan, decides whether changes are needed, and approves a final strategic plan. Senior management should meet regularly to monitor progress against the plan and reevaluate the plan as necessary.

Management Commitment

Management at all levels needs to provide support to approved projects to help ensure their successful completion. This commitment includes assigning a competent project manager and ensuring participation by all staff members who will use the system or whose work will be affected by the project. Management should also strive to keep the same personnel in critical positions throughout a project to ensure accountability and timely completion.

Senior management too often believes that when a project is turned over to an outside contractor, everything is under control. Even with a contractor, a complex application requires substantial effort from internal staff. IT personnel, end users, and others must spend considerable time away from their regular duties to communicate their detailed requirements to the contractor. A certain amount of time will also be needed to monitor and review the contractor's work.

Contracting Process

Organizations often contract with consulting firms for systems acquisition and development services. Management must be familiar with the various laws, regulations, and legal decisions that affect contracting services. Companies must also determine whether a fixed price, cost-plus, or hourly rate contract is more appropriate, the most appropriate type of contract for the situation (e.g., fixed-price or cost-plus-fixed-fee), ensure that contract specifications are sufficiently detailed, and exercise care when evaluating bids.

Basic Features

IT and financial managers should ensure that planned automated applications include the following:

- Automated controls to help ensure the accuracy and reliability of data being input and reports being produced
- Controls to physically safeguard the computer hardware and all storage media
- Controls to logically safeguard the data in the applications and system from a loss of privacy or unauthorized changes
- Audit trails that allow transactions to be traced to the responsible end user
- Flexible inquiry capability to aid in meeting ad hoc needs
- Recording transactions only once
- Automatic matching of related transactions
- Controlled manual procedures needed to correct errors in automatic processing and to handle transactions that defy automatic handling

SDLC Methodology

Applications developed in-house, purchased from software vendors, and acquired freely from the public can be managed through an effective SDLC methodology. A proven methodology is an essential tool in developing high-quality applications. An SDLC methodology is a formal, structured approach to development that outlines and describes sequentially and in substantial technical depth all phases, tasks, and considerations necessary for a successful project.

A methodology provides a framework for ensuring that each development phase is carefully planned, controlled, and approved; that the project complies with standards; that the phases are adequately documented; and that assigned project personnel are competent. Most consulting firms have developed or adopted a systems methodology for their projects. To be fully effective, a systems methodology should take into account all of the critical factors discussed here.

The SDLC methodology should outline the planning, budgeting, and acquisition of the application, including the staff and skills needed to support the system, the space and facilities to house the people and equipment, and the procedures to convert to the new application. An effective methodology ensures that massive and complex projects are carried out segment by segment. Each phase must be completed before the project moves to the next phase. The IT auditor should recognize that certain tasks may begin before a phase is approved, but these should be the exception and not the rule.

Target Dates

Project managers often have a difficult time setting accurate target dates because of the unexpected events that make seeing into the future an art rather than a science. As a result, regular progress reports should be prepared. Target dates set at the beginning of a project should be as realistic as possible; however, variances from early projections may still occur. As the project proceeds and a greater understanding of its scope and complexity evolves, target dates should become more precise and reliable.

Functional Requirements

The functional requirements document is the blueprint for an applications development project. It should contain, directly or by reference, all of the basic information to execute the remainder of the project. This information also needs to be presented clearly to provide for effective tasks and avoid the confusion that leads to lost time and wasted resources. Functional requirements information can be grouped into the following four categories:

1. Data to be input to the application
2. Processing that should occur within the application
3. Reports, documents, cross-feeds to other applications, and any other output the application should produce
4. Data, information, images, and other items that should be stored within the application

The final delivered document must be carefully reviewed and approved before the actual development begins. The functional requirements study is often the most difficult part of a project, consistent with its being the most important. It asks that specialists in three disciplines—business operations, finance, and information technology—work effectively with each other. These specialists will need to work with managers, accountants, and users at all levels who understand the company's true needs to establish these requirements and review the functional requirements document.

Application Documentation

The total investment in an application is at risk if that application is poorly documented, or not documented at all. People cannot be expected to know and remember everything they might possibly need to know to use, operate, and maintain a complex system. When they need to refer to the application documentation, it is most often to solve a problem, and at a time when that problem needs to be fixed. If programmers/analysts need to repair or improve an application, they will need comprehensive technical information about the programs and their interrelationships. This type of information also helps when new personnel, whether technical or end user, are being trained. Adequate documentation usually includes:

- Manuals describing how to use the application
- Manuals describing how to operate the application
- Manuals describing all the technical information about the application programming and any hardware dedicated to that application

Current Technology

Systems development projects should always include time to consider using proven technology, new technology, or both. IT management must keep up with technological innovations that might improve the effectiveness of its application base systems and should use this technology whenever it passes the appropriate cost–benefit test.

Hardware Acquisitions

Requirements should be clearly defined before any hardware is acquired. When possible, applications should be designed to operate on existing equipment. The IT auditor should confirm that, throughout this process, application development projects should be driven by the company's information needs and the overall costs and benefits involved.

Training

Effective training can greatly reduce the tension often associated with major changes in the workplace besides being necessary for operating and using the system. Some positions will change, and sometimes it is impossible to know in advance which ones and to what extent. Training, counseling, and familiarity with the system can greatly smooth the transition and minimize resistance to change. In addition, training is important to ensure that the application's potential is realized to the company's benefit, and to avoid the tendency of many people who prefer to do things the same as in the past.

Acceptance Testing

Acceptance testing is conducted by the end users before a system is placed in operation to ensure that it will perform as designed. Acceptance testing plans should be prepared by the end users, or at least, someone that was not involved in development, to increase the probability of getting valid results. If the developer prepares the acceptance testing plan—particularly if the developer misunderstood the requirements or if there was an error in the final function requirements deliverable—then there is a very high risk that the test plan will not detect the resulting error in the application.

Acceptance testing should always be a formal and well-documented process, with the application's complexity driving the degree of the final documentation. The testing plan should indicate the elements needed to perform the testing, how the tests will be performed, and how the results will be recorded.

Errors, problems, and even simple questions that arise during acceptance testing should be categorized as either needing resolution or not. If an item needs resolution, then the implementation should not proceed until it has been resolved—defined as passing the relevant acceptance testing procedures.

Implementation

Senior management is ultimately responsible for knowing that new applications are developed and tested before implementation to reduce any risk to the overall continuity of the company. They may delegate this responsibility to an IT Steering Committee, but it should never fall below the IT Project Manager level.

The IT auditor should ensure that this responsibility is not delegated to his or her own department. It may be flattering to be asked to participate in every application development project, but this philosophically compromises the auditor's independence. The IT auditor should only participate to the extent needed to reach a conclusion on the controls in the SDLC methodology, to opine on a particularly sensitive project, or to bridge the gap until the company can build effective controls into its processes.

The IT auditor should also remember that it is unrealistic to try and eliminate every potential problem prior to implementation. Some unanticipated problems may occur, and provisions need to be made for resolving these problems as they arise.

The IT auditor should evaluate the company's decision on whether to use parallel processing in the acceptance testing and implementation phases of a project. Parallel processing may be required in many high-risk situations, but there is no doubt that it can produce new applications that are very reliable. The primary parallel processing advantage is that everyone can see if the new application can at least duplicate the existing application. Its disadvantages include its cost, double work for the technical and end users, and potential disruptions to regular work activity.

Quality Control Review

The SDLC methodology should include a review by an individual who has technical knowledge but is not close to the project. This review should focus on problem areas and omissions, but may also take the time to consider better ways of accomplishing the applications work. The independent reviewer should use a checklist to ensure that nothing is missed and to document all relevant points.

(*Note:* Workpaper 3-1 provides self-assessment questions for each of the critical general control areas described in this part.)

Section 2
Reviewing Application Systems

An Automated application review will include some combination of auditors, the application, methods, tools, technical personnel, end users, etc. Audit management is responsible for ensuring that these are in place and effective. This chapter identifies eight areas that should be addressed during the audit process:

- Audit structure
- Internal auditors
- Audit manual
- Audit management
- Audit procedures
- Application development and testing
- Documenting and reporting audit work
- External auditors

THE AUDIT STRUCTURE

The audit director should ensure that there are policies or procedures that are likely to select the auditors best suited to perform a particular review. The audit director retains ultimate responsibility for all work done by the department, and should therefore periodically review and/or approve the following:

- Qualifications and independence of each audit staff member
- Scope and frequency of the audits performed
- Techniques to be used
- The overall condition of the company's controls and operations
- The actual resolution of issues from the final reports developed by the department
- Management actions to resolve material weaknesses cited in audit reports

The IT and financial audit personnel must have sufficient IT expertise to perform the audits, whether IT audit coverage is provided by an internal audit staff, external auditors, or a combination of both. The IT expertise should be commensurate with the degree and sophistication of the IT function. The audit director should utilize internal and external third parties when it is not possible or practical to acquire or develop the internal IT expertise required for a particular assignment.

THE INTERNAL AUDITORS

The internal IT audit function should provide independent appraisals of applications, systems, etc., as needed. IT auditors evaluate the effectiveness of controls to ascertain whether processing is done in compliance with the applicable internally or externally created standards.

IT auditors should produce reports with analyses, appraisals, recommendations, and other pertinent comments concerning the activities reviewed. These comments should help the auditors meet their responsibilities more effectively. The IT auditor is properly concerned with all phases of business activity and must look beyond simple technical or financial issued to obtain a full understanding of the operations under review. The IT auditor's full range of activities should include one or more of the following in each review.

- Reviewing, appraising, and reporting on the adequacy and effectiveness of established controls
- Supporting the implementation of cost-effective controls
- Ascertaining compliance with established policies, procedures, and laws
- Determining the extent to which IT assets are safeguarded
- Ascertaining the reliability and timely processing of statistical data
- Recommending alternatives to correct control deficiencies

Competence

The overall skills required for IT audit tasks depend on the size and complexity of the IT operation. In some instances, the internal IT audit is performed by an individual or group that is only responsible for IT auditing. In other cases, the responsibility for the audit may be placed with a generalist auditor who plans and performs the audits personally or directs staff borrowed from other departments. Whatever the situation, an auditor must possess IT expertise commensurate with the sophistication of the system under audit. The following basic skills are required of any internal auditors with IT audit responsibilities:

- A sound knowledge of company practices and requirements
- A firm understanding of the fundamental principles of internal control
- The ability to schedule and execute specific IT audit functions
- The ability to investigate thoroughly and document the work

- The ability to accurately summarize and report negative findings, and prepare effective and constructive recommendations
- A general understanding of SCLC methodology concepts
- A general knowledge of automated environments
- Awareness of automated application review concepts and techniques

Audit management should be committed to providing a program of continuing education to maintain or improve competence levels, because the automated environment changes with the introduction of new technologies. Available sources of technical audit training include:

- Conferences and seminars sponsored by ISACA, IIA, other professional associations, and private organizations
- Courses sponsored by hardware and software vendors, colleges, universities, and local technical schools
- Self-study and programmed learning courses

The IT auditor's competence will ultimately be evidenced by the quality of the work performed, the ability to communicate the results of that work, and the ability to have deficiencies corrected.

Independence. The audit department's real or perceived independence is likely to have a significant impact on its ability to meet departmental objectives. One quick, although not always accurate, indication of its independence is to determine where the auditor director reports within the organization. Internal auditor departments should report to the board of directors or to the audit committee. The board should ensure that the audit department does not participate in functions that compromise its independence. These areas include such activities as preparing records, developing procedures, or engaging in other duties they would normally review.

Audit department or individual auditor independence can be evaluated by reviewing the appropriate organization charts, evaluating the findings and recommendations actually being presented, and performing other procedures as needed. To be effective, the IT auditor should be given authority to obtain all records necessary to conduct the audit and to require management to respond formally to audit findings. Internal IT and financial auditors have been considered responsible for ensuring that financial and operating management takes corrective action on each recommendation presented. This has more recently been seen as inappropriate because it does not permit the affected management to have the final say in the areas for which they are responsible. The auditor's power comes from the ability to escalate an issue all the way to the Board of Directors if the affected managers do not appear to respond appropriately to particular issue, or group of issues.

THE AUDIT MANUAL

The audit director should oversee the development of a manual that will increase the likelihood that audits performed will be successful and consistent. This manual should be built on an *Internal Audit Charter* that defines the role of the audit department in the organization, describes the philosophies of the Audit Committee, and establishes the authority the department needs to meet its objectives.

The manual and the charter should include sections that similarly define and empower the IT auditing function within the department. These sections should establish appropriate guidelines for auditing data centers, automated applications, and other related controls.

The Board of Directors must approve the Audit Charter for the latter to be meaningful. The Board is less likely to be involved in the audit manual, although it may choose to review and approve it as well. The Board may ask the external auditors to determine whether the standards and procedures it contains meet the requirements to perform an effective audit. Once the manual has been approved, it should provide the audit department with uniform standards and serve as a valuable training aid. In addition, it gives the Board a basis for evaluating the audit department.

The audit manual should contain the following policies, standards, and procedures:

- Administrative personnel policies to the extent not already provided by Human Resources
- Organization structure
- Areas or functions to be audited
- Audit frequency and scheduling guidelines
- Standards for audit workpapers and reports (e.g., content, format, filing, and distribution) and report follow-up

The audit manual must be periodically modified to remain consistent with the company, other business changes, technology changes, etc. The Board should at least review, if not approve, any item that threatens to compromise the audit department's ability to satisfy its chartered responsibilities.

MANAGING THE INDIVIDUAL IT AUDIT

The IT auditor must either know, or else learn, how to manage all of the work involved in performing a specific IT review, beginning with high-level planning and continuing through planning and performing the procedures required for the specific review. The strategic and tactical audit planning process will be covered in detail later in the book, but a summary of the key issues follows below.

Scope and Frequency of Audit Coverage

The Audit Department must perform audits with a scope and frequency sufficient to meet the objectives and responsibilities set forth in the Audit Charter and strategic plans. The scope of any specific IT audit will include one or more of the following.

- Control reviews, covering general controls, application controls, microcomputer controls, or other technical area applicable to the company
- Compliance reviews, covering qualitative or quantitative evaluation of performance against internal and/or external policies, standards, or laws
- Operational reviews, covering effectiveness and efficiency issues that are not directly related to control issues (the IT auditor should note that there will be many situations where control and operational issues are difficult to separate, but the auditor should always try to remember the difference and avoid presenting purely operational issues as strongly as a control issue should be presented for consideration and possible action)

The IT auditor should establish audit frequencies after conducting a risk assessment of the company's possible IT audit areas. Risk assessment considerations include:

- The nature of the specific operation and related assets and liabilities
- The existence of appropriate policies, standards, and procedures
- The effectiveness of supervision
- The potential impact of errors or irregularities
- The results of past reviews

All relevant IT audit areas should be reviewed on a periodic basis, even if it is only once every three years. There is always a certain chance that the risk assessment is flawed, that the assumptions or information supporting the last risk assessment are no longer valid, or that another condition that caused a review to be deferred when there was a problem to be addressed. The Board, or its audit committee, should approve the annual audit schedule. The audit director should also inform them of significant deviations to that schedule. If these changes will cause part of the approved schedule not to be completed, the audit director should revise the schedule and obtain the audit committee's approval.

Planning the Audit. The audit department, and the IT audit function within it, benefits from effective planning just like every other part of the company. Effective planning should produce consistent high-quality results, which the IT auditor should view as an absolute necessity. The planning function should include:

- Setting specific objectives

- Gathering background information and evaluating that information
- Formulating the detail audit program
- Preparing a time and expense budget for the audit
- Arranging for the appropriate staff resources
- Providing a mechanism for any needed revisions

Performing the Audit. The IT auditor responsible for performing a specific IT audit may satisfy this objective in one of three ways, or through a combinations of these three in more complex situations. First, the IT auditor may perform all procedures personally if the total effort is limited or if no one else has the technical expertise to effectively help complete the work. Second, the IT auditor may supervise less-experienced IT or financial auditors as they perform the detail audit program steps. Third, the IT auditor may coordinate the efforts of fellow IT auditors or outside consultants who have the experience to do the audit program steps.

In any case, the IT auditor's responsibility is likely to include most, if not all, of the following.

- Deciding when audit findings warrant additional procedures
- Reviewing the workpapers and deciding when the detail procedures are sufficient to support an opinion
- Meeting with the auditee to discuss audit findings and the items to be included in the audit report
- Preparing and finalizing the audit report, which should include having the IT audit director or audit director review the work, conclusions, and draft report, and distributing the report after it has been signed
- Planning for a follow-up of progress against planned actions in six months or other appropriate interval

IT AUDIT PROCEDURES

IT audit procedures should only vary based on the technical environment and the specific audit scope. The audit procedures should never vary based on the skills of the internal IT audit staff. If the risk assessment identifies an IT audit that no one on the staff has the skill or experience to perform, audit department management is obligated to develop or contract those skills and complete the audit. The audit program steps may include manual procedures, computer-assisted procedures, or fully automated procedures. In most cases, a combination of these techniques is used.

Manual Procedures

The IT auditor utilizes manual procedures when they are more effective than the alternatives, or when they cannot be partially or fully automated. Please note that a procedure that cannot be automated today may be fully automated tomorrow, based on a new technology. Examples of these procedures include:

- Selecting one or more physical documents, such as vendor invoices and comparing the information from them, field by field, with the data stored in the system through to the booking of the documents in the ledger (when possible)
- Driving to one or more vendor addressed to establish at least the existence, if not the legitimacy, of the source of the physical documents from the first example
- Reviewing internal documents for evidence of approval by authorized persons

There are hundreds of other examples that every auditor is probably familiar with, thus no other examples of manual procedures will be discussed.

Computer-Assisted Procedures

The IT auditor uses computer-assisted procedures, also known as Computer Assisted Audit Techniques (CAATs), because they permit the auditor to switch from procedures based on limited, random, or statistical samples of records in a file to procedures that include every record in a file.

The IT auditor may choose to use an audit software package that is designed to support CAATs, or to develop his or her own programs using desktop database or spreadsheet software. In either case, the IT auditor would either request read-only access to the appropriate file or files, or ask to have them downloaded in ASCII or EBCDIC format. The following examples are set in the context of an IT auditor who has received a file of cash disbursement information for testing.

- Total disbursements are computed for the file and compared to ledger and bank records.
- Every record is checked for disbursement amounts equal to or less than zero.
- Every record is checked to see that all required fields contain values.
- For fields that should meet conditions such as numeric values between 10000 and 99999, a check is done for any records with values outside that range.
- The check number field is tested for missing or duplicated values.
- Key items are selected for individual confirmation.

In most cases, CAATs are used to evaluate the data directly, while testing processing indirectly through the data evaluation procedures. It is possible to simulate application processing with a CAAT, but this is still an indirect way of evaluating the actual processing done by an automated application.

Fully Automated Procedures

This term is an oxymoron, as there are no known automated tools that can independently identify, evaluate, discuss, report, and follow up on potential audit issues. It is used to describe tools and techniques that continue to function and produce results automatically after a single development effort. The IT auditor can choose from any of the following based on the requirements of a particular application or situation.

Integrated Test Facility. The audit director asks senior management for permission to have a fictitious master record added to an application. This might be a vendor master record in a purchasing or cash disbursements application. The fictitious record would have to be established without the knowledge of the persons responsible for master file maintenance or transaction processing, or else the reliability of the results would be compromised. Transactions are initiated by the auditor at random or present intervals, are indistinguishable from live transactions, and are processed exactly like live data. The IT auditor must take special care to avoid understating or overstating balance sheet or income statement amounts. In addition, the auditor should also be aware of possible local legal implications or restrictions regarding the use of this procedure.

Parallel Simulation. The IT auditor arranges for application software to be developed, based on the same functional requirements used to develop all or part of an application that is live in production. Once completed, the IT auditor obtains copies of master and/or transaction records that were entered into the production application, along with any related output produced by the application. These master and transaction records are then input to the specially developed application software and processed to see if the output from the independent system bears the same results as the real processing.

Parallel Operations. The IT auditor participates in a procedure that is similar to Parallel Simulation, except that the auditor is an observer in this scenario while the end user or software developer processes a standard set of transactions through both the new and existing application software to see if any differences result. The purpose of these operations is to verify the accuracy of new or revised application programs by processing production data and files, and using the existing and the newly developed programs. Processing results are compared to identify unexpected differences.

Base Case System Evaluation. The IT auditor develops a standard transaction or group of transactions and processes them through the original application. The results are confirmed and recorded, and the IT auditor can now resubmit the transactions to confirm that a change was made, to test whether no changes were made, etc. Such testing may be performed whenever application are modified.

Embedded Audit Data Collection. The IT auditor works with the audit director to obtain senior management's approval for having a special module developed and implemented as part of an automated application. The module would most often be designed to identify master file or transaction data records based on predetermined criteria, standard intervals, random intervals, or any other basis that can be written into a rule. The selected data would then either be automatically displayed or printed for the IT auditor to evaluate.

Extended Records. These records are created by adding a control field to a master record or by creating a special record that is linked to a transaction record. This record or field may include data about all the application programs that processed a transaction, or other data deemed significant in that context.

Whatever the source, any specially developed applications or standalone programs should remain under the strict control of the audit department. For this reason, all documentation, test material, source listings, source and object program modules, and changes to such programs must be strictly controlled. In installations using advanced library management software, audit object programs may be cataloged with password protection. This is acceptable as long as the auditors retain control over the documentation and the appropriate job control instructions necessary to retrieve and execute the object program from its library. If general controls do not provide for strict audit control, audit programs should not be cataloged. The IT auditor should ensure that programs intended for audit use are fully documented to help ensure their continued usefulness and reliability.

The IT auditor should also take reasonable steps to protect the integrity of processing. Appropriate controls can include:

- Maintaining physical control over the audit software, unless it is cataloged in the system and protected appropriately
- Developing independent program controls that monitor or limit the processing of the audit software
- Maintaining control over software specifications, documentation, and job control cards
- Controlling the integrity of files being processed and output generated

APPLICATION DEVELOPMENT AND TESTING

Automated application development projects should be carried out according to a reliable SCLC methodology. Any project is likely to require complete and effective communication between the end users and the developers, whether the project is done in 3 or 12 phases. The IT auditor should work to evaluate controls during development, as it has been generally accepted that modifying a live-production application costs five to ten times more than implementing the desired feature during the development phase. The IT auditor's evaluation could come at or near the end of each phase, or more often if deemed necessary. Guidelines should be developed to facilitate the review of new applications during the requirements definition phase so that controls can be identified for early assessment and potential inclusion.

IT auditors need to be capable of recommending effective controls to user management during the requirements definition and development phases. Such recommendations will not ensure that controls are absolute, but only that the structure is appropriate. Acting in this manner in this capacity, the IT auditor can be viewed as an internal controls consultant. The IT auditor should be careful not to make, or participate in making, any management decisions.

The IT auditor should consider the need to schedule a post-implementation review for each major or identifiable automated application accepted and implemented into the production environment. Reviews that get scheduled should be done within six to nine months of the production implementation. Where the IT auditor originally evaluated the defined and expected controls, he can now evaluate the effectiveness of the controls as implemented.

One indirect benefit from a timely post-implementation review is that any control deficiencies may get worked into the normal code fine-tuning activities that follow the implementation of many automated application development projects.

The IT auditor should also be aware that any serious problems or deviations from the functional requirements deliverable that made it into production are likely to be identified by the end-user personnel responsible for the affected business function faster than almost any audit could do the same.

In larger IT departments, quality assurance or change management personnel may be responsible for performing a post-implementation review for each completed application development project. If this is the case, the IT auditor should consider whether to participate in the planned post-implementation review or conduct his own. Regardless, the IT auditor should request copies of all post-implementations as they should contain information that is important to the audit planning process.

DOCUMENTING AND REPORTING AUDIT WORK

The internal audit manual should include standards for audit workpapers and other standard documents. Since workpapers are the primary evidence of the audit procedures performed, the workpaper package for each audit should be well-organized, clearly written, and address all areas in the audit scope. Audit workpapers should contain sufficient evidence of the tasks performed and conclusions reached, including:

- Audit program with sign-offs
- Planning and administrative documents
- Permanent file including internal control and other carry-forward information
- Workpapers indicating the preparer and reviewer
- Detailed evidence of work performed, results achieved, issues identified, etc.
- Authorized signatures approving the final opinion

Reporting Findings and Conclusions

Potential audit findings should be discussed with the appropriate personnel throughout the course of the audit. Preliminary conclusions and audit findings, normally a subset of the potential findings, should be presented to the auditee during an exit conference and discussed at that time. The draft audit report should be the natural extension of the exit conference materials combined with the discussions that took place during the exit meeting. Once the auditee's responses have been received, the final audit report may be prepared and distributed.

Regardless of whether the IT auditor uses the four-step approach just mentioned or another, the following guidelines should be satisfied.

- All potential audit findings should be documented in the normal course of the audit, discussed with appropriate personnel, and their comments documents as well.
- All potential findings with sufficient merit should be included for discussion at the exit conference as preliminary audit recommendations.
- The exit meeting should document and include auditee comments and questions concerning the preliminary audit recommendations.
- The draft audit report should contain an overall opinion of the audited function, state whether controls have strengthened or weakened since the function was last audited, and summarize the preliminary recommendations and related exposures.

- Written responses to all audit reports should be prepared by line management and provided to audit management on a timely basis.
- The final audit report, including management's responses, should be distributed as soon as possible once those responses have been received.
- Serious control deficiencies or other issues identified during the audit that remain unresolved should be escalated as needed until a satisfactory resolution is reached.
- IT auditors should schedule a follow-up review, even if only done over the phone, whenever the auditor agrees to take action in response to a recommendation.
- All significant audit findings should be periodically summarized and reviewed with senior management and the audit committee.

Audit Follow-up

The IT auditor should schedule follow-up procedures whenever an auditee agrees to take action in response to a specific audit recommendation. The auditor should always be concerned about whether that action is really taken, as there will be a certain percentage of auditees that will agree to take action just to get the audit over with, never intending to make any change. One very real risk is that an auditor's failure to follow up may lead the auditee community to conclude that the audit recommendations are not worth taking seriously, and actually create the problem situation just described. Follow-up procedures may include the following:

- Requesting a written report on the status of the planned changes
- Deciding whether on-site procedures are warranted
- Planning and performing audit procedures to confirm that the planned change was made and to evaluate whether it has met original objective (if not, then an additional recommendation may become appropriate)
- Deciding whether unresolved issues warrant an immediate notification to the audit committee, or special mention during the next scheduled meeting

The IT auditor should remain aware that although the desirability of formal procedures is clear, the auditor should obtain effective responses without overemphasizing haste. Overall audit management should try to ensure that monitoring techniques are effective yet do not arouse antagonism that may impair the department's relationship with operating management. The company may choose to appoint a senior officer formally responsible for audit follow-up to protect the auditor/auditee relationship.

EXTERNAL AUDITORS

The responsibilities of external auditors should be defined clearly for the audit committee, board of directors, and senior management. The external auditors are aware of this need, and will normally submit engagement letters to the board that require a written acceptance before commencing their work. Such letters normally include the scope of the audit, its length, and expected results. In many cases, essential features of the audit are summarized in the letter with schedules attached that describe specific procedures for each area to be audited. The letter may include biographical information on the personnel involved, as well as provisions for disclosure and review of audit workpapers by third parties. In addition, the letter may specify any normal audit procedures to be omitted and whether the auditor is expected to render an opinion on the organization's financial statements.

The external auditor must review IT internal control procedures as part of his evaluation of the overall system of internal control when auditing the organization's financial statements. AICPA standards require auditors to consider the effects of IT activity in each significant financial application.

Generally, the external auditors must review the general controls and application controls that could have a material impact on the financial statements as presented. General controls include IT planning and structure, physical and logical access security, and other controls over the IT environment. Application controls are linked to individual systems, and should ensure that these are adequate controls over input, processing, output, and data storage.

As the external auditors evaluate internal controls, they must determine the extent to which IT is used in each significant accounting application, and thus also determine the need to review IT controls. The AICPA has indicated in the past that: the external auditor is permitted to select the specific procedures they believe are the most effective for evaluating IT controls. Most of the audit forms begin with a questionnaire that gathers most or all of the required background information. Usually, these questionnaires cover:

- Hardware, software, and organization
- User department controls over data processed by automated applications
- IT program and procedural documentation
- Automatic controls over processing
- Backup procedures
- Security
- Contingency planning

As part of their review, external auditors can also decide to perform a variety of substantive audit procedures.

Section 3
Assessing IT Audit Capabilities

The senior IT auditor is likely to consider having a peer review done when an objective evaluation of the internal IT audit capabilities is needed. An internal self-assessment is an effective substitute when the objectivity of a third party is not required. This self-assessment program is divided into three main areas. The first area explains who should conduct the self-assessment, the second describes how, and the third how to analyze the results. The IT auditor performing a self-assessment will not only learn about their capabilities and the capabilities of the IT audit function, but will also gain a better understanding of what the auditees asked to complete self-assessment questionnaire experience.

WHO SHOULD PERFORM THE SELF-ASSESSMENT?

The self-assessment should be performed by the internal IT audit staff. The audit team should include no more than five people. The ideal self-assessment team would include:

- An internal IT audit manager
- A senior IT internal auditor
- A peer review experienced auditor

The team should be responsible for conducting the self-assessment and reporting self-assessment results. While the team approach is preferable, the reality of leaner and more focused audit departments has led to many situations where multi-billion dollar international companies have IT audit functions that include three persons or less. In these situations, it is completely reasonable and appropriate to have a single IT auditor conduct the self-assessment.

The internal IT audit manager, or the audit director if there is no IT manager, should appoint the self-assessment team. If the internal IT audit staff lacks the necessary IT skills, an experienced professional from the IT department may be selected to conduct the assessment. A self-assessment or peer review should be done at least once every three years.

CONDUCTING THE SELF-ASSESSMENT

The self-assessment exercise should cover three areas, as follows:

- The basic technology environment
- The SDLC methodology
- Internal IT audit capabilities

These areas should be reviewed in order, because the environment is the foundation for systems development, and because both must be understood before being able to assess the adequacy of available IT audit skills. For example, the more complex or technically specialized the environment is, the more significant the SDLC methodology becomes, and the required IT audit capabilities grow accordingly.

The self-assessment can be performed and documented using the following workpapers:

- Workpaper 3-1: Self-Assessment of the IT Environment
- Workpaper 3-2: Analysis Worksheet for Workpaper 3-1
- Workpaper 3-3: Self-Assessment of the SDLC methodology
- Workpaper 3-4: Analysis Worksheet for Workpaper 3-3
- Workpaper 3-5: Self-Assessment of Internal IT Audit Capabilities
- Workpaper 3-6: Analysis Worksheet for Workpaper 3-5
- Workpaper 3-7: Statistical Summary of the Analysis Worksheets

The person or team performing the self-assessment should complete the questionnaires without outside assistance. There are two reasons for this: first, this is not an audit, and interviewing IT or other internal professionals could create confusion and second, the self-assessment needs to encompass both skills and knowledge, and the knowledge needs to be sufficient to complete the project.

ANALYSIS AND REPORTING OF RESULTS

The analysis and reporting of self-assessment results includes three tasks.

Task 1: Post Self-Assessment Results to Analysis Worksheets

Each self-assessment questionnaire contains several areas. For example, in the IT environment, the first area is planning. The number of positive and not applicable responses for the questions should be totaled, and the percentage of those responses versus the total number of questions should be calculated. The percentages should be posted to the analysis workpapers.

Task 2: Perform Preliminary Analysis

Using the analysis worksheets, the self-assessment team should review each of the three areas. At this point, the analysis worksheets should be complete, showing the control and audit capabilities for the various areas. A sample preliminary analysis would be as follows:

% Score	Analysis
0–60	Either the controls or capabilities appear to be inadequate. More analysis should be done to determine which one is weak. If it is the IT environment or SDLC methodology, then the timing and scope of the next planned review may require re-evaluation. If it is deficient capabilities, then improvements should be made.
70–80	The controls and capabilities appear to be adequate. Improvements may be worthwhile and should be considered if there is available time.
90–100	The controls and capabilities appear to be more than adequate. No further attention is required.

As was mentioned in the first analysis comment above, each potential problem can have one or more causes. The person or team performing the self-assessment will either have to perform additional analysis to better understand the situation or will have to defer a conclusion on that item until an audit is performed. For example, if an IT audit were being undertaken in the near future, an assessment of the potential weakness could be incorporated into that audit plan.

Task 3: Formulate Final Recommendations

The self-assessment person or team should develop conclusions and prepare recommendations once the work is at least substantially completed. Where additional analysis indicates that there is a problem in the basic technology environment or the SDLC methodology, that information should be input to the overall risk assessment and audit department planning process. Conversely, where the additional analysis indicates a weakness in the IT audit capabilities, specific recommendations should be made to either correct those weaknesses, or to arrange for third parties to participate when IT audits need to be performed on the areas where capabilities are weak.

Internal IT audit functions using this self-assessment exercise should evaluate the effectiveness of the exercise at its conclusion and supplement or modify the exercise as needed to improve its usefulness.

Workpaper 3-1. Self-Assessment Questionnaire (Page 1 of 11)

Assessment Area: IT Environment

Item	Response		
	Yes	No	N/A
Strategic Plan			
1. Does the IT department have a strategic planning process? *Comments:*_____			
2. Is the IT planning process based on the company's planning process? *Comments:*_____			
3. Does the planning process address quality issues? *Comments:*_____			
4. Does the plan help to ensure compatibility between hardware and systems? *Comments:*_____			
5. Do all parts of the company provide input to the planning process? *Comments:*_____			
6. Does the plan encompass IT throughout the company and not just the central IT department? *Comments:*_____			
7. Does the plan include acquired as well as in-house-developed software? *Comments:*_____			
8. Does the plan identify target dates, resources, and personnel needed to accomplish the plan? *Comments:*_____			
9. Are current IT activities consistent with the current plan? *Comments:*_____			
Category totals:			
Combined "Yes" and "NA" total:			
Combined as a % of Total Questions:			

Workpaper 3-1. Self-Assessment Questionnaire (Page 2 of 11)

<u>**Assessment Area: IT Environment**</u>

Item	Response		
	Yes	**No**	**N/A**
Management Commitment			
1. Does IT management accept the responsibility for the success of the IT function? *Comments:* _____ _____			
2. Is the senior management actively involved in significant projects? *Comments:* _____ _____			
3. Does management receive periodic project status reports? *Comments:* _____ _____			
4. Does senior management demonstrate its commitment to the success of IT projects? *Comments:* _____ _____			
5. Is the turnover rate in the IT department reasonable? *Comments:* _____ _____			
6. Does IT management treat its users as customers? *Comments:* _____ _____			
7. Does IT management regularly visit with end users to determine whether needs are being met? *Comments:* _____ _____			
8. Does IT management maintain continuity of personnel in the application projects? *Comments:* _____ _____			
9. Does IT management monitor the quality and status of work by contractors? *Comments:* _____ _____			
Category totals:			
Combined "Yes" and "NA" total:			
Combined as a % of Total Questions:			

Workpaper 3-1. Self-Assessment Questionnaire (Page 3 of 11)

<u>Assessment Area: IT Environment</u>

	Response		
Item	**Yes**	**No**	**N/A**
Contracting Process			
1. Does the IT department have a policy on contracting? *Comments:* _____ _____			
2. Does the IT department have a list of approved contractors? *Comments:* _____ _____			
3. Is any quality or reliability data gathered and analyzed for vendors? *Comments:* _____ _____			
4. Does the organization have skilled, competent individuals to perform the contracting function? *Comments:* _____ _____			
5. Are the individuals involved in contracting familiar with contracting laws and regulations? *Comments:* _____ _____			
6. Does anyone regularly visit with the contractors and vendors to evaluate their capabilities and performance? *Comments:* _____ _____			
7. Do vendor contracts include performance standards? *Comments:* _____ _____			
8. Do the contracts for hardware and software include at least an evaluation of ongoing vendor support and maintenance? *Comments:* _____ _____			
9. Does the IT organization use contractors effectively? *Comments:* _____ _____			
10. *Comments:* _____			
Category totals:			
Combined "Yes" and "NA" total:			
Combined as a % of Total Questions:			

Workpaper 3-1. Self-Assessment Questionnaire (Page 4 of 11)

<u>**Assessment Area: IT Environment**</u>

Item	Response		
	Yes	No	N/A
Basic Features			
1. Are there procedures on how to develop effective controls? *Comments:* _____ _____			
2. Is security included as a basic feature? *Comments:* _____ _____			
3. Are procedures in place for developing and maintaining audit trails? *Comments:* _____ _____			
4. Are procedures in place for providing controls over automated financial systems? *Comments:* _____ _____			
5. Are there basic features to control data entry? *Comments:* _____ _____			
6. Are there features that support the identification and correction of potentially invalid transactions? *Comments:* _____ _____			
7. Are there file control procedures, such as labeling or reconciliation? *Comments:* _____ _____			
8. Are procedures in place for governing the responsibilities of transactions from the point of origin to the point of final use of transaction data? *Comments:* _____ _____			
9. Are there procedures for tracing transactions through information systems, even without formal audit trails? *Comments:* _____ _____			
10. *Comments:* _____ _____			
Category totals:			
Combined "Yes" and "NA" total:			
Combined as a % of Total Questions:			

Workpaper 3-1. Self-Assessment Questionnaire (Page 5 of 11)

<u>Assessment Area: IT Environment</u>

Item	Response		
	Yes	**No**	**N/A**
SDLC Methodology			
1. Does the organization use a systems development life cycle methodology? *Comments:* _____ _____			
2. Is normal maintenance included in that methodology? *Comments:* _____ _____			
3. Is the methodology divided into a reasonable number of phases? *Comments:* _____ _____			
4. Are there checkpoints at the end of each phase? *Comments:* _____ _____			
5. Are the systems analysts and programmers taught how to use the methodology? *Comments:* _____ _____			
6. Is the methodology consistent with other IT standards? *Comments:* _____ _____			
7. Does the methodology include features that will ensure compliance, or at least detect material noncompliance? *Comments:* _____ _____			
8. Is the methodology sufficiently flexible to be used in developing all types of application systems? *Comments:* _____ _____			
9. Are software tools integrated, where appropriate, into the methodology? *Comments:* _____ _____			
10. Does IT management understand the SDLC methodology and how to effectively utilize it? *Comments:* _____ _____			
Category totals:			
Combined "Yes" and "NA" total:			
Combined as a % of Total Questions:			

Workpaper 3-1. Self-Assessment Questionnaire (Page 6 of 11)

Assessment Area: IT Environment

Item	Response		
	Yes	No	N/A
Target Dates			
1. Does the company regularly establish target dates? *Comments:* _____ _____			
2. Is the estimating process reliable by itself, or as reliability related to the personnel? *Comments:* _____ _____			
3. Does the estimating process consider the quality of the systems to be produced? *Comments:* _____ _____			
4. Do procedures include monitoring estimates versus actual status or progress? *Comments:* _____ _____			
5. Are significant variances from schedules properly responded to? *Comments:* _____ _____			
6. Are project status reports tied to a scheduling system? *Comments:* _____ _____			
7. Are the estimates and schedules revised as projects change to maintain consistency between the two? *Comments:* _____ _____			
8. Do IT and senior management act firmly and fairly when dealing with slippage and delays? *Comments:* _____ _____			
9. *Comments:* _____ _____			
10. *Comments:* _____ _____			
Category totals:			
Combined "Yes" and "NA" total:			
Combined as a % of Total Questions:			

Workpaper 3-1. Self-Assessment Questionnaire (Page 7 of 11)

Assessment Area: IT Environment

Item	Response		
	Yes	No	N/A
Application Systems Documentation			
1. Are IT systems personnel trained to prepare documentation? *Comments:* _____			
2. Is the application design normally documented? *Comments:* _____			
3. Are programs documented? *Comments:* _____			
4. Is the testing methodology documented? *Comments:* _____			
5. Are operations procedures documented? *Comments:* _____			
6. Are user manuals prepared? *Comments:* _____			
7. Do manuals normally include procedures for handling exceptions? *Comments:* _____			
8. Are the methods for preparing documentation sufficient to produce clear and complete information? *Comments:* _____			
9. Are the methods by which documentation will be prepared described in sufficient detail so that the documentation will be complete and understood by the user? *Comments:* _____			
10. Are there procedures to update documentation when an application changes? *Comments:* _____			
Category totals:			
Combined "Yes" and "NA" total:			
Combined as a % of Total Questions:			

Workpaper 3-1. Self-Assessment Questionnaire (Page 8 of 11)

<u>**Assessment Area: IT Environment**</u>

Item	Response		
	Yes	**No**	**N/A**
Current Technology			
1. Has a strategic hardware plan been established? *Comments:* _____ _____			
2. Is the plan reasonable, considering the company's ability to use new technology? *Comments:* _____ _____			
3. Are the uses of new technology adequately defined before the technology is acquired? *Comments:* _____ _____			
4. Does the organization have an individual or group in charge of selecting new technology? *Comments:* _____ _____			
5. Is the technology used by the company compatible with the technology used throughout the industry? *Comments:* _____ _____			
6. Does senior management understand the risks and implications associated with acquiring new technology? *Comments:* _____ _____			
7. Is a cost/benefit analysis performed to support the decision on whether to acquire the new technology? *Comments:* _____ _____			
8. Is the use of new technology monitored to ensure that expected benefits are achieved? *Comments:* _____ _____			
9. *Comments:* _____ _____			
10. *Comments:* _____ _____			
Category totals:			
Combined "Yes" and "NA" total:			
Combined as a % of Total Questions:			

Workpaper 3-1. Self-Assessment Questionnaire (Page 9 of 11)

<u>**Assessment Area: IT Environment**</u>

Item	Response		
	Yes	No	N/A
Hardware Acquisition and Maintenance			
1. Does the IT organization have anyone who is responsible for strategic and/or tactical capacity planning? *Comments:*			
2. Is there an effective preventive maintenance program in place for all significant equipment? *Comments:*			
3. Is equipment downtime kept within reasonable limits (<5%)? *Comments:*			
4. Is a reasonable effort made to acquire data center and networking hardware that is compatible with the existing environment? *Comments:*			
5. Have standards been established to create an appropriate level of consistency in the end-user computing environment? *Comments:*			
6. Are vendors qualified or otherwise reviewed to ensure their reliability? *Comments:*			
7. Is anyone in the IT organization responsible for identifying potentially unneeded equipment and taking appropriate action? *Comments:*			
8. Is a formal inventory of all IT hardware available? *Comments:*			
Category totals:			
Combined "Yes" and "NA" total:			
Combined as a % of Total Questions:			

Workpaper 3-1. Self-Assessment Questionnaire (Page 10 of 11)

<u>Assessment Area: IT Environment</u>

Item	Response		
	Yes	**No**	**N/A**
Training			
1. Does the IT department have a training plan for its staff? *Comments:* _____			
2. Has anyone been made responsible for the IT department training program? *Comments:* _____			
3. Do the training alternatives encompass an adequate range of alternatives such as on- and off-site seminars, self-study programs, professional society memberships, etc.? *Comments:* _____			
4. Is the training director or person responsible for training knowledgeable in training principles and concepts? *Comments:* _____			
5. Is there approval to ensure that the approved trained programs are consistent with the needs of the business? *Comments:* _____			
6. Are vendors used to conduct training whenever possible? *Comments:* _____			
7. Is any of the training directed at defect reduction or quality improvement? *Comments:* _____			
8. Is the amount of funds allocated to training reasonable? *Comments:* _____			
9. *Comments:* _____			
10. *Comments:* _____			
Category totals:			
Combined "Yes" and "NA" total:			
Combined as a % of Total Questions:			

Workpaper 3-1. Self-Assessment Questionnaire (Page 11 of 11)

Assessment Area: IT Environment

Item	Response		
	Yes	No	N/A
Quality Control			
1. Do procedures require quality control reviews during the development of application systems? *Comments:*_____			
2. Are quality control reviews performed by, or least supervised by, persons trained in quality control review procedures? *Comments:*_____			
3. Have checklists been prepared? *Comments:*_____			
4. Is consideration given to selecting personnel that are knowledgeable about the business issues? *Comments:*_____			
5. Are quality control review personnel familiar with the SDLC methodology? *Comments:*_____			
6. Are review recommendations incorporated before the application moves to the next phase? *Comments:*_____			
7. Are quality control review reports prepared for each review? *Comments:*_____			
8. Are quality control review recommendations regularly reviewed, and worthwhile recommendations implemented before the development continues into the next phase? *Comments:*_____			
9. Are any peer or quality reviews done over the quality control review itself? *Comments:*_____			
10. Is the adequacy of quality control reviews periodically checked by quality assurance personnel or equivalent managers? *Comments:*_____			
Category totals:			
Combined "Yes" and "NA" total:			
Combined as a % of Total Questions:			

Workpaper 3-2. Analysis Summary for Workpaper 3-1

IT Environment	# of Yes and N/A	# of Questions	% of Total
1	3	5	60%
2	3	5	60%
3	3	5	60%
4	3	5	60%
5	3	5	60%
6	3	5	60%
7	3	5	60%
8	3	5	60%
9	3	5	60%
10	3	5	60%
11	3	5	60%
12	3	5	60%
13	3	5	60%
14	3	5	60%
Response totals	42	70	60%

Workpaper 3-3. Self-Assessment Questionnaire (Page 1 of 5)

<u>Assessment Area: SDLC Methodology</u>

Item	Response		
	Yes	**No**	**N/A**
Requirements Definition			
1. Has a standard for defining requirements been established? *Comments:*_____			
2. Is the procedure followed for defining requirements consistent with the standard? *Comments:*_____			
3. Does the end user have to agree with these before the project proceeds? *Comments:*_____			
4. Does the end user participate when developing the requirements? *Comments:*_____			
5. Are the requirements changed as the project moves through the development cycle, or are they held constant? *Comments:*_____			
6. Do the functional requirements need any special justification? *Comments:*_____			
7. Are the original requirements traced through development and acceptance testing and into implementation? *Comments:*_____			
8. Does the methodology include procedures to validate the requirements? *Comments:*_____			
9. Are requirements completed before design begins? *Comments:*_____			
10. Is there a management checkpoint at the end of the requirements definition phase to evaluate those requirements and confirm the validity of the original development and implementation plan? *Comments:*_____			
Category totals:			
Combined "Yes" and "NA" total:			
Combined as a % of Total Questions:			

Workpaper 3-3. Self-Assessment Questionnaire (Page 2 of 5)

<u>**Assessment Area: SDLC Methodology**</u>

Item	Response		
	Yes	**No**	**N/A**
Input and Application Processing			
1. Are edit tests built into data input programs to ensure that all entries are valid? *Comments:* _____			
2. Do input routines trap the userid, logon, or other element that permits authorized persons to identify the end user responsible for that element? *Comments:* _____			
3. Are controls in place to ensure that all items entered can be accounted for, such as having the system automatically attach a sequential number to each item? *Comments:* _____			
4. Are there procedures in place to help ensure that all successfully entered transactions are processed fully or followed-up to ensure their proper final disposition? *Comments:* _____			
5. Does the application include procedures that should ensure transactions are recorded into the proper period? *Comments:* _____			
6. Does the application include control features to help ensure that only specifically authorized persons can input transactions and master data into the system? *Comments:* _____			
7. Does the application system include automated or manual procedures to identify transactions designed to circumvent automated controls? An example would be submitting two or more small purchase orders to avoid the approval required for the total amount of the purchase. *Comments:* _____			
8. *Reserved for future use.* *Comments:* _____			
Category totals:			
Combined "Yes" and "NA" total:			
Combined as a % of Total Questions:			

Workpaper 3-3. Self-Assessment Questionnaire (Page 3 of 5)

Assessment Area: SDLC Methodology

Item	Response		
	Yes	No	N/A
Data Storage Within the Application			
1. Does the application system include controls and procedures designed to ensure that data stored in the application is protected from unauthorized changes or deletion? *Comments:* _____			
2. Does the application system include controls designed to ensure that only authorized persons are able to display and/or output data? *Comments:* _____			
3. Does the application system have automated or manual features designed to back up all or changed application system data at regular intervals? *Comments:* _____			
4. Prior to implementation, and at regular intervals afterward, will the data backup processes mentioned in #3 above be restored on a test basis to ensure that the backups are reliable? *Comments:* _____			
5. If there are any controls the IT auditor would normally expect to see omitted from the application system, is their omission supported by a reasonable analysis that supports the decision to omit them? *Comments:* _____			
6. *Reserved for future use.* *Comments:* _____			
7. *Reserved for future use.* *Comments:* _____			
8. *Reserved for future use.* *Comments:* _____			
Category totals:			
Combined "Yes" and "NA" total:			
Combined as a % of Total Questions:			

Workpaper 3-3. Self-Assessment Questionnaire (Page 4 of 5)

Assessment Area: SDLC Methodology

Item	Response		
	Yes	No	N/A
Development and Acceptance Testing			
1. Are procedures in place to ensure independent validation of application systems prior to acceptance? *Comments:* _____ _____			
2. Are end users or customers involved in this independent acceptance? *Comments:* _____ _____			
3. Is a test plan developed for each application system being implemented that includes acceptance testing? *Comments:* _____ _____			
4. Does the test plan include testing documentation to verify its accuracy? *Comments:* _____ _____			
5. Are the independent testing results documented and a summary report prepared? *Comments:* _____ _____			
6. Does acceptance testing encompass all features of the application, or only the features deemed critical? *Comments:* _____ _____			
7. Do acceptance testing procedures appear to cover internal controls with the application? *Comments:* _____ _____			
8. Do the persons responsible for acceptance testing normally appear to understand the business implications of the application? *Comments:* _____ _____			
9. *Comments:* _____ _____			
10. *Comments:* _____ _____			
Category totals:			
Combined "Yes" and "NA" total:			
Combined as a % of Total Questions:			

Workpaper 3-3. Self-Assessment Questionnaire (Page 5 of 5)

<u>Assessment Area: SDLC Methodology</u>

Item	Response		
	Yes	No	N/A
Implementation			
1. Are procedures designed to ensure that all significant errors are resolved prior to implementation? *Comments:*_____			
2. Are end users involved in deciding which errors do not have to be corrected prior to implementation? *Comments:*_____			
3. Are procedures designed to ensure that the correct version of each program within the application system is moved to production? *Comments:*_____			
4. Are training programs completed for all persons involved in running the application system prior to implementation? *Comments:*_____			
5. Is parallel processing used to support the implementation of highly complex or high-risk application systems? *Comments:*_____			
6. Are application system implementations executed according to sufficiently detailed implementation plans? *Comments:*_____			
7. Is all required security functionality implemented concurrent with the initial implementation of the application? *Comments:*_____			
8. Have formal error/response procedures been developed and documented, to the extent possible or practical, prior to implementing the application system? *Comments:*_____			
9. *Comments:*_____			
10. *Comments:*_____			
Category totals:			
Combined "Yes" and "NA" total:			
Combined as a % of Total Questions:			

Auditor: _____

Review: _____

Date: _____

Workpaper 3-4. Analysis Summary for Workpaper 3-3

SDLC Methodology	# of Yes and N/A	# of Questions	% of Total
1	3	5	60%
2	3	5	60%
3	3	5	60%
4	3	5	60%
5	3	5	60%
6	3	5	60%
7	3	5	60%
8	3	5	60%
9	3	5	60%
10	3	5	60%
11	3	5	60%
12	3	5	60%
13	3	5	60%
14	3	5	60%
Response totals	42	70	60%

Workpaper 3-5. Self-Assessment Questionnaire (Page 1 of 10)

Internal IT Audit Capabilities

Item	Response		
	Yes	No	N/A
Audit Structure			
1. Does the company utilize IT auditors in the IT audit function? *Comments:* _____			
2. If financial or operational auditors are used in IT audits, is there any requirement for them to have basic computer skills? *Comments:* _____			
3. Does the IT audit manager ensure that skill weaknesses on the part of auditors are compensated for in some way? *Comments:* _____			
4. Are the IT auditors trained to effectively use IT audit tools and techniques? *Comments:* _____			
5. Are highly technical IT audits only done by IT auditors with comparable skills? *Comments:* _____			
6. Does the IT audit staff provide technical support of the financial and operational auditors? *Comments:* _____			
7. Is the IT audit function subject to periodic peer reviews (or equivalent evaluation)? *Comments:* _____			
Category totals:			
Combined "Yes" and "NA" total:			
Combined as a % of Total Questions:			

Workpaper 3-5. Self-Assessment Questionnaire (Page 2 of 10)

<u>**Internal IT Audit Capabilities**</u>

Item	Response		
	Yes	No	N/A
IT Audit Scope			
1. Does the IT audit include an analysis of all the transactions processed by the applications option? *Comments:*_____ _____			
2. Does the IT audit include an analysis of internal control? *Comments:*_____ _____			
3. Does the IT audit manager ensure that skill weaknesses on the part of the auditors are compensated for in some way? *Comments:*_____ _____			
4. Does the IT audit include an assessment of the application option documentation? *Comments:*_____ _____			
5. Does the IT audit include an assessment of compliance with the company's policies, procedures, and standards? *Comments:*_____ _____			
6. Does the IT audit include an assessment of compliance with IT departmental policies, procedures, and standards? *Comments:*_____ _____			
7. Does the IT audit include an assessment as to whether transactions are completely and correctly processed on a timely basis? *Comments:*_____ _____			
8. Does the IT audit include an operational review of the application system's performance, including manual and automated parts? *Comments:*_____ _____			
9. Does the IT audit include an assessment of whether the end users have the skills required to effectively utilize the application system? *Comments:*_____ _____			
Category totals:			
Combined "Yes" and "NA" total:			
Combined as a % of Total Questions:			

Workpaper 3-5. Self-Assessment Questionnaire (Page 3 of 10)

<u>Internal IT Audit Capabilities</u>

Item	Response		
	Yes	No	N/A
Internal IT Auditor Independence			
1. Do IT auditors understand the SDLC methodology? *Comments:*_____			
2. Do the auditors understand the business functions and requirements the application system should satisfy? *Comments:*_____			
3. Are the IT auditors involved in reviews where specialized hardware is used required to have an understanding of that technology? *Comments:*_____			
4. Do the IT auditors employ the proper IT audit tools and techniques needed to maintain their Independence? *Comments:*_____			
5. Are the IT auditors organizationally independent of the function under review? *Comments:*_____			
Category totals:			
Combined "Yes" and "NA" total:			
Combined as a % of Total Questions:			

Workpaper 3-5. Self-Assessment Questionnaire (Page 4 of 10)

Internal IT Audit Capabilities

Item	Response		
	Yes	No	N/A
IT Audit Manual (If there is no IT audit manual, then all the following should be answered with a "No" rather than an "N/A")			
1. Does the IT audit manual contain an index? *Comments:* _____			
2. Does the IT audit manual contain a glossary of items? *Comments:* _____			
3. Does the IT audit manual contain a self-assessment section? *Comments:* _____			
4. Does the IT audit manual contain pro forma working papers? *Comments:* _____			
5. Does the IT audit manual contain instructions on how to complete the pro forma? *Comments:* _____			
6. Does the IT audit manual contain procedures for auditing application systems as they are being developed? *Comments:* _____			
7. Does the IT audit manual contain procedures for evaluating all relevant general control areas? *Comments:* _____			
8. Is the IT audit manual based on ISALA's standards for the practice of professional IT auditing? *Comments:* _____			
9. Is the audit manual updated regularly? *Comments:* _____			
Category totals:			
Combined "Yes" and "NA" total:			
Combined as a % of Total Questions:			

Workpaper 3-5. Self-Assessment Questionnaire (Page 5 of 10)

Internal IT Audit Capabilities

Item	Response		
	Yes	No	N/A
Planning and Performing the Audit			
1. Is a plan prepared for each IT audit? Comments: _____			
2. Does the plan include a set of objectives and basic procedures for accomplishing those objectives? Comments: _____			
3. Does the plan include a budget? Comments: _____			
4. Does the plan include the assigned resources and the expected IT audit schedule? Comments: _____			
5. Does the plan include a detailed audit program for accomplishing the planned objectives? Comments: _____			
6. Is someone assigned responsibility for each audit plan? Comments: _____			
7. Does internal IT audit management monitor each audit to ensure its compliance with the plan? Comments: _____			
8. Is each IT audit plan consistent with the IT department's and profession's standards and procedures? Comments: _____			
9. Is each IT audit supervised by someone possessing the necessary skills? Comments: _____			
10. Do the supervisors ensure that IT workpapers are adequate and comprehensible? Comments: _____			
Category totals:			
Combined "Yes" and "NA" total:			
Combined as a % of Total Questions:			

Workpaper 3-5. Self-Assessment Questionnaire (Page 6 of 10)

<u>**Internal IT Audit Capabilities**</u>

Item	Response		
	Yes	**No**	**N/A**
Audit Procedures			
1. Is there a control questionnaire designed to facilitate any basic application system review? *Comments:* _____ _____			
2. Is the IT auditor required obtain or develop a narrative and flowchart for each automated application system reviewed? *Comments:* _____ _____			
3. Do the IT audit procedures require the IT auditor to identify files, transactions, and documents related to the audit? *Comments:* _____ _____			
4. Do the IT audit procedures require the IT auditor to obtain the application's detailed record layouts and field definitions? *Comments:* _____ _____			
5. Are IT auditors trained to use CAATs? *Comments:* _____ _____			
6. Do the IT auditors have specialized audit programs or reference material related to the company's actual hardware and software? *Comments:* _____ _____			
Category totals:			
Combined "Yes" and "NA" total:			
Combined as a % of Total Questions:			

Workpaper 3-5. Self-Assessment Questionnaire (Page 7 of 10)

<u>Internal IT Audit Capabilities</u>

Item	Response		
	Yes	No	N/A
SDLC Methodology			
1. Do the IT auditors review the SDLC methodology as a stand-alone item for effectiveness and adequacy of controls? *Comments:* _____			
2. If so, are the results of those SDLC methodology reviews available to the IT auditors performing application systems development a regular application system reviews? *Comments:* _____			
3. Do IT auditors ever participate in applications systems development? *Comments:* _____			
4. If an application system was reviewed during development and is identified for a review once implemented, are different IT auditors assigned to support the objective of independence? *Comments:* _____			
5. Do IT audits in this area normally encompass the system of internal controls? *Comments:* _____			
6. Do IT audits in this area normally evaluate IT documentation? *Comments:* _____			
7. Do IT audits of application system development projects include quantitative compliance testing? *Comments:* _____			
8. If #7 is yes, are any meaningful situations presented to IT management for evaluation and response? *Comments:* _____			
9. Do IT application development reviews evaluate compliance with legal and statutory conditions identified during Requirements Definition? *Comments:* _____			
Category totals:			
Combined "Yes" and "NA" total:			
Combined as a % of Total Questions:			

Workpaper 3-5. Self-Assessment Questionnaire (Page 8 of 10)

<u>Internal IT Audit Capabilities</u>

Item	Response		
	Yes	No	N/A
Documenting and Reporting IT Audit Work			
1. Do the IT audit working papers include a copy of the detailed audit program? *Comments:*_____			
2. Do the IT audit working papers include an approved audit planning memo or other documents indicating the planned audit scope and testing? *Comments:*_____			
3. Are the IT auditors instructed to provide detailed cross-references between the audit program and the working papers? *Comments:*_____			
4. Are the IT auditors instructed to document the work performed, findings, and other analysis to ensure their work can be followed at any subsequent time and the same conclusions reached? *Comments:*_____			
5. Do procedures require that all findings be documented so that the IT auditor's decision whether or not to include a recommendation related to that finding can be reviewed? *Comments:*_____			
6. Are the IT auditors instructed to assess the implications of each potential findings in the process of deciding whether to propose a recommendation for change? *Comments:*_____			
7. Do IT audit procedures require that the IT auditor obtain comments from an appropriate auditee for each documented finding? *Comments:*_____			
8. Is the IT auditor instructed to indicate the final resolution of each finding, whether included in a final recommendation or not, on the original workpaper? *Comments:*_____			
9. Are procedures in place requiring that all IT audit workpapers are reviewed by IT or general audit superiors to ensure that standards were sufficiently completed and conclusions supported? *Comments:*_____			
10. Do IT audit reports normally include information about the audit scope, objections, procedures, findings, and recommendations? *Comments:*_____			
Category totals:			
Combined "Yes" and "NA" total:			
Combined as a % of Total Questions:			

Workpaper 3-5. Self-Assessment Questionnaire (Page 9 of 10)

Internal IT Audit Capabilities

Item	Response		
	Yes	No	N/A
IT Audit Followup			
1. Are IT auditors instructed to prepare or update permanent or carryforward file documentation with status information to ensure that no final recommendations are left unresolved? _Comments:_ _____			
2. Is the IT auditor instructed to include and specifically to identify recommendations from prior IT audits that remain unresolved on the current audit report? _Comments:_ _____			
3. Are final audit reports distributed to an appropriate group of auditor and company management? _Comments:_ _____			
4. Are the detailed audit reports, or at least a summary of the audit performed and the most significant findings, provided to the audit committee and other selected members of senior management? _Comments:_ _____			
5. Are IT audit reports made available to the external auditors? _Comments:_ _____			
6. Do IT audit procedures require that all significant recommendations are followed up to ensure that management's responses were put into effect, and in a way which met the objective(s)? _Comments:_ _____			
7. Do IT audit procedures require that significant findings which direct management refuses to address are escalated through predefined channels and to the Board of Directors if necessary? (The IT auditor should remember that if the Board chooses to accept a risk, rather than act, then there is nothing else to be done. One of the few exceptions would be when doing nothing was potentially criminal, and that type of problem would probably be handled differently from the beginning.) _Comments:_ _____			
8. Do IT audit procedures require the IT auditor to obtain copies of prior audit reports and related follow-up materials? _Comments:_ _____			
Category totals:			
Combined "Yes" and "NA" total:			
Combined as a % of Total Questions:			

Workpaper 3-5. Self-Assessment Questionnaire (Page 10 of 10)

Internal IT Audit Capabilities

Item	Response		
	Yes	**No**	**N/A**
Relationship with External Audit			
1. Do the external auditors attempt to place any reliance on the work done by the overall internal audit department, whose activities would normally duplicate at least some of their own procedures? *Comments:* _____ _____			
2. If the internal auditors perform no procedures the external auditors performing some of these procedures simply to take advantage of total internal cost per hour rates that can be much lower than the external auditor's billing rates? *Comments:* _____ _____			
3. a) Does the external auditor participate directly in the strategic and tactical internal audit and IT audit planning? b) Do the external auditors receive a copy of all internal audit strategic and tactical plans? *Comments:* _____ _____			
4. Does the internal audit department provide copies of all internal audit reports to the external auditors? *Comments:* _____ _____			
5. If the IT auditors and external auditors are planning to perform different reviews involving one set of auditors, is the work planned to minimize the auditors description, either by working concurrently or clearly separating the timing of the two reviews? *Comments:* _____ _____			
6. Does senior management regularly or probably ask the external auditors to evaluate IT audit standards and procedures? *Comments:* _____ _____			
7. Does senior management ask the internal audit director to assess and comment on the work done by the external auditors? *Comments:* _____ _____			
8. Does senior management ask the external auditors to assess and comment on the work done by the internal auditors and IT auditors? *Comments:* _____ _____			
Category totals:			
Combined "Yes" and "NA" total:			
Combined as a % of Total Questions:			

Auditor: _____

Review: _____

Date: _____

Workpaper 3-6. Analysis Summary for Workpaper 3-5

IT Audit Capabilities	# of Yes and N/A	# of Questions	% of Total
1	3	5	60%
2	3	5	60%
3	3	5	60%
4	3	5	60%
5	3	5	60%
6	3	5	60%
7	3	5	60%
8	3	5	60%
9	3	5	60%
10	3	5	60%
11	3	5	60%
12	3	5	60%
13	3	5	60%
14	3	5	60%
Response totals	42	70	60%

Auditor: _____

Review: _____

Date: _____

Workpaper 3-7. Analysis Summary for Workpapers 3-2, 3-4, and 3-6

IT Assessment Category	# of Yes and N/A	# of Questions	% of Total
IT Environment	42	70	60%
SDLC Methodology	42	70	60%
IT Audit Capabilities	42	70	60%
Response totals	126	210	60%

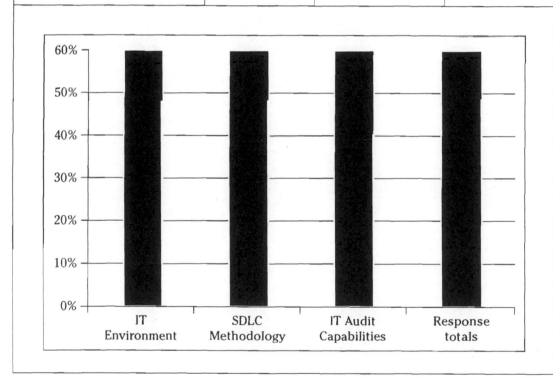

Part II
Developing the IT Audit Plan

The IT audit planning process involves developing a strategic annual audit plan and tactical plans for the individual audits. Both types of planning are discussed here. The overall objectives of IT application audit planning include:

- Determining which audit tasks must be performed
- Determining the priority for performing audit tasks
- Acquiring the necessary staff to perform the audit
- Budgeting the needed resources to perform the audit
- Demonstrating to the independent auditors the scope of internal auditing
- Effectively managing the audit function

OVERVIEW OF COMPUTER APPLICATIONS AUDIT PLANNING STANDARDS AND PROCESSES

The auditing standards issued by all professional audit organizations include audit planning information. The standards that relate to planning define what the planning process should include but do not specify the procedures for meeting planning standards. Because the standards related to planning from all professional audit groups are similar, this section uses the Standards for the Professional Practice of Internal Auditing, as issued by the Institute of Internal Auditors. This approach is supported by the Information Systems Audit and Control Association Standard for Information Systems Auditing number 050.010, which requires the Information Systems auditor to comply with applicable professional auditing standards.

Section 520 of the Institute's professional standards states that the director of internal auditing should establish plans to carry out the responsibilities of the internal auditing department. Although this standard does not divide planning into annual planning and individual planning, it does indicate that the plans should he consistent with the department's charter. Most businesses run on an annual cycle; therefore, the standard is consistent with the audit charter that a plan coincide with the organization's annual plan and that each individual audit be planned.

The specific content of Section 520 of the Institute's standards states: The planning process involves establishing:

- Goals
- Audit work schedules
- Staffing plans and financial budgets
- Activity reports

The goals of the internal auditing department should be capable of being accomplished within specified operating plans and budgets *and*, to the extent possible, should be measurable. They should be accompanied by measurement criteria and targeted dates of accomplishment.

Audit work schedules should include which activities are to be audited, when they will be audited, and the estimated time required, taking into account the scope of the audit work planned and the nature and extent of audit work performed by others. Matters to be considered in establishing an audit work schedule should include the date and results of the last audit; financial exposure; potential loss and risk; requests by management; major changes in operations, programs, systems, and controls; opportunities to achieve operating benefits; and changes to and capabilities of the audit staff. The work schedules should be sufficiently flexible to cover unanticipated demands on the internal auditing department.

Staffing plans and financial budgets, including the number of auditors and the knowledge, skills, and disciplines required to perform their work, should be determined from audit work schedules, administrative activities, education and training requirements, and audit research and development efforts.

Activity reports should be submitted periodically to management and to the board. These reports should compare performance with the department's goals and audit work schedules and compare expenditures with financial budgets. They should explain the reasons for major variances and indicate any action taken or needed.

Part II covers all aspects of the planning process except activity reporting. Activity reports are, however, an important part of the planning process and auditors must ensure that these reports are prepared and measured against the plan. Audit management makes adjustments to annual and individual audit plans on the basis of these activity reports.

Annual Audit Planning

The annual audit plan that audit management performs should include an IT audit plan for computer applications. This part of the planning process can be performed as an independent planning process and then integrated into the audit group's annual audit plan.

A five-task process is proposed here to meet the internal auditing standards for planning the annual audits of computer applications. This plan begins with guidance from the overall audit planning process and adheres to the following outline:

- Task 1: Identify potential audit areas—Identifies the computer applications subject to audit by creating an inventory of the organization's automated applications.
- Task 2: Develop a work priority scheme—Pinpoints the applications to be audited and the risks or exposures faced by these applications.
- Task 3: Determine the audit's scope—Determines the scope of computer applications audits, including the amount of resources required to perform the audit.
- Task 4: Select and schedule audits—Selects and schedules the applications to he audited in the following year on the basis of the population of potential computer applications, the degree of risk within those applications, the amount of resources required for the audit, and the amount of resources available.
- Task 5: Merge audit plans—Integrates the annual audit plan for computer applications into the audit group's annual audit plan, in some instances introducing changes into one or both plans.

Individual Audit Planning

Planning for individual audits occurs when audit management determines that it is time to begin a specific audit. The individual audit planning is constrained by the components of the annual audit plan. The purpose of the individual audit plan is to prepare for the detailed fieldwork. As such, individual audit planning is a two-part process. The first part, which is covered in this section, deals with the planning that occurs before fieldwork begins. This planning is usually done by audit management or the auditor in charge of the audit. The second part of this process occurs immediately prior to the fieldwork. This planning usually takes place at the auditee location and includes the performance of a preliminary survey and a review of auditee documentation.

The planning that occurs prior to visiting the auditee site is a six-task process. A description of the tasks follows:

- Task 1: Assigning an auditor-in-charge—Selects the individual who is to run the fieldwork, which may be the same individual who performs the remaining five planning tasks.

- Task 2: Performing application fact-gathering—Involves gathering background information about the application to be audited before visiting the auditee work areas.
- Task 3: Analyzing application audit risk—Uses the risk analysis performed in the annual audit planning as a base and then extends the analysis of risk to materials gathered through fact-gathering and risk investigation.
- Task 4: Developing and ranking measurable audit objectives—Develops specific measurable audit objectives and ranks those objectives in order of importance.
- Task 5: Developing an administrative plan to accomplish objectives—Determines the amount of resources, skill levels, and special needs required to perform each of the measurable audit objectives developed in task 4.
- Task 6: Writing audit assignment—Develops the audit assignment that is the basis for performing the fieldwork. Part III of this book describes how to conduct the fieldwork, which is based on the audit assignment developed in this individual audit planning step.

Updating Annual and Individual Audit Plans

The creation of these plans occurs at a single point in time; however, the plans should he continually updated on the basis of changing information. Audit management updates the annual plan, and the individual audit plan is updated by the auditor-in-charge.

The events that can cause an audit plan to he changed include:

- Change in the business or operating environment (e.g., the addition of a new line of business, significant changes in the volume of business, or perceived problems in a specific line of business)
- Change in allocation of work between the independent auditors and the internal auditors
- Change in the size or skill of the internal audit staff
- Change in scope of audits based on individual audit planning or findings during the audit fieldwork
- Audit judgment or experience indicating that the business risks and exposures have changed and thus the type or scope of audits should change.

Whenever one of these events causes changes to occur, the plan should be updated. The plan is a document that is used by audit management and the auditor-in-charge to determine the completion of the audit effort. If the plan is not updated as activities change, audit management has lost the tool to perform its function.

Section 4
IT Audit Planning

IT audit planning should address strategic and tactical considerations. This planning should ultimately satisfy the following objectives:

- Identifying the general controls reviews, application reviews, and other specialized reviews that could be performed to better understand the potential risks
- Evaluating and prioritizing the reviews from the prior objective
- Arranging the human and other resources needed to perform the selected reviews
- Monitoring progress against the approved plan
- Responding to unplanned projects and deviations from the plan

OVERVIEW OF STANDARDS FOR IT AUDIT PLANNING

The standards issued by professional audit organizations include audit planning. These standards normally define the basic planning process without specifying the process to follow. This section uses the Standards for the Professional Practice of IT Auditing, as issued by the Information Systems Audit and Control Association. The ISACA standards are extended by Standard 050.010, which requires the IT auditor to comply with all applicable professional auditing standards.

General Planning

Institute of Internal Auditors (IIA) standards indicate that the Internal Audit Director is ultimately responsible for all planning within the department. Although the IIA standard does not divide planning into strategic and tactical components, it does indicate that the plans should be consistent with the internal audit department charter. Most strategic plans are at least one year in scope, to match the most common business cycle. Tactical planning is most often done within the timeline of a single business cycle.

The most senior IT auditor on staff should be responsible for IT audit strategic and tactical planning. The IT audit planning activities should coincide with and compliment internal audit planning to support effective overall department functioning.

The IT audit strategic and tactical plans should be realistic, supported by the personnel, budgets, and other necessary resources, and measurable from an actual versus plan perspective.

Tactical IT audit plans should indicate what will be audited, when the audit is set to take place, and how much time is required. The IT auditor or internal auditor responsible for developing the tactical plans should consider most, if not all, of the following:

- When the most recent IT audit was performed
- Results of the most recent IT audit
- Results of the most recent risk assessment
- Magnitude of specific financial exposures
- Changes in the operations
- Requests from management

IT auditors should develop tactical plans that include specific objectives, staffing plans, financial budgets, administrative activities, training requirements, and encompass other appropriate activities.

The IT audit director and lead IT auditor should regularly prepare combined status and activity reports, and provide them to senior management, and, if appropriate, to the audit committee and the board of directors. The reports should include a comparison of actual to planned performance, and actual to planned expenditures. The report should also include the reasons for major variances, whether plan adjustments are needed, and what decisions, if any senior management and the board need to make.

Part II covers strategic and tactical planning, except for activity reporting. These reports are important to the planning process, and auditors should ensure that they are prepared. Senior management, the audit committee, and the board of directors should only approve changes to strategic or tactical plans based on these reports or other equally authoritative information.

Section 5
Strategic IT Audit Planning

The IT audit department plans should include IT components, and within these components should be plans for auditing automated application systems. This section focuses on application system audit planning, which follows the same pattern as the overall planning, and which should be running concurrently.

The IT auditor following the described four-step process should comply with all applicable professional standards for planning. This plan begins with guidance from the overall audit planning process and adheres to the following outline.

- Step 1: Identify all potential reviews. The IT auditor should obtain or, if unavailable, create an inventory of the company's automated application systems.
- Step 2: Prioritize the potential reviews. The IT auditor assesses the absolute and relative risk between applications based on the period since the last review, results of that review, levels of inherent risk, and other appropriate factors. The IT auditor concludes this step by preparing a prioritized list of automated application reviews.
- Step 3: Prepare initial review estimate. The IT auditor should estimate the time and resources required for at least the top third of the potential reviews.
- Step 4: Integrate plans. The IT auditor initially integrates the automated application review plan with general controls and other IT audit focus areas, and that integrated plan is then merged with the overall departmental plan.

Specific Audit Planning

There are several very different, but equally effective, models for detailed planning. The model presented includes two phases, which may run consecutively. The first phase is designed to establish a framework for the review, gather additional background information, attempting to support or extend the original risk analysis, developing the specific measurable objectives, and summarizing the phase, often in an Audit Planning Memo (APM).

The first detailed planning phase should almost always be performed and completed before spending any time in the field. The second phase can be performed in the office or the field, although the IT auditor will often find that being in the field facilitates completing the second phase. Second-phase procedures should confirm the APM or lead to its revision, and should also result in a final detailed audit program, whether it is developed or simply finalized in this phase.

At one time, this second phase was known to the public accounting forms as "interim procedures." The IT auditors updated all carryforward files, reviewed permanent workpapers, performed walkthroughs to validate procedural narratives, and performed tests of transactions to evaluate both narrative accuracy and quantitative compliance with established procedures.

Phase 1 specific audit planning includes the following steps:

- Step 1.1: Assigning an Auditor in Charge (AIC).
- Step 1.2: Reviewing background information. Includes reviewing permanent files, carryforward documents prior audit reports, etc.
- Step 1.3: Extending the risk analysis. Based in step 2, the original risk analysis should be reviewed and extended to reflect any new or additional information the IT auditor identified.
- Step 1.4: Defining measurable IT audit objectives. This objectivity should be closely related to all the prior steps, and be clearly stated to help ensure that the audit is successfully executed.
- Step 1.5: Write the APM. The IT auditor should be able to complete this task having begun it earlier and based on the results of steps 1.1 through 1.4. Once written, the IT audit manager should review and approve it on a timely basis. Work can proceed without this approval, but the work is at risk of the IT audit manager should decide on a scope adjustment that is inconsistent with the work already done or in progress.
- Step 2: Writing the detailed audit program. Refines the nature of all activities needed to meet the previously established objectives.

Updating IT Planning Deliverables

The IT audit planning process has been described as a single thread activity—develop, document, and monitor progress. However, the plans should be periodically updated to reflect significant changes in assumptions or underlying information.

Significant changes requiring plan maintenance:

- Business or operating environment changes: adding a new product line; significant unexpected changes in business volume, or problems in some part of the business.

- Work reallocations between internal audit and external audit. Change in allocation of work between the independent auditors and the internal auditors.
- IT audit staffing changes.
- Detail IT audit changes, both in terms of audits performed and their scope, that arise over time.

Plans should be updated as needed whenever one of these events occurs. Internal audit and IT audit management, along with each AIC, use the plans to manage the audit effort. All these persons will be less effective if plans are not properly maintained.

THE ANNUAL IT AUDIT PLANNING PROCESS

The annual IT audit plan is usually prepared by the most senior IT auditor on staff. This plan is a subset of the internal audit's annual planning process. IT audit planning is properly separated due to its unique issues and objectives, although all auditing planning must be coordinated to help ensure that all top-level objectives are met. (Throughout this section, we will generically refer to the senior IT auditor as the IT audit manager for convenience.)

The IT audit manager should already know or gather the following information before preparing the annual IT audit plan.

- The talent, shell, and capacity of the current IT audit staff
- The potential for acquiring additional resources of these are problems that could prevent eventual completion of the plan
- The IT annual plan
- Expected external audit scope, historical support provided by IT audit, and the level and nature of coordination expected for the coming year
- Expected changes in the business or operating environment
- Any planned changes in the IT audit or internal audit function

The IT audit manager, armed with the above information, should prepare the plan by following the four-step methodology described earlier in the text.

STEP 1: IDENTIFY ALL POTENTIAL REVIEWS

The IT audit manager will find that the vast majority of IT reviews will fall into one of two categories: automated application reviews or general controls reviews. This author feels that almost every conceivable review falls into one of these categories, except for special topics like fraud investigations. In most normal situations, the IT auditor will be focused on a processing environment, making the work a general controls review, or on how the activity within or across environments meets general business objectives, making the work an automated application review.

Information Sources

The IT auditor should consider reviewing at least the following items to identify potential reviews. The IT auditor should first request these items. If they are not available, then IT personnel should be asked to develop them. The IT auditor should only personally develop any such item as a last resort, and should also consider drafting a recommendation that the IT function maintain this information.

- Annual IT plan
- An automated application inventory
- A systems software inventory
- A summarized or high-level hardware inventory

IT auditor should consider reviews related to applications and environments that the IT function only has limited responsibility for. Furthermore, the IT auditor should always be alert for systems and applications where the IT function is not responsible, or possibly not even aware of them.

STEP 2: EVALUATE AND PRIORITIZE POSSIBLE REVIEWS

The IT auditor's foundation for this step is performing an accurate risk assessment of the potential reviews. The risk assessment is normally a highly customized activity, as the accuracy of the results are directly correlated with how well the risk assessment model reflects the issues and conditions that will determine the company's future success. The risk assessment process usually produces a numerical score or other value that can be used to compare items that are otherwise unrelated or are difficult to compare.

The final risk value or score enables the IT auditor to rank the potential reviews by the degree of risk to the company. The IT auditor should find that many elements of the risk assessment are objective, and produce the most easily defended results. Unfortunately for the auditor, there will almost always be significant subjective, or judgmental, elements included in the risk assessment. There will also be situations where the judgmental elements clearly outweigh the objective elements.

The risk assessment model presented on the following pages includes both objective and subjective elements. The IT auditor should also consider the idea that even identifying objective and subjective elements can create conflict, as the classification of an element is often a matter of opinion. The IT audit director will normally establish the basic definitions for objective and subjective while developing the departmental strategic planning framework. The included risk assessment model will not go beyond defining possible elements and providing examples for using them.

The IT audit manager needs to work closely with all of the appropriate constituencies in the company. Reflecting their concerns and opinions in the risk assessment model is likely to increase their acceptance of the tactical audit plan. Their acceptance, in turn, is likely to be a significant contributing factor in determining whether the IT audit effort is successful.

The IT audit manager may enter the risk assessment step with an extremely long list of potential automated application reviews and general controls reviews. It may be reasonable in that situation for the IT audit manager to perform an initial risk assessment to quickly separate the potential review list into two or three sections. A two-section split could be as basic as include versus exclude, and a three-section list divided as being high, medium, and low risk. The text does not describe procedures for an initial risk assessment, as it represents a subset of a complete risk assessment.

An IT audit manager in a small company, in having little time, or supported with limited resources, may choose to use a limited risk assessment for the company and not go farther. That inherently subjective division will ultimately be supported or overturned by the IT audit director, and then by senior management.

IT auditors may choose to reduce or extend the number of elements and the analysis done for each one. In any event, the final risk assessment model should match up well to the company.

The Task Process

The risk assessment model described in the text is developed and used in three phases. Phase 1 includes risk factor identification and weighting. Phase 2 includes assigning the risk value to each risk factor, whether it is determined subjectively or objectively. Phase 3 combines the total risk score, and is the phase where the accumulated scores are used to rank the potential reviews.

The IT auditor should always consider the following issues and items prior to beginning a risk assessment. If the IT auditor finds that too many of these represent problems or exceptions, then others should be selected.

- A complete systems and applications inventory is available or can be developed to establish the audit universe.
- A readily available inventory may have one or more of the following problems: it may not reflect recent production environment changes, it may exclude automated application reviews that are still in development and testing, or strategic and tactical changes planned for the hardware and equipment environment.

- Other unauthorized changes, whether accidental or intentional, may cause customer-provided information to be anything from slightly incomplete to completely invalid.
- The internal audit department, senior management, and audit customers may be better serviced if an IT auditor is involved who has the appropriate technical background.
- The IT auditor who fails to include the appropriate number of company managers, technical employees, end users, and other auditees is likely to develop a model that is at least rejected, or at most fatally flawed.
- Judgment, whether the IT auditor's or from another constituency, is an inherent and necessary part of any risk assessment. Even choosing only monetary risk factors in an attempt to avoid subjectivity is founded on the *opinion* that monetary factors are objective.

The above list is not meant to be all-inclusive, and should always be tailored to the facts and circumstances of the company or situation.

If the IT auditor is not familiar with the risk assessment process, he or she should take extra time to become familiar with the process. One should also consider asking IT auditors from other companies, or other knowledgeable third parties, to periodically review progress and plans, and provide other needed support.

Review the internal audit risk assessment model. Normal IT audit planning should complement the internal audit departmental process, with which the IT audit manager should be familiar. The three-step risk assessment described earlier will be apparent in almost every model as either the actual structure, or as a central theme, of the internal audit risk assessment model.

The risk assessment model in Exhibit 5-1 begins with some of the nontechnical areas the IT audit manager should review to identify relevant risk factors.

- Regularity issues: SEC, IRS, and other federal and state agencies
- Company policies and procedures: policies and procedures may be established within a company, and even within a company at the subsidiary, division, department, or other level
- Business environment: current opportunities or limitations of the economy and overall competitive pressures
- Market position: are there unusual or even unique circumstances to consider, or is the company positioned to compete in a low-cost commodity-type market?
- Geopolitical issues: are there current or potential events that could significantly impact the company such as hyperinflation, civil unrest, or regional instability?

Exhibit 5-1. Risk Assessment Model (100-Point System)

RISK ASSESSMENT MODEL			ITEM 1	ITEM 2	ITEM 3	ITEM 4	ITEM 5
Category	Description	Overall Points					
A	FIRST CATEGORY	25	22.5	4.5	4.3	4.0	3.8
B	SECOND CATEGORY	25	21.0	0.5	0.8	1.0	1.3
C	THIRD CATEGORY	20	12.4	1.4	1.6	1.8	2.0
D	FOURTH CATEGORY	17	13.3	2.0	2.2	2.4	2.6
E	FIFTH CATEGORY	13	11.7	2.2	2.3	2.5	2.6
TOTAL OVERALL RISK SCORE		100	80.9	10.7	11.2	11.7	12.2

A	FIRST CATEGORY		ITEM 1	ITEM 2	ITEM 3	ITEM 4	ITEM 5
1	SUBCATEGORY	13	11.7	2.3	2.2	2.1	2.0
2	SUBCATEGORY	13	11.7	2.3	2.2	2.1	2.0
3	SUBCATEGORY	6	5.4	1.1	1.0	1.0	0.9
4	SUBCATEGORY	10	9.0	1.8	1.7	1.6	1.5
5	SUBCATEGORY	10	9.0	1.8	1.7	1.6	1.5
6	SUBCATEGORY	6	5.4	1.1	1.0	1.0	0.9
7	SUBCATEGORY	1	0.9	0.2	0.2	0.2	0.2
8	SUBCATEGORY	20	18.0	3.6	3.4	3.2	3.0
9	SUBCATEGORY	6	5.4	1.1	1.0	1.0	0.9
10	SUBCATEGORY	15	13.5	2.7	2.6	2.4	2.3
	Total Compliance To Technical Specs.	100	90.0	18.0	17.0	16.0	15.0

1 SUBCATEGORY

			ITEM 1	ITEM 2	ITEM 3	ITEM 4	ITEM 5
a	Characteristic 1	19	18.0	18.0	17.0	16.0	15.0
b	Characteristic 2	18	17.0				
c	Characteristic 3	17	16.0				
d	Characteristic 4	16	15.0				
e	Characteristic 5	15	14.0				
f	Characteristic 6	5	4.0				
g	Characteristic 7	4	3.0				
h	Characteristic 8	3	2.0				
i	Characteristic 9	2	1.0				
j	Characteristic 10	1	—				
	TOTAL	100	90.0	18.0	17.0	16.0	15.0

- Internal resources limitations: these could result from temporary or long-term considerations, and could have a profound impact on the company's agility and responsiveness

The entire IT audit plan may be driven by nontechnical issues. External constraints may require that certain audits be performed on a predetermined schedule, and these could consume 100 percent of the available resources. A limited risk assessment model may still be useful for sequencing and refining the required reviews.

It is more likely that the majority of the available IT audit resources can be spent on discretionary reviews. This appears to support having the IT audit manager perform a risk assessment, including additional internal and technical considerations.

Define the Risk Assessment Model. The included model groups the universe of potential risk factors into five categories. The IT audit manager may group or break down these categories as necessary, and also restrict or extend the breadth and depth of the risk factors in each category. The categories are summarized below.

- Criticality: This may be best understood by considering the potential impact of the automated application system or hardware being *unavailable*. Simply put, the closer an outage comes to stopping the business, the more critical it is.

- Complexity: This should be separated because there is no inherent direct relationship between how complex and how critical an automated application system is. There is a direct relationship between complexity and the risk of failure, and that risk is the focus in this category. The size of a hardware or hardware system is often included in the evaluation of complexity, but it can be included elsewhere. The relationship between size and complexity can be high, but it can also be quite low.

- Technology: This is an important, but equally difficult, category for assessing risk. Technology is important because the right technology should efficiently and effectively support business activities. The wrong technology could easily lead to missed opportunities and wasted resources. The IT auditor trying to assess technology issues is further confounded by having no means to objectively determine the "right" technology for each company and related nuances.

- Control environment: This is where any prior IT reviews are included. The IT auditor, whether experienced director or first-year staff, is likely to be most comfortable and confident working in this category. The IT auditor should be careful not to over-emphasize the control environment due to that comfort factor.

- Integration: The more tightly integrated the systems are with the business activity, the greater the business risk if there is a problem. The irony is that weakly integrated systems represent an almost automatic IT audit recommendation.

Develop Risk Factor Weighting. The IT audit manager creates a weighting methodology to complement and support the risk factor categories defined for the risk assessment model. There are numerous alternatives available, but the text utilizes a basic automatic approach on a 100-point scale.

The 100 point system is one of a wide range of alternative implementations of the arithmetic model. There are also at least three different ways to implement the 100 point system. The first method illustrated in Exhibit 5-1, assumes that each group of categories or subcategories must total 100 points. The total score achieved in a subcategory group is reduced when the score moves up to the next level.

The second method is built on the assumption that there are only 100 points, and they are allocated across the full range of categories and subcategories. The method illustrated in Exhibit 5-2. The third method is based on the idea that each individual category, a subcategory, is scored on the same scale, such as 1 to 100, or 1 to 10. The actual score is multiplied by a weighting factor. This method is illustrated in Exhibit 5-3.

All three exhibits include sample data as if each of the methods were used to evaluate a single automated application system. The IT auditor should notice that all three methods lead to the same final risk score. The method selected may be more closely linked to the experience and personal preference of the auditor than anything else.

Proponents of the first method, which combines the other two methods, believe that it allows the IT auditors performing the risk assessment see the complete situation without over complicating the risk scoring process.

Proponents of the second method believe it to be the most realistic because there are no secondary in automatic calculations. There are only 100 points to be had, and each category's contribution to the total is clearly visible.

Proponents of the third method believe that its advantage is based on the fact that the IT auditor performing the review evaluates each category or subcategory on the same scale, and that repetition and consistency will lead to better results.

The first method, the 100-point must system, is portrayed in Workpaper 5-1. This workpaper is structured with one automated application system or general controls review per column, and the categories and subcategories down the left side. This structure is probably better suited to those situations where there are a limited number of automated application systems and general controls reviews. This workpaper is designed with the categories as columns, and the list of potential automated application systems and general controls review reviews appear down the left side of the risk assessment model.

There is no single set of risk factors that encompass every situation the IT auditor may encounter. The following lists illustrate some of the risk factors that might be included in each category. Criticality (defined as the impact of a system outage on):

- The company's mission
- The well-being, safety, or interest of third parties
- The company's competitive advantage
- The public's confidence in the company or product
- The ability to provide privacy, confidentiality, or security
- The interfaces with internal or external third parties

Complexity:

- Number of users
- Number of interfaces
- Network complexity
- Number of input items
- Number of physical files
- Number of logical files
- Number of simultaneous interactive queries
- Complexity of core programming language
- Number of time zones supported
- Number of devices
- Transaction volumes
- Complexity of individual transactions

Technology:

- Number of technology platforms:
  —Mainframe
  —Midrange
  —Client/server
- Number of hardware vendors
- Number of software providers

General controls, including:

- IT administrations
- Physical access controls
- Logical access controls
- SDLC methodology
- Backup and recovery

Step 4. The risk assessment model can be used in both developing and production automated application systems. The results are comparable because the potential risk can be assessed for systems being developed.

Exhibit 5-2. Risk Assessment Model (Weighted System)

RISK ASSESSMENT MODEL			ITEM 1	ITEM 2	ITEM 3	ITEM 4	ITEM 5
Category	Description	Overall Points					
A	FIRST CATEGORY	60	0	0	0	0	0
B	SECOND CATEGORY	10	0	0	0	0	0
C	THIRD CATEGORY	10	0	0	0	0	0
D	FOURTH CATEGORY	10	0	0	0	0	0
E	FIFTH CATEGORY	10	0	0	0	0	0
TOTAL OVERALL RISK SCORE		100	—	—	—	—	—

A	FIRST CATEGORY						
	1	SUBCATEGORY	13	—	—	—	—	—
	2	SUBCATEGORY	13	—	—	—	—	—
	3	SUBCATEGORY	6	—	—	—	—	—
	4	SUBCATEGORY	10	—	—	—	—	—
	5	SUBCATEGORY	10	—	—	—	—	—
	6	SUBCATEGORY	6	—	—	—	—	—
	7	SUBCATEGORY	2	—	—	—	—	—
	8	SUBCATEGORY	0	—	—	—	—	—
	9	SUBCATEGORY	0	—	—	—	—	—
	10	SUBCATEGORY	0	—	—	—	—	—
		Total Compliance To Technical Specs.	60	—	—	—	—	—

1 SUBCATEGORY

a	Characteristic 1	2					
b	Characteristic 2	2					
c	Characteristic 3	3					
d	Characteristic 4	1					
e	Characteristic 5	1					
f	Characteristic 6	2					
g	Characteristic 7	1					
h	Characteristic 8	1					
i	Characteristic 9	0					
j	Characteristic 10	0					
	TOTAL	13	—	—	—	—	—

The difference between the two really only relates to evaluation, there controls as the systems in development cannot be evaluated.

The IT auditor has been shown how to use a risk assessment model in both an absolute and a relative sense. Each automated application system in the example was scored independently for each objective or subjective

Exhibit 5-3. Risk Assessment Model (10-Point System)

Category	Description	Overall Points	ITEM 1	ITEM 2	ITEM 3	ITEM 4	ITEM 5
RISK ASSESSMENT MODEL							
A	FIRST CATEGORY	25	13.8	2.3	2.0	1.8	1.5
B	SECOND CATEGORY	25	20.5	0.7	1.1	1.4	1.8
C	THIRD CATEGORY	20	11.3	2.3	2.7	3.0	3.3
D	FOURTH CATEGORY	17	13.0	2.6	2.8	3.0	3.2
E	FIFTH CATEGORY	13	9.0	1.3	1.2	1.0	0.7
TOTAL OVERALL RISK SCORE		100	67.5	9.1	9.7	10.2	10.5

A	FIRST CATEGORY		ITEM 1	ITEM 2	ITEM 3	ITEM 4	ITEM 5
1	SUBCATEGORY	100	55.0	9.0	8.0	7.0	6.0
2	SUBCATEGORY	100	55.0	9.0	8.0	7.0	6.0
3	SUBCATEGORY	100	55.0	9.0	8.0	7.0	6.0
4	SUBCATEGORY	100	55.0	9.0	8.0	7.0	6.0
5	SUBCATEGORY	100	55.0	9.0	8.0	7.0	6.0
6	SUBCATEGORY	100	55.0	9.0	8.0	7.0	6.0
7	SUBCATEGORY	100	55.0	9.0	8.0	7.0	6.0
8	SUBCATEGORY	100	55.0	9.0	8.0	7.0	6.0
9	SUBCATEGORY	100	55.0	9.0	8.0	7.0	6.0
10	SUBCATEGORY	100	55.0	9.0	8.0	7.0	6.0
	Total Compliance To Technical Specs.	1000	550.0	90.0	80.0	70.0	60.0

1 SUBCATEGORY			ITEM 1	ITEM 2	ITEM 3	ITEM 4	ITEM 5
a	Characteristic 1	10	10.0	9.0	8.0	7.0	6.0
b	Characteristic 2	10	9.0				
c	Characteristic 3	10	8.0				
d	Characteristic 4	10	7.0				
e	Characteristic 5	10	6.0				
f	Characteristic 6	10	5.0				
g	Characteristic 7	10	4.0				
h	Characteristic 8	10	3.0				
i	Characteristic 9	10	2.0				
j	Characteristic 10	10	1.0				
	TOTAL	100	55.0	9.0	8.0	7.0	6.0

criteria—an absolute evaluation. Once the scores are compared, the evaluation is on a relative basis.

The IT auditor may consider short-cutting the process and moving directly into a relative risk assessment model, where each automated application systems is ranked versus the others (Exhibit 5-4). The IT auditor

Workpaper 5-1. Risk Assessment Model (100-Point System)

			ITEM 1	ITEM 2	ITEM 3	ITEM 4	ITEM 5

RISK ASSESSMENT MODEL

Category	Description	Overall Points	ITEM 1	ITEM 2	ITEM 3	ITEM 4	ITEM 5
A	FIRST CATEGORY	25	22.5	4.5	4.3	4.0	3.8
B	SECOND CATEGORY	25	21.0	0.5	0.8	1.0	1.3
C	THIRD CATEGORY	20	12.4	1.4	1.6	1.8	2.3
D	FOURTH CATEGORY	17	13.3	2.0	2.2	2.4	2.6
E	FIFTH CATEGORY	13	11.7	2.2	2.3	2.5	2.6
TOTAL OVERALL RISK SCORE		100	80.9	10.7	11.2	11.7	12.2

A	FIRST CATEGORY		ITEM 1	ITEM 2	ITEM 3	ITEM 4	ITEM 5
	1	SUBCATEGORY	13	11.7	2.3	2.2	2.1	2.0
	2	SUBCATEGORY	13	11.7	2.3	2.2	2.1	2.0
	3	SUBCATEGORY	6	5.4	1.1	1.0	1.0	0.9
	4	SUBCATEGORY	10	9.0	1.8	1.7	1.6	1.5
	5	SUBCATEGORY	10	9.0	1.8	1.7	1.6	1.5
	6	SUBCATEGORY	6	5.4	1.1	1.0	1.0	0.9
	7	SUBCATEGORY	1	0.9	0.2	0.2	0.2	0.2
	8	SUBCATEGORY	20	18.0	3.6	3.4	3.2	3.0
	9	SUBCATEGORY	6	5.4	1.1	1.0	1.0	0.9
	10	SUBCATEGORY	15	13.5	2.7	2.6	2.4	2.3
		Total Compliance To Technical Specs.	100	90.0	18.0	17.0	16.0	15.0

1 SUBCATEGORY

	Description	Points	ITEM 1	ITEM 2	ITEM 3	ITEM 4	ITEM 5
a	Characteristic 1	19	18.0	18.0	17.0	16.0	15.0
b	Characteristic 2	18	17.0				
c	Characteristic 3	17	16.0				
d	Characteristic 4	16	15.0				
e	Characteristic 5	15	14.0				
f	Characteristic 6	5	4.0				
g	Characteristic 7	4	3.0				
h	Characteristic 8	3	2.0				
i	Characteristic 9	2	1.0				
j	Characteristic 10	1	—				
	TOTAL	100	90.0	18.0	17.0	16.0	15.0

Workpaper 5-1. Risk Assessment Model (100-Point System) (Continued)

RISK ASSESSMENT MODEL			ITEM 1	ITEM 2	ITEM 3	ITEM 4	ITEM 5

2 SUBCATEGORY

			ITEM 1	ITEM 2	ITEM 3	ITEM 4	ITEM 5
a	Characteristic 1	19	18.0	18.0	17.0	16.0	15.0
b	Characteristic 2	18	17.0				
c	Characteristic 3	17	16.0				
d	Characteristic 4	16	15.0				
e	Characteristic 5	15	14.0				
f	Characteristic 6	5	4.0				
g	Characteristic 7	4	3.0				
h	Characteristic 8	3	2.0				
i	Characteristic 9	2	1.0				
j	Characteristic 10	1	—				
	TOTAL	100	90.0	18.0	17.0	16.0	15.0

3 SUBCATEGORY

			ITEM 1	ITEM 2	ITEM 3	ITEM 4	ITEM 5
a	Characteristic 1	19	18.0	18.0	17.0	16.0	15.0
b	Characteristic 2	18	17.0				
c	Characteristic 3	17	16.0				
d	Characteristic 4	16	15.0				
e	Characteristic 5	15	14.0				
f	Characteristic 6	5	4.0				
g	Characteristic 7	4	3.0				
h	Characteristic 8	3	2.0				
i	Characteristic 9	2	1.0				
j	Characteristic 10	1	—				
	TOTAL	100	90.0	18.0	17.0	16.0	15.0

4 SUBCATEGORY

			ITEM 1	ITEM 2	ITEM 3	ITEM 4	ITEM 5
a	Characteristic 1	19	18.0	18.0	17.0	16.0	15.0
b	Characteristic 2	18	17.0				
c	Characteristic 3	17	16.0				
d	Characteristic 4	16	15.0				
e	Characteristic 5	15	14.0				
f	Characteristic 6	5	4.0				
g	Characteristic 7	4	3.0				
h	Characteristic 8	3	2.0				
i	Characteristic 9	2	1.0				
j	Characteristic 10	1	—				
	TOTAL	100	90.0	18.0	17.0	16.0	15.0

Workpaper 5-1. Risk Assessment Model (100-Point System) (Continued)

RISK ASSESSMENT MODEL				ITEM 1	ITEM 2	ITEM 3	ITEM 4	ITEM 5
5 SUBCATEGORY								
a	Characteristic 1		19	18.0	18.0	17.0	16.0	15.0
b	Characteristic 2		18	17.0				
c	Characteristic 3		17	16.0				
d	Characteristic 4		16	15.0				
e	Characteristic 5		15	14.0				
f	Characteristic 6		5	4.0				
g	Characteristic 7		4	3.0				
h	Characteristic 8		3	2.0				
i	Characteristic 9		2	1.0				
j	Characteristic 10		1	—				
	TOTAL		100	90.0	18.0	17.0	16.0	15.0

6 SUBCATEGORY								
a	Characteristic 1		19	18.0	18.0	17.0	16.0	15.0
b	Characteristic 2		18	17.0				
c	Characteristic 3		17	16.0				
d	Characteristic 4		16	15.0				
e	Characteristic 5		15	14.0				
f	Characteristic 6		5	4.0				
g	Characteristic 7		4	3.0				
h	Characteristic 8		3	2.0				
i	Characteristic 9		2	1.0				
j	Characteristic 10		1	—				
	TOTAL		100	90.0	18.0	17.0	16.0	15.0

7 SUBCATEGORY								
a	Characteristic 1		19	18.0	18.0	17.0	16.0	15.0
b	Characteristic 2		18	17.0				
c	Characteristic 3		17	16.0				
d	Characteristic 4		16	15.0				
e	Characteristic 5		15	14.0				
f	Characteristic 6		5	4.0				
g	Characteristic 7		4	3.0				
h	Characteristic 8		3	2.0				
i	Characteristic 9		2	1.0				
j	Characteristic 10		1	—				
	TOTAL		100	90.0	18.0	17.0	16.0	15.0

Workpaper 5-1. Risk Assessment Model (100-Point System) (Continued)

RISK ASSESSMENT MODEL			ITEM 1	ITEM 2	ITEM 3	ITEM 4	ITEM 5
8 SUBCATEGORY							
a	Characteristic 1	19	18.0	18.0	17.0	16.0	15.0
b	Characteristic 2	18	17.0				
c	Characteristic 3	17	16.0				
d	Characteristic 4	16	15.0				
e	Characteristic 5	15	14.0				
f	Characteristic 6	5	4.0				
g	Characteristic 7	4	3.0				
h	Characteristic 8	3	2.0				
i	Characteristic 9	2	1.0				
j	Characteristic 10	1	—				
	TOTAL	100	90.0	18.0	17.0	16.0	15.0

9 SUBCATEGORY							
a	Characteristic 1	19	18.0	18.0	17.0	16.0	15.0
b	Characteristic 2	18	17.0				
c	Characteristic 3	17	16.0				
d	Characteristic 4	16	15.0				
e	Characteristic 5	15	14.0				
f	Characteristic 6	5	4.0				
g	Characteristic 7	4	3.0				
h	Characteristic 8	3	2.0				
i	Characteristic 9	2	1.0				
j	Characteristic 10	1	—				
	TOTAL	100	90.0	18.0	17.0	16.0	15.0

10 SUBCATEGORY							
a	Characteristic 1	19	18.0	18.0	17.0	16.0	15.0
b	Characteristic 2	18	17.0				
c	Characteristic 3	17	16.0				
d	Characteristic 4	16	15.0				
e	Characteristic 5	15	14.0				
f	Characteristic 6	5	4.0				
g	Characteristic 7	4	3.0				
h	Characteristic 8	3	2.0				
i	Characteristic 9	2	1.0				
j	Characteristic 10	1	—				
	TOTAL	100	90.0	18.0	17.0	16.0	15.0

Workpaper 5-1. Risk Assessment Model (100-Point System) (Continued)

RISK ASSESSMENT MODEL				ITEM 1	ITEM 2	ITEM 3	ITEM 4	ITEM 5
B	**SECOND CATEGORY**							
	1	Characteristic 1	10	9.0	2.0	3.0	4.0	5.0
	2	Characteristic 2	10	10.0				
	3	Characteristic 3	10	6.0				
	4	Characteristic 4	15	6.0				
	5	Characteristic 5	15	15.0				
	6	Characteristic 6	20	20.0				
	7	Characteristic 7	20	18.0				
	8	Unused						
	9	Unused						
	10	Unused						
		TOTAL	100	84.0	2.0	3.0	4.0	5.0

				ITEM 1	ITEM 2	ITEM 3	ITEM 4	ITEM 5
C	**THIRD CATEGORY**							
	1	Characteristic 1	17	6.0	7.0	8.0	9.0	10.0
	2	Characteristic 2	17	11.0				
	3	Characteristic 3	17	17.0				
	4	Characteristic 4	17	14.0				
	5	Characteristic 5	17	5.0				
	6	Characteristic 6	15	9.0				
	7	Unused						
	8	Unused						
	9	Unused						
	10	Unused						
		TOTAL	100	62.0	7.0	8.0	9.0	10.0

				ITEM 1	ITEM 2	ITEM 3	ITEM 4	ITEM 5
D	**FOURTH CATEGORY**							
	1	Characteristic 1	25	11.0	12.0	13.0	14.0	15.0
	2	Characteristic 2	25	20.0				
	3	Characteristic 3	30	28.0				
	4	Characteristic 4	20	19.0				
	5	Unused						
	6	Unused						
	7	Unused						
	8	Unused						
	9	Unused						
	10	Unused						
		TOTAL	100	78.0	12.0	13.0	14.0	15.0

Workpaper 5-1. Risk Assessment Model (100-Point System) (Continued)

RISK ASSESSMENT MODEL				ITEM 1	ITEM 2	ITEM 3	ITEM 4	ITEM 5
E		FIFTH CATEGORY						
	1	Characteristic 1	10	10.0	17.0	18.0	19.0	20.0
	2	Characteristic 2	15	15.0				
	3	Characteristic 3	20	19.0				
	4	Characteristic 4	15	14.0				
	5	Characteristic 5	8	7.0				
	6	Characteristic 6	8	4.0				
	7	Characteristic 7	8	7.0				
	8	Characteristic 8	8	8.0				
	9	Characteristic 9	8	6.0				
	10	Unused						
		TOTAL	100	90.0	17.0	18.0	19.0	20.0

should be careful in taking this path because it hides the absolute analysis that is still being done. Consider even a question that seems completely relative, such as 'so is today hotter than yesterday?' One could not answer without knowing that "hot" refers to temperature, which is measured on one of several scales.

If one did not know what temperature was for each day, then one might decide which day felt hotter. Returning to the audit risk assessment, the auditor should try to document the absolute items whenever possible, as it builds a stronger and more defendable foundation in case the risk assessment results are challenged. This does not preclude the auditor from including judgment in the risk assessment model, but only strives to separate both the objective/subjective and the mechanical/judgmental elements.

Preventing and solving problems. There are problems that might inhibit the IT auditor's ability to use risk assessment techniques. These problems include:

- Significant data collection resources
- Inadequate IT planning
- Lack of credibility in the risk assessment model
- Insufficient time to analyze the collected data
- Inadequate skills in IT to perform the initial risk scoring

Potential solutions include:

- Simplify the questionnaire and procedures
- Encourage IT personnel to plan by helping them to develop a basic plan

Workpaper 5-2. Risk Assessment Model (Weighted System)

RISK ASSESSMENT MODEL			ITEM 1	ITEM 2	ITEM 3	ITEM 4	ITEM 5
Category	Description	Overall Points					
A	FIRST CATEGORY	25	—	—	—	—	—
B	SECOND CATEGORY	25	—	—	—	—	—
C	THIRD CATEGORY	20	—	—	—	—	—
D	FOURTH CATEGORY	17	—	—	—	—	—
E	FIFTH CATEGORY	13	—	—	—	—	—
TOTAL OVERALL RISK SCORE		100	—	—	—	—	—

A	FIRST CATEGORY			ITEM 1	ITEM 2	ITEM 3	ITEM 4	ITEM 5
	1	SUBCATEGORY	100	—	—	—	—	—
	2	SUBCATEGORY	100	—	—	—	—	—
	3	SUBCATEGORY	100	—	—	—	—	—
	4	SUBCATEGORY	100	—	—	—	—	—
	5	SUBCATEGORY	100	—	—	—	—	—
	6	SUBCATEGORY	100	—	—	—	—	—
	7	SUBCATEGORY	100	—	—	—	—	—
	8	SUBCATEGORY	100	—	—	—	—	—
	9	SUBCATEGORY	100	—	—	—	—	—
	10	SUBCATEGORY	100	—	—	—	—	—
		Total Compliance To Technical Specs.	1000	—	—	—	—	—

1 SUBCATEGORY

		Overall Points	ITEM 1	ITEM 2	ITEM 3	ITEM 4	ITEM 5
a	Characteristic 1	10					
b	Characteristic 2	10					
c	Characteristic 3	10					
d	Characteristic 4	10					
e	Characteristic 5	10					
f	Characteristic 6	10					
g	Characteristic 7	10					
h	Characteristic 8	10					
i	Characteristic 9	10					
j	Characteristic 10	10					
	TOTAL	100	—	—	—	—	—

Workpaper 5-2. Risk Assessment Model (Weighted System) (Continued)

RISK ASSESSMENT MODEL			ITEM 1	ITEM 2	ITEM 3	ITEM 4	ITEM 5

2 SUBCATEGORY

a	Characteristic 1	10					
b	Characteristic 2	10					
c	Characteristic 3	10					
d	Characteristic 4	10					
e	Characteristic 5	10					
f	Characteristic 6	10					
g	Characteristic 7	10					
h	Characteristic 8	10					
i	Characteristic 9	10					
j	Characteristic 10	10					
	TOTAL	100	—	—	—	—	—

3 SUBCATEGORY

a	Characteristic 1	10					
b	Characteristic 2	10					
c	Characteristic 3	10					
d	Characteristic 4	10					
e	Characteristic 5	10					
f	Characteristic 6	10					
g	Characteristic 7	10					
h	Characteristic 8	10					
i	Characteristic 9	10					
j	Characteristic 10	10					
	TOTAL	100	—	—	—	—	—

4 SUBCATEGORY

a	Characteristic 1	10					
b	Characteristic 2	10					
c	Characteristic 3	10					
d	Characteristic 4	10					
e	Characteristic 5	10					
f	Characteristic 6	10					
g	Characteristic 7	10					
h	Characteristic 8	10					
i	Characteristic 9	10					
j	Characteristic 10	10					
	TOTAL	100	—	—	—	—	—

Workpaper 5-2. Risk Assessment Model (Weighted System) (Continued)

RISK ASSESSMENT MODEL			ITEM 1	ITEM 2	ITEM 3	ITEM 4	ITEM 5

5 SUBCATEGORY

			ITEM 1	ITEM 2	ITEM 3	ITEM 4	ITEM 5
a	Characteristic 1	10					
b	Characteristic 2	10					
c	Characteristic 3	10					
d	Characteristic 4	10					
e	Characteristic 5	10					
f	Characteristic 6	10					
g	Characteristic 7	10					
h	Characteristic 8	10					
i	Characteristic 9	10					
j	Characteristic 10	10					
	TOTAL	100	—	—	—	—	—

6 SUBCATEGORY

			ITEM 1	ITEM 2	ITEM 3	ITEM 4	ITEM 5
a	Characteristic 1	10					
b	Characteristic 2	10					
c	Characteristic 3	10					
d	Characteristic 4	10					
e	Characteristic 5	10					
f	Characteristic 6	10					
g	Characteristic 7	10					
h	Characteristic 8	10					
i	Characteristic 9	10					
j	Characteristic 10	10					
	TOTAL	100	—	—	—	—	—

7 SUBCATEGORY

			ITEM 1	ITEM 2	ITEM 3	ITEM 4	ITEM 5
a	Characteristic 1	10					
b	Characteristic 2	10					
c	Characteristic 3	10					
d	Characteristic 4	10					
e	Characteristic 5	10					
f	Characteristic 6	10					
g	Characteristic 7	10					
h	Characteristic 8	10					
i	Characteristic 9	10					
j	Characteristic 10	10					
	TOTAL	100	—	—	—	—	—

Workpaper 5-2. Risk Assessment Model (Weighted System) (Continued)

RISK ASSESSMENT MODEL

			ITEM 1	ITEM 2	ITEM 3	ITEM 4	ITEM 5

8 SUBCATEGORY

			ITEM 1	ITEM 2	ITEM 3	ITEM 4	ITEM 5
a	Characteristic 1	10					
b	Characteristic 2	10					
c	Characteristic 3	10					
d	Characteristic 4	10					
e	Characteristic 5	10					
f	Characteristic 6	10					
g	Characteristic 7	10					
h	Characteristic 8	10					
i	Characteristic 9	10					
j	Characteristic 10	10					
	TOTAL	100	—	—	—	—	—

9 SUBCATEGORY

			ITEM 1	ITEM 2	ITEM 3	ITEM 4	ITEM 5
a	Characteristic 1	10					
b	Characteristic 2	10					
c	Characteristic 3	10					
d	Characteristic 4	10					
e	Characteristic 5	10					
f	Characteristic 6	10					
g	Characteristic 7	10					
h	Characteristic 8	10					
i	Characteristic 9	10					
j	Characteristic 10	10					
	TOTAL	100	—	—	—	—	—

10 SUBCATEGORY

			ITEM 1	ITEM 2	ITEM 3	ITEM 4	ITEM 5
a	Characteristic 1	10					
b	Characteristic 2	10					
c	Characteristic 3	10					
d	Characteristic 4	10					
e	Characteristic 5	10					
f	Characteristic 6	10					
g	Characteristic 7	10					
h	Characteristic 8	10					
i	Characteristic 9	10					
j	Characteristic 10	10					
	TOTAL	100	—	—	—	—	—

Workpaper 5-2. Risk Assessment Model (Weighted System) (Continued)

RISK ASSESSMENT MODEL				ITEM 1	ITEM 2	ITEM 3	ITEM 4	ITEM 5
B	SECOND CATEGORY							
	1	Characteristic 1	10					
	2	Characteristic 2	10					
	3	Characteristic 3	10					
	4	Characteristic 4	10					
	5	Characteristic 5	10					
	6	Characteristic 6	10					
	7	Characteristic 7	10					
	8	Unused						
	9	Unused						
	10	Unused						
		TOTAL	70	—	—	—	—	—
C	THIRD CATEGORY							
	1	Characteristic 1	10					
	2	Characteristic 2	10					
	3	Characteristic 3	10					
	4	Characteristic 4	10					
	5	Characteristic 5	10					
	6	Characteristic 6	10					
	7	Unused						
	8	Unused						
	9	Unused						
	10	Unused						
		TOTAL	60	—	—	—	—	—
D	FOURTH CATEGORY							
	1	Characteristic 1	10					
	2	Characteristic 2	10					
	3	Characteristic 3	10					
	4	Characteristic 4	10					
	5	Unused						
	6	Unused						
	7	Unused						
	8	Unused						
	9	Unused						
	10	Unused						
		TOTAL	40	—	—	—	—	—

Workpaper 5-2. Risk Assessment Model (Weighted System) (Continued)

RISK ASSESSMENT MODEL				ITEM 1	ITEM 2	ITEM 3	ITEM 4	ITEM 5
E		FIFTH CATEGORY						
	1	Characteristic 1	10					
	2	Characteristic 2	10					
	3	Characteristic 3	10					
	4	Characteristic 4	10					
	5	Characteristic 5	10					
	6	Characteristic 6	10					
	7	Characteristic 7	10					
	8	Characteristic 8	10					
	9	Characteristic 9	10					
	10	Unused						
		TOTAL	90	—	—	—	—	—

- Understand the reasons for credibility problems and react to those reasons
- Simplify the analysis
- Borrow internal expertise or employ consulting support to complete the scoring.

The IT auditor should be willing to risk over-simplification, as it is much easier to expand and improve the next effort than it is to fail to complete the first one.

STEP 3: SETTING PRELIMINARY SCOPES

The IT auditor should now be able to set a preliminary scope for the application reviews identified for inclusion in the current plan. The auditor should include all of the information should include all of the information gathered or developed thus far to support the current analysis.

Task 1: Set Review Scope

The IT auditor must set a specific audit scope for each planned review. The decisions to make are which elements of each selected application will be done for each selected element. The IT auditor should perform a general review of the application as part of every selected review.

Task 2: Estimate Audit Resources

The IT auditor estimates the audit time and expenses required to perform the audit. The time estimates includes the following considerations:

Workpaper 5-3. Risk Assessment Model (10-Point System)

RISK ASSESSMENT MODEL			ITEM 1	ITEM 2	ITEM 3	ITEM 4	ITEM 5
Category	Description	Overall Points					
A	FIRST CATEGORY	1000	0.0	0.0	0.0	0.0	0.0
B	SECOND CATEGORY	70	0.0	0.0	0.0	0.0	0.0
C	THIRD CATEGORY	60	0.0	0.0	0.0	0.0	0.0
D	FOURTH CATEGORY	40	0.0	0.0	0.0	0.0	0.0
E	FIFTH CATEGORY	90	0.0	0.0	0.0	0.0	0.0
TOTAL OVERALL RISK SCORE		1260	0.0	0.0	0.0	0.0	0.0

A	FIRST CATEGORY						
1	SUBCATEGORY	100	0.0	0.0	0.0	0.0	0.0
2	SUBCATEGORY	100	0.0	0.0	0.0	0.0	0.0
3	SUBCATEGORY	100	0.0	0.0	0.0	0.0	0.0
4	SUBCATEGORY	100	0.0	0.0	0.0	0.0	0.0
5	SUBCATEGORY	100	0.0	0.0	0.0	0.0	0.0
6	SUBCATEGORY	100	0.0	0.0	0.0	0.0	0.0
7	SUBCATEGORY	100	0.0	0.0	0.0	0.0	0.0
8	SUBCATEGORY	100	0.0	0.0	0.0	0.0	0.0
9	SUBCATEGORY	100	0.0	0.0	0.0	0.0	0.0
10	SUBCATEGORY	100	0.0	0.0	0.0	0.0	0.0
	Total Compliance To Technical Specs.	1000	0.0	0.0	0.0	0.0	0.0

1 SUBCATEGORY

a	Characteristic 1	10					
b	Characteristic 2	10					
c	Characteristic 3	10					
d	Characteristic 4	10					
e	Characteristic 5	10					
f	Characteristic 6	10					
g	Characteristic 7	10					
h	Characteristic 8	10					
i	Characteristic 9	10					
j	Characteristic 10	10					
	TOTAL	100	0.0	0.0	0.0	0.0	0.0

Workpaper 5-3. Risk Assessment Model (10-Point System) (Continued)

RISK ASSESSMENT MODEL				ITEM 1	ITEM 2	ITEM 3	ITEM 4	ITEM 5
2 SUBCATEGORY								
a	Characteristic 1		10					
b	Characteristic 2		10					
c	Characteristic 3		10					
d	Characteristic 4		10					
e	Characteristic 5		10					
f	Characteristic 6		10					
g	Characteristic 7		10					
h	Characteristic 8		10					
i	Characteristic 9		10					
j	Characteristic 10		10					
	TOTAL		100	0.0	0.0	0.0	0.0	0.0

3 SUBCATEGORY								
a	Characteristic 1		10					
b	Characteristic 2		10					
c	Characteristic 3		10					
d	Characteristic 4		10					
e	Characteristic 5		10					
f	Characteristic 6		10					
g	Characteristic 7		10					
h	Characteristic 8		10					
i	Characteristic 9		10					
j	Characteristic 10		10					
	TOTAL		100	0.0	0.0	0.0	0.0	0.0

4 SUBCATEGORY								
a	Characteristic 1		10					
b	Characteristic 2		10					
c	Characteristic 3		10					
d	Characteristic 4		10					
e	Characteristic 5		10					
f	Characteristic 6		10					
g	Characteristic 7		10					
h	Characteristic 8		10					
i	Characteristic 9		10					
j	Characteristic 10		10					
	TOTAL		100	0.0	0.0	0.0	0.0	0.0

Workpaper 5-3. Risk Assessment Model (10-Point System) (Continued)

RISK ASSESSMENT MODEL			ITEM 1	ITEM 2	ITEM 3	ITEM 4	ITEM 5

5 SUBCATEGORY

			ITEM 1	ITEM 2	ITEM 3	ITEM 4	ITEM 5
a	Characteristic 1	10					
b	Characteristic 2	10					
c	Characteristic 3	10					
d	Characteristic 4	10					
e	Characteristic 5	10					
f	Characteristic 6	10					
g	Characteristic 7	10					
h	Characteristic 8	10					
i	Characteristic 9	10					
j	Characteristic 10	10					
	TOTAL	100	0.0	0.0	0.0	0.0	0.0

6 SUBCATEGORY

			ITEM 1	ITEM 2	ITEM 3	ITEM 4	ITEM 5
a	Characteristic 1	10					
b	Characteristic 2	10					
c	Characteristic 3	10					
d	Characteristic 4	10					
e	Characteristic 5	10					
f	Characteristic 6	10					
g	Characteristic 7	10					
h	Characteristic 8	10					
i	Characteristic 9	10					
j	Characteristic 10	10					
	TOTAL	100	0.0	0.0	0.0	0.0	0.0

7 SUBCATEGORY

			ITEM 1	ITEM 2	ITEM 3	ITEM 4	ITEM 5
a	Characteristic 1	10					
b	Characteristic 2	10					
c	Characteristic 3	10					
d	Characteristic 4	10					
e	Characteristic 5	10					
f	Characteristic 6	10					
g	Characteristic 7	10					
h	Characteristic 8	10					
i	Characteristic 9	10					
j	Characteristic 10	10					
	TOTAL	100	0.0	0.0	0.0	0.0	0.0

Workpaper 5-3. Risk Assessment Model (10-Point System) (Continued)

RISK ASSESSMENT MODEL			ITEM 1	ITEM 2	ITEM 3	ITEM 4	ITEM 5
8 SUBCATEGORY							
a	Characteristic 1	10					
b	Characteristic 2	10					
c	Characteristic 3	10					
d	Characteristic 4	10					
e	Characteristic 5	10					
f	Characteristic 6	10					
g	Characteristic 7	10					
h	Characteristic 8	10					
i	Characteristic 9	10					
j	Characteristic 10	10					
	TOTAL	100	0.0	0.0	0.0	0.0	0.0

9 SUBCATEGORY							
a	Characteristic 1	10					
b	Characteristic 2	10					
c	Characteristic 3	10					
d	Characteristic 4	10					
e	Characteristic 5	10					
f	Characteristic 6	10					
g	Characteristic 7	10					
h	Characteristic 8	10					
i	Characteristic 9	10					
j	Characteristic 10	10					
	TOTAL	100	0.0	0.0	0.0	0.0	0.0

10 SUBCATEGORY							
a	Characteristic 1	10					
b	Characteristic 2	10					
c	Characteristic 3	10					
d	Characteristic 4	10					
e	Characteristic 5	10					
f	Characteristic 6	10					
g	Characteristic 7	10					
h	Characteristic 8	10					
i	Characteristic 9	10					
j	Characteristic 10	10					
	TOTAL	100	0.0	0.0	0.0	0.0	0.0

Workpaper 5-3. Risk Assessment Model (10-Point System) (Continued)

RISK ASSESSMENT MODEL				ITEM 1	ITEM 2	ITEM 3	ITEM 4	ITEM 5
B	**SECOND CATEGORY**							
	1	Characteristic 1	10					
	2	Characteristic 2	10					
	3	Characteristic 3	10					
	4	Characteristic 4	10					
	5	Characteristic 5	10					
	6	Characteristic 6	10					
	7	Characteristic 7	10					
	8	Unused						
	9	Unused						
	10	Unused						
		TOTAL	70	0.0	0.0	0.0	0.0	0.0

RISK ASSESSMENT MODEL				ITEM 1	ITEM 2	ITEM 3	ITEM 4	ITEM 5
C	**THIRD CATEGORY**							
	1	Characteristic 1	10					
	2	Characteristic 2	10					
	3	Characteristic 3	10					
	4	Characteristic 4	10					
	5	Characteristic 5	10					
	6	Characteristic 6	10					
	7	Unused						
	8	Unused						
	9	Unused						
	10	Unused						
		TOTAL	60	0.0	0.0	0.0	0.0	0.0

RISK ASSESSMENT MODEL				ITEM 1	ITEM 2	ITEM 3	ITEM 4	ITEM 5
D	**FOURTH CATEGORY**							
	1	Characteristic 1	10					
	2	Characteristic 2	10					
	3	Characteristic 3	10					
	4	Characteristic 4	10					
	5	Unused						
	6	Unused						
	7	Unused						
	8	Unused						
	9	Unused						
	10	Unused						
		TOTAL	40	0.0	0.0	0.0	0.0	0.0

Workpaper 5-3. Risk Assessment Model (10-Point System) (Continued)

RISK ASSESSMENT MODEL				ITEM 1	ITEM 2	ITEM 3	ITEM 4	ITEM 5
E		FIFTH CATEGORY						
	1	Characteristic 1	10					
	2	Characteristic 2	10					
	3	Characteristic 3	10					
	4	Characteristic 4	10					
	5	Characteristic 5	10					
	6	Characteristic 6	10					
	7	Characteristic 7	10					
	8	Characteristic 8	10					
	9	Characteristic 9	10					
	10	Unused						
		TOTAL	90	0.0	0.0	0.0	0.0	0.0

- Risk level, as higher risks are likely to require either higher skills or more time
- Budget and actual results from previous audits

The expense estimate is normally driven by any travel cost incurred to audit a non-local site. Other typical expenses include computer hours, supports groups, and unusual administrative support.

Task 3: Identify Special Audit Needs

The IT auditor must define special audit needs, including unique audit skills (e.g., knowledge of a particular DBMS), special knowledge of certain business activities, and operational knowledge of special tools (e.g., audit software).

STEP 4: SELECT AND SCHEDULE IT AUDITS

The IT auditor selects the computer applications that are to be audited during the coming year and then schedules the time when these audits will be performed.

The auditor must select the audits that should be performed during the coming year. General guidelines should be developed to enable the auditor to set priorities for the audit to be performed. An example of these guidelines follows:

- First priority: high-risk applications
- Second priority: medium-risk applications
- Third priority: low-risk applications, beginning with those controlling a high dollar volume of resources

Workpaper 5-4. Risk Assessment Model (100-Point Total System)

Category	Description	Overall Points	ITEM 1	ITEM 2	ITEM 3	ITEM 4	ITEM 5
A	FIRST CATEGORY	60	0	0	0	0	0
B	SECOND CATEGORY	10	0	0	0	0	0
C	THIRD CATEGORY	10	0	0	0	0	0
D	FOURTH CATEGORY	10	0	0	0	0	0
E	FIFTH CATEGORY	10	0	0	0	0	0
TOTAL OVERALL RISK SCORE		100	—	—	—	—	—

A	FIRST CATEGORY						
	1	SUBCATEGORY	13	—	—	—	—	—
	2	SUBCATEGORY	13	—	—	—	—	—
	3	SUBCATEGORY	6	—	—	—	—	—
	4	SUBCATEGORY	10	—	—	—	—	—
	5	SUBCATEGORY	10	—	—	—	—	—
	6	SUBCATEGORY	6	—	—	—	—	—
	7	SUBCATEGORY	2	—	—	—	—	—
	8	SUBCATEGORY	0	—	—	—	—	—
	9	SUBCATEGORY	0	—	—	—	—	—
	10	SUBCATEGORY	0	—	—	—	—	—
		Total Compliance To Technical Specs.	60	—	—	—	—	—

1 SUBCATEGORY

a	Characteristic 1	2					
b	Characteristic 2	2					
c	Characteristic 3	3					
d	Characteristic 4	1					
e	Characteristic 5	1					
f	Characteristic 6	2					
g	Characteristic 7	1					
h	Characteristic 8	1					
i	Characteristic 9	0					
j	Characteristic 10	0					
	TOTAL	13	—	—	—	—	—

Workpaper 5-4. Risk Assessment Model (100-Point Total System) (Continued)

RISK ASSESSMENT MODEL			ITEM 1	ITEM 2	ITEM 3	ITEM 4	ITEM 5

2 SUBCATEGORY

			ITEM 1	ITEM 2	ITEM 3	ITEM 4	ITEM 5
a	Characteristic 1	2					
b	Characteristic 2	2					
c	Characteristic 3	3					
d	Characteristic 4	1					
e	Characteristic 5	1					
f	Characteristic 6	2					
g	Characteristic 7	1					
h	Characteristic 8	1					
i	Characteristic 9	0					
j	Characteristic 10	0					
	TOTAL	13	—	—	—	—	—

3 SUBCATEGORY

			ITEM 1	ITEM 2	ITEM 3	ITEM 4	ITEM 5
a	Characteristic 1	1					
b	Characteristic 2	1					
c	Characteristic 3	1					
d	Characteristic 4	1					
e	Characteristic 5	1					
f	Characteristic 6	1					
g	Characteristic 7	0					
h	Characteristic 8	0					
i	Characteristic 9	0					
j	Characteristic 10	0					
	TOTAL	6	—	—	—	—	—

4 SUBCATEGORY

			ITEM 1	ITEM 2	ITEM 3	ITEM 4	ITEM 5
a	Characteristic 1	2					
b	Characteristic 2	1					
c	Characteristic 3	2					
d	Characteristic 4	1					
e	Characteristic 5	1					
f	Characteristic 6	2					
g	Characteristic 7	1					
h	Characteristic 8	0					
i	Characteristic 9	0					
j	Characteristic 10	0					
	TOTAL	10	—	—	—	—	—

Workpaper 5-4. Risk Assessment Model (100-Point Total System) (Continued)

RISK ASSESSMENT MODEL			ITEM 1	ITEM 2	ITEM 3	ITEM 4	ITEM 5

5 SUBCATEGORY

			ITEM 1	ITEM 2	ITEM 3	ITEM 4	ITEM 5
a	Characteristic 1	1					
b	Characteristic 2	3					
c	Characteristic 3	2					
d	Characteristic 4	1					
e	Characteristic 5	3					
f	Characteristic 6	0					
g	Characteristic 7	0					
h	Characteristic 8	0					
i	Characteristic 9	0					
j	Characteristic 10	0					
	TOTAL	10	—	—	—	—	—

6 SUBCATEGORY

			ITEM 1	ITEM 2	ITEM 3	ITEM 4	ITEM 5
a	Characteristic 1	1					
b	Characteristic 2	1					
c	Characteristic 3	1					
d	Characteristic 4	1					
e	Characteristic 5	1					
f	Characteristic 6	1					
g	Characteristic 7	0					
h	Characteristic 8	0					
i	Characteristic 9	0					
j	Characteristic 10	0					
	TOTAL	6	—	—	—	—	—

7 SUBCATEGORY

			ITEM 1	ITEM 2	ITEM 3	ITEM 4	ITEM 5
a	Characteristic 1	1					
b	Characteristic 2	1					
c	Characteristic 3	0					
d	Characteristic 4	0					
e	Characteristic 5	0					
f	Characteristic 6	0					
g	Characteristic 7	0					
h	Characteristic 8	0					
i	Characteristic 9	0					
j	Characteristic 10	0					
	TOTAL	2	—	—	—	—	—

Workpaper 5-4. Risk Assessment Model (100-Point Total System) (Continued)

RISK ASSESSMENT MODEL			ITEM 1	ITEM 2	ITEM 3	ITEM 4	ITEM 5

8 SUBCATEGORY

a	Characteristic 1	0					
b	Characteristic 2	0					
c	Characteristic 3	0					
d	Characteristic 4	0					
e	Characteristic 5	0					
f	Characteristic 6	0					
g	Characteristic 7	0					
h	Characteristic 8	0					
i	Characteristic 9	0					
j	Characteristic 10	0					
	TOTAL	0	—	—	—	—	—

9 SUBCATEGORY

a	Characteristic 1	0					
b	Characteristic 2	0					
c	Characteristic 3	0					
d	Characteristic 4	0					
e	Characteristic 5	0					
f	Characteristic 6	0					
g	Characteristic 7	0					
h	Characteristic 8	0					
i	Characteristic 9	0					
j	Characteristic 10	0					
	TOTAL	0	—	—	—	—	—

10 SUBCATEGORY

a	Characteristic 1	0					
b	Characteristic 2	0					
c	Characteristic 3	0					
d	Characteristic 4	0					
e	Characteristic 5	0					
f	Characteristic 6	0					
g	Characteristic 7	0					
h	Characteristic 8	0					
i	Characteristic 9	0					
j	Characteristic 10	0					
	TOTAL	0	—	—	—	—	—

Workpaper 5-4. Risk Assessment Model (100-Point Total System) (Continued)

RISK ASSESSMENT MODEL				ITEM 1	ITEM 2	ITEM 3	ITEM 4	ITEM 5
B	**SECOND CATEGORY**							
	1	Characteristic 1	3					
	2	Characteristic 2	2					
	3	Characteristic 3	1					
	4	Characteristic 4	1					
	5	Characteristic 5	1					
	6	Characteristic 6	1					
	7	Characteristic 7	1					
	8	Unused						
	9	Unused						
	10	Unused						
		TOTAL	10	—	—	—	—	—

C	**THIRD CATEGORY**							
	1	Characteristic 1	2					
	2	Characteristic 2	2					
	3	Characteristic 3	2					
	4	Characteristic 4	2					
	5	Characteristic 5	1					
	6	Characteristic 6	1					
	7	Unused						
	8	Unused						
	9	Unused						
	10	Unused						
		TOTAL	10	—	—	—	—	—

D	**FOURTH CATEGORY**							
	1	Characteristic 1	3					
	2	Characteristic 2	3					
	3	Characteristic 3	2					
	4	Characteristic 4	2					
	5	Unused						
	6	Unused						
	7	Unused						
	8	Unused						
	9	Unused						
	10	Unused						
		TOTAL	10	—	—	—	—	—

Workpaper 5-4. Risk Assessment Model (100-Point Total System) (Continued)

RISK ASSESSMENT MODEL				ITEM 1	ITEM 2	ITEM 3	ITEM 4	ITEM 5
E.		FIFTH CATEGORY						
	1	Characteristic 1	2					
	2	Characteristic 2	1					
	3	Characteristic 3	1					
	4	Characteristic 4	1					
	5	Characteristic 5	1					
	6	Characteristic 6	1					
	7	Characteristic 7	1					
	8	Characteristic 8	1					
	9	Characteristic 9	1					
	10	Unused						
		TOTAL	10	—	—	—	—	—

Auditors should schedule the audits for a year in groups by quarter. The scheduling considerations for determining which quarter to perform audits include:

- Annual audits: scheduling at least three quarters from the last audit
- Related applications: auditing in the sequence in which data logically flows through the application (e.g., a cash receipt system is audited before the accounts receivable system to which that cash is applied)
- Applications in out-of-town locations: auditing concurrently to reduce travel expenses
- Audits of application with widely fluctuating volumes: scheduling during either high- or low-volume periods, depending on audit objectives and special audit needs (e.g., the availability of project staff to work with auditors).

Additional considerations include the availability of special audit staff to assist in the conduct of the audit and the ability to coordinate with independent public accountants and other auditee area personnel.

STEP 5: MERGER AUDIT PLANS

This task merges the IT audit plan with other audit plans to create an overall internal audit department plan.

During this task, the IT auditor must integrate multiple audit plans from various parts of the audit department into a single audit plan. The process usually depends on the available audit resources. Thus, the overall audit plan must meet the following organizational constraints:

Exhibit 5-4. Risk Assessment Model (100 Point Total System)

RISK ASSESSMENT MODEL			ITEM 1	ITEM 2	ITEM 3	ITEM 4	ITEM 5
Category	Description	Overall Points					
A	FIRST CATEGORY	1000	550.0	90.0	80.0	70.0	60.0
B	SECOND CATEGORY	70	57.5	2.0	3.0	4.0	5.0
C	THIRD CATEGORY	60	34.0	7.0	8.0	9.0	10.0
D	FOURTH CATEGORY	40	30.5	6.0	6.5	7.0	7.5
E	FIFTH CATEGORY	90	62.0	9.0	8.0	7.0	5.0
TOTAL OVERALL RISK SCORE		1260	734.0	114.0	105.5	97.0	87.5

A	FIRST CATEGORY						
1	SUBCATEGORY	100	55.0	9.0	8.0	7.0	6.0
2	SUBCATEGORY	100	55.0	9.0	8.0	7.0	6.0
3	SUBCATEGORY	100	55.0	9.0	8.0	7.0	6.0
4	SUBCATEGORY	100	55.0	9.0	8.0	7.0	6.0
5	SUBCATEGORY	100	55.0	9.0	8.0	7.0	6.0
6	SUBCATEGORY	100	55.0	9.0	8.0	7.0	6.0
7	SUBCATEGORY	100	55.0	9.0	8.0	7.0	6.0
8	SUBCATEGORY	100	55.0	9.0	8.0	7.0	6.0
9	SUBCATEGORY	100	55.0	9.0	8.0	7.0	6.0
10	SUBCATEGORY	100	55.0	9.0	8.0	7.0	6.0
	Total Compliance To Technical Specs.	1000	550.0	90.0	80.0	70.0	60.0

1 SUBCATEGORY

a	Characteristic 1	10	10.0	9.0	8.0	7.0	6.0
b	Characteristic 2	10	9.0				
c	Characteristic 3	10	8.0				
d	Characteristic 4	10	7.0				
e	Characteristic 5	10	6.0				
f	Characteristic 6	10	5.0				
g	Characteristic 7	10	4.0				
h	Characteristic 8	10	3.0				
i	Characteristic 9	10	2.0				
j	Characteristic 10	10	1.0				
	TOTAL	100	55.0	9.0	8.0	7.0	6.0

- Number of available staff auditors days
- Number of specialized audit skills (e.g., IT audit specialist)
- Available travel funds
- Available funds for computer resources
- Available funds for specialized tools and assistance

Administrative activities (e.g., training and staff meetings) should be incorporated through other parts of the annual audit planning process.

This task produces an annual audit department plan that closely parallels the IT plan. If specific items are included in the organization's annual audit planning documents that are not included in the audit planning process presented in this section, the auditor should modify these workpapers to include the other needed information.

Section 6
Specific Audit Planning

Specific audit planning is divided into two parts: part one occurs before the fieldwork and part two occurs during the fieldwork. This section deals with audit planning that occurs before commencing the fieldwork.

The prefieldwork individual audit planning is usually performed by the auditor-in-charge. In addition, the planning involves sources of information other than what can be readily acquired from the auditee (e.g., the results of previous audits, consultation with corporate management and key staff groups, and industrial and risk analysis). This differentiates prefieldwork audit planning from the planning that occurs through preliminary investigation of the auditee area, although some audit groups combine both types of individual audit planning.

STEP 1: ASSIGN AN AUDITOR-IN-CHARGE

The IT audit manager should assign auditor-in-charge for this specific audit. The auditor-in-charge then begins to plan for the specific audit.

The IT auditor manager must first become familiar with the individual audit application and audit the risk involved. The annual audit usually provides the auditor with the necessary information.

The manager should assign an auditor-in-charge on the basis of the audit risk, audit scope, and application area. The considerations in assigning an auditor-in-charge include:

- Degree of experience needed to address the audit risk
- Familiarity with the application area
- Specific skills the auditor-in-charge must possess
- Availability of personnel for auditor-in-charge assignments

STEP 2: PERFORM APPLICATION FACT-GATHERING

The auditor-in-charge gathers sufficient background data on the audit to help the plan address the major risk and exposure areas. This fact-gathering task includes visiting and obtaining information from all areas except the auditee areas. In addition, if the information processing area is not visited during the audit, it should be visited as part of this step.

The auditor-in-charge must examine as much background material and interview as many knowledgeable staff members as time permits and potential audit risks warrant. Interviewing large groups for short periods of time usually causes concerns to surface and reveals facts that are helpful in identifying problems. Any and all parties involved in the auditee's business should be interviewed.

The audit department should develop procedures for performing this fact-gathering process. The most logical individuals to interview include:

- The prior year's auditor-in-charge
- The prior year's key audit staff
- The following key company officials:
  —Comptroller
  —Chief information officer
  —Administrative vice president
  —Operations vice president
  —Corporate security officer
  —Corporate legal officer
  —Corporate officer in charge of the auditee area
  —CPAs and the CPA firm audit partner or manager

These interviews need not be extensive in length, but should include the following types of questions.

- What areas of concern do you have about the auditee area?
- Are there any questions that you personally would like answered as a result of conducting an audit in this area?
- Have there been any significant changes in the area under audit that should be examined or might be potential problems?
- Have you heard any discussions, pro or con, from other departments regarding the operations of the auditee area?
- Have you received correspondence or telephone calls from individuals or organizations interacting with the auditee area regarding problems or unsatisfactory service?
- Do you have any documentation or complaint letters that you could give me as a basis to use in conducting the audit?
- What do you personally believe is the greatest risk that the auditee area faces?
- If you were auditor-in-charge of this audit, what is the first thing you would want to investigate?

The following sources are helpful in gathering background information.

- Audit suggestions for improving the audit made by the prior year's audit team or suggestions made by auditors concerned with related areas of the business.
- Correspondence arriving in customer service groups or problem groups about the auditee area.
- Newspaper, magazine, and industry reports about the business area in which the auditee is involved.

A final technique that is helpful in fact-gathering is to organize a group of key audit personnel and brainstorm about the potential problems in the auditee area. This process usually takes about an hour. The group members list their concerns and then consolidate and rank them in order of importance. The result is a risk list that is used by the audit staff.

STEP 3: ANALYZE APPLICATION AUDIT RISK

The auditor-in-charge documents, from previous planning, the risks associated with this application; analyzes the severity of those risks using auditor judgment; and translates the specific risk concerns into criteria for field-work audit objectives.

The auditor-in-charge should have at least these three tasks.

Task 1: Document Audit Risks

Using the results of previous planning steps, the auditor-in-charge must document the risk criteria from the application system. This information is usually transferred from one workpaper to another; however, it may be easier to cross-reference available workpapers, particularly if they are lengthy.

Task 2: Perform an Analysis of the Audit Risk

The auditor-in-charge must use the risk score, risk dimensions, and audit issues gathered during the planning process to create a form that can be used by the audit team. This task converts that data into a summary analysis that familiarizes the audit staff with the concerns that they must address and is used as one of the primary bases for developing audit objectives.

Task 3: Define Specific Risk Concerns

This task is the key task in computer application risk analysis. The auditor extracts the key concerns from the audit risk analysis and the risk information, and then translates them into specific audit objectives (see Step 4).

This step depends heavily on audit judgment and experience. The auditor-in-charge should pose the following questions to determine the audit's risk concerns.

- Are there aspects of risk which subject the organization to high financial or negative publicity exposure?
- Do new risks exist that have not been addressed in previous audits?
- Are there risk concerns for which the auditor does not believe there are adequate controls to reduce that risk to an acceptable level?
- Based on the auditor's knowledge of the business, is the risk one that could have already turned into a significant loss?
- Is there reasonable supporting evidence to substantiate that the risk is significant to the organization?

STEP 4: DEVELOP AND RANK MEASURABLE AUDIT OBJECTIVES

The auditor-in-charge develops a set of specific objectives that are to be accomplished during the performance of the application audit. These objectives drive the audit; when the objectives have been completed, the audit is considered to be complete.

Two tasks are performed as part of this task.

Task 1: Define Audit Objectives

Only those audit procedures that support the audit objectives should be performed. The audit objectives are the basis and purpose for performing the audit; when they have been accomplished, the audit is complete. There are three basic types of audit objectives, as follows:

- Administrative objectives: including compliance to auditing standards and procedures and other administrative criteria.
- Application-specific audit objectives: for example, verifying the correctness of the account balances controlled by the application and tracing it to the general ledger.
- Risk-related objectives: including the objectives developed through risk analysis.

Each objective should be described in as measurable a format as possible so that the auditor knows when the audit is complete.

Task 2: Define the Priority for Each Audit Objective

Audits are often constrained by time, staff availability, and budgets. During the performance of the audit, it may be necessary to emphasize some objectives and de-emphasize others. This system of setting priorities provides the audit team with guidance as to which objectives should be accomplished first if there is a shortage of time.

STEP 5: DEVELOP ADMINISTRATIVE PLAN

This step ensures that the proper staff, resources, tools, and skills are available to perform the audit. During this step, the auditor must first determine the administrative staffing resources needed to perform each audit objective. This requires the auditor-in-charge to apply the staffing resources, tools, and audit approach previously defined for the audit to each specific audit objective. In some instances, the previous data may need to be expanded and, in other cases, that data may be applied to the specific audit objective.

The second project for the auditor is to identify and acquire audit staff. On the basis of the administrative analysis of the resource requirements for performing each audit objective, staff members should be identified and acquired to accomplish these objectives. This information is used during the performance of the audit to assign specific objectives to individuals.

STEP 6: WRITE AUDIT PROGRAM

The auditor-in-charge transcribes all of the planning information into an audit program. This audit program is used as a basis for performing the audit.

Once the audit program has been prepared, the fieldwork can commence. Other parts of this book commence at the point that the audit program has been issued.

Part III
Assessing General IT Controls

The IT Auditor can only perform effective reviews of automated application systems after evaluating the general controls underlying and supporting the proper functioning of those applications. These general controls affect the operation of every application running on a system, and inadequate or missing general controls have the potential to compromise the controls in all automated application systems.

Part III guides the IT auditor through the general controls areas that should be evaluated in a normal systems environment review. This approach to the general controls review groups all possible controls into the following five categories:

- Information Technology administration. Controls should ensure that IT activities are based on strategic and tactical plans that are coordinated with those same plans for the business, and that those IT activities support the needs of the business (see Section 7).
- Physical security. Controls should ensure that the physical equipment comprising the system is reasonably safeguarded from harm (see Section 8).
- Logical security. Controls should ensure that only authorized persons have access to the system and that these authorized persons only have the access required for their responsibilities (see Section 9).
- Systems development. Controls should ensure that new systems and functional enhancements are prepared in ways that are likely to produce systems that meet end-user expectations and that keep applications operating and available during the business day (see Section 10).
- Backup, recovery, and contingency planning. Controls should ensure that the IT department develops the plans and performs the necessary system backups to ensure that the organization has the ability to recover from major and minor disruptions with little or no risk to the continuity of the organization. Data center operations can be separated into another category, but it is included here due to the reduced support requirements of today's automated application systems (see Section 11).

These categories are discussed in Sections 7 through 11, and are included in a set of fully articulated workpapers at the end of Section 12.

Section 7
Information Systems Administration

Controls over IT administration should ensure that the function is managed in a way that efficiently and effectively supports strategic and tactical business activities. The controls in this area often include:

- Strategic planning
- Tactical planning
- IT standard setting

The common element among these controls is that none of them has any direct association with an automated application system. The idea of an indirect relationship is familiar to first-time managers as they realize that they may no longer be doing any "work," at least not as they have known it in the past. They draw their salary based on the direction and guidance they provide.

These administrative responsibilities provide the guidance needed to move both individual and functional activities in the appropriate directions. Guidance takes many forms, some of which are further defined in the sections that follow.

STRATEGIC PLANNING

The Information Technology (IT) department should always be aware of advances and changes in technology that can affect the hardware and software that the company uses in meeting its objectives. A strategic plan usually looks at least one year ahead, then continuing as far into the future as appropriate.

The Strategic Plan

The strategic plan ensures that company executives and managers are able to establish the overall systems direction for the enterprise. This knowledge permits other management levels to determine how their individual areas will be supported or identifies where changes should be made in their tactical activities. The IT auditor should be cognizant that having a strategic

Exhibit 7-1. Sample IT Strategic Plan

GENERIC DOMESTIC COMPANY
Technology activities within the Domestic Company will be conducted in accordance with the following guidelines. Any deviations from these guidelines must be approved in advance of making any contractual or financial commitments. All transaction processing systems will have a single storage location for all primary data files, whether the systems are mainframe, midrange, or client/server based. Hardware changes will be to appropriate IBM equipment to maximize our corporate ability to negotiate discounts on acquisition and maintenance of technical hardware. The use of conversion tables to interface incompatible data structures will be eliminated as part of the company's effort to move toward seamless integration and an enterprise model. Electronic commerce is becoming increasingly important to the company's business, and all Electronic Data Interchange (EDI) will be done in compliance with ANSI standards, while Internet and World Wide Web activity will be guided by provisions of the Internet guidelines currently being developed. Personal computers will only be purchased from an approved vendor to improve our ability to provide for effective support and maintenance, and will be purchased with one of the approved application suites specified by the Information Technology department.

plan is important, but it should not unreasonably limit individual decisions or prevent needed day-to-day changes.

Exhibit 7-1 is an example of a strategic IT plan. For another company this exhibit might only be a vision statement. There are no rules concerning the degree of detail appropriate for strategic planning, but the IT auditor should evaluate strategic plan provisions based on the answers to these questions:

- Can the plan's provisions be understood by professionals and nonprofessionals?
- Will these provisions be long-lived or require frequent updating?
- Do these provisions complement strategic plans developed in other parts of the company?
- Is anything missing, based on either the IT auditor's knowledge of other information from within the enterprise or general changes in technology?
- Has the strategic plan been endorsed by senior management?

The IT auditor should use caution when reviewing a strategic plan, particularly if it has already been publicized, due to the potential political implications of suggesting that it be changed and re-issued. Although independence should be preserved, the auditors should make an extra effort in this area to ensure their participation during development of the strategic plan. The auditor's suggestions during plan development are likely to be much better received than if they are made later in the process.

TACTICAL PLANNING

The tactical IT plan, which can also be referred to as the short-term plan, should be based on the strategic plan and identify specific activities to be performed and objectives to be met over the next 12 to 24 months. The tactical plan can be divided by operating unit, product line, department, or other internal division of the entity.

The tactical plan is often the product of both IT and end-user personnel. This is a joint effort because the end users often must prioritize their open and in-process requests. End-user prioritization is necessary if their requests require more development and implementation hours than are available based on the tactical planning horizon and the number of resources available to satisfy those hours.

The tactical plan can also be changed more easily than the strategic plan, and it must be changed to reflect changing circumstances and shifts in the overall focus of the company The tactical plan should also include specific elements of each activity such as estimated work effort and implementation date. If the tactical plan does not include those elements, they should be readily available from another source, and be available to all parties with a specific interest in that information.

Exhibit 7-2 is an example of a tactical plan. This sample tactical plan is not complete and represents only a fictitious first page of such a report. The report would most likely also include sections for those items expected to be completed within the tactical planning horizon, prioritized items that would be worked on next if a project is completed early or taken off of the list, and a group of nonprioritized items that had been submitted but deemed to have a priority low enough that they are not being considered at all for planning purposes.

INFORMATION TECHNOLOGY STANDARD SETTING

The IT auditor in many organizations dedicates a certain amount of time to persuading members of the IT staff as to what constitutes adequate or minimum control in a particular situation. An example is the minimum length for passwords. The IT auditor is evaluating logical access controls and

Exhibit 7-2. Sample IT Tactical Plan

		GENERIC DOMESTIC COMPANY FOR 199X AND 199Y			
Request	**User**	**Description**	**Est. Hours**	**Hours to Date**	**Hours to Complete**
9Y-011	Smith	Enhance credit module functionality to permit direct interface to external business rating services to increase the number of new customer transactions that can be handled interactively.	250	130	200
9X-005	Jones	Determine reason that general ledger journal entries set up as recurring entries are not included in automatic monthly close processing in subsequent months and make necessary corrections.	75	20	35
9X-103	Bruce	Modify the customer balance inquiry screen so that current balances in excess of established credit limits appear in red.	16	0	16
9Y-051	Ng	Modify the accounts receivable module so that pending orders reduce the available credit balance when entered instead of when shipped to prevent orders from being accepted that are actually over the customer's established limit.	130	42	115
9Y-050	Rand	Add another level of subtotals on the open accounts payable report so that the report includes grand totals, regional totals, customer totals, and customer/location totals.	30	10	20

determines that end users can set a password as short as one character when they are prompted to change their password by the system. The IT auditor should conclude that a minimum length of one is not sufficient to limit the probability of someone else easily guessing an end user's password. The auditor then has to decide what minimum length is appropriate and subsequently persuade the IT staff of that requirement.

Most experienced IT auditors can describe the futility of these experiences because they will often attempt to be consistent between employer locations or even between employers, and those different groups often have their own opinions concerning what is necessary and what is effective. This does not mean that every situation will trigger a disagreement, but the issue of minimum password length selected for the example represents something that is truly opinion and not fact.

In most areas, company policy on a topic should eliminate the need to discuss alternatives and reach a consensus, because it would represent the codification of senior executive management's opinion for a specific subject. And senior management's opinion should normally be adequate to create change at lower levels. If IT management would adopt a security policy, for example, it can simplify the IT auditor's work by at least one order of magnitude.

The IT auditor can focus on reviewing the policy, making comments during policy development, or suggesting that IT management make changes to the policy during the next normal updating cycle. Working in this manner changes the IT auditor's fieldwork because much of the time that can be lost to working out basic control issues is recovered for more valuable activities. Control issues become a simple matter of compliance. Thus, the IT auditor has more time to focus on complex issues that have more potential to add value to the organization.

Exhibit 7-3 is a sample IT security policy, which is important for two reasons:

- It provides the foundation for the standard general controls questionnaire.
- It incorporates a number of elements of effective policy statements with which IT auditors should become familiar.

Exhibit 7-3. Sample IT Security Plan

SPECIFIC SECURITY PROVISIONS
1. - - - D Unauthorized entry to the computer room shall be prevented by locks, automatic admission checking system, or guards. If the computer room is on the ground floor, the windows shall be of an unbreakable type, preferably also opaque and not possible to open.
2. - B C D Fire extinguishers of carbon dioxide or Halon gas shall be located in the computer room and in the adjacent room. Where applicable, the fire control organization should be consulted, and they should make periodic inspections.

The complete policy that the exhibit was taken from is included as Workpaper 7-1. This sample security policy was originally designed for a holding company with a large number of operating units and a variety of hardware platforms. Its basic structure has many elements in common with other organizations, even small ones, where it is more common to find independent personal computers, network or client/server installations, and a central transaction processing system. Even if the network or client/server is responsible for transaction processing, two distinct levels of controls should be considered.

The sample security policy incorporates the following critical elements.

- *Sensitivity to size.* A size-based classification is presented, and policy statements are keyed to those classes.
- *Clarity.* The policy statements are very clear, which reduces the risk of misunderstanding and subsequent noncompliance.
- *Recognizing variations in risk.* Several policy provisions have more than one relevant statement because one installation class is required to take action, and smaller classes are only required to consider action.
- *Delegating responsibility.* The policy requires local managers, whether in information technology services or other areas, to review the policy and either take action or determine that action is not needed on an item-by-item level.
- *Providing for circumstances.* Allowing individual managers to request variances empowers those persons by giving them a method to deal with their individual concerns other than simply choosing to deviate from corporate policy.

Other elements should be added, but any policy containing at least the most significant elements described is likely to be effective and thus improve general controls.

Workpaper 7-1. Complete Sample IT Security Policy

This security manual has been developed to provide both general and specific guidance on security-related matters to company personnel. Management believes that this is necessary so that all of our personnel can have access to the information required to be properly enabled to address security concerns and issues as they arise.

This policy document is oriented toward safeguarding the company's investment in hardware, software, and data. Without such a policy, it has not been practical to provide management the assurance it desires that only authorized system access is permitted, that systems activities are consistent with business activities, and so on.

This manual has been developed with some sensitivity to the variety of computer systems now in place and supporting some part of our total business. We have established the following classes based on the installed workstations. You *must* address all items for your installation class. The items for each class are the minimum requirements, but we encourage you to review them all, as items from other classes might benefit your installation. Requests for variations from this policy, if submitted in writing to this department, will be considered and formally responded to.

CLASS CODE/INSTALLATION SIZE

A. PCs with large files or sensitive material or used for administrative routines like order processing
B. 1–5 workstations or FIT PCs used for CAD
C. 6–25 workstations
D. 26–150 workstations
E. More than 150 workstations (for class E, all measures marked D shall be carried out and also any others that are appropriate to the size and type of installation)

SPECIFIC SECURITY PROVISIONS

1.- - - D

Unauthorized entry to the data center shall be prevented by locks, automatic admission checking system, or guards. If the data center is on the ground floor, the windows shall be of an unbreakable type, preferably also opaque and not possible to open.

YES _____ NO _____ N/A _____

_____

_____

2. - B C D

Fire extinguishers of carbon dioxide or Halon gas shall be located in the data center and in the adjacent room. Where applicable, the fire control organization should be consulted, and they should make periodic inspections.

YES _____   NO _____   N/A _____

_____

_____

3. - - - D

Automatic fire extinguishing installations, smoke detectors, and fire alarms are strongly recommended. However, in most countries, Halon will be forbidden within the first half of the 1990s. The technological developments must be observed. **Before deciding for a new automatic Halon installation, corporate approval must be obtained.**

YES _____   NO _____   N/A _____

_____

_____

4. - B C D

Sprinklers might be a suitable alternative if they are combined with an automatic power shut-off to the data center before the sprinklers are released.

YES _____   NO _____   N/A _____

_____

_____

5. - - C D

When constructing a data center, sewer and water pipes should be removed or the material changed to an anticorrosive material. If there is any risk of leakage, flooding, or water rising from the drainage system, there shall be (automatic) shut-off valves and gutters.

YES _____   NO _____   N/A _____

_____

_____

6. - - - D

A water or moisture alarm should be installed.

YES _____   NO _____   N/A _____

_____

_____

7. - B C D

Where needed, air conditioning equipment shall be installed. If suitable, the capacity should be divided into at least two units.

YES _____   NO _____   N/A _____

_____

_____

8. - - - D

Equipment for alarm and power shut-off at unsuitable temperatures or humidity should be installed.

YES _____   NO _____   N/A _____

_____

_____

9. A B C D

An Uninterruptible Power Supply (UPS) should be installed where power disruptions are frequent and recovery takes a long time or where disruptions incur significant costs.

YES _____   NO _____   N/A _____

_____

_____

10. A B C D

Stabilizers should be used where voltage or frequency is not stable.

YES _____   NO _____   N/A _____

_____

_____

11. A B C D

When sending data media containing payment transactions, special security measures shall be taken to prevent the media from being altered. Such measures could be a fixed timetable for the conveyance, transport in a locked box, and an electronic seal on a tape.

YES _____   NO _____   N/A _____

_____

_____

12. A B C D

Backup copies shall be taken so frequently that the time for a recovery procedure is relatively short. The recovery should not take more than four hours or create business disturbances or incur significant costs. For frequently used files, backup shall be at least daily. A full backup including low-frequency files and system and application software shall be performed at least monthly.

YES _____   NO _____   N/A _____

_____

_____

13. A B C D

The backup copies shall be stored in such a way that they cannot be destroyed or stolen at the same time as the computer. They should either be stored in another building or in a fireproof cupboard in another room away from the computer. The backup copies shall be kept under lock and key.

YES _____   NO _____   N/A _____

_____

_____

14. A - - -

At least two generations of backup shall be kept.

YES _____   NO _____   N/A _____

_____

_____

15. - B C D

At least three generations of backup shall be kept.

YES _____   NO _____   N/A _____

_____

_____

16. A B C D

Surplus output material should be destroyed and sensitive information shall be shredded or destroyed in some other manner that ensures security.

YES _____   NO _____   N/A _____

_____

_____

17. A B C D

Forms used for training and testing should be specially identified, in particular regarding payment routines.

YES _____ NO _____ N/A _____

_____

_____

18. - B C D

Output that includes sensitive information should be stored in locked cupboards before distribution.

YES _____ NO _____ N/A _____

_____

_____

19. A B C D

Users shall be reminded yearly, through training or campaigns, about their responsibility for EDP security.

YES _____ NO _____ N/A _____

_____

_____

20. A B C D

Passwords shall be individual, secret, and difficult to guess.

YES _____ NO _____ N/A _____

_____

_____

21. A - - -

Using a password or unlocking a physical lock shall give access to a PC system.

YES _____ NO _____ N/A _____

_____

_____

22. - B - -

A combination of at least user identity and password shall be required to authorize the use of the system.

YES _____ NO _____ N/A _____

_____

_____

23. - - C D

User identity and password shall be used for authorization to specified objects (resources). This also implies access to SPOOL files.

YES _____ NO _____ N/A _____

_____

_____

24. - - C D

In certain cases, such as the work of the security officer, a combination of user identity and password shall give authorization for transactions to be handled on a specified terminal.

YES _____ NO _____ N/A _____

_____

_____

25. A B C D

Standard passwords installed by the supplier shall be altered before using the system.

YES _____ NO _____ N/A _____

_____

_____

26. - B C D

The passwords shall be changed every second or third month. Reuse of old passwords shall not be allowed.

YES _____ NO _____ N/A _____

_____

_____

27. A B C D

User identity, including passwords, shall be deleted promptly when employees leave the company.

YES _____ NO _____ N/A _____

_____

_____

28. - B C D

For emergency and backup purposes, the security officer's password shall be kept in a secure area. Access to the password should be allowed only in an emergency situation.

YES _____ NO _____ N/A _____

_____

_____

29. - B C D

After three attempts with illegitimate combinations of user identity and password, further attempts shall automatically be prevented.

YES _____ NO _____ N/A _____

_____

_____

30. A B C D

When leaving the terminal for more than a short period, the user shall log off the terminal or set it in a standby position, where a new log-on is required.

YES _____ NO _____ N/A _____

_____

_____

31. - - C D

As a support to the users, the following functions should be installed where possible. After a certain time (20–30 minutes) with no work at the terminal, it should automatically be set in a standby position or be shut off. Further use of the terminal should require a new sign-on procedure.

YES _____ NO _____ N/A _____

_____

_____

32. A - - -

For virus protection, diskettes or files from unknown sources (especially games) shall not be used.

YES _____ NO _____ N/A _____

_____

_____

33. A - - -

To protect confidential information, one of the following methods shall be used.

1. Data shall be stored on diskettes that are kept under lock and key.
2. If data is stored on a hard disk, a security system shall be implemented. It shall have functions for password security and hard disk encryption, and it shall prevent "booting" from diskettes.

YES _____   NO _____   N/A _____

_____

_____

34. - B C D

For file transfer data communication, the available password functions shall be used. A receipt shall be issued and sent back when a file has been received and stored.

YES _____   NO _____   N/A _____

_____

_____

35. A B C D

For interactive data communication, the security measures items 20–32 shall be included.

YES _____   NO _____   N/A _____

_____

_____

36. A B C D

The use of encryption should be decided jointly by the personnel responsible for security at the sending and the receiving companies. Their feasibility study shall include sensitivity of data, risks, and costs. **Before deciding for encryption, corporate approval must be obtained.**

YES _____   NO _____   N/A _____

_____

_____

37. A B C D

For synchronous communication, the identities shall be unique.

YES _____   NO _____   N/A _____

_____

_____

38. A B C D

Dial-up asynchronous communication, X21 and X25, must be specially secured against unauthorized access. The following methods may be used:

1. Call back, so that the final connection is always established from the minicomputer or the mainframe (not from a personal computer).

2. Dynamic passwords, changed each time the communication is used (this requires some special hardware).
3. Encryption. **Before deciding for encryption, corporate approval must be obtained.** Direct access to data with a simple password as the only security measure is not suitable.

YES _____   NO _____   N/A _____

_____

_____

39. A B C D

For each application where data communication is being used, fallback alternatives to the communication and its routines shall be developed and tested.

YES _____   NO _____   N/A _____

_____

_____

40. - B C D

Investigations have shown that the risk of loss is as great in the area of swindle and sabotage as it is for fire and water damage. In light of these facts, the background of those who will be employed in sensitive positions should be carefully checked.

YES _____   NO _____   N/A _____

_____

_____

41. A B C D

The employment agreement for IT personnel should include a paragraph stating, "Programs made in working hours or otherwise made for the employer are the property of the employer and cannot be sold or given away without written permission from the employer."

YES _____   NO _____   N/A _____

_____

_____

43. - - C D

A logbook of disturbances shall be kept. It should contain the time when the disturbance was discovered, the kind of disturbance and where it occurred, the time for notification of error, and the time when the system was working again.

YES _____   NO _____   N/A _____

_____

_____

44. - - C -

A contingency plan should be worked out and kept updated.

YES _____   NO _____   N/A _____

_____

_____

45. - - - D

A contingency plan must be worked out and kept updated.

YES _____   NO _____   N/A _____

_____

_____

46. - - C D

The computer installations should have insurance against fire. Water and extra cost insurance is often recommended. For leased equipment, check whether the leasing company or the Group company is responsible for taking out the insurance policy.

YES _____   NO _____   N/A _____

_____

_____

47. A B C D

A complete system and operation documentation shall be kept up to date. One copy of it shall be kept in a fireproof place.

YES _____   NO _____   N/A _____

_____

_____

48. - B C D

Before putting a new system or a new version into production, a thorough test shall be carried out. This

YES _____   NO _____   N/A _____

_____

_____

49. - - C D

A test system or a test company should be installed, so that tests and education will not affect the production environment.

YES ____   NO ____   N/A ____

50. A B C D

Methods shall be applied to ensure that all input allowed and nothing else is entered into the system. Such methods are automatic checking of batch sums or serial numbers and a split input by two clerks and a comparison between the two input files.

YES ____   NO ____   N/A ____

51. A B C D

Quality checks of data entry shall be used, such as check digits, format, and reasonableness checks, combination controls, matching checks, and batch totals.

YES ____   NO ____   N/A ____

YES _____ NO _____ N/A _____

30. A B C D

Methods shall be applied to ensure that all input allowed and nothing else is entered into the system. Such methods are automatic checking of batch numbers of serial numbers and split input by two checks and split input between the two input files.

YES _____ NO _____ N/A _____

31. A B C D

Quality checks of data entry shall be used such as check digit, format, and reasonableness checks, prohibition in partial batching, batch, and hash totals.

YES _____ NO _____ N/A _____

Section 8
Physical Access Security

Controls over physical security should ensure that only authorized access is permitted to computer hardware, peripheral devices, and any other equipment that may indirectly affect the operation of the computer hardware. Controls should also ensure that the physical risks to the equipment have been addressed, whether the appropriate managers have chosen to eliminate the risk, compensate for the risk at some intermediate level, or accept the risk in the normal course of doing business.

THE DATA CENTER

The room used to house the computer should be designed and built consistently with the hardware to be placed there and the risks relevant in the particular circumstances of that installation. These circumstances include the size of the computer; requirements for electricity, cooling, and other utilities; and the number of people expected to attend to that hardware. The range of potential issues is covered item by item in the text.

Many of these items are predicated on the belief that the computer should be kept in a separate area, whether the computer is a mainframe, midrange, or microcomputer. This may seem excessive, particularly when the central computer is a microcomputer but, under any circumstances, if the central computer is an integral part of the business activity, it should at least be protected from accidental harm.

Having transaction processing interrupted simply because someone carrying a box or other package ended up stumbling into the data center and damaging the computer could prove embarrassing to the person responsible for the computer, let alone the individuals responsible for the business.

The data centers should be physically separated from other areas of the building by making it a separate fire zone. This generally means that the construction is floor-to-ceiling concrete block and that any wires, conduits, or other through-the-wall items have been plugged with a fire-resistant material. The objective is to prevent or significantly slow the progress of a fire or other physical event from outside the data center or vice versa. The building code in any particular state, county, or municipality is the source of more specific requirements.

DOOR LOCKS

Data center door locks are important because the lock should provide for all appropriate security, and the incorrect lock will most often result in the door being propped or left open. If the door lock causes the door to be open, the control objectives have been compromised, and the organization has to be concerned not only with individual noncompliance, but also with institutional noncompliance.

In selecting the appropriate door lock, or evaluating one already installed, the difference between the risk for internal and external sources should be considered. If the risk is only from an outside agency, it is reasonable to use a lock that would be used only during those times when no one was present in the data center. If a risk also exists from insiders, it is normal to use a lock that is always in service.

A risk-based decision process is illustrated in Exhibit 8-1. This may appear overly complicated for deciding what type of door lock is required, but it allows us to easily see how risk assessment plays an important role in control-based decision support situations.

Regardless of the type of lock used, the IT auditor should consider that:

- Once a door is open, no one can know who passes through, or how many, unless there is a camera or a guard
- Once someone is inside, almost every door can be opened from the inside to let additional persons through
- It should never be assumed that only authorized persons can unlock the door unless, as previously mentioned, there is a camera or a guard

Types of Door Locks

The three types of locks commonly available today are: key-operated locks, combination locks, and magnetic or electronic locks. How they work and their advantages and disadvantages are discussed in the following paragraphs.

Key Locks. Key-operated locks can range from simple, single knob locks found in most homes to the laminated deadbolt style more often used to lock double doors at the entrance to a business. Many of these locks have keys that can be duplicated for almost no cost at any hardware store or convenience store. Even those keys stamped "DO NOT DUPLICATE" are so stamped because they can be duplicated. That message is supposed to prevent scrupulous persons from making copies; it does little to deter the unscrupulous.

Exhibit 8-1. Risk-Based Decision Support Process

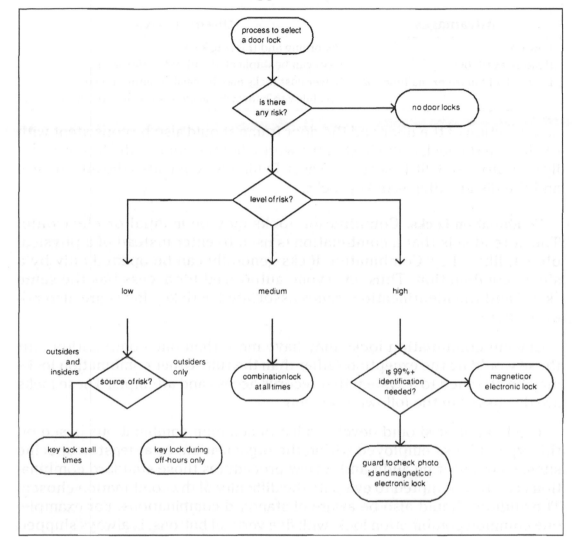

Other keys have special beveled ridges that standard key duplicating machines cannot copy. The number of machines capable of copying these keys is far less than standard machines, and they are not normally available to the general public. This may deter the person who would copy the key just because he or she was curious or for a prank, but it would not stop someone determined to copy the key to gain unauthorized access to a data center. Such a person could make a copy of the key on a standard machine, which would produce the necessary peaks and valleys, but would then have to bevel each one manually. This is difficult to do, but certainly not impossible.

Key locks should also prevent against the use of a credit card or other stiff object being used to depress the lock plunger find thus open the door. The

Exhibit 8-2. Evaluation of Key Locks

Advantages	Disadvantages
Low cost	Recording and tracking keys
Readily available	Keys can be duplicated without authorization
Low risk of failure or malfunction	Lower cost locks may be easily compromised
	No ability to know who accesses the area being secured

construction of the door and the door frame should also be consistent with the lock. If the lock is the best in the world, but the door or the frame is easily compromised, little security exists. Exhibit 8-2 compares the advantages and the disadvantages of key locks.

Combination Locks. Combination locks may be manual or electronic. The core idea is that a combination is used to enter instead of a physical object, like a key. Combination locks generally can be opened only by a single combination. Thus, everyone authorized for access has the same "key," and the identification issues associated with key locks are also relevant here.

Certain combination locks may have more than one combination, but those would be the exception rather than the rule. Other combination locks may be attached to a system that records access and attempts. These locks are discussed in the following section.

The IT auditor should develop a list of common combinations based on the type of locks employed within the organization, or at least at specific sites, so that during audit and review procedures those standard combinations can be attempted to evaluate the difficulty of the combination chosen. The auditor should also be aware of standard combinations. For example, one common combination lock, with five vertical buttons, is always shipped from the factory with the same combination. The manual and instructions that come with the lock indicate that the first action to take after installing the lock is to change the combination. This is not always done, and being able to walk up to that lock and open it with that combination is an attention-getter.

The IT department must be in control of changing the combination (periodically or whenever an employee leaves the organization) and designating someone to be responsible for deciding who is authorized for the combination and subsequent access. The ironic element in choosing a combination lock over a key lock is that a combination is duplicated much more easily than a key.

The most important advantages and disadvantages to combination locks are shown in Exhibit 8-3.

Exhibit 8-3. Evaluation of Mechanical Combination Locks

Advantages	Disadvantages
Relatively low cost	Changing combinations periodically or when someone leaves
Readily available	
Combination is usually simple enough to remember	Risk of malfunction (although a manual override is often built into lock)
Some locks may be able to lock out any access after too many unsuccessful attempts	No ability to know who accesses the area being secured
	Combinations can be easily duplicated

Magnetic or Electronic Locks. Magnetic and electronic locks are the most sophisticated and practical alternative. These locks also represent the first opportunity for the enterprise to determine who is unlocking the door and entering the authorized personnel area. This improved control is made possible because these locks are usually opened by a card that may have any one of the following characteristics:

- Visible magnetic strip
- Invisible magnetic or chemical strip
- Embedded microchip or transmitter
- Visible magnetic strip
- Invisible magnetic or chemical strip
- Embedded microchip or transmitter

In every instance, the card is unique and identifies to the system who is entering based on which card is being activated. Of course, the enterprise likes to think that it knows who is entering but, unless there is a camera or a guard on duty, the system cannot determine who is holding the card and actually gaining access to the secured area. The compensation for this continuing inability to ensure that the enterprise knows in advance who is entering is twofold: responsibility and event identification. In this situation, responsibility means that each user must be responsible for his or her card such that anything that happens associated with that card is the responsibility of that person. However, assigning this responsibility does not make these cards a 100 percent reliable control. Event identification means that the enterprise can know when an access attempt is made and initiate a secondary response, such as having a fixed camera take a picture of the entrance or a fixed video camera tape a few moments to capture the entry activity. The system makes a secondary response possible because the system takes the card coding and checks it in realtime against the access database, returning either the signal to open the door or the signal not to open the door and to trigger the red light or other mechanism indicating that access is being denied (if that feature is available or enabled).

Exhibit 8-4. Evaluation of Electronic and Magnetic Locks

Advantages	Disadvantages
Locks do not require changing unless there is a personnel change, and then the change is usually only logical and made through a terminal Lock management system can track who accesses secured areas along with the time and date of each access Secondary security responses can be activated based on entry system activity	Relatively high cost Identification still not assured

The significant advantages and disadvantages to using magnetic or electronic locks are summarized in Exhibit 8-4.

WINDOWS

Many data centers have windows. The windows may open to an interior area, to the outside, or both. Typically, the windows are present because of one of the following three reasons.

- The computer was placed in a room that already had windows.
- The windows were designed for the data center room to provide light for employees working in that area.
- The windows were put in the data center room to display the equipment to customers and employees.

Corresponding reasons exist to place the computer in a room that does not have any windows, interior or exterior.

- What someone cannot see, he or she may not think to damage.
- The computer and its operators do not need exterior light or a view for job satisfaction or performance.
- The windows may be the weakest link in the data center construction.

The IT auditor is likely to encounter windows in the majority of data centers where physical security is being evaluated. The first task is to understand what risks are relevant for the data center under review. The primary risks to consider are:

- the hardware damage after someone enters the room or uses the window to get a foreign object into the room
- the theft of computer hardware that may be salable on the black market
- access to the computer by someone who wants to do something that is not possible from a terminal

Although these may not seem like common occurrences, not many of the security risks addressed by effective general controls are frequent events. This is clearly one of the areas in which the IT auditor should work to ensure that effective controls are in place because the controls will not require maintenance or followup. These controls will simply be in place, working to reduce or eliminate risk at all times.

If the IT auditor does not believe that these issues should be addressed, or if there is a resistance from the customer, consider the following events.

- During an extended strike, one frustrated union member prepared a Molotov cocktail and threw it at the window through which a computer that the member believed belonged to the employer could be seen. The explosive device went through the plate-glass window and landed on the data center floor of the company adjacent to the employer of the disgruntled employee.
- During a wildcat strike at a Midwest employer, someone fired a shot into the data center through the wire-reinforced glass in an attempt, it is believed, to damage the computer. No one was injured, and there was so little damage to the glass that it was not replaced. Management left the punctured glass in place as a testament to what could, but should not, happen in such a situation. It was never determined if one of the strikers or someone else fired the shot.
- An employer in the Southwest had personal computers being serviced stored in the data center. The room was not in use after the end of the day Friday until early Monday morning. Over one weekend, someone broke the plate-glass window and stole the personal computers. The good news was that the thief or thieves did not recognize that a brandnew midrange computer that could be the server for a network, valued at more than $200,000, was still in the box adjacent to where the personal computers were located.

Replacement Glass Alternatives

The IT auditor has three alternatives when considering replacements for standard tempered or plate glass windows: wire-reinforced glass, shatterproof glass, or Plexiglas.

Wire-Reinforced Glass. Wire-reinforced glass has been the least expensive alternative, providing for increased security. The glass can be broken, but it is very difficult to clear the glass away from the wire to be able to cut the wire. Without taking the time to get the wire cut, the only entry to the room can be made by objects smaller than the gaps in the wire, usually not more than an inch apart.

Plexiglas. Plexiglas, although more costly than wire-reinforced glass, offers a material that is much more difficult to break and is not susceptible to small objects because the material is uniform throughout. The drawback to Plexiglas is that in certain installations it can discolor or slightly distort the image seen through it, which may compromise the business objectives of improving the work environment for the staff or having the computer on display for clients and customers.

Shatterproof or Bulletproof Glass. Shatterproof, or bulletproof, glass combines the consistency of Plexiglas with the visual quality of regular glass. Its drawbacks are its high cost, along with its extra thickness and proportional weight. The exact thickness and weight cannot be determined until a decision is made about just how strong the glass must be. The decision has to be based on an analysis of the possible risks and effects in the situation.

DATA CENTER FLOOR

The mainframe computer was a machine that, particularly in its infancy, generated a tremendous amount of heat. System engineers typically responded to this problem by installing appropriate cooling, and then placing the computer on a raised floor. The raised floor, normally 6 to 16 inches above the actual floor, provided underfloor ventilation that exited the floor directly underneath the computers. This caused the chilled air to blow directly into the system, thus keeping the operating temperatures within a reasonable range.

As the raised floor became common, computer technicians recognized an opportunity to eliminate the mass of wires and cables needed to interconnect data center equipment, as well as terminals and other remote devices that had been left lying on the floor surrounding the equipment. The raised floors generally left enough room for cable runs, and the computer manufacturers responded by redesigning their hardware to have those cables exit at the base of each unit near the floor. The new design created a new risk because there were now electrical and other connections either at or very close to floor level such that any water accumulation could affect the connections. This situation was amplified when people started running electrical cable under the raised floor, including standard extension cables for ancillary or other indirect equipment. The IT auditor should look under the raised floor, particularly on a first-time review, to see what is under the floor and what risks are relevant to the circumstances.

ALARM SYSTEM

The IT auditor should consider the need for an alarm system for the data center or for, at least, the area where the computer is kept. The cost of a system may be difficult to justify if the computer does not warrant being kept in a separate location. However, the evaluation should not be overlooked. The alarm system can have two different purposes: one related to environmental issues and the other to unauthorized persons.

Any evaluation of an alarm system should cover the need for identification, notification, and response, although the sequence of response and notification can be varied based on the nature of the problem encountered. This section discusses environmental issues from identification through response, followed by issues related to unauthorized activity.

A wide range of items can be considered part of environmental issues. They may be as small as a bad filter on the heating, ventilation, and air conditioning (HVAC) system or as big as a tornado. The greater issues surrounding a total loss of the data center, or a total loss of availability, should trigger the business recovery plan, and are not discussed here. An environmental event can only be addressed after it is identified.

Identification and Detection

Two practical methods exist for identifying environmental events. First is physical observation by employees, which may be effective during working hours, but only so long as the affected area has someone present and the event takes place where it can be observed. The second method relies on detection equipment. This equipment has the advantage of always being on duty and of having a specific threshold for action.

The IT auditor should always remember that most detection equipment requires electricity to function, and may either be battery powered or wired directly into an electrical source. If any of the devices is battery powered, it should have a feature that indicates when the battery power begins to diminish, and there should be a procedure to require the regular periodic replacement of the batteries. The company's interests are not served if the detector is in place, but the event went unrecognized because of a dead battery.

Fire Detection. The alarm system should have at least one method of fire detection, whether it is smoke or particle detection. In either case, it is not the heat that triggers the detector, but one of the two primary products of combustion: smoke or particulate matter floating up in the heat from the fire. Smoke or particle detection is considered more effective than heat detection because the smoke and particulate matter usually precede the full conflagration that would be sufficient to trigger a heat-based fire detection system.

Heat Detection. Although heat detection is not an effective means of identifying fire, it is important to have a heat detector as part of the alarm system. The heat detector works to protect the equipment, because most computer equipment has a normal operating range of temperatures that should not be exceeded. Malfunctions can result if the operating temperature is too high or too low, although equipment damage is more likely when the temperature is above the normal operating range.

The IT auditor should be familiar with the hardware being used because some manufacturers have begun to build thermal sensors into their equipment. If these sensors identify an out-of-range condition that meets any other criteria that may have been established, the equipment will automatically shut down. These automatic shutdowns usually minimize potential data loss to the company. If a temperature condition causes a computer to shut down in an unplanned or uncontrolled manner, data loss is much more likely. There may also be a delay in recovery operations, which will trigger the business resumption plan.

Heat is normally the focus of deletion systems as opposed to cold. Too much heat can be caused by fire, an air conditioning failure, or malfunctioning equipment; too much cold results only if central heating is lost in a location experiencing sub-zero conditions. In such a case, turning the computer off would probably be a result, because everyone would have stopped working.

Water Detection. Water is the most common problem experienced by a computer, although the causes are not the floods that the systems professional may be quick to ensure will not happen. A leaking roof, failure of pipes running over the data center, unexpected sprinkler discharge, or drainage failure causing water to back into the data center are more frequent causes of water destruction than floods.

Water detectors generally work on a simple principle. Two contacts are placed in very close proximity to the floor, preferably in a low spot. As the water begins to rise up to those contacts, they short out and cause the attached alarm to sound. Water detectors may be the most important device to wire directly into an electrical source because they are generally the most difficult to access. Difficult to access means difficult to check or change the batteries, and there is an increased chance of having a dead battery when an unexpected water accumulation takes place.

Event Notification

The importance of the alarm system notification feature cannot be understated. The IT auditor can verify that all necessary detectors are in place, but if those detectors do not bring an immediate response, their effectiveness is compromised. The IT auditor cannot assume that a comprehensive alarm system costing any amount of money, and providing every conceivable feature will actually be connected to a guard station or to the police and fire departments.

Local Siren. The local siren is a good method of notification because the personnel on site may be able to respond to the situation and resolve it immediately or very quickly. It also places on-duty personnel on notice as to the existence of a problem even if their only response is to vacate the area, which accomplishes the primary objective in these situations—to protect life.

Guard Location. The IT auditor may find guards that are on site or there may be an off-site guard service connected to the company's alarms. In either case, an alarm sounding at a guard's location should cause company personnel to begin responding according to their emergency procedures manual.

Community Services. The company may include procedures to have the guards notify the applicable public service, such as the police or fire department, or the system may be set up with a direct connection to these services. In either case, the setup is designed to ensure that the necessary community services are notified as quickly as possible to accelerate the required response.

Automatic Call-Out. Touch-pulse and touch-tone dialing technology has an unexpected benefit—machines/computers can dial the telephone. This improves the capabilities of physical detection systems. One of the improvements is the ability to establish a calling list. The system uses this list, based on the nature of the detected event, to make phone calls to the appropriate persons on the calling list. When the phone call is answered, the system announces its identify, the type of event, and any other relevant information.

For example, the system call might announce that: "This is the XYZ Company data center alert system. The heat detector has been activated because the room temperature was XXX degrees and is currently YYY degrees. Successful calls have been placed to...." The system tracks successful calls based on a response code that the recipient would be expected to enter after hearing the message.

Event Response

Once the environmental event has been identified and the appropriate parties notified, an appropriate response is required. These responses fall into three categories:

- *Administrative responses.* Once an environmental event takes place and the appropriate company personnel have been notified, it is likely that one or more emergency procedures will be activated. The extent of those procedures is likely to vary according to the nature and severity of the problem encountered. All personnel should be familiar with the emergency procedures so that they can be implemented quickly with minimal effort.
- *Community service response.* Once notified, the typical community service response will be to activate the appropriate equipment and personnel who will respond to the scene. Once there, they will have their own procedures to follow, and can generally be expected to take care of themselves.
- *On-site manual and automated responses.* The on-site manual response should be directed by an emergency procedures manual. The IT auditor should look for such a manual, and make a recommendation that one be developed if one does not exist. Usually, the risk management or facility personnel are responsible for drafting emergency procedures.

The on-site automated response is almost entirely focused on fires, at least in terms of there being alternatives from which to choose. The alarm system may have the capability of being connected to the computer such that an orderly shutdown could be initiated. That would be almost the only automated response to a temperature or water problem:

- *A temperature problem.* A temperature problem identified by the alarm system usually indicates a failure of the HVAC system. For example, the HVAC thermostat controlling the heat and cooling mechanisms is probably not going to be able to react to the problem. In that case, someone will have to get in and either find a way to at least temporarily correct the problem or else shut down the computer.
- *A water problem.* A water problem is particularly difficult to address, unless the company has deemed the risk important enough to warrant having an installed pump that can be turned on by the alarm system. In this situation, having the system effect an orderly shutdown is strongly recommended to reduce the risk of data loss and other problems.

FIRE SUPPRESSION SYSTEMS

A fire problem has a number of solutions. The number of solutions, the range in costs to implement and maintain those solutions, and changing regulations require careful analyses of the resolution of fire problems. However, there are two primary fire suppression systems: chemical and water. Many IT professionals continue to be convinced that water has no place in a data center, although numerous companies, such as IBM, have approved and supported a switch to water-based systems for many of their own sites, and suggested water as one of the acceptable alternatives for protecting data centers.

Water-Based Fire Suppression Systems

Two reasons for the switch to water-based systems are: computer construction has changed over time so they are much less susceptible to water damage, and fires in data centers do not usually start with the computer, but with other equipment or materials in the room that are best extinguished by water.

The original sprinkler systems were very simple, turning on only when the temperature increased until a piece of lead would melt, and the sprinkler head would activate. Some of the problems with sprinkler systems include:

- Ballast failure causing unnecessary water release and associated damage
- Water releasing over an area that is not on fire because air circulation patterns moved heated air to another area
- The imprecision of the response such that equipment and facilities that were not at risk were damaged

The desirability of water sprinklers has led to continuing advances in that particular technology; advances that were facilitated by microprocessor technology. Fire detection systems became more sophisticated, gaining the ability to determine the location of a potential fire more precisely. Three new types of water sprinkler-based fire suppression systems that have evolved include:

- Computer-controlled wet pipe
- Computer-controlled dry pipe
- Pre-action dry pipe

Computer-Controlled Wet Pipe. The computer-controlled wet pipe system continues to have the sprinkler water pipes running over the data center charged with water at all times. The first difference is that the sprinkler heads are not controlled by lead ballast, but by microprocessors. In most cases, the sprinkler heads are retracted into the ceiling until the system orders one to discharge when it first drops down from the ceiling.

The second difference is that the company has direct control over what conditions have to be met before the system activates, as well as control over the parameters of the system response. The increased control creates a new issue for the IT auditor because he or she will have to evaluate the established settings for such a system.

Computer-Controlled Dry Pipe. The computer-controlled dry pipe system adds one improvement to the computer-controlled wet pipe system previously described. The improvement is the addition of a master valve that controls all of the sprinkler pipes for the data center. This valve keeps the overhead pipes without water until sensor activations meeting established parameters cause the valve to open.

The valve opening permits water to flow up to the individual sprinkler heads, but that is where the water stops. The individual sprinkler heads are still controlled by the microprocessor that will determine which heads are active and when that will happen. The difference may appear to be minor. However, this system virtually eliminates any chance of an accidental water discharge over the equipment in the data center.

Pre-action Dry Pipe. The advantages of the two computer-controlled systems previously described are diminished by the high cost of these systems, and many companies are unwilling to incur the cost. However, the mechanical nature of a sprinkler system provides for a less costly and less technologically advanced alternative. The pre-action dry pipe system includes the master control valve principle from the prior system, but it retains the same lead ballast sprinkler heads that have been in use for decades.

Control over the master valve may be through mechanical or microprocessor technology, although the way it works is unchanged. An inert gas is kept in the overhead pipes at all times to prevent corrosion and to provide a means for monitoring system integrity. If a pipe or connection were to fail, the system pressure would drop, triggering an alarm.

Maintaining pressure is also important because it works to keep the lead ballast properly positioned in the sprinkler heads. After a pressure failure, the sprinkler heads must be checked to ensure that they will function as expected in an emergency. The pre-action system normally controls pressure by pumping the inert gas out as water is released into the system such that the pressure is kept effectively constant.

Chemical Fire Suppression Systems

Computer systems in the not too distant past were much more susceptible to damage from a sprinkler system discharge than they are today. Engineers developed a number of alternative systems using dry chemicals or gases to suppress fires, although only two of those systems made any significant penetration into the market. The two chemicals providing a foundation for these alternatives are Halon and carbon dioxide.

Halon. The chemical compound Halon was developed by DuPont in response to the need for a non-lethal fire suppression chemical. Its formulation includes items that make Halon part of the chlorofluorocarbon (CFC) family. Halon is an ozone-depleting chemical, as are most members of the CFC family, and is already banned in several countries around the world.

The United States has signed at least one agreement that will affect the legality and availability of Halon after the year 2000. DuPont and other chemical companies are working constantly to develop alternative chemicals that do not have the same ozone-depleting potential (ODP) as Halon that can be deployed by using the same delivery systems. If a complete infrastructure replacement ends up being needed, many companies plan to change back to a water-based system.

Carbon Dioxide. This naturally occurring gas does not promote combustion and will prevent or extinguish a fire if present in sufficient levels in the atmosphere of a room or area. Unlike Halon, carbon dioxide is generally harmful to humans if present in sufficient levels to be effective as a fire suppression agent. Many companies that had selected carbon dioxide for their data centers have changed to Halon, although there are carbon dioxide systems that continue to be used.

Common Elements of Chemical Fire Suppression Agents. Halon, carbon dioxide, and other chemical fire suppression agents have a number of common elements or issues that include the following:

Atmospheric Concentration. Chemical fire suppression agents are consistently based on the idea that reducing or eliminating the available oxygen in the protected area puts out fires. Experience and testing has supported the validity of that idea. The volume of the data center must be determined very accurately so that the delivery system, quantity of the selected chemical agent, and configuration are properly installed.

Data Center Seal Integrity. The data center must be designed or modified so that its doors close automatically and that the HVAC system capacities are sufficient. If the data center doors do not close automatically, a risk is certain, particularly if the computer operators or any other persons who are evacuating the room do not take the time to ensure that the doors are fully closed. Most chemical systems discharge their contents very quickly under very high pressure. If the doors are not closed tightly, it is very likely that they will be forced open.

The opened doors increase the effective volume of the data center to include all of the adjacent areas. The increased actual volume reduces the concentration of the chemical agent, probably below effective levels, and the fire continues to burn. It is unreasonable to include sufficient extra quantities to cover an additional area because the extra amount could be 300 to 400 percent more than the original. And even ignoring the financial considerations, releasing all the chemical into the original room volume, assuming it was sealed, could blow doors or windows out and create the problem it was intended to solve.

System Delay. Almost every system has a built-in delay from the time it is activated until the contents are discharged. This delay has several objectives:

- It permits personnel to evacuate, which is essential if the chemical agent is harmful or fatal.
- It provides time to confirm the problem and abort if needed.
- It provides time for any other emergency procedures appropriate to the situation.

The IT executive is likely to have a choice regarding the length of the delay, and it is a matter that deserves consideration. The number of people normally in the data center, the chemical agent chosen, the speed with which a fire might spread, and other parts of the business that might be harmed are some of the most important considerations in setting the delay. The executive should also consult internal risk management and external insurance personnel, assuming that there is some external coverage in effect related to the particular computer installation.

The risks of setting the wrong delay are clear. Too little delay time and personnel may not be able to react according to their training and emergency procedures. An incomplete evacuation may compromise the seal integrity and lead to a failure to extinguish the fire. If the delay is too long, the fire may spread beyond the ability of the chemical agent to extinguish it. The delay normally incorporates the companion feature of an abort switch.

Abort Switch. Most, if not all, chemical systems include an abort switch. The abort switch gives company personnel the chance to prevent a system discharge if they know that there is no emergency or that there is another reason that the discharge should not be permitted to take place. There are minor variations based on building codes, vendor, and company discretion, but most abort switches are deadman switches, i.e., the switch only operates as long as someone is there to press it.

Once the switch is released, the system may continue to count down from the point it had reached when the switch was pressed, or a new count may begin. This factor is very significant because these switches are routinely located inside the data center. If it is inside the data center and if the delay timer does not reset, it may leave very little time for someone to evacuate the area if he/she has pressed the abort switch to allow others to leave and are now ready to go themselves. In addition, as described earlier, if the data center door is open when the chemical system activates, the system could fail to extinguish the fire.

One very different scenario is a false alarm in which someone knows that a system discharge is unnecessary and uses the abort button. Of course, this action does not reset the system, so someone with that capability must be summoned.

Telephone. A telephone and a directory, at least with the numbers of emergency response personnel, should be located within easy reach of the abort switch. Anyone who finds it necessary to press the switch can then call for any assistance believed necessary to reset the system, investigate the potential emergency, provide assistance to another employee who may be unable to evacuate, or other similar situation.

Backup System Considerations. There are a number of situations when a fire suppression system may fail, although it is more likely with a chemical system. The company should consider, and the IT auditor should verify, that the need for a second system has been considered and an appropriate decision reached. A chemical system can be supplemented by a water system that is ultimately supported by the local fire department.

Training and Documentation. Selecting and installing a system for physical security is only half the battle. Unless the appropriate employees are fully trained on alarm system operations, options, and responses, there is a risk that the control objectives will not be met in an emergency situation. The information provided during training should be provided in writing with one copy by the abort switch and telephone, one with the guard (if there is a guard), and other copies as needed.

THE DETECTION OF AND RESPONSE TO UNAUTHORIZED ACTIVITY

All of the environmental situations covered in the preceding pages could be generalized under the topics "accidental" or "acts of God." Several of them, most likely fire, could be the result of unauthorized activity. Such activity could also result in equipment being stolen, damaged, reconfigured, or simply used for unauthorized or fraudulent activities. The data center room construction discussions covered the basics of preventive controls over unauthorized physical activity. The focus of this section is the detection of and the response to unauthorized physical activity in the data center.

Mechanical Detection Devices

To monitor the activity in and surrounding the data center, companies have several mechanical and human options. The mechanical options include the use of security cameras, motion sensors, and door and window sensors. The alternative to or supplement of these options is to hire guards who are posted in and around the computer facility at all times.

The Security Camera. The company can have a security camera installed if there is an internal guard service or external guard service with direct monitoring capabilities. This may not ensure that unauthorized activity is detected in real time, but should ensure that if such activity takes place and is not detected in realtime, subsequent detection should be possible.

A Motion Sensor. Anyone successfully entering the data center without authorization will almost certainly move about the room, even if it is only once to get to the desired location and a second time to exit the room. If a motion sensor is installed, it should be reasonable to expect that any unauthorized activity during off-hours will activate the sensor. The sensor should be connected outside the data center just like the rest of the alarm system. It would be management's decision as to whether a motion sensor activation will sound an alarm in the data center. The reason to sound the alarm is to attempt to interrupt the unauthorized activity and to prevent problems at the risk of not catching the person or persons involved. Conversely, the reason to not sound the alarm is to provide time for the response personnel to reach the scene and capture the persons responsible for the unauthorized activity.

Door and Window Sensors. Sensors can also be installed that provide coverage for both the windows and the doors, whether they are broken or simply opened enough to permit access. The decisions about what alarms to sound and what responses to initiate must be made by the appropriate managers.

Having Guards in the Data Center

Companies that have full- or part-time internal guard services often require those guards to walk through the guarded areas periodically. These walk-throughs may be scheduled or unscheduled. In either case, there may be an electronic or manual system in place that the guard interacts with to prove with certainty that the walk-through was completed through the designated areas.

One of the guarded areas is likely to be the data center. The issue arises based on the location of the guard's check-in point. It is recommended not to place the check-in point inside the data center, but at a point outside that gives the guard an opportunity to look in and check through internal windows, even if the only internal window is part of the door. The reasons for having the check-in point inside the data center may include one or more of the following:

- The guard is more likely to detect an environmental problem like fire or heat from inside the data center.
- The company wants the guards to be in a position to identify potential medical problems of systems personnel and to initiate the appropriate response.
- The guards should be in any area where they are expected to provide the most effective service.

The recommended responses to these items are:

- The guard is only present for a few minutes an hour at the most. Implementing a physical sensor and alarm system provides constant monitoring, which the guard can supplement from outside the room. The guard should know the number of persons expected to be on duty and should look in and determine that they are not experiencing any problems.
- The guard will be in the area if the check-in point is just outside the data center. In addition, it is not recommended to prevent them from entering the data center; rather, they should not be required to enter during every walk-through.
- Having untrained personnel in the data center is not a recommended practice in general. No exception should be made for the guards. It is possible for them to cause a problem accidentally, such as bumping into a piece of equipment and turning it off.

Section 9
Logical Access Security

Controls over logical access security should ensure that all programs and data stored on computer systems are protected from unauthorized access and execution. It is a business decision as to the level of security implemented and to what extent that security will either compensate for or eliminate in terms of logical access risks. The two most fundamental logical access control objectives are that:

- Users must be identified and authenticated *before* receiving any access
- The authentication methods used must provide the desired level of assurance that the identification is accurate

Subsequent to adopting these two fundamental objectives, the enterprise should determine which levels of access should be controlled. Logical access controls may be able to control access at one or more of the following levels:

- *System.* Once identified and authenticated, the user may access any data, function, or resource within the computer.
- *Application.* Once identified and authenticated, the end user accesses all capabilities within an automated application system like accounts receivable, but has no access to the sales system or the general ledger.
- *Function.* The access within the accounts receivable application includes adding new customers, but not deleting existing customers.
- *Screen.* The end user can create and enter the basic name and address information for a new customer, but cannot access the credit screen to input that information.
- *Field.* The end user adding a new customer has all of the fields related to that task on one screen, but either cannot see the credit fields or can see those fields but cannot access them.

The access to system resources can also be managed based on the type of access. Depending on the situation, this may supplement or replace other techniques. Access types include:

- The ability only to see and read information
- The ability to add new information
- The ability to change existing information
- The ability to delete existing information

• The ability to print reports or get information out of the system into another format, whether written or electronic media

USER IDENTIFICATION

The majority of systems begin the sign-on process by requesting an identification code. The system will read the code and attempt to match that code against the security master files. Most systems will be configured to refuse access if that code cannot be matched against these files. The IT auditor should be aware that many systems have an operating condition where an unmatched code does not prevent access, and another where the unmatched code is added to the master file.

If a password requirement has been established, the matched user code acts as the link from the entered password to the stored password. The password would then be entered and matched just as the code had been. The same configuration issues discussed for the user code would also apply to the user password.

The IT auditor should assess the reliability of user identification codes in terms of meeting the appropriate control objectives. The IT auditor's ability to assess this will partially rely on his or her understanding of the differences between a single-level sign-on process and a two-level sign-on process. The single-level sign-on process only requires a user identification code for both identification and authentication. A two-level sign-on process uses the end-user identification code, sometimes referred to as a user ID, for identification and the password to authenticate the identification.

Single-Level Sign-on Environment

In a single-level sign-on environment, it is critical that the user identification code not have any correlation to other information about the user. If the user identification code is the end user's initials, or last name and first initial, it is extremely likely that one end user or a third party could guess the identification code of another end user, and successfully sign on to the system by using that other identification code.

The company's application software may provide logging capabilities that include capturing the user identification code with each transaction entered into the system. This logging is important if the enterprise values the ability to investigate application transactions and to know which end user is responsible for a particular transaction. The problem created by logging the user identification code in a single-level sign-on environment is that the logged code values must be accessible to be useful. If it is accessible, anyone having access to the logged codes has the ability to sign on using any of those other values.

Another drawback is associated with the usefulness of the logged code values. If the values are randomly or otherwise generated such that there is no association with the actual end user, anyone expected to review the transaction logs will have to have some access to information concerning which end user is associated with each code value. If this information is not available, it should not be possible for anyone reviewing transaction logs to ascertain which end user is identified by the logged code value.

Another issue in the single-level sign-on environment concerns the idea of period code value changes. If the user identification code values change periodically, the control objectives related to logging transactions and the associated end-user code are partially or fully compromised. If the codes never change, there is a significant risk that over time end users will accidentally or intentionally let their identification code become known to someone else, which effectively fully compromises the related control objectives.

The IT auditor will often be faced with situations in which the potential harm related to accidental or intentional events must be considered. The auditor's problem is often determining whether something was done accidentally or intentionally. A well-designed system should reduce the risk of errors and, thus, facilitate the determination just described. Poorly designed systems will do just the opposite.

Two-Level Sign-on Environment

The two-level sign-on environment often employs a user identification code that is associated with end users, such as their initials, for the first level. The second level is the password, which should not be associated with the end user and should be kept private at all times. This approach supports transaction logging activities because the end-user identification code for a particular end user should not change, and anyone reviewing a transaction log should be able to identify the logged identification codes and quickly determine which end user to contact with questions.

The enterprise's (and the auditor's) ability to rely on the concept that a logged end-user identification code actually identifies the person responsible for a particular transaction or other event is critical, particularly in online environments in which end users may be responsible for entering some or all of their own transactions. The security features related to passwords in many systems are in place just to support the reliability of the user authentication process in a two-level sign-on environment.

User Authentication

The issues related to passwords in a two-level sign-on environment can be divided into three groups. First are the password characteristics such as minimum and maximum length. Second are the rules for entering or using passwords, such as how many guesses or attempts are permitted, and what happens when the maximum number of attempts have been made and the end user has not successfully completed the sign-on process. Third are other issues such as how often (or when) an end user should have to re-enter his or her password or how many different passwords should an end user have to perform his or her assigned responsibilities.

Password Characteristics. Enterprise senior management or information systems management personnel decide what the password characteristics will be as systems are implemented. These characteristics are likely to include many of the following items, and may occasionally include characteristics not discussed in the subsequent sections.

Password Length. The security subsystem may permit setting both minimum and maximum lengths. Passwords should rarely have a minimum length of less than four or five positions because short passwords are both easier to guess and easier to observe over an end user's shoulder. Mathematically, a single-character password where any letter or number was permitted would provide 36 choices.

The IT auditor may find it difficult to believe that anyone would attempt to guess the password of another end user 1000 times, and impossible to imagine 1 million or more attempts. Programmers have written applications that will begin with the first one-character password and continue to try passwords until one is found that grants access. Moreover, these applications have all of the patience required to make thousands, millions, or more attempts if permitted by the system.

Minimum Password Length. No laws or regulations dictate what minimum length for a password is sufficient to reduce the risk to an acceptable level of having someone guess an end user's password. Over time, IT auditors have reached general concurrence that four or five positions as the minimum password length reduces the risk to acceptable levels, particularly if combined with log-in controls, discussed later in this section.

Maximum Password Length. This illustration is not intended to suggest that more is necessarily better. A password length of ten positions permits more than 3.5 quadrillion possible passwords, which is likely to be more than enough to frustrate even the most persistent password guesser, even if the frustration is only from waiting for the password guessing program to be successful. Thus, the IT auditor should carefully consider any situation in which passwords of more than ten, or even eight, positions are permitted. If the system provides for setting a minimum length for passwords, it is likely to also provide for setting a maximum length.

Other Password Characteristics. The password length is in some ways the easiest item to control. Other characteristics that may be controlled are repeating characters in passwords, sequential characters in passwords, and requiring special characters to be included in passwords.

Repeating Characters. End users generally do not view passwords as one of the best parts of their experience working with information systems. Because of this, end users may occasionally select passwords that are easy to remember rather than passwords that are not easily guessed. Setting a password that is comprised of a single character repeated until the minimum length is reached may be the simplest password. If the security software permits this, the security administrator should enable it as a simple and direct way to improve the reliability of passwords.

Sequential Characters. The end user may weaken the password as a control by selecting passwords that are sequential, whether the sequence is numeric (123) or alphabetic (ABC). If the security software permits this, the security administrator should block this type of password construction. If available, this restriction may also eliminate the palindrome, which is a character string that is the same forward or backward (i.e., albla).

Special Characters. The 36 choices mentioned previously represent the digits 0 through 9 and the characters a through z. The standard computer character set for personal computers includes 128 characters, many of which are intended for graphical or system use only. The ones available for use can be found on a standard keyboard and include #, A, /, ?, and }, among others.

Some security software permits the security administrator to require the inclusion of one of these special characters in a particular position or positions. This increases the number of alternatives available for a single position from 36 to 46 or more. At one time, using this feature was considered effective. There may continue to be many situations when it increases security. The risk is that it will over-complicate the password, causing the user to write it down and increasing the risk of lost privacy password characteristics.

Required Positions. Another option that makes passwords more difficult to guess also reduces the number of unique possible passwords is one that permits the security administrator to specify what type of character must appear in each password position. The security administrator might set the following positional rule: ANS??AV:

A Alphabetic character
N Alphanumeric character
V Numeric character

S Special character
? Any character

Positional password rules should be implemented in a way that eliminates the need for turning on some of the other password control features previously discussed. The IT auditor should always remember that there is nothing to ensure that the need for the other features will be eliminated, or that if the other features are not needed that they will be turned off. These rules may conflict with each other if no strategic direction to provide for consistency and effectiveness exists.

IT auditors should take care to understand the security functions of their systems. Some systems handle rule or parameter conflicts based on preprogrammed hierarchies that determine which features take precedence in a conflict. Other systems simply eliminate all of the conflicting features, which can leave the enterprise exposed, although anyone auditing or reviewing system security software settings will only find what appear to be settings that should be securing the systems environment.

END-USER LOG-IN CONSIDERATIONS

As previously described, the two most common end-user sign-on techniques are single-level and multiple-level sign-ons. Once the enterprise chooses the log-in technique, several more decisions follow. The decisions required by a single-level sign-on are much less complex than those required by a multiple-level sign-on.

Single-Level Log-in

The end user types his or her identification code into the indicated field on the screen and takes whatever action is required for the computer to process the entry. The computer should take the entered information and compare it with the security database. If the end-user identification code is found, access should be granted as provided for in the security database. The IT auditor should note that a successful log-in in this situation means that one of three things is true:

1. An end user correctly entered his or her own identification code.
2. An end user incorrectly entered the identification code for another end user.
3. An unauthorized person correctly entered the identification code of a legitimate end user and gained access to the system.

If the end-user identification code provided during the log-in process is not found in the security database, there is one choice. The security application or function can either let the end user log-in despite the invalid end-user identification code or reject the log-in attempt. Permitting the log-in to take place is not generally recommended unless that access can be controlled in some other fashion.

Invalid End-User Identification Code Accepted

The security software should be able to do at least two of the following if the enterprise is going to permit any access to end users providing invalid end-user identification codes:

- Restrict the end user to an area that gives him or her no options other than signing off or else very limited read-only access in the system. This has the benefit of informing an end user that entered an invalid identification code that a mistake has been made.
- Perform additional logging to enable the security administrator to perform a complete review of what the unidentified user did while having access to the system.
- Immediately signal the security administrator and possibly someone in operations so they can investigate and take any action deemed necessary.

Notwithstanding the preceding items, the single-level log-in approach should be avoided if at all possible. The enterprise does not have the ability to rely on the authenticity of users accessing company systems, and there is the risk of end-user identification codes being compromised due to the accidental entry of an invalid identification that happens to be the identification code of another user.

Invalid Identification Code Rejected

If the security administrator sets the security software to reject an invalid end-user identification code, the rejection will probably require other settings to be established. These settings may include, but are not limited to, one or more of the following items:

- Limit on unsuccessful attempts
- Action to be taken
  - —Temporary device lockout
  - —Permanent device lockout
- Notification

Limit on Unsuccessful Attempts. The security software may have the capability to track unsuccessful log-in attempts. This feature is designed to detect potential attempts to gain unauthorized access in which the unauthorized access is based on password guessing. If the number of attempted sign-ons reaches the threshold value in the security software, the system will respond.

The system response in an environment with a single-level sign-on technique cannot be based on or associated with the end-user identification code, because someone guessing at codes will not be using the same one twice. Any response can be based only on the device in use when the log-in is attempted. The system typically only has two options for a device: locking it out temporarily or locking it out permanently.

Temporary Device Lockout. Locking out the device temporarily has the effect of delaying the person or program attempting to access the system without completely blocking an authorized user who is only having trouble logging onto the system properly. The temporary response is more appropriate in situations in which personnel may be working on second or third shift, or on the weekend, when no one may be present in operations. The end user can continue trying to sign on to the system without having to go to another area or take some other potentially inefficient alternative.

Permanent Device Lockout. The security administrator may choose to establish a permanent lockout of the device for those situations in which security considerations require a more definitive response, or where someone is present to reset a device for the end user who accidentally disabled the device through unsuccessful access attempts.

Notification. The security software should include at least one feature providing for the notification of the system operator, security administrator, security guard, third-party security service, or other party responsible for monitoring activity at the covered location. The notification could be as simple as an indicator that there has been a violation without specification. It could also be complex, providing detailed information about the violation, the physical location, time, and user identification code.

Two-Level Log-in

The end user types his or her identification code into the indicated field on the screen and either takes whatever action is required for the computer to process the entry, or enters the password and then prompts the computer system to take action. The computer should take the entered end-user identification code and compare it with the security database. If the end-user identification code is found, the password kept in the system is compared with the password entered by the end user. The IT auditor should grant access based on established rules in the case of a match.

The IT auditor should be aware that there are systems that permit an end user entering an invalid end-user identification code to log into the system. Even further, these systems can create a new end-user profile based on the entered information. The IT auditor is urged to resist this approach, which may reduce security effectiveness to zero.

IT auditors should note that a successful log-in in this situation indicates that the most likely occurrence was one of the following:

- An end user correctly entered his or her own identification code and password.
- An unauthorized person correctly entered the identification code and password of a legitimate end user and gained access to the system.

If the end-user identification code provided during the log-in process is not found in the security database, there are two options. The security application or function can either let the end user log-in despite the invalid end-user identification code or reject the log-in attempt. Permitting the log-in to take place is not generally recommended, unless that access can be controlled.

Invalid End-User Identification Code Accepted

The security software should be able to do at least two of the following if the enterprise is going to permit any access to end users providing invalid end-user identification codes:

- Restrict the end user to an area that gives him or her no options other than signing off or else very limited read-only access in the system. This has the benefit of informing an end user that entered an invalid identification code that a mistake has been made.
- Perform additional logging to enable the security administrator to perform a complete review of what the unidentified user did while accessing the system.
- Immediately signal the security administrator and possibly someone in operations so he or she may investigate and take any necessary action.

Notwithstanding these items, this approach should be avoided if at all possible. The enterprise does not have the ability to rely on the authenticity of users accessing company systems, and that risk should not be accepted.

Invalid Identification Code Rejected

If the security administrator sets the security software to reject an invalid end-user identification code, the rejection will probably require other settings to be established. These settings may include, but are not limited to, one or more of the following:

- Limit on unsuccessful attempts
- Action to be taken

—Temporary device lockout
—Permanent device lockout
—Temporary end-user lockout
—Permanent end-user lockout
• Notification

There is no discussion of the situation when the system would either accept or reject an invalid password in a two-level sign-on environment. The reason is that if the end-user identification code is accepted when invalid, the password is invalid by default and there is no issue. In addition, consider the situation in which the end-user identification code is verified against the security file but the password is not validated. That is effectively a single-level sign-on environment, which has been previously discussed.

Limit on Unsuccessful Attempts. The security software may have the capability to track unsuccessful log-in attempts. This feature is designed to detect potential attempts to gain unauthorized access in which the unauthorized access is based on password guessing. If the number of attempted sign-ons reaches the threshold value in the security software, the system will respond.

The system response in a two-level sign-on environment can be based on either the end-user identification code or the device identification, unlike the single-level sign-on environment, which can only be associated with the device. In the two-level environment, anyone attempting to gain unauthorized access to the system would be using the same end-user identification code with different passwords.

System Responses Associated with the Device. The system typically has two options for a device: locking it out temporarily or locking it out permanently.

Locking the device out temporarily has the effect of delaying the person or program attempting to access the system without completely blocking an authorized user who is only having trouble logging onto the system properly. The temporary response is more appropriate in situations in which personnel may be working on a second or third shift, or on the weekend, when no one may be present in operations. The end user can continue trying to sign on to the system without having to go to another area or take some other potentially inefficient alternative.

The security administrator may choose to establish a permanent lockout of the device for those situations in which security considerations require a more definitive response, or in which someone is present to reset a device for the end user who accidentally disabled the device through unsuccessful access attempts.

System Responses Associated with the End User. The security software will usually have two alternatives for the end user: temporarily or permanently blocking access to the indicated end-user identification code:

- *Temporary end-user lockout.* Locking out the end user temporarily delays the person attempting to sign on to the system without requiring any third-party intervention to either give that person more chances or reset his or her password and let that person try again the next day. The extent of the delay and how that reason for the delay is expressed on the system is dependent on the security software in use.
- *Permanent end-user lockout.* The security software may be set to block completely the offending end-user profile if the threshold number of unsuccessful access attempts is exceeded. The decision to choose a permanent lockout instead of a temporary lockout should be based on general security issues within the organization. There may even be situations in which the security administrator will choose to establish different rules for a specific end user than for the rest of the organization.

If the security software permits setting exception rules for a particular purpose, the IT auditor has to ensure that the exceptions established are reasonable and proper. This includes determining if the systems professionals have established settings for themselves that are less stringent than those for the general population. If that is the case, the auditor has to note this fact, although there is the ongoing risk that the less stringent rules will be reestablished at any time after the audit is completed.

The IT auditor, in this circumstance, has to determine the extent of management's concern. If management chooses not to be concerned about this situation, there is little the auditor can do, because it is not practical for the IT auditor to monitor the situation continuously. If management chooses to be interested, the auditor may be able to show them the procedures involved to monitor the situation themselves on at least a random basis.

Notification. The security software should include at least one feature that provides for the notification of the system operator, security administrator, security guard, third-party security service, or other party responsible for monitoring activity at the covered location. The notification could be as simple as an indicator that there had been a violation without specification. It could also be complex, providing detailed information about the violation, the location, time, and user identification code.

Multiple Sign-on Requirements

The continuing technology penetration into business methods has led to an increasing percentage of end users having to keep track of two, three, or more user identification codes and associated passwords. Each system has its own rules, potentially different password expiration periods, and password syntax. In these situations, it is common for end users to record all of their identification codes and passwords.

Writing down identification codes and passwords should be a violation of company security policy, although the risk exposure comes not from recording the information but from deciding where to keep that information. If the enterprise could be assured that the information would be with the end user at all times, the risk is considerably different than if the information is kept in the end user's work area or desk, or taped to his or her monitor or terminal.

Single Sign-on

In response to this situation, there has been a new development in access technology referred to as single sign-on. Under single sign-on technology, the end user has only to remember one end-user identification code and password. Two types of single sign-on technology are available to most enterprises:

- *Native single sign-on.* The native approach describes a situation in which all of the involved systems have the capability to have the same password and other access control settings, parameters, and values. These systems also have incorporated the capability to communicate between systems so that if an end user changes his or her end-user identification code or related password, it is changed on all of the systems at the same time.
- *Pseudo single sign-on.* This artificial approach is based on an application that, after installation, takes its place in front of the true security processing in terms of what programs get processed before others by the central processing unit. The application can be programmed with the specifications of the security software of each system, and can respond interactively with each of those applications just as the end user would. This front-end software can handle most requests for end-user identification codes and passwords and can attempt to handle any other responses that are required.

One common problem for this type of application arises when the actual access security routine asks for a new password from the end user. In this situation, the front-end program will present a screen to the end user that is identical in appearance to the screen that would normally be presented by the true access security software. The end user completes the screen; then the front-end program both passes the new password through to the underlying security software so that the new password is set and also records the new password so that it may accurately perform the sign-on process the next time the end user needs to access the system involved in the processing previously described.

Section 10
Systems Development Process

Controls over applications development should ensure that applications are only developed or acquired in ways that support the appropriate strategic or tactical interests of the organization. The process of developing an application is often described as the Systems Development Life Cycle (SDLC). The subject is covered at length in P07, and is one half of the purpose for this publication. It is included here because gaining a basic understanding of SDLC methodology while reviewing the general controls environment should facilitate future application reviews.

This process is a cycle because there are common elements to every development effort. The elements may have different specifications and levels of formality, but the same objectives are generally satisfied by the end of the cycle.

The common elements can be described as:

- Recognize a need or opportunity.
- Identify and evaluate alternatives.
- Decide whether to implement. If yes:
  - Develop or acquire a solution.
  - Test and implement the solution.
  - Plan for maintenance and enhancement.
  - Perform post-implementation review.

GENERAL OBJECTIVES

The following objectives should apply to all application development activities, regardless of their size, as defined by the internal and external resources required to complete their development. The development effort size has an effect on what is required to meet these objectives because it is not reasonable to hold a project taking 40 hours to the same standard as one requiring 4000 hours. General objectives are:

- Development activities should always support either the strategic or tactical objectives of the enterprise.

- Development projects requiring approval for funding and resources through a capital expenditure request (or other similar) process should include mechanisms to ensure that all costs are captured and monitored in a manner that is consistent with company guidelines.
- Application security should complement the overall security approach taken within the enterprise.
- Application design and testing should ensure that the application will be available and responsive to the needs of the involved end users of the application.

SPECIFIC OBJECTIVES

Each one of the following systems development life cycle elements should meet specific objectives to increase the likelihood that the general objectives previously described are met by the time an application has been implemented. The following objectives generally can be tailored to fit the specifics of a particular situation:

Recognizing Needs or Opportunities. The enterprise should develop mechanisms to promote this recognition so that problems are solved and opportunities are capitalized on in an effective manner. Company employees should be trained so that they can effectively recognize these situations, because they can be advantageous to both the employee and to the enterprise.

Evaluating Alternatives and Details. The enterprise should have a policy that provides for assessing the proposed application that includes general business issues, specific business issues, and the expected effect on revenues and expenses. This policy should include a form or format for all of the appropriate information so that anyone reviewing the proposed application can see that all preliminary work has been completed before submitting the request. Any form or process used should reduce or eliminate the risk that applications will never be considered because of the effort or difficulty involved in performing this evaluation.

Making a Decision. There should be a place to record the authorization of the person or persons making the decision for accountability in the event of a question. The authorization should be on the form or attached to the forms defining the application and the work being requested to reduce the risk of misunderstanding or erroneous approval of the wrong specifications.

Develop or Acquire the Solution. Procedures should be in place to see that a solution is developed or acquired on a timely basis. All costs should be in accordance with the approved request, and any potential overruns exceeding a predetermined threshold should go back to the persons authorizing the original activity so that any approval or denial of additional expenditures is consistent with the original decision.

Detailed specifications should be developed so that whether the application is acquired or developed, the information is available to make the application most effective in terms of meeting the needs as specified.

Test and Implement the Solution. Testing procedures should be included that test both individual programs and functions of the application but also the application taken as a whole, including the interfaces to other systems. Application data should be converted or migrated in a way that ensures the integrity of that information and eliminates the risk of loss to the enterprise. Implementation procedures should include making the change overnight, on a weekend, or after a financial closing or other time when the problems resulting from an incomplete implementation are minimized.

The implementation procedures should include a method for stopping the process, backing out changes, and falling back to the prior application if necessary, and if possible, to reduce the risk that the enterprise will be without the functionality of the application in the event of a problem.

Final Documentation. The systems, operations, and end-user documentation that is being developed throughout the development project should be finalized once the application is considered to be fully implemented so that it will reflect all final changes and corrections as well as a complete understanding of the lessons learned through the final development and implementation activities.

Post-implementation Review of the Application. Conducting a review after an application is implemented seems to contradict many of the modern business initiatives related to total quality and continuous improvement. Performing such a review is critical if the enterprise personnel are to learn to perform future development activities more effectively. The risk in performing these reviews is that they can become punitive instead of informative.

The IT auditor should conduct a basic review of the systems development process by using the sequence of information in the subsequent paragraphs. A preliminary review to gather and evaluate the basic information should be prepared as part of the general controls review.

Basic information can be gathered by obtaining answers to this list of questions:

- Is there a methodology?
- Is it documented?
  —What are the phases?

—Are there deliverables?

—Are samples or examples provided?

—What compliance or enforcement method is in place?

—Does it include the recognition of need, authorization for expenditure or project justification, development of specifications, programming and testing, training and documentation, and implementation and conversions?

• Is anything in place for emergency maintenance?

• Are any change management procedures in place?

• Are post-implementation reviews conducted?

• How are priorities established and changes accommodated?

Methodology

The company should have a methodology to ensure that systems are implemented using techniques designed to provide effective systems without taking unacceptable risks that would hamper the enterprise's ability to do business. If there is no methodology, the IT auditor is likely to be told that the enterprise is relying on the IT employees to implement the systems properly.

Even without having any personal knowledge of the people on the IT staff, the IT auditor can be assured that the systems staff is likely to have differing beliefs about what the most effective development and implementation approach is for the enterprise. Beyond this, the individual pressures to perform are likely to lead the IT auditor to take shortcuts and to fail to comply with even their own set of proper procedures.

Documentation

"Is it documented?" is an important follow-up question when the IT auditor is told that a methodology is in place and followed. A documented methodology is available to all of the systems developers, and it should not be necessary to interpret oral instructions. If the plan is not documented, the IT auditor will not be able to rely on the methodology because compliance cannot be tested and measured.

An undocumented methodology does not mean that the audit is finished, but that almost no other circumstances exist in which the IT auditor can come to a *positive* conclusion about the systems development area. The auditor still needs to discuss the answers to the remaining questions so that a preliminary opinion can be formed. A preliminary opinion gives the auditor the opportunity to advise the IT staff on whether formalizing their informal methodology will be sufficient or whether they should consider changes or improvements before making the effort to formalize the existing procedures.

The Phases of Systems Development Methodology

The common elements of systems development methodology discussed earlier in this section are present in some form in every development methodology unless someone in the enterprise has specifically decided to eliminate it for business or cultural reasons. Variations between projects, such as not comparing alternatives in a situation in which a completely new idea is being pursued and believing that no competition exists, are more likely.

The phases also differ based on the type of systems methodology that the enterprise uses. The methodology may have eight or more phases if it has its roots 10 to 15 years in the past when it was considered more important to have every activity and decision fully documented, reviewed, and formally approved by two or more persons. On the other hand, the entire process may have only three phases in today's environment of total quality, continuous improvement, and employee empowerment.

Either of these alternatives can be well controlled and completely appropriate for an enterprise, as well as myriad other alternatives in between. The number of people in the information systems department and how many of them are assigned to systems development is also likely to be significant. Until the number is large enough to reach critical mass, any formal methodology is likely to be unreliable due to a lack of segregation of duties through the program implementation and change control process.

The number of people required to reach critical mass is not a fixed value. Therefore, the IT auditor must exercise judgment when forming an opinion on the development methodology, the adequacy of the development staff size, and what recommendations are appropriate for the circumstances.

The Deliverables

Deliverables are important because they have the potential to provide substantial value to the enterprise. Each systems development life cycle phase represents a milestone in that certain objectives should have been met, decisions made, and data gathered or analyzed. The smallest deliverable may be a one- or two-paragraph memo that documents a subjective decision made without any other support, but even that decision can be evaluated if needed.

The IT auditor evaluates the deliverables based on the circumstances, although certain assumptions can be made. The minimum deliverables should be defined in advance, and examples provided so that the person preparing the deliverable has complete information and the opportunity to develop an effective deliverable efficiently.

Providing Sample Deliverables. Example documents ensure that project by project deliverables are of the appropriate quality. In addition, the IT auditor can review the sample deliverables and establish a benchmark for auditing the deliverables in specific systems development projects. By reviewing the sample deliverables, the IT auditor has the opportunity to form opinions and develop recommendations that could affect the deliverables on any active and all potential future projects. This review may also foster improved relations with the internal customers because the review of a sample is objective, and the review of a deliverable in any specific project will more directly affect the involved information systems personnel.

System Compliance and Change Management Procedures

Systems development life cycle deliverables, being closely associated with project milestones, are more reliable when they are mandatory and not optional. For many enterprises, it has not been considered unreasonable to require a completed deliverable, including time for review and approval, before any work on the next phase can begin. Without such a requirement for production, there is a risk that other priorities will displace the deliverable, or at least delay it such that it has little value other than for providing information about the phase long after it is over and the next phase has begun.

Change Management Procedures. Most IT auditors should be familiar with the phrase "program change controls" because this phrase covers the identity of persons able to move programs into the production environment and specifies the procedures that must be followed. Program change controls developed with a limited focus on one type of change within the IT function. Over time, this focus expanded to encompass all of the changes that could affect information systems, with an emphasis on the ones that could affect or disrupt the production environment on the system. This expanded focus is referred to as "change management." Change management should cover any change within the IT function that has the potential, directly or indirectly, to have a negative effect on the operating environment.

The environmental effects the IT auditor is most concerned about are those that could cause system functioning to be unexpectedly disrupted; those that could cause existing approved programs to function in unexpected and potentially unauthorized ways; and those that result in unauthorized programs being introduced into the systems environment and then functioning in an unauthorized fashion.

Emergency Maintenance Procedures. In every situation, whether applications are completely custom coded or purchased and processed without any customization or changes, applications can fail without warning and require immediate attention to resume normal processing. This attention or maintenance is therefore usually performed with little notice, performed in isolation, and performed while violating any standards program change control procedures.

The IT auditor should determine whether procedures for identifying emergency maintenance situations and for performing at least some of the critical control procedures after the fact exist. These emergency maintenance procedures should limit the exposure of an enterprise to an unauthorized change because the person making the change should easily be identified if there is a subsequent problem with the emergency change made.

Post-Implementation Reviews. Post-implementation reviews can be an effective technique with total quality and continuous improvement benefits if conducted in a positive manner. Emphasizing the positives protects individual personalities and gives people a chance to obtain the information that they need to perform more effectively during the next systems development life cycle project. Performing more effectively on the next systems development life cycle includes:

- Producing higher quality deliverables
- Reducing development costs
- Creating a shorter total life cycle time

Section 11
Backup and Recovery

The IT auditor must understand the difference between backup and recovery issues. Backup issues are focused on what information should be saved, when it should be saved, and how it should be saved. Recovery issues are focused on how to use those backups in the event of a data loss or system interruption.

Controls over backup and recovery should ensure that all designated applications and data continue to be available to the organization even after an event in which the entire system, both hardware and software, has been lost. Backup and recovery are issues that are addressed in completely different ways, which is why many IT auditors deal with them as two independent topics or controls areas.

APPROACHES TO MAKING BACKUPS

There are only three primary alternatives for making backups:

- *Full backups.* These are made when every item in the system is copied to the backup media. Making a full backup may take minutes or hours and can take up to several hundred tapes.
- *Incremental backups.* These represent a backup of all files on a system that have changed since the last full or incremental backup was made. To use the incremental backups made each evening, it is necessary to have the most recent full backup and all incremental backups made subsequent to the full backup.
- *Differential backups.* These represent a backup of all files on a system that have changed since the last full backup. Therefore, to use these backup tapes for a complete restoration, the most recent full backup and only the most recent differential backup is needed.

MEDIA UTILIZED TO MAKE BACKUPS

Backups may be created using any of the following media combinations:

- *Disk to diskettes.* This would only be used on a system that did not have a tape drive. It is considered to be relatively inefficient because most diskettes have very little capacity in comparison with tapes.

- *Disk to tape.* This has been, and continues to be, the most common method of making backups. Tapes can hold a lot of information and are considered to be the most cost-efficient medium.
- *Disk to disk (optional second step of disk to tape or other media).* This is the quickest way to make backups, but requires the IT department to have a lot of available space for the backup files. The disk-to-disk approach permits the online and interactive systems to be reactivated quickly and to have the backups transferred to tape or diskette, making the disk space available once again.

RECOVERY ISSUES

Any time backup issues are discussed, recovery issues should either accompany or precede them. The *only* business reason to make a backup copy of something is to be able to restore that "something" after it is lost or damaged.

The IT auditor's historical emphasis has focused on how often backups are made, how the backup media are cared for, how many versions are retained, and other similar items. In many reviews, including some done by this author (a long time ago), little or no emphasis was placed on the use of backups. The IT auditor's emphasis was on their existence.

Business Contingency Planning, or disaster recovery planning, became more important to the company and to the IT auditor as Automated Application Systems became more integrated with daily business activities. This growing importance led to auditors identifying two critical questions:

1. Have we done a test recovery to ensure that our backups contain all the information and files needed to restart company systems?
2. How will we maintain our business activities (production, sales, etc.) and restore the transaction and master data activity that took place after the last backup was taken through the time the automated application systems or data center went down?

While the IT auditor should always keep compensating controls and mitigating circumstances in mind, the wrong answers to these questions should set alarms off for the auditor. And if the automated application systems and system have so little value that their loss has no meaningful impact, why are they even being evaluated?

Companies are increasingly interested in reducing the dependence on end users being able to move backward in time and recreate their work for two reasons: it does not work, and integrated highly complex systems require not only completeness but also proper sequencing of re-entered transactions.

One example of the importance of sequencing is the order fulfillment department of a retail store with a catalog or phone order processing function. As orders are entered into the system, stock availability is determined, that information is provided to the customer, the system allocates the appropriate stock, and shipping plans are made. Without addressing the issue of sequencing, the problems an organization can encounter include differing availabilities, differing allocations, differing customer promised and actual dates, and the potential impossibility of processing the transactions as originally processed with those same transactions as recovered following the problem.

A new approach to backups that attempts to reduce the time lag between backups includes fault-tolerant equipment such as dual write controllers and redundant array of independent disk (RAID) hard disk technology. These techniques and technologies are reducing the dependence of the organization on end users to be able to go backward in time to the last backup, or last usable backup, and restore the lost transactions from the backup used to the point in time when the system or application failed.

The following section is a basic but still comprehensive approach for business continuity planning. An audit program constructed on the same framework is included as Workpaper 11-1.

Business Continuity Planning

The strategic objective of business continuity planning, also known as disaster recovery planning, is to ensure that the enterprise has the ability to suffer disasters of various magnitudes with very low risk that the enterprise will fail as a result.

I. Business Impact Analysis
    A. A cross-function internal team should perform a study that:
        1. Identifies relevant risks, or events, that could strike the enterprise.
        2. Investigates all possible alternatives for reacting, or responding, to the identified events.
        3. Determines the duration of any business interruption until recovery activities could restore normal operations, whether that interruption affected company personnel, company systems, or both.
        4. Estimates the impact of having business partially or fully interrupted based on the outage duration information from the prior step. The impact or effect could take the form of:
            a. unplanned direct costs associated with the event
            b. increased normal operating costs
            c. lost or delayed revenues

      d. changes in intangibles such as market share, public perception, etc.

    5. Determines or estimates the unplanned costs, increased normal operating costs, lost revenues, and effect on intangibles associated for each recovery alternative.

  B. Study results should be documented and presented to management along with a recommendation for which of the alternative recovery strategies should be selected. This document is often called "The Business Impact Analysis Report."

  C. Management should select a strategy based on the Business Impact Analysis Report and any other information it believes is appropriate for the situation. The strategy selected may be anywhere in the range between simply waiting for a disaster to happen and establishing an identical fully staffed and equipped facility remote facility with duplicate personnel, systems, and infrastructure whose only purpose is to take over business without interruption when a disaster takes place.

II. Recovery Strategy

  A. The recovery strategy selected by management should be identified in a policy statement so that management's interests and intentions are clearly communicated to company personnel.

  B. The approved recovery strategy should be documented, and the document, or at least certain parts of it, should be distributed to all company personnel.

III. The Recovery Plan

  A. Damage assessment, plan activation, and salvage activities.

    1. Local managers should be directly involved in assessment activities so they have the information needed to make the decision on whether to activate the plan; and if activating the plan, to what extent it should be activated.

    2. The decision to activate the plan should be done first orally to any critical parties like hot-site providers, to the affected local personnel, and then communicated in writing to those parties identified in the plan.

    3. Any potential salvage procedures must be implemented as quickly as possible as most of them have a very limited window during which they are effective. Salvage procedures may cover documents, drawings, and other filed or reference information, office equipment, microcomputers, furniture, fixtures, etc.

  B. Hardware restoration. The plan should:

    1. Include a complete hardware inventory.

    2. Include vendor information, lead times, and other needed purchasing information.

3. Indicate in detail the process for acquiring, installing, configuring, and otherwise restoring hardware support for business activities.

C. Alternate office facilities. Plans designed to support a complete recovery of the business should consider the potential for needing to rearrange or relocate company personnel during a disaster situation. Company personnel, whether focused on the disaster or on continuing business activities, will need someplace to work, equipment and supplies to work with, and services such as the telephone and fax.

D. Data Recovery. This part of the plan should have two components: backward and forward data recovery. Backward recovery includes all transactions entered or received by the system and then lost due to the disaster. Forward recovery takes in all the transactions that were in the entry process or that occurred after the disaster happened and could not be entered.

1. Backward recovery issues include identifying lost transactions, having them sequenced if necessary, and then re-entering and processing them. Care should be taken to ensure that activities kicked off when a transaction is entered, or because of it, are not done twice.

2. Forward recovery issues include capturing those transactions that are in the entry process when the disaster happens, transactions occurring and being handled while systems are being restored, and reconciliation and review activities designed to ensure that system files are complete and accurate.

E. Personnel issues. Personnel health and safety are company priorities. During and after a disaster, there are additional risks that should be considered.

1. The plan should include a complete employee listing so that rolls can be checked, calls to employees with instructions can be made expeditiously, and, in the most extreme circumstances, families can be notified of injuries and other problems.

2. The Employee Assistance Program is likely to come into play and some consideration should be given to providing for counselors to be available on-site and at employee residences both during and after the disaster.

IV. Plan Testing and Maintenance

A. The plan should be tested on a regular schedule to ensure management's ability to rely on it.

B. The plan should be tested based on predetermined scenarios that include the situation, the test procedures, who will perform those procedures, and the expected results.

C. The actual test should be conducted based on the predetermined scenarios with all participants keeping a log of the things that happen, both as expected and not. One person should be responsible for the official log of the overall test.

D. The plan should be regularly updated to reflect the test results and any other change, event, or information that has an effect on the plan strategy or tactics. Once maintained, either the entire plan or just the updated portions should be distributed as they had been previously.

Workpaper 11-1. Standard Business Continuity Planning Audit Program

Audit:		Auditor/Date:	
Date:		Reviewed/Date:	

Program Step			Description	Done by	Date	W/P
1			Evaluate the Business Impact Analysis			
	A		Assess the extent to which the following issues have been addressed:			
		1	Identify relevant risks or events that could strike the enterprise.			
		2	Investigate all possible alternatives for reacting or responding to those events.			
		3	Determine the duration of any business interruption until recovery activities could restore normal operations, whether that interruption affected company personnel, company systems, or both.			
		4	Estimate the effect of having the business partially or fully interrupted based on the outage duration information from the prior step. The effect could take the form of: a. unplanned direct costs associated with the event b. increased normal operating costs c. lost or delayed revenues d. changes intangibles such as market share and public perception			
		5	Determine or estimate the unplanned costs, increased normal operating costs, lost revenues, and effect on intangibles associated for each recovery alternative.			
	B		Review final analysis and recommendations presented to management.			
2			Evaluate the Recovery Strategy			
	A		The recovery strategy selected by management should be identified in a policy statement so that management's interests and intentions are clearly communicated to company personnel.			
	B		The approved recovery strategy should be documented and distributed to appropriate company personnel.			

Workpaper 11-1. Standard Business Continuity Planning Audit Program (Continued)

Audit:		Auditor/Date:	
Date:		Reviewed/Date:	

Program Step				Description	Done by	Date	W/P
3				Evaluate the Recovery Plan			
	A			Damage assessment, plan activation, and salvage activities.			
		1		Determine local management's knowledge of plan and assessment activities required to decide whether to activate the plan, and, if activating the plan, to what extent it should be activated.			
		2		Determine the timing, communication process, and sequence of activation steps.			
		3		Review assessment of critical time deadlines needed to secure high-value transactions and data elements.			
	B			Hardware restoration. Review plan for:			
		1		Complete inventory of hardware that should be recovered.			
		2		Vendor, item, and other necessary purchasing information.			
		3		Details for acquiring, installing, configuring, and otherwise restoring hardware support for business activities.			
	C			Alternate office facilities. Review any plans designed to support a complete recovery of the business that require rearranging or relocating company personnel during a disaster situation. Evaluate the scope of plans for required support tools such as equipment and telecommunication.			
	D			Data recovery. Review plan for two components: backward and forward data recovery. Backward recovery includes all those transactions entered or received by the system and then lost due to the disaster. Forward recovery takes in all the transactions that were in the entry process or that occurred after the disaster happened and could not be entered.			

Workpaper 11-1. Standard Business Continuity Planning Audit Program (Continued)

Audit:		Auditor/Date:	
Date:		Reviewed/Date:	

Program Step			Description	Done by	Date	W/P
		1	Review backward recovery issues such as identifying lost transactions, having them sequenced if necessary, and then re-entering and processing them. Ensure that checks are in place to avoid duplication.			
		2	Review forward recovery issues such as capturing those transactions that are in the entry process when the disaster happens, transactions occurring and being handled while system files are complete and accurate.			
	E		Personnel issues. Review procedures to address employee safety and accessibility.			
		1	Review plan for a complete employee list so that rolls can be checked, calls to employees with instructions can be made expeditiously, and, that in the most extreme circumstances, families can be notified of injuries or other problems.			
		2	Review support contact lists that would include key vendors, customers, and other emergency contacts.			
4			Evaluate Plan Testing and Maintenance			
	A		Review frequency and thoroughness of testing plans.			
	B		Determine if the plan is tested based on predetermined scenarios that include the situation, the test procedures, which will perform those procedures, and the expected results.			
	C		Evaluate the documentation and reporting process surrounding testing.			
	D		Evaluate the frequency and causes of plan updates that should ensure that plan strategic and tactical information is current. Confirm that the plan is redistributed after any material change.			
			Audit Program for Backup, Recovery, and Contingency Planning.			

Section 12
Auditing the Mainframe

The first business computers were all mainframe computers. Mainframe computers were easily recognized because they filled large rooms if not entire buildings, and the personnel to support them could require twice the space of the system itself. At that time, the IT auditor had a very daunting task when attempting to assess the controls present in that environment.

The difficulty was driven by the technical understanding required to do the work, and the fact that controlling what happened in the computer was very closely tied to evaluating the personnel having access to the system. Physical access security was the primary audit concern because it was the foundation on which processing and other controls were built.

This is no longer true, because logical access security has replaced physical access security as a cornerstone to other controls in the mainframe computer. In the past, anyone wanting to process programs or access data required access to the data center and the tape library. Today's online interactive environments provide both program and data access from any workstation connected to the physical computer. The audit process, or at least one alternative approach, can be described in three steps: planning, fieldwork, and finalization.

This process is supported by a comprehensive set of fully articulated working papers:

- Data Processing Control Environment Questionnaire (Workpaper 12-1). This general controls self-assessment questionnaire is designed to be completed by the auditee and reviewed by the IT auditor.
- General Controls Audit Program (Workpaper 12-2). This audit program is closely aligned with the self-assessment questionnaire to increase the effectiveness of the standard program. Where practical, the audit program includes references to a standard workpaper set.
- General Controls Workpapers (Workpaper 12-3). This complete workpaper set is designed to optimize auditor productivity by laying out the workpapers normally required for an audit, supplying an appropriate workpaper header to eliminate the need to prepare all of them separately, and supplying basic text and formatting on the individual workpapers to facilitate their completion.

PLANNING THE AUDIT

The IT auditor should always begin with planning and should be careful to put the proper effort into planning every audit, even if he or she has performed the same basic review many times in the past. Every audit may be different, and failing to allocate to each audit assignment the appropriate amount of planning time can lead to unreliable audit results.

Contacting the Auditee

The IT auditor should make initial contact with the auditee by phone if possible, because it is less formal than sending a letter or even a note by electronic mail. Once the audit timing or scope is committed to paper, even as a draft, it can create subsequent problems for the systems auditor. The auditor should begin by communicating the areas to be reviewed, which can include all or a portion of the following:

- IT administration
- Physical security
- Logical security
- Operations
- Backup and recovery
- Systems development

The auditor should contact the head of the IT department initially, unless it has previously been agreed to that contact at a lower level is more appropriate. In the latter instance, it is appropriate to copy the head IT person once the scope and schedule of the audit have been determined. The mainframe environment is likely to require at least several work weeks of effort, to a maximum that is only limited by the auditor's decision to discontinue detailed testing.

The mainframe environment is also likely to contain subfunctions reporting to different managers, so that the IT auditor has to coordinate the review with each of the affected managers. The auditor may have to contact each manager individually to complete the audit planning process if the primary contact is unable to perform the necessary coordination tasks.

The IT auditor should send a letter to each manager or designated contact to confirm the planning details. This letter should be made available to the audit field personnel at least two weeks in advance of fieldwork so that any questions or comments can be communicated, researched, and resolved before starting fieldwork.

Preliminary Office Planning Before Fieldwork

The IT auditor should complete the following procedures while still in the office before initiating fieldwork procedures:

- Prepare an audit planning memo, including these elements:
  —Location background
  —Prior audit scope and results
  —Detailed list of prior recommendations
  —Current planned scope and timing
  —Planned staffing
  —Time budgets
- Define the specific audit program based on the standard program, the intended objectives based on the audit department's planning and selection of the audit, and the planning conversations held with location personnel.
- Send out the Information Technology Internal Control Questionnaire (Workpaper 12-1), specifying a date for its completion that will permit time for it to be returned and reviewed before fieldwork. (If there is a questionnaire from a previous audit, and if it is not materially different from the questionnaire currently in use, copy it and have the location personnel update the previous form.)
- Obtain prior audit reports related to this location and place a copy in the workpapers.
- Review past audit files for permanent and carry-forward information, and incorporate any previous findings into the current workpapers.
- Set up any necessary files on the personal computer or laptop that will facilitate the performance of fieldwork.

PERFORMING FIELDWORK PROCEDURES

Fieldwork may be done in one continuous sequence or be completed over multiple visits. The IT auditor must take the time to ensure that there is a workable schedule and that all involved parties are aware of it. The general items that should be completed in the field that do not relate to any of the specific areas are:

- Conduct an entrance conference and document the results of that meeting. It may be necessary to have multiple meetings in a mainframe review, based on audit areas, physical locations, and other considerations.
- Prepare a list of all issues from the prior audit and determine the current status of those items by contacting the appropriate personnel, performing detailed procedures if necessary. Document the current status of those items in the workpapers. The auditor's effort to complete this step is not related to the environment as much as it is to the nature and extent of prior audit recommendations.
- Take a plant tour, noting any unusual items or observations. This gives the IT auditor an opportunity to become acquainted with the business and to gain some indirect information about how that particular business

or location is operating, which may be useful when the auditor is evaluating potential recommendations and their cost/benefit considerations. The tour, observations, and other items that the auditor deems important should be documented in the workpapers.

AUDITING SPECIFIC PROCEDURES BY AUDIT AREA

The IT auditor should be ready to begin specific detailed audit procedures once the planning and the general office procedures have been covered. The audit tasks are discussed in the subsequent sections followed by the estimated time to complete and additional comments if necessary.

IT Administration

The IT administration has eight tasks and should take a minimum of $7^1/2$ hours to a maximum of $14^1/2$ hours to complete, exclusive of testing.

Task 1: Review Security and Control Questionnaire. The IT auditor should make a copy of the IT administration portion of the security and control questionnaire so that the original completed questionnaire can be kept whole in the carryforward workpapers. The auditor should evaluate the questionnaire responses and document any items that require additional investigation or follow-up. The estimated time is three hours to complete this procedure. The audit of the mainframe environment should include most of the controls covered in the questionnaire.

Task 2: Review the Organization Chart. The IT auditor should obtain a copy of the top-level organization chart and review the placement of IT in the organization in terms of its overall effectiveness. The estimated time to complete this task is 30 minutes.

Task 3: Evaluate the Long-Range IT Plan. The IT auditor should obtain the long-range IT plan and evaluate it in terms of supporting business objectives, its consistency with the business plan, the likelihood of meeting management's objectives, and its being properly developed in terms of scope, detail, quantitative analysis, and responsibility. Partially depending on the extent of the plan, the time estimate to complete this review is two to three hours. The mainframe environment is the most critical for having a plan, because the investment in personnel, hardware, software, and other resources is likely to be the most significant of the three environments covered in this supplement.

Task 4: Audit Expense and Budget Statements. The IT auditor should obtain and review appropriate expense and budget statements, paying particular attention to significant fluctuations between periods or any unusual items.

The time estimated to complete this area is between two and six hours, based on the detail and extent of the budget and actual information.

Task 5: Examine Job Descriptions. The IT auditor should obtain and evaluate the IT department's job descriptions based on the business structure and observed regular responsibilities. The time estimate for this is one hour, although more time may be needed if the IT auditor determines that the job descriptions are too general or are inconsistent with the responsibilities that IT personnel have been assigned.

Task 6: Review and Evaluate the IT Standards Manual. The IT auditor should obtain and evaluate the IT standards manual in terms of scope, timeliness, and general qualitative usefulness. The standards manual is important in a large mainframe shop because it provides a foundation for consistent activities by different persons if there is substantial compliance with the procedures in the manual. The estimated time to complete this step depends on the level of testing the IT auditor decides to perform, and could vary between 2 and 80 hours. If no manual is in place, the ITA should spend at least one hour to one day to assess the need for a standards manual and to prepare the related recommendation with a sample document or, at least, a sample table of contents.

Task 7: Perform a Complete Inventory of All IT-Related Hardware. The IT auditor should obtain a complete inventory of all IT-related hardware used at the audited location and this inventory should be included in the permanent workpapers. This inventory should be tested based on a judgmental sample in both directions: from the inventory to the actual hardware, and from selected hardware to the inventory. This procedure should take no more than one hour including the preparation of the workpapers. One potential difficulty in auditing the mainframe environment is that a large number of components may be part of the central processing unit. Operations assistance may be required to determine the location of a particular hardware item.

Task 8: Prepare a Summarization Memo. The IT auditor should prepare a memo summarizing the work performed in the IT Administration area, all potential findings, and any other information deemed important. This task should take between one and three hours, depending on the extent and nature of the included items.

Physical Security

The review of physical security has five tasks and should take a minimum of six hours to complete.

Task 1: Review Security and Control Questionnaire. The IT auditor should make a copy of the physical security portion of the security and control questionnaire so that the original completed questionnaire can be kept whole in the carry-forward workpapers. The IT auditor should evaluate the questionnaire responses and document any items that required additional investigation or follow-up. The estimated time is two to four hours to complete this procedure. The mainframe environment should include most of the controls covered in the questionnaire.

Task 2: Test to Ensure that All Security Features Are Operational. The IT auditor should test the procedures identified in task 1 to ensure that all of the appropriate security features are in place and functioning. This procedure should take between two and eight hours to complete, depending on the extent of the testing required.

Task 3: Review Physical Security Layout of Data Center. The IT auditor should obtain a layout diagram of the data center, review it for completeness and accuracy, and ensure that it identifies all key security features. This task should take approximately one hour.

Task 4: Determine Any Additional Audit Procedures. The IT auditor should consider the need for additional procedures based on his or her judgment, observations made during fieldwork, and results of the other audit procedures performed. The time required for this task cannot be estimated until the auditor reviews his or her findings over the course of the fieldwork.

Task 5: Prepare a Summarization Memo. The IT auditor should prepare a memo summarizing the work performed in the physical security area, including any potential findings and any other information deemed important. This task should take between one and three hours, depending on the extent and nature of the included items.

Logical Security

The review of logical security has eight tasks and should take a minimum of 12 hours to complete.

Task 1: Review Security and Control Questionnaire. The IT auditor should make a copy of the IT administration portion of the security and control questionnaire so that the original completed questionnaire can be kept whole in the carry-forward workpapers. The IT auditor should evaluate the questionnaire responses and document any items that require additional investigation or follow-up. The estimated time is three hours to complete this task. The mainframe environment should include most of the controls covered in the questionnaire.

Task 2: Audit the List of Logical Security Values Obtained from the System and Security Software. The IT auditor should, if possible, obtain the list of the logical security values from the system and security software and trace the values from the questionnaire to the list. Any differences should be noted and followed up to determine what the correct value should be and why the difference between the document and the list exists. This task should take no longer than two hours.

Task 3: Identify All Standard Security Profiles Supplied with the System and Security Package. The IT auditor should determine if there are any standard security profiles supplied with the system and security package. There is a risk that, if these are not reset, anyone familiar with the system will be able to use one of these standard profiles to access the system and potentially perform unauthorized activities. The auditor should attempt to log onto the system by using the standard profiles to ensure that the profiles were reset. This task should take no longer than one hour to complete.

Task 4: Test Password Controls. The IT auditor should also test other password controls to the extent possible to evaluate their functioning. The results of these tests should be documented in the workpapers. This testing can normally be completed while sitting at a terminal and should take no longer than one or two hours.

Task 5: Identify and Document Access Privileges. The IT auditor should ascertain the details of how persons within the enterprise are granted access to the system. That process should be documented if that information is not already documented. The process of granting access should then be tested by selecting a judgmental sample of users from the system and a similar sample of users from the files, and by confirming that the documents authorizing their access are present and properly completed. The estimated time for this task is two to four hours.

Task 6: Test User Profiles. The IT auditor should select a cross-sample of user profiles on the system and review them for consistency in the way that they are set up and authorized to use the system; any special capabilities given; and exceptions to established password management rules. The results of this review should be documented in the workpapers. The estimated time for this task is approximately two hours for each ten users selected for testing.

Task 7: Determine Any Additional Audit Procedures. The IT auditor should consider the need for additional procedures based on his or her judgment, observations made during fieldwork, and results of the other audit procedures performed. The time required for this task cannot be estimated until the auditor reviews his or her findings over the course of the fieldwork.

Task 8: Prepare a Summarization Memo. The IT auditor should prepare a memo summarizing the work performed in the logical security area, including any potential findings and any other information deemed important. This task should take between one and three hours, depending on the extent and nature of the included items.

Change Management

The review of change management has five tasks and should take a minimum of 17 hours to complete.

Task 1: Review Security and Control Questionnaire. The IT auditor should make a copy of the change management and systems development portion of the security and control questionnaire so that the original completed questionnaire can be kept whole in the carry-forward workpapers. The auditor should evaluate the questionnaire responses and document any items that require additional investigation or follow-up. The estimated time is two to four hours to complete this task. The mainframe environment should include most of the controls covered in the questionnaire.

Task 2: Test to Ensure that All Change Control Features are Operational.
The IT auditor should test the procedures identified in task 1 to ensure that all of the appropriate control features are in place and functioning. This procedure should take between two and eight hours to complete, depending on the extent of the testing required.

Task 3: Test the Change Control Management Process. The IT auditor must determine the extent of testing that is desirable for the current audit, which is most likely based on the need to reach a conclusion on the reliability of the change management process. Once the extent of testing is determined, the auditor should perform the tests that address reviewing the changed code, evaluating the authorization process, and verifying the testing and documentation that was done. The time to complete this process is contingent on the plan for testing and can vary between 12 and 80 hours.

Task 4: Review and Evaluate the Questionnaire Responses. The auditor should, before preparing the conclusion memo for this area, review the control questionnaire responses to determine if any of them has not been reviewed or tested in any way. Any items identified during this task should either be further evaluated or noted in the workpapers to indicate why no evaluation was needed. The time to complete this task cannot be estimated in advance for auditing the mainframe environment.

Task 5: Prepare a Summarization Memo. The IT auditor should prepare a memo summarizing the work performed in the control change management area, including any potential findings and any other information deemed important. This task should take between one and three hours, depending on the extent and nature of the included items.

Backup, Recovery, and Contingency Planning

The review of backup, recovery, and contingency planning has five tasks and should take between 13 and 47 hours to complete.

Task 1: Review Security and Control Questionnaire. The IT auditor should make a copy of this portion of the security and control questionnaire so that the original completed questionnaire can be kept whole in the carry-forward workpapers. The auditor should evaluate the questionnaire responses and document any items that required additional investigation or follow-up. The estimated time is three hours to complete this task. The mainframe environment should include most of the controls covered in the questionnaire.

Task 2: Identity, Test, and Document Backup Procedures. The IT auditor should identify the strategy for making periodic backups as it relates to the business conducted by the locations served by the installation. The results should be documented. In the mainframe environment, this task should take between two and four hours, and the testing of the information obtained should require no more than an additional eight hours.

Task 3: Obtain and Evaluate the Corporate Business Continuity Plan. The IT auditor should obtain and evaluate the business continuity plan for the data center under review and for the business location by using the audit program included as Workpaper 11-1. If a plan is in place, even if the plan only covers the recovery of the data center, the estimated time to complete this task is between 8 and 40 hours. A comprehensive business plan could add 40 hours to the review. As with other control areas, the final time required for this task is dependent on the level of testing desired and the results of those testing procedures.

Task 4: Review Questionnaire Responses. The IT auditor should, before preparing the conclusion memo for this area, review the questionnaire responses to determine if any of them have not been reviewed or tested in any way. Any items identified during this task should either be evaluated or noted in the workpapers to indicate why no further evaluation was needed. The time to complete this task cannot be estimated in advance for the mainframe environment.

Task 5: Prepare a Summarization Memo. The IT auditor should prepare a memo summarizing the work performed in the backup, recovery, and contingency planning area, including potential findings and any other information deemed important. This task should take between one and three hours, depending on the extent and nature of the included items.

AUDIT FINALIZATION

The IT auditor should review the workpapers for clarity and completeness. This task should not take more than two hours. The IT auditor should have the workpapers reviewed by a manager and clear all manager's review notes. The time will vary between 4 and 40 hours, based on the review notes received.

The IT auditor should perform the following tasks to issue the final report:

1. Prepare a draft report.
2. Have the draft reviewed, clearing all questions and comments.
3. Mail the draft to the auditee for review and response development.
4. If the responses are not received as scheduled, contact the auditee by telephone to determine when the responses can be expected.
5. Evaluate the responses for adequacy; add them to the draft report; and review them with Internal Audit management as needed.
6. Based on the preceding tasks, prepare a final report.

The auditor should complete the audit program and any other remaining pieces of the audit and submit the final workpapers for filing and appropriate retention.

Workpaper 12-1. Generic Questionnaire

GENERIC DOMESTIC COMPANY

IT INTERNAL AUDIT

IT CONTROL ENVIRONMENT QUESTIONNAIRE

COMPANY   _____

DIVISION   _____

CITY/STATE   _____

PREPARED BY   DATE   APPROVED   DATE

_____   _____   _____   _____

_____   _____   _____   _____

_____   _____   _____   _____

INFORMATION NOT FOR REPRODUCTION OR DISTRIBUTION

DEVELOPED FOR INTERNAL IT AUDIT USE ONLY

IT DEPARTMENT INFORMATION REQUEST FORM
GENERIC DOMESTIC INTERNAL IT AUDIT

This questionnaire is based on the Parent Company IT Security Manual, and the numbered items are drawn from the manual. These items are not in sequence because they have been reorganized into subject areas.

The class code for each question has been retained. The class code definitions are listed below. You <u>must</u> address all items for your installation class. The items for each class are the <u>minimum</u> requirements, but we encourage you to review them all, as items from other classes might benefit or relate to your installation.

CLASS CODE/INSTALLATION SIZE

A. PCs with large files or sensitive material or used for administrative routines like order processing.
B. 1–5 work stations or RT PCs used for CAD.
C. 6–25 workstations.
D. 26–150 workstations.
E. More than 150 workstations. For class E, all measures marked D shall be carried out and also any others that are appropriate to the size and type of installation.

Please review each of the questions and mark the appropriate space, whether the answer is "yes," "no," or "N/A." The Security Manual includes both specific requirements and general suggestions. Your response to the specific requirements should show if you are in compliance or not. Your response to general suggestions could indicate either your compliance or your consideration of the item, even if no specific action was taken. There is a space for comments after each question.

We added supplemental questions to include topics not in the Security Manual, and to gather other information needed for a complete audit. These questions are lettered instead of numbered, to make them readily identifiable.

GENERAL INFORMATION ITEMS

1. Please attach documents covering the following: Please check the items that are attached.
   computer and peripheral hardware listing _____
   purchased and written software listing _____
   data processing organization chart _____
   data center and department floor plan _____
   departmental position descriptions _____
   network diagram _____

PHYSICAL SECURITY

1. - - - D

Unauthorized entry to the data center shall be prevented by locks, automatic admission checking system, or guards. If the data center is on the ground floor, the windows shall be of an unbreakable type, preferably also opaque and not possible to open.

YES _____   NO _____   N/A _____

_____

_____

1a   Is the data center locked at all times? _____
1b   What type of lock is used? _____
     For combination and card type locks, how often is it changed to a new number or card? _____

2. - B C D

Fire extinguishers of carbon dioxide or Halon gas shall be located in the data center and in the adjacent one. Where applicable, the fire control organization should be consulted and it should make inspections.

YES _____   NO _____   N/A _____

_____

_____

3. - - - D

Automatic fire extinguishing installations, smoke detectors, and fire alarms are strongly recommended. However, in most countries, Halon will be forbidden within the first half of the 1990s. The technological developments must be observed. **Before deciding for a new automatic Halon installation, corporate approval must be obtained.**

YES _____   NO _____   N/A _____

_____

_____

4. - B C D

Sprinklers might be a suitable alternative if they are combined with an automatic power shut-off to the computer before the sprinklers are released.

YES _____   NO _____   N/A _____

_____

_____

A   What controls exist for the risk of fires in the data center or surrounding areas? Check all that apply.

Halon system _____   Smoke alarms _____
Sprinkler _____   Extinguisher _____
Other _____   Halon extinguisher _____

Will the activation of any of the above trigger a central alarm for times when the room is not manned? _____

5. - - C D

When constructing a data center, sewer and water pipes should be removed or the material changed to an anticorrosive material. If there is any risk of leakage, flooding, or water rising from the drainage system, there shall be (automatic) shut-off valves and gutters.

YES _____   NO _____   N/A _____

6. - - - D

A water or moisture alarm should be installed.

YES _____   NO _____   N/A _____

*   6a   Is water damage a risk in the data center? _____
*   6b   Is there a raised floor? _____ If so, how high? _____ Are underfloor sprinklers needed? _____ in place? _____

7. - B C D

Where needed, air conditioning equipment shall be installed. If suitable, the capacity should be divided into at least two units.

YES _____   NO _____   N/A _____

8. - - - D

Equipment for alarm and power shut-off at unsuitable temperature or humidity should be installed.

YES _____   NO _____   N/A _____

9. A B C D

UPS, Uninterruptible Power Supply, should be installed where power disruptions are frequent and recovery takes a long time or where disruptions incur significant costs.

YES _____   NO _____   N/A _____

_____

_____

*   9a   Do you have a UPS? _____ If yes, then .....
        how many minutes of backup does it provide? _____
        is it linked to the CPU? _____
        what items are protected? _____

10. A B C D

Stabilizers should be used where voltage or frequency is not stable.

YES _____   NO _____   N/A _____

_____

_____

11. A B C D

When sending data media containing payment transactions, special security measures shall be taken to prevent the media from being altered. Such measures could be a fixed timetable for the conveyance, transport in a locked box, and an electronic seal on a tape.

YES _____   NO _____   N/A _____

_____

_____

B   What position is the CPU console keyswitch normally kept in? _____ Where is the key kept? _____ Who has access to the key? _____

Continued with OPERATIONS on the following page.

OPERATIONS

12. A B C D

Backup copies shall be taken so frequently that the time for a recovery procedure is relatively short. The recovery should not take more than four hours or create business disturbances or incur significant costs. For frequently used files, backup shall be at least daily. A full backup including low frequency files and system and application software shall be taken at least monthly.

YES _____   NO _____   N/A _____

_____

_____

13. A B C D

The backup copies shall be stored in such a way that they cannot be destroyed or stolen at the same time as the computer. This means that they should either be stored in another building or in a fireproof cupboard in another room than the computer. The backup copies shall be kept under lock and key.

YES _____   NO _____   N/A _____

_____

_____

14. A - - -

At least two generations of backup shall be kept.

YES _____   NO _____   N/A _____

_____

_____

15. - B C D

At least three generations of backup shall be kept.

YES _____   NO _____   N/A _____

_____

_____

*   15a Please indicate the appropriate information about making and storing backup files:

File type	# of cycles	when taken (daily, etc.)	which are off-site?
Application data	_____	_____	_____
Application program	_____	_____	_____
Operating system	_____	_____	_____
Utilities	_____	_____	_____
Other	_____	_____	_____

Where is your off-site storage? _____

16. A B C D

Surplus output material should be destroyed, sensitive information shall be shredded or destroyed in some other manner that ensures security.

YES _____   NO _____   N/A _____

_____

_____

*   16a Do you have a shredder or other means to destroy confidential reports? _____ If so, is there a policy or other documentation explaining what is sensitive information and how it is to be handled for the employees? _____ If there is something, please attach a copy of it.

17. A B C D

Forms used for training and testing should be specially identified, in particular regarding payment routines.

YES _____   NO _____   N/A _____

_____

_____

18. - B C D

Output that includes sensitive information should be stored in locked cupboards before distribution.

YES _____   NO _____   N/A _____

_____

_____

C.   Is anything done to monitor system utilization? _____ If so, describe what is done, how the data is used, and attach an example of one of the reports.

_____

_____

39. A B C D

For each application where data communication is being used, fall-back alternatives to the communication and its routines shall be developed and tested.

YES _____   NO _____   N/A _____

_____

_____

43. - - C D

A log book of disturbances shall be kept. It should contain time when the disturbance was discovered, kind of disturbance and where it occurred, time for notification of error, and time when the system was working again.

YES _____   NO _____   N/A _____

_____

_____

44. - - C -

A contingency plan should be worked out and kept updated.

YES _____   NO _____   N/A _____

_____

_____

45. - - - D

A contingency plan must be worked out and kept updated.

YES _____   NO _____   N/A _____

_____

_____

46. - - C D

The computer installations should have insurance against fire. Water and extra cost insurance is often recommended. For leased equipment, check whether the leasing company or the Group company is responsible for taking out the insurance policy.

YES _____   NO _____   N/A _____

_____

_____

47. A B C D

A complete system and operation documentation shall be kept up-to-date. One copy of it shall be kept in a fireproof place.

YES _____   NO _____   N/A _____

_____

_____

Continued with LOGICAL SECURITY on the following page.

LOGICAL SECURITY

19. A B C D

Users shall be reminded yearly, through training or campaigns, about their responsibility for EDP security.

YES _____ NO _____ N/A _____

_____

_____

D   Indicate the names of the individuals who have the authority to add, change, or delete user profiles and access rules.

_____

_____

E   Is there a standard form used for adding and maintaining user profile information? _____
If so, attach a copy. Also, is the form retained in a central place? _____
Please describe. _____

20. A B C D

Passwords shall be individual and secret, and difficult to find out.

YES _____ NO _____ N/A _____

_____

_____

20a Please describe the syntax of user passwords:
minimum/maximum length _____/_____
required alpha or numeric characters? _____

21. A - - -

Using password or unlocking a physical lock shall give access to a PC system.

YES _____ NO _____ N/A _____

_____

_____

22. - B - -

A combination of at least user identity and password shall be required to authorize the use of the system.

YES _____ NO _____ N/A _____

_____

_____

23. - - C D

User identity and password shall be used for authorization to specified objects (resources). This also implies access to SPOOL files.

YES _____   NO _____   N/A _____

_____

_____

24. - - C D

In certain cases, such as the work of the security officer, a combination of user identity and password shall give authorization for transactions to be handled on a specified terminal.

YES _____   NO _____   N/A _____

_____

_____

25. A B C D

Standard passwords installed by the supplier shall be altered before using the system.

YES _____   NO _____   N/A _____

_____

_____

26. - B C D

The passwords shall be changed every second or third month. Reuse of old passwords shall not be allowed.

YES _____   NO _____   N/A _____

_____

_____

27. A B C D

User identity including passwords shall be deleted promptly when employees leave the company.

YES _____   NO _____   N/A _____

_____

_____

*   27a Are written procedures in place to ensure that data processing is notified of transfers and terminations on a timely basis so that any necessary changes can be made to security? _____ If so, attach a copy of the procedures.

28. - B C D

For emergency and backup purposes, the security officer's password shall be kept in a secure area. Access to the password should be allowed only in an emergency situation.

YES _____ NO _____ N/A _____

_____

_____

29. - B C D

After three attempts with illegitimate combinations of user identity and password, further attempts shall automatically be prevented.

YES _____ NO _____ N/A _____

_____

_____

30. A B C D

When leaving the terminal for more than a short while, the user shall log off the terminal or set it in a standby position, where a new log-on is required.

YES _____ NO _____ N/A _____

_____

_____

31. - - C D

As a support to the users the following functions should be installed where possible. After a certain time (20–30 minutes) with no work at the terminal, it should automatically be set in a standby position or be shut off. Further use of the terminal should require a new sign-on procedure.

YES _____ NO _____ N/A _____

_____

_____

F   Are inactive user profiles (users that have not logged in for at least 90 or 120 days) automatically revoked? _____ After how long? _____

G   Is the system log or other report reviewed for security violations or other potential problems with the system? _____ If so, describe the review procedures, including the frequency of review, who does the review, and if the review is documented.

_____

_____

H   Are programmers restricted from accessing company data on an update or control basis? _____

34. - B C D

For file transfer data communication, available password functions shall be used.

YES _____   NO _____   N/A _____

_____

_____

35. A B C D

For interactive data communication, the security measures items 20–32 shall be included.

YES _____   NO _____   N/A _____

_____

_____

36. A B C D

The use of encryption should be decided jointly by the personnel responsible for security at the sending and the receiving companies. Their feasibility study shall include sensitivity of data, risks, and costs. **Before deciding for encryption, corporate approval must be obtained.**

YES _____   NO _____   N/A _____

_____

_____

37. A B C D

For synchronous communication, the identities shall be unique.

YES _____   NO _____   N/A _____

_____

_____

38. A B C D

Dial-up asynchronous communication, X21 and X25, must be specially secured against unauthorized access. The following methods may be used.

1   Call back, so that the final connection is always established from the mini computer or the mainframe (not from a PC).
2   Dynamic passwords, changed each time the communication is used (this requires some special hardware).

3   Encryption. **Before deciding for encryption, corporate approval must be obtained.**

Direct access to data via a simple password as the only security measure is not suitable.

YES ____   NO ____   N/A ____

IT ADMINISTRATION

40. - B C D

Investigations have shown that the risk of loss is as great in the area of swindle and sabotage as it is for fire and water damage. In light of these facts, the background of those who will be employed in sensitive positions should be carefully checked.

YES _____   NO _____   N/A _____

_____

_____

41. A B C D

The employment agreement for IT personnel should include a paragraph stating "Programs made in working hours or otherwise made for the employer are the property of the employer and cannot be sold or given away without written permission from the employer."

YES _____   NO _____   N/A _____

_____

_____

I   Are you expecting any significant changes to hardware or software that have not been covered by other questions? _____
Please describe below:

_____

_____

J   Do you have a written standards manual, or other document describing the normal practices for departmental employees to follow? _____
If so, please attach a copy (if small) or else just the table of contents.

K   Are continuing education seminars a required part of a continuing employment requirement for data processing personnel? _____ If so, what is the annual minimum? _____ And, is this information recorded anywhere?

_____

_____

L   Is departmental chargeback (or other allocation of data processing costs) done? _____ If so, what is the basis for the charges? And, is there a separate calculation for usage and development?

_____

_____

N   Do you have a written short- or long-range plan for data processing activities? _____ If so, please attach a copy.

ASSESSING GENERAL IT CONTROLS

O   Is there a management steering committee that oversees data processing projects and priorities? _____ If so, how often does the committee meet? _____

AUTOMATED APPLICATION SYSTEMS

48. - B C D

Before taking a new system or a new version into production, a thorough test shall be carried out. This also applies to program alterations. Both the EDP function and users should participate in system testing.

YES _____   NO _____   N/A _____

_____

_____

49. - - C D

A test system or a test company should be installed, so that tests and education will not affect the production environment.

YES _____   NO _____   N/A _____

_____

_____

50. A B C D

Methods shall be applied to ensure that all input allowed and nothing else is entered into the system. Such methods are automatic checking of batch sums or serial numbers and a split input by two clerks, and a comparison between the two input files.

YES _____   NO _____   N/A _____

_____

_____

51. A B C D

Quality checks of data entry shall be used, such as check digits, format, and reasonableness checks, combination controls, matching checks, and hash and batch totals.

YES _____   NO _____   N/A _____

_____

_____

P   Is there a standard form used to request additions and/or changes to existing and proposed systems? _____ If so, please attach a copy of the blank form, and a copy of one that has been filled out and the project completed. Are there written procedures for using it? _____ Again, please attach a copy.

Q   If there are no written procedures for requesting projects, please
     describe the process below:

     _____

     _____

     _____

R   Are there separate libraries for:
         program development?   _____
         program testing?   _____
         production programs?   _____

S   Is there a standard procedure within data processing for approving a
     new or changed program? _____ If yes, please attach a copy of the
     standard procedure.

T   Is there a review of the source code to evaluate the actual changes
     made by the programmer? _____ If so, describe how it is done and any
     documentation retained.

     _____

     _____

U   Is systems documentation required to be prepared or updated? _____
     If so, please describe the documentation required and attach an exam-
     ple of it.

     _____

     _____

V   Is user documentation required as part of this process? _____ If so,
     indicate who has responsibility for preparing and maintaining it. Also
     attach an example of several pages from such documentation.

     _____

     _____

W   Describe the normal procedures for testing new and/or enhanced sys-
     tems prior to their going into production.

     _____

     _____

     _____

X   Are programmers restricted from adding new or changed programs
     directly into production libraries? _____ If so, describe how that is
     accomplished.

     _____

     _____

     _____

Y   Are source programs recompiled after being transferred into the production library? _____

Z   Is a log or standard form kept for all additions and changes to the production environment? _____ If so, attach an example of a completed log sheet or form.

AA   Are testing or acceptance procedures for purchased programs different from those for in-house programs? _____ If so, please describe the difference.

_____

_____

AB   How are updates to purchased application software made?

_____

_____

AC   Is user training a part of the systems development and maintenance process? _____ If so, describe the training procedures in the area below.

_____

_____

AD   Indicate what documentation is usually present for company applications.

system narrative	_____	printer layouts	_____
system flowchart	_____	operator instructions	_____
program listing	_____	program narratives	_____
program history	_____	data descriptions	_____
other (specify)		_____	

AE   Are there any programs for which the source code is not available? _____ If so, indicate which ones, and how any necessary maintenance is done.

_____

_____

AF   Is there a practice of conducting post-implementation reviews for significant projects? _____ If so, please describe the process, what deliverables it has, and what happens to the information. Also, provide one example of the report from such a review.

_____

_____

_____

Thank you for your time and cooperation in completing this information request form. If you have any questions or comments regarding this survey, please contact [INSERT APPROPRIATE AUDITOR NAME, INSERT DEPARTMENT, at (xxx)-xxx-xxxx.]

Workpaper 12-2. Generic Program

Please note that wherever possible the standard workpaper reference for the workpaper addressing a particular audit program step has been indicated in parentheses and boldface type. If a procedure has not been performed, the reason for that will either be indicated on the audit program itself or else on the indicated workpaper.

I. Planning the audit

A. Contact the location personnel responsible for coordinating the audit to confirm the basic scope of the expected procedures and the timing of the various audit phases.

B. Send a letter to the primary contact at the location confirming the information discussed in the prior step. **(AA-11.2)**

C. Prepare an audit planning memo based on the expected scope of the audit, a review of the previous report and workpapers, and any other items as needed. **(AA-1)**

D. Define the specific audit program for the engagement. This may be done directly from the standard program for this area (noting any steps not being done due to scope or time limitations) or developed specifically for the engagement. **(AA-2)**

E. Send out the IT Internal Control Questionnaire, specifying a date for its completion that will permit time to have it returned and to review it before leaving for the field. (If there is a questionnaire from a previous audit, and it is not materially different from the questionnaire currently in use, copy it and have the location personnel update the prior form.)

F. Obtain prior audit reports related to this location, and place a copy in the workpapers. **(AA-6.2)**

G. Review past audit files for permanent and carryforward information, and incorporate any found into the current workpapers. **(AA-3)**

H. Set up any necessary files that will facilitate performance of fieldwork.

II. Performing field procedures

A. Conduct an entrance conference, and document the results of the meting. **(AA-4)**

B. Prepare a listing of all issues from the prior audit, and indicate the current status of each of those items. **(AA-6.1)**

C. Take a plant tour, noting any unusual items or observations. **(AA-7)**

D. Document all audit finding and potential exceptions in the audit point section of the workpapers. **(APSUM)**

III. Specific procedures by audit area

A. IT Administration

1. Evaluate the questionnaire responses in this area and document any items that required additional investigation/follow-up. **(A-1)**
2. Review the placement of data processing in the organization in terms of its overall effectiveness. **(A-2)**
3. Evaluate the long-range plan in terms of supporting business objectives, consistency with the business plan, meeting management's objectives, and being properly developed in terms of scope, detail, quantitative analysis, and responsibility. **(A-3)**
4. Obtain and review appropriate expense and budget statements, paying particular attention to significant fluctuations between periods or any unusual items. **(A-4)**
5. Evaluate the job descriptions based on the business structure and observed regular responsibilities. **(A-5)**
6. Evaluate the IT standards manual in terms of scope, being up to date, and general qualitative usefulness. **(A-6)**
7. Test the data processing hardware inventory using a judgmental sample. Document the process and the results. **(A-7)**
8. Test the responses not covered by the specific steps above by observation and any other measures deemed appropriate, and document the work done. **(A-99)**
9. Formulate a conclusion regarding the adequacy of controls in this area. **(A-MEMO)**

B. Physical Security

1. Evaluate the questionnaire responses in this area and document any items that required additional investigation/follow-up. **(B-1)**
2. Review the data center layout in the carryforward workpapers and ensure that all security features are clearly identified. **(CF-??)**
3. Test the responses by observation and any other measures deemed appropriate, and document the work done. **(B-2)**
4. Test the responses not covered by the specific steps above by observation and any other measures deemed appropriate, and document the work done. **(B-99)**
5. Formulate a conclusion regarding the adequacy of controls in this area. **(B-MEMO)**

C. Logical Security

1. Evaluate the questionnaire responses in this area and document any items that required additional investigation/follow-up. **(C-1)**
2. Cross-reference the questionnaire responses with the system values printout, noting and investigating any differences. **(C-6)**

3. Attempt to sign on with vendor supplied profiles to insure that the passwords were changed since the hardware was installed. **(C-2)**

4. Test other password controls to the extent possible, and document the results. **(C-3)**

5. Test the user profile management process for appropriate documentation, approval, and profile information consistent with the original authorization. **(C-4)**

6. Review all user profiles for consistency in the way they are set up and authorized to use the system; any special capabilities given, exceptions to established password management rules, etc. Document the results of this review. **(C-5)**

7. Obtain an extract of the history log with, review for noteworthy or unusual items, and document the procedures performed and the results obtained. **(C-7)**

8. Test the responses not covered by the specific steps above by observation and any other measures deemed appropriate, and document the work done. **(C-99)**

9. Formulate a conclusion regarding the adequacy of controls in this area. **(C-MEMO)**

IV.

A. Change Management

1. Evaluate the questionnaire responses in this area and document any items that required additional investigation/follow-up. **(D-1)**

2. To the extent possible, perform tests of the change management system that will address reviewing the changed code, evaluating the authorization process, and checking the testing and documentation that was done. **(D-2)**

3. Test the responses not covered by the specific steps above by observation and any other measures deemed appropriate, and document the work done. **(D-99)**

4. Formulate a conclusion regarding the adequacy of controls in this area. **(D-MEMO)**

B. Backup, Recovery, and Contingency Planning

1. Evaluate the questionnaire responses in this area and document any items that required additional investigation/follow-up. **(E-1)**

2. Evaluate the backup strategy as it relates to the business done by the locations served by the installation, and document the results. **(E-2)**

3. Evaluate the disaster recovery plan, and document the results. **(E-3)**

4. Evaluate the overall recovery strategy. **(E-4)**

5. Test the responses not covered by the specific steps above by observation and any other measures deemed appropriate, and document the work done. **(E-99)**

6. Formulate a conclusion regarding the adequacy of controls in this area. **(E-MEMO)**

C. Operations

1. Evaluate the questionnaire responses in this area and document any items that required additional investigation/follow-up. **(F-1)**

2. Evaluate the operations run manual considering being up to date, complete, well organized, and addressing other local factors as needed. **(F-2)**

3. Test the responses by observation and any other measures deemed appropriate, and document the work done. **(F-3)**

4. Test the responses not covered by the specific steps above by observation and any other measures deemed appropriate, and document the work done. **(F-99)**

5. Formulate a conclusion regarding the adequacy of controls in this area. **(F-MEMO)**

D. Application review—Automated Application System 1

1. Obtain and/or prepare flowcharts, narratives, and other documents to describe the applications and functions under review. This documentation should be clearly marked to indicate control points, strengths, and weaknesses, and include the following:
   a. Identification of key transactions
   b. Identification of controls over those transactions
   c. Identification of key files
   d. Identification of controls over those files
   e. Access controls over the applications and its functions
   f. Backup, recovery, and restart procedures

2. Evaluate the information obtained in the prior step in terns of potential opportunities for more efficient business practices.

3. Perform substantive testing, either on a walkthrough, judgmental, or statistical sample basis, to confirm the understanding and information obtained from the two previous steps.

4. Formulate a conclusion regarding the adequacy of controls in this area.

E. Application review—Automated Application System 2

1. Obtain and/or prepare flowcharts, narratives, and other documents to describe the applications and functions under review.

This documentation should be clearly marked to indicate control points, strengths, and weaknesses, and include the following:

a. Identification of key transactions
b. Identification of controls over those transactions
c. Identification of key files
d. Identification of controls over those files
e. Access controls over the applications and its functions
f. Backup, recovery, and restart procedures

2. Evaluate the information obtained in the prior step in terns of potential opportunities for more efficient business practices.
3. Perform substantive testing, either on a walkthrough, judgmental, or statistical sample basis, to confirm the understanding and information obtained from the two previous steps.
4. Formulate a conclusion regarding the adequacy of controls in this area.

V. Audit Finalization

1. Review the workpapers for clarity and completeness.
2. Have the workpapers reviewed, and clear all review notes.
3. Reporting procedures
   a. Prepare a draft report.
   b. Have the draft reviewed, clearing all questions and comments.
   c. Mail the draft to the auditee for review and response development.
   d. If the responses are not received as scheduled, contact the auditee by telephone to determine when the responses can be expected.
   e. Evaluate the responses for adequacy; add them into the draft report, and review with Internal Audit management as needed.
   f. Based on the above, prepare a final report.

4. Complete the audit program and any other remaining pieces of the audit, and submit the final workpapers for filing and appropriate retention.

I have successfully completed all of the audit procedures in the above sections and documented the results of those procedures in the workpapers. All significant observations, findings, and exceptions have been noted.

Name: _____   Date: _____

Workpaper 12-3. Generic Workpaper Set

MASTER WORKPAPER INDEX   W/P Reference   0-0

Prepared by / date ___AUDITOR___ _99/month/day

Approved by / date _____ _99/____/____

SRM	Summary review memorandum
FAR	Final audit report
DAR	Draft audit reports
APSUM	Audit point summary listing
AA	Audit administration
CF	Carryforwards
A	Information Technology administration
B	Physical security
C	Logical security
D	Change management
E	Backup, recovery, and contingency planning
F	Operations
G	not used
H	not used
I	Personal computers
J	not used
K	Application review

WORKPAPER INDEX - CARRYFORWARDS   CF-Index

Prepared by / date ___AUDITOR___ _96/month/day

Approved by / date _____ _96/___/___

CF-10   General controls questionnaire booklet

CF-20   Data processing inventory documents
    CF-20.1   hardware inventory
    CF-20.2   software inventory
    CF-20.3   organization chart
    CF-20.4   contingency recovery plan
    CF-20.5   network diagram
    CF-20.6   control manuals
    CF-20.7   job descriptions
    CF-20.8   personal computer inventory
    CF-20.9   data processing long-range plan
    CF-20.10   MIS service/programming request form
    CF-20.11   user profile maintenance form
    CF-20.12   current project backlog listing
    CF-20.13   systems development and maintenance standards
    CF-20.14   data processing budget
    CF-20.15   sample programmer documentation
    CF-20.16   sample user documentation
    CF-20.17   system utilization analyses
    CF-20.18   data processing error log
    CF-20.19   personal computer user guidelines
    CF-20.20   human resources transfer/termination document
    CF-20.21   testing procedures for fire security systems
    CF-20.22   continuing education records

CF-30   System value listing

CF-40   Not currently in use

CF-50   Not currently in use

CF-60   Other carryforward materials
    CF-60.1   physical layout of the location
    CF-60.2   phone list(s)
    CF-60.3   specific maps for the entity
    CF-65.0   _____

WORKPAPER INDEX - AUDIT ADMINISTRATION AA-Index

Prepared by / date ___AUDITOR___ _96/month/day

Approved by / date _____ _96/___/___

AA-Legend	Master legend
AA-1	Audit planning memo
AA-2	Audit program
AA-3	Review of carryforward documentation
AA-4	Entrance conference
AA-5	Resolution of entrance conference questions/issues
AA-6	Status of prior recommendations
AA-7	Facility tour memo
AA-8	Exit conference
AA-9	Audit point summary listing
AA-10	NOT USED
AA-11	Other audit correspondence

MASTER TICK MARK LEGEND   AA-Legend

Prepared by / date ___AUDITOR___ _96/month/day

Approved by / date _____ _96/____/____

This tick mark legend applies to all of the workpapers for this engagement. Supplemental legends may be found in individual audit areas or on specific workpapers.

F   footed (if below)/crossfooted (if beside)

SF   scan footed

√   indicated attribute tested without exception

wp ref. ⇒   (traced from the indicated workpaper

⇒ wp ref.   traced to the indicated workpaper

AUDIT PLANNING MEMO   AA-1

Prepared by / date ___AUDITOR___ _96/month/day

Approved by / date _____ _96/____/____

OVERVIEW

The audit of __ in __, __ will take place during the week of __. The audit will have the following emphases:

data center general controls; and
a telecommunications overview.

Field time is __ days, with __ manager(s), __ senior auditor(s); and __ staff auditor(s) assigned to the fieldwork.

SPECIFIC OBJECTIVES

The objectives for this assignment are to evaluate IT general controls: 1. administration; 2. physical security; 3. logical security; 4. change management; 5. backup, recovery, and contingency planning; 6. data center operations.

APPROACH

The approach selected will begin with the information technology control questionnaire appropriate to this location (or having the most recent one updated, if appropriate); getting the current information on prior recommendations and carryforward documents, and basic discussions with the client. This is followed by fieldwork, which should include discussions, documentation reviews, direct testing, and other procedures as deemed necessary.

Local personnel will be kept informed at all times regarding the status and potential findings related to the procedures performed. This will culminate in an exit conference with appropriate local personnel. Materials distributed during the exit meeting may be any appropriate combination of the audit point summary, a summarized agenda format, or a preliminary audit report draft.

Final audit report development and issuance will follow standard audit procedures.

LOCAL CONTACTS

Plant manager
Controller

IT manager
Programmer/Analyst

STAFFING

The staff personnel assigned to this job include:

Manager(s):
Senior(s):
Staff:

TIMING

The audit will be executed with a total budget of ___ days; ___ days in the field during the week(s) of ___; with the balance allocated to office time for administrative matters and report issuance.

Submitted to file,

__Auditor__

__Title____

AUDIT PROGRAM   AA-2

Prepared by / date ___AUDITOR___ _96/month/day

Approved by / date _____ _96/____/____

REVIEW OF CARRYFORWARD DOCUMENTATION AA-3

Prepared by / date ___AUDITOR___ _96/month/day

Approved by / date _____ _96/___/___

I have reviewed the carryforward workpapers. My observations/comments/questions/etc. are shown below, organized in the order of the items included in the carryforward workpapers.

Note: Strike out any items not available or excluded from review.

CF-10   General controls questionnaire booklet

CF-20   Data processing inventory documents
      CF-20.1   hardware inventory
      CF-20.2   software inventory
      CF-20.3   organization chart
      CF-20.4   contingency recovery plan
      CF-20.5   network diagram
      CF-20.6   control manuals
      CF-20.7   job descriptions
      CF-20.8   personal computer inventory
      CF-20.9   data processing long-range plan
      CF-20.10   MIS service/programming request form
      CF-20.11   user profile maintenance form
      CF-20.12   current project backlog listing
      CF-20.13   systems development and maintenance standards
      CF-20.14   data processing budget
      CF-20.15   sample programmer documentation
      CF-20.16   sample user documentation
      CF-20.17   system utilization analyses
      CF-20.18   data processing error log
      CF-20.19   personal computer user guidelines
      CF-20.20   human resources transfer/termination list
      CF-20.21   testing procedures for fire security systems
      CF-20.22   continuing education records

CF-30   System value listing

ENTRANCE CONFERENCE   AA-4

Prepared by / date ___AUDITOR___ _96/month/day

Approved by / date _____ _96/____/____

An entrance meeting was held on _____ with the following personnel:

-
-
-
-
- (myself)

We discussed the following items:

- the audit scope (described in the A-1 planning memo)
- the expected audit timing (as shown in the A-11 correspondence)
- personnel to talk to in regards to the various scope items
- audit finalization and reporting procedures

They posed the following questions and potential scope adjustments for the audit:

-
-
-
-

No other noteworthy matters took place during the meeting.

RESOLUTION OF ENTRANCE CONFERENCE QUESTIONS / ISSUES   AA-5

Prepared by / date ___AUDITOR___ _96/month/day

Approved by / date _____ _96/___/___

STATUS OF PRIOR RECOMMENDATIONS   AA-6

Prepared by / date ___AUDITOR___ _96/month/day

Approved by / date _____ _96/____/____

I have reviewed the prior audit report which is included as AA-6.2 in these workpapers. There were two areas of recommendation in that report.

FACILITY TOUR   AA-7

Prepared by / date ___AUDITOR___ _96/month/day

Approved by / date _____ _96/____/____

I was taken on a plant tour by _??_ on _ Month _ Day _ , _ Year _. During that tour, I noted the following:

- Item 1
- Item 2
- Item 3
- Item 4
- Item 5

EXIT CONFERENCE   AA-8

Prepared by / date ___AUDITOR___ _96/month/day

Approved by / date _____ _96/____/____

An exit meeting was held on __ with the following personnel:

-
-
-
-
- (myself)

We discussed the following items: (basically a repeat of the entrance meeting)

- the audit scope (described in the AA-1 planning memo)
- the expected audit timing (as shown in the AA-11 correspondence)
- personnel to talk to in regards to the various scope items
- audit finalization and reporting procedures

We then discussed the audit findings, which included items that are expected to be dropped, included in a secondary private letter to local management, and included in the formal draft audit report.

-
-
-
-

No other noteworthy matters took place during the meeting.

NOT USED   AA-10

Prepared by / date ___AUDITOR___ _96/month/day

Approved by / date _____ _96/____/____

OTHER AUDIT CORRESPONDENCE   AA-11.1

Prepared by / date ___AUDITOR___ _96/month/day

Approved by / date _____ _96/____/____

AA-11.2   Audit initiation/announcement letter
AA-11.3   other
AA-11.4   other

WORKPAPER INDEX - IT ADMINISTRATION   A-Index

Prepared by / date ___AUDITOR___ _96/month/day

Approved by / date _____ _96/___/___

A-Memo	Summary memo for this audit area
A-Point	Audit point(s) for this audit area
A-1	Review of questionnaire responses
A-2	Review of IT department placement in the organization
A-3	Review of short- and long-range plans
A-4	Analytical review of budgeted and actual expenses
A-5	Evaluation of job descriptions
A-6	Evaluation of the standards manual
A-7	Verification procedures for the hardware inventory listing
A-8	unused
A-9	unused
A-99	Other procedures

QUESTIONNAIRE RESPONSE REVIEW - IT ADMINISTRATION   A-1.1

Prepared by / date ___AUDITOR___ _96/month/day

Approved by / date _____ _96/___/___

I have reviewed the responses to the questionnaire section dealing with information technology administration. A copy of that section follows this working paper as 1.2. All of the items requiring further discussion, investigation, or other follow-up are described below, and referenced by the letter (and audit point reference where appropriate) shown in the left column.

Reference	Audit Point	Description

REVIEW OF IT PLACEMENT IN THE ORGANIZATION   A-2

Prepared by / date ___AUDITOR___ _96/month/day

Approved by / date _____ _96/____/____

I have reviewed the top level organization charts, included in the carryforward workpapers, which show the placement of information technology in the overall organization. Based on that review, it is my opinion that information technology **is/not** properly placed in the structure of the overall organization.

REVIEW OF IT PLANNING   A-3

Prepared by / date ___AUDITOR___ _96/month/day

Approved by / date _____ _96/___/___

l have reviewed the short-term and long-term plans for information technology, which are attached to this working paper, made the following observations, and followed up as needed.

Observations:

- Item 1
- Item 2
- Item 3

ANALYTICAL REVIEW OF THE BUDGET AND ACTUAL EXPENSES   A-4

Prepared by / date ___AUDITOR___ _96/month/day

Approved by / date _____ _96/___/___

EVALUATION OF JOB DESCRIPTIONS   A-5

Prepared by / date ___AUDITOR___ _96/month/day

Approved by / date _____ _96/____/____

EVALUATION OF STANDARDS MANUAL A-6

Prepared by / date ___AUDITOR___ _96/month/day

Approved by / date _____ _96/____/____

VERIFICATION OF HARDWARE INVENTORY   A-7

Prepared by / date ___AUDITOR___ _96/month/day

Approved by / date _____ _96/____/____

Note: Modify as needed based on the actual procedures performed.

I selected the five items for verification. Those items are shown on the hardware resource list enclosed in the carryforward working papers as **CF-20.1**. The existence of these items was confirmed by visual observation and by matching the serial numbers indicated on the working paper to the item described. One of the memory cards is integrated with the processor, and cannot be separately identified. No exceptions were noted. No further procedures were performed.

OTHER PROCEDURES   A-99

Prepared by / date ___AUDITOR___ _96/month/day

Approved by / date _____ _96/___/___

SUMMARY MEMO - IT ADMINISTRATION   A-Memo

Prepared by / date ___AUDITOR___ _96/month/day

Approved by / date _____ _96/____/____

OBJECTIVE

The objective for auditing IT administration was to ensure that the information technology function is managed in a way that protects the information assets of the company.

CONCLUSION

Based on the work done in this area, my opinion is that the controls over IT administration _??_ ensure that the activities of the department are properly coordinated with and focused on the plans and needs of the business.

FINDINGS

The conclusion(s) above were made considering the following specific findings:

-
-
-

PROCEDURES

To satisfy the audit program the following procedures were done.

- reviewed the responses to the general controls questionnaire
- evaluated the placement of the IT function in the organization
- evaluated the short and long range information technology planning
-
-

Submitted to file,

__Auditor__

__Title____

WORKPAPER INDEX - PHYSICAL SECURITY   B-Index

Prepared by / date ___AUDITOR___ _96/month/day

Approved by / date _____ _96/____/____

B-Memo	Summary memo for this audit area
B-Point	Audit point(s) for this audit area
B-1	Review of questionnaire responses
B-2	Physical security testing procedures
B-3	
B-4	
B-5	
B-6	
B-7	
B-8	
B-9	
B-99	Other facility issues

REVIEW OF QUESTIONNAIRE RESPONSES   B-1.1

Prepared by / date ___AUDITOR___ _96/month/day

Approved by / date _____ _96/___/___

I have reviewed the responses to the questionnaire section dealing with physical security. A copy of that section follows this working paper as 1.2. All of the items requiring further discussion, investigation, or other follow-up are described below, and referenced by the letter (and audit point reference where appropriate) shown in the left column.

Reference	Audit Point	Description

TESTING OF PHYSICAL SECURITY FEATURES   B-2

Prepared by / date ___AUDITOR___ _96/month/day

Approved by / date _____ _96/____/____

Note: Review and update as needed based on work performed.

I have tested the following security features that were identified in the internal control questionnaire and identified on the data center diagram included in the carryforward workpapers. The results are summarized below:

Door locks:	I tried 10 combinations on the lock, working with simple sequential combinations, the factory default combination, and other combinations I have seen used in the past. I was not successful in opening the door.
Fire extinguishers:	I examined all of the extinguishers in the data center and the surrounding area noting that all of them had the appropriate inspection cards attached, that all of them had a current inspection, and that all of the gages were in the green.
Water detectors	I tested the water detectors by shorting one of them out with an insulated handle screw driver. (Note that the monitoring personnel were notified in advance, and that local management approved the testing before being done. This also applies to tests of the other detector systems with an annunciation feature.)
Heat/smoke sensors:	I tested these directly using the included test feature/by reviewing the testing documentation from the outside security service responsible for the system. All items functioned as expected.
Control panel:	I checked the control panel using the test function button included in the system without exception. I also confirmed that a sensor activation will be shown on the monitoring panels with the guards and the third-party security service.

OTHER PROCEDURES   B-99

Prepared by / date ___AUDITOR___ _96/month/day

Approved by / date _____ _96/____/____

SUMMARY MEMO - AREA   B-Memo

Prepared by / date ___AUDITOR___ _96/month/day

Approved by / date _____ _96/____/____

OBJECTIVE

The objective in this area was to determine the adequacy of controls over physical security.

CONCLUSION

Based on the work done in this area, my opinion is that: the controls over the physical security of the installation __ protect the personnel and equipment from relevant local risks.

FINDINGS

The conclusion(s) above were made considering the following specific findings:

-
-
-

PROCEDURES

To satisfy the audit program the following procedures were done.

- The internal control questionnaire responses related to physical security were reviewed and discussed with appropriate personnel.
- Additional observations were made directly during the course of the audit.
- Limited testing of available security features was done while on-site.

Submitted to file,

__Auditor__

__Title___

WORKPAPER INDEX - LOGICAL SECURITY   C-Index

Prepared by / date ___AUDITOR___ _96/month/day

Approved by / date _____ _96/___/____

C-Memo	Summary memo for this audit area
C-Point	Audit point(s) for this audit area
C-1	Review of internal control questionnaire responses
C-2	Testing of vendor-supplied profiles/passwords
C-3	Testing of password syntax and control parameters
C-4	Testing of user profile management procedures
C-5	Comparison of user profile setup
C-6	Comparison of questionnaire responses and the system value listing
C-7	Evaluation of security items from the system history log
C-8	
C-9	
C-99	Other logical access related procedures

REVIEW OF QUESTIONNAIRE RESPONSES   C-1.1

Prepared by / date ___AUDITOR___ _96/month/day

Approved by / date _____ _96/___/___

I have reviewed the responses to the questionnaire section dealing with logical access controls. A copy of that section follows this working paper as 1.2. All of the items requiring further discussion, investigation, or other follow-up are described below, and referenced by the letter (and audit point reference where appropriate) shown in the left column.

Reference	Audit Point	Description

VENDOR SUPPLIED PASSWORDS   C-2

Prepared by / date ___AUDITOR___ _96/month/day

Approved by / date _____ _96/___/___

I tested whether the vendor supplied profiles and passwords have been changed since the system has been implemented. The ones identified tested are shown below:

VP1   not/successful
VP2   not/successful
VP3   not/successful
VP4   not/successful

No further procedures were deemed necessary.

PASSWORD SYNTAX TESTING   C-3

Prepared by / date   ___AUDITOR___   _96/month/day

Approved by / date _____ _96/____/____

I have tested the following password control parameters:

- **Periodic required changes:**   System parameters indicate changes are due at least every XX days.

- **Minimum password length:**   Using the XXX sign-on, I attempted to set a password less than the indicated minimum length of XX characters and was (not) successful.

- **Maximum password length:**   Using the XXX sign-on, I attempted to set a password longer than the indicated maximum length of XX characters and was (not) successful.

- **Maximum attempts:**   Using the XXX sign-on, I attempted to sign on with the indicated password more than the XX maximum attempts indicated in the internal control questionnaire and was not successful.

No further procedures were deemed necessary.

USER PROFILE MANAGEMENT   C-4

Prepared by / date ___AUDITOR___ _96/month/day

Approved by / date _____ _96/____/____

I selected a random sample of ten user profiles from the population of all system users to validate the profile management procedures at this location. The profiles selected and the testing results are summarized in the table below:

User profile	Name	Authorization form was present	Authorization form was approved

No exceptions were noted. No further procedures were deemed necessary.

USER PROFILE REVIEW   C-5

Prepared by / date ___AUDITOR___ _96/month/day

Approved by / date _____ _96/____/____

Note: Update as needed.

SUMMARY LISTING

I have reviewed the user profile summary listing which follows as **C-5.1** for consistency in the setup of user profiles. All profiles were scanned, and no unusual items were noted.

PREVIOUS SIGN-ON DATE

I obtained the listing of users by previous sign-on date that is enclosed as working paper **C-5.2.2.** An aging by date has been summarized on working paper **C-5.2.1.** My opinion is that the user base is (not) being kept relatively current, and will keep the related audit point, **C 12**, to the exit meeting only.

LAST PASSWORD CHANGE DATE

I obtained the listing of users by last password change date to use as support for the results of the **C-5.2** work that was done. There should be a high consistency in the aging of the two reports. Based on the listing (**C-5.3.2**) and the summary (**C-5.3.1**), the results are consistent, and no further work was performed.

USERS WITH EXPIRED PASSWORDS

I have reviewed the appropriate listing that is included in the working papers as **C-5.4,** noting that there are not users with expired passwords. Based on that information, the summary worksheet for this subsection was not prepared.

COMPARISON OF RESPONSES TO THE SYSTEM VALUES LISTING   C-6.1

Prepared by / date ___AUDITOR___ _96/month/day

Approved by / date _____ _96/____/____

I have highlighted the appropriate system values on the attached copy of the system values listing, taken from the original that is included in the carryforward working papers as **CF-30**. Those highlighted items were compared to the questionnaire excerpt included as **C-1.2** noting no exceptions. No further procedures were performed.

REVIEW OF SECURITY ITEMS IN THE HISTORY LOG C-7.1

Prepared by / date ___AUDITOR___ _96/month/day

Approved by / date _____ _96/___/___

l have reviewed the enclosed extract from the system history log. Based on my review of those items, l noted the following:

OTHER PROCEDURES C-99

Prepared by / date ___AUDITOR___ _96/month/day

Approved by / date _____ _96/___/___

SUMMARY MEMO—LOGICAL ACCESS CONTROLS   C-Memo

Prepared by / date ___AUDITOR___ _96/month/day

Approved by / date _____ _96/___/___

Note: Update as needed.

OBJECTIVES

The objectives in this area were to:

- Ensure that only authorized users can access the systems
- Users will be encouraged to reasonably manage their own passwords
- Users are restricted to only those items they require access to

CONCLUSION

Based on the work done in this area, my opinion is that the controls over logical access to system programs and data ____.

FINDINGS

The conclusion(s) above were made considering the following specific findings:

-
-
-

PROCEDURES

To satisfy the audit program, the following procedures were done.

- Questionnaire responses were reviewed
- Vendor-supplied passwords, password syntax and change parameters, and user profile management procedures were tested
- Profiles were compared for consistency and exceptions

Submitted to file,

__Auditor__

__Title___

WORKPAPER INDEX - CHANGE MANAGEMENT   D-Index

Prepared by / date ___AUDITOR___ _96/month/day

Approved by / date _____ _96/____/____

D-Memo   Summary memo for this audit area

D-Point   Audit point(s) for this audit area

D-1   Review of questionnaire responses

D-2   Testing of change management procedures

D-3

D-4

D-5

D-6

D-7

D-8

D-9

D-99   Other procedures

REVIEW OF QUESTIONNAIRE RESPONSES D-1.1

Prepared by / date ___AUDITOR___ _96/month/day

Approved by / date _____ _96/___/___

I have reviewed the responses to the questionnaire section dealing with change management. A copy of that section follows this working paper as 1.2. All of the items requiring further discussion, investigation, or other follow-up are described below, and referenced by the letter (and audit point reference where appropriate) shown in the left column.

Reference	Audit Point	Description

TESTING OF CHANGE MANAGEMENT PROCEDURES   D-2

Prepared by / date ___AUDITOR___ _96/month/day

Approved by / date _____ _96/____/____

I have selected a judgmental sample of ten program changes that took place over the last 12 months preceding the audit for testing. These changes were tested for reasonable business purpose for the change, evidence of documentation and testing, and appropriate IT or user management's approval.

Changed program	Business reason	Documentation and testing	Management approval

Based on the procedures performed and results obtained, my opinion is that _____ .

WORKPAPER TITLE   D-3

Prepared by / date   ___AUDITOR___ _96/month/day

Approved by / date   _____ _96/____/___

WORKPAPER TITLE   D-4

Prepared by / date ___AUDITOR___ _96/month/day

Approved by / date _____ _96/___/___

OTHER PROCEDURES D-99

Prepared by / date ___AUDITOR___ _96/month/day

Approved by / date _____ _96/___/___

SUMMARY MEMO - CHANGE MANAGEMENT   D Memo

Prepared by / date ___AUDITOR___ _96/month/day

Approved by / date _____ _96/____/____

OBJECTIVE

The objective in this area was to determine if changes to the system hardware and software are being managed in such a way as to minimize or eliminate the risk of disruption or other problem to the production environment.

CONCLUSION

Based on the work done in this area, my opinion is that the controls over change management are/not adequate.

FINDINGS

The conclusion(s) above were made considering the following specific findings:

-
-
-

PROCEDURES

To satisfy the audit program, the following procedures were done.

- The internal control questionnaire responses were reviewed
- Change management procedures were tested to the extent possible
-

Submitted to file,

__Auditor__

__Title___

WORKPAPER INDEX - BACKUP, RECOVERY, ...   E-Index

Prepared by / date ___AUDITOR___ _96/month/day

Approved by / date _____ _96/___/___

E-Memo   Summary memo for this audit area

E-Point   Audit point(s) for this audit area

E-1   Review of questionnaire responses

E-2   Evaluation and testing of backups

E-3   Evaluation and testing of disaster recovery plan

E-4   Evaluation and testing of overall recovery strategy

E-5

E-6

E-7

E-8

E-9

E-99   Other procedures

REVIEW OF QUESTIONNAIRE RESPONSES   E-1.1

Prepared by / date ___AUDITOR___ _96/month/day

Approved by / date _____ _96/___/___

I have reviewed the responses to the questionnaire section dealing with backup, recovery, and contingency planning. A copy of that section follows this working paper as 1.2. All of the items requiring further discussion, investigation, or other follow-up are described below, and referenced by the letter (and audit point reference where appropriate) shown in the left column.

Reference	Audit Point	Description

BACKUP STRATEGY: EVALUATION AND TESTING   E-2

Prepared by / date ___AUDITOR___ _96/month/day

Approved by / date _____ _96/___/___

Note: Delete or strike out unneeded lines.

Based on discussions with the information systems manager, the backup strategy has been summarized below:

Daily:
- All changed objects in the production libraries (programs and data)
- All changed objects
- All production objects
- All objects

Weekly:
- All changed objects in the production libraries (programs and data)
- All changed objects
- All production objects
- All objects

Monthly:
- All changed objects in the production libraries (programs and data)
- All changed objects
- All production objects
- All objects

Quarterly:
- All changed objects in the production libraries (programs and data)
- All changed objects
- All production objects
- All objects

Annually:
- All changed objects in the production libraries (programs and data)
- All changed objects
- All production objects
- All objects

To test the information above, I judgmentally selected a total of ___items, half from the backup records and half from the backups to make a comparison of what they believe they have in backups and what they actually have in backups. The items tested and the test results are summarized in the following table.

Based on the procedures performed and results obtained, my opinion is that _____ .

DISASTER RECOVERY PLAN: EVALUATION AND TESTING   E-3

Prepared by / date ___AUDITOR___ _96/month/day

Approved by / date _____ _96/____/____

I have reviewed the disaster recovery plan that is included in the carryforward workpapers. Based on that review I noted the following:

- Item 1
- Item 2
- Item 3
- Item 4
- Item 5

RECOVERY STRATEGY: EVALUATION AND TESTING   E-4

Prepared by / date ___AUDITOR___ _96/month/day

Approved by / date _____ _96/___/___

Note: Correct the statements below as needed.

I asked the information systems manager for a summary of his/her recovery strategy, which has been summarized in the paragraphs below.

1. Backups are taken such that there should be no more than one business day's worth of information lost in the event of a problem.
2. A physical security system has been installed and is maintained for the data center to prevent or reduce the actual data center damage in the event of a disaster.
3. A disaster recovery plan has been developed to support the objective of fully restoring processing capabilities after no more than a 24-hour outage.

Based on the procedures performed and results obtained, my opinion is that _____ .

WORKPAPER TITLE   E-5

Prepared by / date ___AUDITOR___ _96/month/day

Approved by / date _____ _96/___/___

WORKPAPER TITLE   E-6

Prepared by / date ___AUDITOR___ _96/month/day

Approved by / date _____ _96/___/___

OTHER PROCEDURES E-99

Prepared by / date ___AUDITOR___ _96/month/day

Approved by / date _____ _96/___/___

SUMMARY MEMO—BACKUP, RECOVERY, AND ..... E-Memo

Prepared by / date ___AUDITOR___ _96/month/day

Approved by / date _____ _96/____/____

Note: Correct the statements below as needed.

OBJECTIVES

The objectives in this area were to:

- Evaluate the current backup strategy for effectiveness and compliance
- Evaluate the current recovery strategy for effectiveness and compliance
- Evaluate the disaster recovery plan for adequacy

CONCLUSION

Based on the work done in this area, my opinion is that:

- The current backup strategy should meet the needs for the business
- The backup strategy as described is functioning
- The recovery plan appears complete and reasonable
- The disaster recovery plan is sufficient for their needs

FINDINGS

The conclusion(s) above were made considering the following specific findings:

-
-
-

PROCEDURES

To satisfy the audit program, the following procedures were done.

- The completeness of the backups taken was tested
- The disaster recovery plan was reviewed

Submitted to file,

__Auditor__

__Title___

WORKPAPER INDEX - DATA CENTER OPERATIONS   F-Index

Prepared by / date ___AUDITOR___ _96/month/day

Approved by / date _____ _96/___/___

F-Memo   Summary memo for operations

F-Point   Audit point(s) for operations (duplicates listing at the beginning
            of the working papers)

F-1   Review of questionnaire responses

F-2   Evaluation of the operations run book

F-3

F-4

F-5

F-6

F-7

F-8

F-9

F-99   Other procedures

REVIEW OF QUESTIONNAIRE RESPONSES - OPERATIONS F-1.1

Prepared by / date ___AUDITOR___ _96/month/day

Approved by / date _____ _96/____/____

I have reviewed the responses to the questionnaire section dealing with data center operations. A copy of that section follows this working paper as 1.2. All of the items requiring further discussion, investigation, or other follow-up are described below, and referenced by the letter (and audit point reference where appropriate) shown in the left column.

Reference	Audit Point	Description

EVALUATION OF OPERATIONS RUN BOOK   F-2

Prepared by / date ___AUDITOR___ _96/month/day

Approved by / date _____ _96/____/____

I have reviewed the operations run book noting the following:

- Item 1
- Item 2
- Item 3
- Item 4

Based on these observations it is my opinion that _____ .

WORKPAPER TITLE   F-3

Prepared by / date ___AUDITOR___ _96/month/day

Approved by / date _____ _96/____/____

WORKPAPER TITLE   F-4

Prepared by / date ___AUDITOR___ _96/month/day

Approved by / date _____ _96/____/____

OTHER PROCEDURES   F-99

Prepared by / date ___AUDITOR___ _96/month/day

Approved by / date _____ _96/____/____

SUMMARY MEMO - DATA CENTER OPERATIONS   F-Memo

Prepared by / date   ___AUDITOR___ _96/month/day

Approved by / date   _____   _96/____/____

OBJECTIVE

The objective in this area is to evaluate the operation of the system/systems to ensure that they will support the business activities as needed.

CONCLUSION

Based on the work done in this area, my opinion is that the controls over data center operations __ ensure that the computer is operated as expected by both information systems and general business management.

FINDINGS

The conclusion(s) above were made considering the following specific findings:

-
-
-

PROCEDURES

To satisfy the audit program the following procedures were done.

- Questionnaire responses were reviewed
- Run book was reviewed and evaluated

Submitted to file,

__Auditor__

__Title___

WORKPAPER INDEX - NAME HERE   G-Index

Prepared by / date ___AUDITOR___ _96/month/day

Approved by / date _____ _96/____/____

Note: This blank working paper section is provided so the IT auditor might duplicate from it to create additional sections as needed.

G-Memo   Summary memo for this audit area

G-Point   Audit point(s) for this audit area

G-1

G-2

G-3

G-4

G-5

G-6

G-7

G-8

G-9

G-10

WORKPAPER TITLE   G-1

Prepared by / date ___AUDITOR___ _96/month/day

Approved by / date _____ _96/____/____

WORKPAPER TITLE　　　　G-2

Prepared by / date ___AUDITOR___ _96/month/day

Approved by / date _____ _96/____/____

WORKPAPER TITLE   G-3

Prepared by / date ___AUDITOR___ _96/month/day

Approved by / date _____ _96/___/___

WORKPAPER TITLE   G-4

Prepared by / date ___AUDITOR___ _96/month/day

Approved by / date _____ _96/___/___

WORKPAPER TITLE   G-5

Prepared by / date ___AUDITOR___ _96/month/day

Approved by / date _____ _96/____/____

WORKPAPER TITLE   G-6

Prepared by / date ___AUDITOR___   _96/month/day

Approved by / date _____ _96/___/___

WORKPAPER TITLE   G-7

Prepared by / date ___AUDITOR___ _96/month/day

Approved by / date _____ _96/___/___

WORKPAPER TITLE   G-8

Prepared by / date ___AUDITOR___ _96/month/day

Approved by / date _____ _96/____/____

WORKPAPER TITLE   G-9

Prepared by / date ___AUDITOR___ _96/month/day

Approved by / date _____ _96/___/___

WORKPAPER TITLE   G-10

Prepared by / date ___AUDITOR___ _96/month/day

Approved by / date _____ _96/___/___

SUMMARY MEMO - NAME HERE G-Memo

Prepared by / date ___AUDITOR___ _96/month/day

Approved by / date _____ _96/____/____

OBJECTIVES

The objective for auditing

CONCLUSION

Based on the work done in this area, my opinion is that the controls

FINDINGS

The conclusion(s) above were made considering the following specific findings:

-
-
-

PROCEDURES

To satisfy the audit program, the following procedures were done.

-
-
-

Submitted to file,

__Auditor__

__Title___

Section 13
Auditing the Midrange Computer

The mainframe computer was simply too expensive for many companies, and they looked for solutions that were more consistent with their size. Vendors began to respond by developing scaled-down versions of the mainframe. Companies first saw the minicomputer, and later the microcomputer, both carefully named to indicate their relationship to the mainframe computer. These computers were designed for small companies that were not in the market for a mainframe computer but still wanted to gain the benefits of automation. Minicomputers, like IBM's System 32, differed from the mainframes of that era by fitting into a fraction of the space, with all of their components contained in as little as one piece of hardware.

Another significant change from the mainframe architecture was the bundling of operating system software components into a single offering. Mainframes had come with a base operating system only, requiring customers to purchase other components, such as security software, separately. These previously separate components began to be bundled into a single offering.

Minicomputers clearly supported a different market and could be easily outgrown, leading companies into the mainframe market. Technical advances significantly increased the capabilities of the minicomputer, and the name for these systems changed to "midrange" as more descriptive of their capabilities fitting between the mainframe and microcomputer markets.

The IT auditor has a less daunting task auditing midrange computers because experience with one specific midrange computer type can almost always be directly applied to another similar system, as the software components are generally the same. The IT auditor still needs technical expertise because the security and control capabilities between midrange systems, even from a single manufacturer, can vary significantly.

Physical access security is still extremely important, but logical access security clearly becomes the more important element because midrange systems increase the direct reliance on end-user input and control for data entry and maintenance instead of these functions being performed centrally. The primary control problem in the midrange environment is change management because the midrange computers are often supported by small staffs that do not have the number of personnel required for effective segregation of duties. Therefore, IT auditors must consider compensating controls as a primary control mechanism because end-user actions and responsibilities offset the segregation weakness within the IT department.

The audit process can be described in three steps: planning, fieldwork, and finalization. Most, if not all, of the audit concerns, considerations, and tasks for the mainframe environment can be applied to the midrange environment.

PLANNING THE AUDIT

The IT auditor should always begin with planning and should be careful to put the proper effort into planning every audit, even if the auditor has performed the same basic review many times in the past. Every audit may be different, and failing to allocate to each audit assignment the appropriate amount of planning time can lead to unreliable audit results.

Contacting the Auditee

The IT auditor should make initial contact with the auditee by phone, if possible, because it is less formal than sending a letter or even a note by electronic mail. Once the audit timing or scope is committed to paper, even as a draft, it can create subsequent problems for the systems auditor. The auditor should begin by communicating the areas to be reviewed, which can include all or a portion of the following:

- IT administration
- Physical security
- Logical security
- Operations
- Backup and recovery
- Systems development

The auditor should contact the head of the IT department initially, unless it has previously been agreed to that contact at a lower level is more appropriate. In the latter instance, it is appropriate to copy the head IT person once the scope and schedule of the audit have been determined. The midrange environment is likely to require at least one to three weeks of effort, to a maximum that is only limited by the auditor's decision to discontinue testing.

The midrange environment is likely to contain subfunctions reporting to no more than two different managers, so that the auditor has to do less coordinating. The IT auditor should send a letter to the primary director or manager to confirm the planning details. This letter should be made available to the field personnel at least two weeks in advance of fieldwork so that any questions or comments can be communicated, researched, and resolved before starting fieldwork.

Preliminary Office Planning Before Fieldwork

The IT auditor should complete the following procedures while still in the office before initiating fieldwork procedures:

- Prepare an audit planning memo, including these elements:
  —Location background
  —Prior audit scope and results
  —Detailed list of prior recommendations
  —Current planned scope and timing
  —Planned staffing
  —Time budgets
- Define the specific audit program based on the standard program, the intended objectives based on the audit department's planning and selection of the audit, and the planning conversations held with location personnel.
- Send out the Information Technology Internal Control Questionnaire (Workpaper 5-1), specifying a date for its completion that will permit time for it to be returned and reviewed before fieldwork. (If there is a questionnaire from a previous audit, and if it is not materially different from the questionnaire currently in use, copy it and have the location personnel update the previous form.)
- Obtain prior audit reports related to this location and place a copy in the workpapers.
- Review past audit files for permanent and carry-forward information, and incorporate any previous findings into the current workpapers.
- Set up any necessary files on the personal computer or laptop that will facilitate the performance of fieldwork.

PERFORMING FIELDWORK PROCEDURES

Fieldwork is more likely to be done in one visit, or at most two. The IT auditor must take the time to ensure that there is a workable schedule and that all involved parties are aware of it. The general items that should be completed in the field that do not relate to any of the specific areas are:

- Conduct an entrance conference and document the results of that meeting. It may be necessary to have multiple meetings in a midrange review, but not as likely as when performing a mainframe review.
- Prepare a list of all issues from the prior audit and determine the current status of those items by contacting the appropriate personnel, performing detailed procedures if necessary. Document the current status of those items in the workpapers. The auditor's effort to complete this

step is not related to the environment as much as it is to the nature and extent of prior audit recommendations.

- Take a plant tour, noting any unusual items or observations. This gives the IT auditor an opportunity to become acquainted with the business and to gain some indirect information about how that particular business or location is operating, which may be useful when the auditor is evaluating potential recommendations and their cost/benefit considerations. The tour, observations, and other items that the auditor deems important should be documented in the working papers.

AUDITING SPECIFIC PROCEDURES BY AUDIT AREA

The IT auditor should be ready to begin specific detailed audit procedures once the planning and the general office procedures have been covered. The audit tasks are discussed in the subsequent sections, followed by the estimated time to complete and additional comments if necessary.

IT Administration

The IT administration has eight tasks and should take a minimum of four to a maximum of eight hours to complete, exclusive of testing.

Task 1: Review Security and Control Questionnaire. The IT auditor should make a copy of the IT administration portion of the security and control questionnaire so that the original completed questionnaire can be kept whole in the carry-forward working papers. The auditor should evaluate the questionnaire responses and document any items that required additional investigation or follow-up. The estimated time is one to two hours to complete this procedure. The audit of the midrange environment should include a substantial portion of the controls covered in the questionnaire.

Task 2: Review the Organization Chart. The IT auditor should obtain a copy of the top-level organization chart and review the placement of IT in the organization in terms of its overall effectiveness. The estimated time to complete this task is 15 minutes.

Task 3: Evaluate the Long-Range IT Plan. The IT auditor should obtain the long-range IT plan and evaluate it in terms of supporting business objectives, its consistency with the business plan, the likelihood of meeting management's objectives, and its being properly developed in terms of scope, detail, quantitative analysis, and responsibility. Partially depending on the extent of the plan, the time estimate to complete this review is one hour. The midrange environment should also be covered by a plan, because the investment in personnel, hardware, software, and other resources is still likely to be significant.

Task 4: Audit Expense and Budget Statements. The IT auditor should obtain and review appropriate expense and budget statements, paying particular attention to significant fluctuations between periods or any unusual items. The time estimated to complete this area is between one and two hours, based on the detail and extent of the budget and actual information.

Task 5: Examine Job Descriptions. The IT auditor should obtain and evaluate the IT department's job descriptions based on the business structure and observed regular responsibilities. The time estimate for this is one hour or less, although more time may be needed if the auditor determines that the job descriptions are too general or are inconsistent with the responsibilities that IT personnel have been assigned.

Task 6: Review and Evaluate the IT Standards Manual. The IT auditor should obtain and evaluate the IT standards manual in terms of scope, timeliness, and general qualitative usefulness. The standards manual is still important as the value of consistent practices is clear, and a staff with two or more is subject to variations. The estimated time to complete this step depends on the level of testing the IT auditor decides to perform, and could vary between 1 and 20 hours. If no manual is in place, the auditor should spend at least one hour to assess the need for a manual and to prepare the related recommendation with a sample document or, at least, a sample table of contents.

Task 7: Perform a Complete Inventory of All IT-Related Hardware. The IT auditor should obtain a complete inventory of all IT-related hardware used at the audited location and this inventory should be included in the permanent working papers. This inventory should be tested based on a judgmental sample in both directions, from the inventory to the actual hardware and from selected hardware to the inventory. This procedure should take no more than one hour, including the preparation of the workpapers.

Task 8: Prepare a Summarization Memo. The IT auditor should prepare a memo summarizing the work performed in the IT administration area, all potential findings, and any other information deemed important. This task should take between one and two hours, depending on the extent and nature of the included items.

Physical Security

The review of physical security has five tasks and should take a minimum of two hours to complete.

Task 1: Review Security and Control Questionnaire. The IT auditor should make a copy of the physical security portion of the security and control questionnaire so that the original completed questionnaire can be kept whole in the carry-forward working papers. The auditor should evaluate the questionnaire responses and document any items that required additional investigation or follow-up. The estimated time is two to four hours to complete this procedure. The midrange environment should include many of the controls covered in the questionnaire.

Task 2: Test to Ensure that All Security Features Are Operational. The IT auditor should test the procedures identified in task 1 to ensure that all of the appropriate security features are in place and functioning. This procedure should take between one and two hours to complete, depending on the extent of the testing required.

Task 3 - Review Physical Security Layout of Data Center. The IT auditor should obtain a layout diagram of the data center, review it for completeness and accuracy, and ensure that it identifies all key security features. This task should take less than one hour.

Task 4: Determine Any Additional Audit Procedures. The IT auditor should consider the need for additional procedures based on his or her judgment, observations made during fieldwork, and results of the other audit procedures performed. The time required for this task cannot be estimated until the auditor reviews the actual findings.

Task 5: Prepare a Summarization Memo. The IT auditor should prepare a memo summarizing the work performed in the physical security area, including any potential findings and any other information deemed important. This task should take between one and two hours, depending on the extent and nature of the included items.

Logical Security

The review of logical security has eight tasks and should take a minimum of four hours to complete.

Task 1: Review Security and Control Questionnaire. The IT auditor should make a copy of the IT administration portion of the security and control questionnaire so that the original completed questionnaire can be kept whole in the carry-forward working papers. The auditor should evaluate the questionnaire responses and document any items that require additional investigation or follow-up. The estimated time is one hour to complete this task. The midrange environment should include many of the controls covered in the questionnaire.

Task 2: Audit the List of Logical Security Values Obtained from the System and Security Software. The IT auditor should, if possible, obtain the list of the logical security values from the system and security software and trace the values from the questionnaire to the list. Any differences should be noted and followed up to determine what the correct value should be and why the difference between the document and the list exists. This task should take no longer than one hour.

Task 3: Identify All Standard Security Profiles Supplied with the System and Security Package. The IT auditor should determine if there are any standard security profiles supplied with the system and security package. There is a risk that, if these are not reset, anyone familiar with the system will be able to use one of these standard profiles to access the system and potentially perform unauthorized activities. The auditor should attempt to log onto the system using the standard profiles to ensure that the profiles were reset. This task should take no longer than one hour to complete.

Task 4: Test Password Controls. The IT auditor should also test other password controls to the extent possible to evaluate their functioning. The results of these tests should be documented in the working papers. This testing can normally be completed while sitting at a terminal and should take no longer than one hour.

Task 5: Identify and Document Access Privileges. The IT auditor should ascertain the details of how persons within the enterprise are granted access to the system. That process should be documented if that information is not already documented. The process of granting access should then be tested by selecting a judgmental sample of users from the system and a similar sample of users from the files, and by confirming that the documents authorizing their access are present and properly completed. The estimated time for this task is one to two hours.

Task 6: Test User Profiles. The IT auditor should select a cross-sample of user profiles on the system and review them for consistency in the way that they are set up and authorized to use the system; any special capabilities given; and exceptions to established password management rules. The results of this review should be documented in the working papers. The estimated time for this task is approximately two hours for each 10 users selected for testing.

Task 7: Determine Any Additional Audit Procedures. The IT auditor should consider the need for additional procedures based on his or her judgment, observations made during fieldwork, and results of the other audit procedures performed. The time required for this task cannot be estimated until the auditor reviews the actual audit results.

Task 8: Prepare a Summarization Memo. The IT auditor should prepare a memo summarizing the work performed in the logical security area, including any potential findings and any other information deemed important. This task should take less than two hours, depending on the extent and nature of the included items.

Change Management

The review of change management has five tasks and should take a minimum of four hours to complete.

Task 1: Review Security and Control Questionnaire. The IT auditor should make a copy of the change management and systems development portion of the security and control questionnaire so that the original completed questionnaire can be kept whole in the carry-forward working papers. The auditor should evaluate the questionnaire responses and document any items that required additional investigation or follow-up. The estimated time is less than two hours to complete this task. The midrange environment is not likely to include most of the controls covered in the questionnaire.

Task 2: Test to Ensure that All Change Control Features Are Operational. The IT auditor should test the procedures identified in task 1 to ensure that all of the appropriate control features are in place and functioning. This procedure should take between two and eight hours to complete, depending on the extent of the testing required.

Task 3: Test the Change Control Management Process. The IT auditor must determine the extent of testing that is desirable for the current audit, which is most likely based on the need to reach a conclusion on the reliability of the change management process. Once the extent of testing is determined, the auditor should perform the tests that address reviewing the changed code, evaluating the authorization process, and verifying the testing and documentation that was done. The time to complete this process is contingent on the plan for testing and can vary between 4 and 20 hours.

Task 4: Review and Evaluate the Questionnaire Responses. The IT auditor should, before preparing the conclusion memo for this area, review the control questionnaire responses to determine if any of them have not been reviewed or tested in any way. Any items identified during this task should either be further evaluated or noted in the working papers to indicate why no evaluation was needed. The time to complete this task should be less than two hours.

Task 5: Prepare a Summarization Memo. The IT auditor should prepare a memo summarizing the work performed in the control change management area, including any potential findings and any other information deemed important. This task should take less than one hour, depending on the extent and nature of the included items.

Backup, Recovery, and Contingency Planning

The review of backup, recovery, and contingency planning has five tasks should take between 2 and 12 hours to complete.

Task 1: Review Security and Control Questionnaire. The IT auditor should make a copy of this portion of the security and control questionnaire so that the original completed questionnaire can be kept whole in the carry-forward working papers. The auditor should evaluate the questionnaire responses and document any items that require additional investigation or follow-up. The estimated time is three hours to complete this task. The midrange environment should include most of the controls covered in the questionnaire.

Task 2: Identity, Test, and Document Backup Procedures. The IT auditor should identify the strategy for making periodic backups as it relates to the business conducted by the locations served by the installation. The results should be documented. In the midrange environment, this task should take between one and two hours, and the testing of the information obtained should require no more than an additional eight hours.

Task 3: Obtain and Evaluate the Corporate Business Continuity Plan. The IT auditor should obtain and evaluate the business continuity plan for the data center under review and for the business location by using the audit program illustrated in Workpaper 11-1. If a plan is in place, even if the plan only covers the recovery of the data center, the estimated time to complete this task is between 4 and 20 hours. A comprehensive business plan could add 30 hours to the review. As with other control areas, the final time required for this task is dependent on the level of testing desired and the results of those testing procedures.

Task 4: Review Questionnaire Responses. The IT auditor should, before preparing the conclusion memo for this area, review the questionnaire responses to determine if any of them have not been reviewed or tested in any way. Any items identified during this task should either be evaluated or noted in the working papers to indicate why no further evaluation was needed. The time to complete this task should be less than two hours for the midrange environment.

Task 5: Prepare a Summarization Memo. The IT auditor should prepare a memo summarizing the work performed in the backup, recovery, and contingency planning area, including potential findings and any other information deemed important. This task should take less than one hour, depending on the extent and nature of the included items.

AUDIT FINALIZATION

The IT auditor should review the workpapers for clarity and completeness. This task should not take more than two hours. The auditor should have the workpapers reviewed by a manager and clear all manager's review notes. The time will vary between 2 and 20 hours, based on the review notes received.

The auditor should perform the following tasks to issue the final report:

1. Prepare a draft report.
2. Have the draft reviewed, clearing all questions and comments.
3. Mail the draft to the auditee for review and response development.
4. If the responses are not received as scheduled, contact the auditee by telephone to determine when the responses can be expected.
5. Evaluate the responses for adequacy; add them to the draft report; and review them with Internal Audit management as needed.
6. Based on the preceding tasks, prepare a final report.

The auditor should complete the audit program and any other remaining pieces of the audit and submit the final workpapers for filing and appropriate retention.

Workpaper 13-1. Midrange Questionnaire (AS/400)

GENERIC DOMESTIC COMPANY

IT Internal Control Questionnaire

(AS/400 Version)

SEGMENT _____

DIVISION _____

CITY/STATE _____

PREPARED BY   DATE

_____   _____

_____   _____

_____   _____

_____   _____

INTRODUCTION

This questionnaire was developed to gather the basic data required to evaluate information systems internal controls. We appreciate your timely completion of this questionnaire. The time spent completing it will greatly reduce our insight time interviewing people and documenting this information.

ASSUMPTIONS

1. A "No" or "NA" does not automatically identify a problem.
2. The "comments" sections provided at the end of a question, or group of questions, can be used for comments, explanations, or even questions to be followed up when we are on site.
3. **This is not a policy document.** You should not interpret the questions as requiring compliance, unless the question references established policies within Generic Domestic Company.

INSTRUCTIONS

This document is divided into several sections, each containing three types of questions. There are questions requiring a specific response, which have a space for the data. Other questions require a response of "Yes," "No," or "NA," and have a response block and space for your comments, explanations, or questions. There are also tables that should be self-explanatory. This document is set up in table format. All responses can be included in the document itself (with the exception of requested attachments).

GENERAL INFORMATION ITEMS

Please attach documents covering the following topics and check the items that are attached.

_____ Computer and peripheral hardware listing

_____ Purchased and written software listing

_____ Organization chart and position descriptions

_____ Data center and department floor plan

_____ Network diagram

TABLE OF CONTENTS

A. INFORMATION SYSTEMS ADMINISTRATION

Organization

1. Personnel   (If Part Time)

		Number	Hours/Week
a.	Managers		
b.	Technical Support Programmers		
c.	Systems Analysts		
d.	Analyst/Programmers		
e.	Programmers		
f.	Computer Operators		
g.	Other		

Annual Budget or Estimated/Actual Expenditures

2. Hardware (CPU, printers, etc.)   Budget or Actual Dollars

    a. Lease/Rental Expense
    b. Maintenance Fee/Charges
    c. Depreciation
    d. Other
3. Software (packages, support programs)
    a. License, Rent, Maintenance Fees
    b. Amortization of Purchased Package
    c. Other
4. Personnel (hourly/salary wages)
5. Supplies (paper, ribbons, etc.)
6. Total Budget or Approximate Expense for Information Systems Department

Computer Hardware

7.	Item	Quantity	Model	Size
	a. Processors			
	b. Disk Units			
	c. Tape Units			
	d. Printers			
	e. Other			

8.	Item	Install Date	Acquisition
	a. Processors		Buy or Lease
	b. Disk Units		Buy or Lease
	c. Tape Units		Buy or Lease
	d. Printers		Buy or Lease
	e. Other		Buy or Lease

A. INFORMATION SYSTEMS ADMINISTRATION (CONT'D)

Computer Software

	Purchase Price	Vendor Maintenance Cost/Year
9. System Support Software		
a. Operating System(s)		
b. Telecommunications Access System		
c. Database System(s)		
d. Decision Support System(s)		
e. Office System(s)		
f. System Development Aid(s)		
g. System Security Software		
h. Utilities		
i. Other		

Application Software

	Purchase Price	Vendor Maintenance Cost/Year
10. Application		

_____

_____

_____

_____

_____

_____

_____

11. Planned Use of Staff		Staff Days
a. New Systems Development and Training		
b. Maintain/Support Existing Systems		
12. Computer Operations Schedule	Days/Week	Hours/Day
a. Computer is operational		
b. Computer support is staffed		

13. **IT Planning**

Y/N   a. Do you have a written short- or long-range plan for information technology activities?

Y/N   b. Is there a management steering committee that oversees information technology projects and priorities?
If so, how often does the committee meet?

Y/N   c. Is there an annual plan for scheduled application projects? Please attach a copy.

COMMENTS

A.   INFORMATION SYSTEMS ADMINISTRATION (CONT'D)

Y/N   14. Is departmental charge-back (or other allocation of information technology costs) used?
What is the basis for the charges?

Y/N   Is there a separate calculation for production usage versus development charges?

COMMENTS

Y/N   15. Do you have a written standards manual, or other document, that describes the normal practices for departmental employees to follow?
Please attach a copy (if small) or the table of contents.

COMMENTS

16. **Personnel Issues**

Y/N   a.   Investigations have shown that the risk of loss is as great in the area of swindle and sabotage as it is for fire and water damage. In light of these facts, is the background of those who will be employed in sensitive positions carefully checked?

Y/N   b.   Is continuing education a requirement for information systems personnel?
What is the annual minimum hours of training?
Is training information recorded anywhere?

Y/N   c.   Is the IT staff cross-trained and expected to cover other functions in the department?

Y/N   d.   Have all employees taken at least five days of vacation in the past year?

COMMENTS

17. Are the following functions segregated from each other within the IT department? (Note that this may not be practical at smaller installations.)

Y/N   a.   Systems analysis and design?

Y/N   b.   Programming?

Y/N   c.   Physical library of tapes and disks?

Y/N   d.   Operating the computer?

COMMENTS

A. INFORMATION SYSTEMS ADMINISTRATION (CONT'D)

Y/N18.Are any outside consultants or time-sharing services in use? If yes, please identify those in use, and provide an estimate of the total payments made to them in the past year.

COMMENTS

Y/N 19. Is there a practice of conducting post-implementation reviews for significant projects?
Please describe the process (comments section), what deliverables it has, and what happens to the information. Also, provide an example report from such a review.

COMMENTS

B. PHYSICAL SECURITY

Data center Access

1. How many entrances/exits are there?
Y/N 2. Do all doors have locks?
Y/N 3. Are the doors locked at all times the room is unattended?
4. What types of locks are used?
a. How often are they changed?
Y/N b. Are they changed automatically when someone leaves?
Y/N 5. Is the data center a separate fire zone (e.g., floor to ceiling walls, etc.)?
Y/N 6. Does security patrol the IT area?

COMMENTS

Data Center Room Sensor/Alarm System

Please indicate which of the following are in place and functioning.

Y/N 7. Smoke detectors
Y/N 8. Heat sensors
Y/N 9. Particle sensors
Y/N 10. Water detectors
Y/N a. Is water damage a risk in the data center?
Y/N b. Is there a raised floor?
If yes, how high is the floor from the subfloor?

A.   INFORMATION SYSTEMS ADMINISTRATION (CONT'D)

Y/N   c. Are under-floor sprinklers needed?

Y/N   Installed?

Y/N   d. Does the data center have a drainage system?

Y/N   Is there any risk of flooding due to water rising out of the drainage system?

Y/N   Are automatic shut-off valves used?

Y/N   11. Are any or all of these sensors connected to the guard or other outside monitoring systems such that the triggering of any of these devices will require timely investigation?

Y/N   12. Are any or all of these systems tested regularly?

Y/N   How often is testing performed?

Y/N   Who does the testing?

Y/N   Are the results of the testing recorded?

COMMENTS

Fire Suppression Systems—Please note which of the following you have.

Y/N   13. Halon system

Y/N   Is there a prevent discharge button?

Y/N   Are there posted instructions by the prevent discharge button to ensure it is used properly?

Y/N   14. CO_2 system

Y/N   15. Sprinkler system

Wet   Is it a wet or dry pipe system?

Dry

       16. If you have a Halon system, is there a plan to replace it with a non-CFC chemical?

COMMENTS

Electrical Considerations

Y/N   17. Do you have an uninterruptible power source (UPS)?

       How many minutes of backup does it provide?

       What items are protected?

Y/N   Are the UPS and CPU logically linked to manage the power outage?

Y/N   18. Is the room air conditioned?

Y/N   Is it on a separate system or systems?

Y/N   Are air ducts closed automatically?

COMMENTS

A. INFORMATION SYSTEMS ADMINISTRATION (CONT'D)

Y/N 19. Is there an emergency power cutoff switch for the room?
Where is it located?

Y/N   Is it protected from accidental contact?

COMMENTS

Y/N 20. Is the data center on a dedicated circuit breaker?

Y/N   Is the breaker protected from accidental shut-off?

Y/N 21. Is there battery powered lighting in place?

COMMENTS

System Console Keyswitch

22. What position is the console keyswitch in? _____
(This switch has four settings—secure, auto, normal, and manual. The secure position permits the system to be powered down but does not permit the system to be restarted unless the key is inserted and the keyswitch is turned into one of the other positions. The auto position permits an automatic system restart based on established parameters. The normal position also allows a certain amount of intervention in the IPL, but does not permit the system values to be changed. The manual position permits manual intervention, changes to system values, or the use of IBM's Dedicated Service Tools—all of which present a significant risk to the established security and control settings. You may refer to IBM *publication "Security Concepts and Planning" for more information.)*

Y/N 23. Is the key removed from the key lock to avoid unauthorized changes to the key lock switch?

COMMENTS

Other Physical Security Considerations

Y/N 24. Is smoking permitted in the data center?

Y/N 25. Is trash removed promptly so that the risk of fire and accidents is minimized?

26. Who cleans the data center?

Y/N   If an outside cleaning service is used, are the employees supervised?

A. INFORMATION SYSTEMS ADMINISTRATION (CONT'D)

Y/N 27. Are cables and electrical wires either under a raised floor or covered to prevent accidents?

COMMENTS

C. LOGICAL SECURITY

1. **Security Master Officer** (QSECOFR)

Y/N a. Has one individual (and possibly an alternate) been designated as the master security officer? (The system provides a userid upon delivery that is defined as the security officer (QSECOFR). Additional security officers can be defined by assigning a user to the user class QSECOFR. The system also provides the ability to establish a person as a security administrator (user class *SECADM), rather than a security officer, with less capability than the security officer.)

Y/N b. Is a copy of the master security password written down and locked in a secure location?

COMMENTS

2. What security level has been set for the system? (QSECURITY) *(This variable can be 10, 20, 30, or 40. At setting 10, no password verification is performed, and user profiles are created as the user logs on to the system. At level 20, password verification is performed, but users still have access to every resource on the system. Level 30 enables resource security. Level 40 will cause failures if certain instructions are attempted that could compromise system integrity. Level 40 is recommended only after successful operation at level 30, since level 40 will cause failures that are only logged at level 30.)*

3. Have procedures and approvals been defined to authorize users to access the system?

Y/N *[These procedures could encompass new hires (adding a profile), job changes (linking a user profile to a different group profile), and separations (changing the user password to *NONE upon separation and removal of the user profile after any objects owned by the user are transferred to another user.)]*

COMMENTS

A. INFORMATION SYSTEMS ADMINISTRATION (CONT'D)

4. User Profile Management

Y/N   a. Is each user assigned a unique profile?

Y/N   b. Is a new user required to change his/her password at first sign-on? (QPWDEXP)

Y/N   c. Do all users change their passwords regularly? (QPWDEXPITV) What is the maximum number of days between password changes?

Y/N   d. Are end users of the system confined to menus?

Y/N   e. Is there a limit on unsuccessful access attempts (QMAXSIGN)? What is the limit? (Note that in OS/400 Release 2, it is possible to suspend the user profile after a predetermined number of invalid sign-on attempts.)

Y/N   f. Are terminal users notified of their last sign-on and the number of invalid sign-on attempts each time they access the system? (QDSPSGNINF)

COMMENTS

Y/N   5. Are inactive user profiles (i.e., no sign-ons for XXX days) automatically revoked? After how many days?

COMMENTS

Y/N   6. Are terminal users limited to one terminal at a time? (QLMTDEVSSN) Restricting users to one terminal session per userid may reduce the sharing of user accounts. *System variable QLMTDEVSSN = 1 will restrict users to one session. The default is 0, unlimited. If it is necessary to have a limited number of users that can sign on to multiple sessions, this can be specified in the user profiles for those users, rather than allowing all users to have multiple sessions.*

COMMENTS

Y/N   7. Have all user profiles been appropriately assigned to a class: Security Officer (*SECOFR); Security Administrator (*SECADM); Programmer (*PGMR); System Operator (*SYSOPR); or End User (*USER)?

     8. Password Syntax—Are the following being used?

Y/N   a. Password minimum length (QPWDMINLEN) What length is specified? ___

A.   INFORMATION SYSTEMS ADMINISTRATION (CONT'D)

Y/N   b. Restricted characters (QPWDLMTCHR)
        This can be useful in preventing common words or names by
        restricting use of vowels. Up to ten characters.

Y/N   c. Consecutive digits (QPWDLMTAGC)
        This can be used to prevent use of phone numbers, birthdays, etc.

Y/N   d. Repeated characters (QPWDLMTREP)
        This can prevent the use of passwords like MMM, 0000, etc.

Y/N   e. Required digits (QPWDRQDDGT)
        This is also directed at preventing the use of common words or
        names by requiring that at least one digit is required some-
        where in the password.

Y/N   f. Password reuse (QPWDRQDDIF)
        This feature will cause the system to record the last 32 pass-
        words used by each user, and prevent any of those 32 from
        being used again.

COMMENTS

Y/N 9. Are terminal users automatically signed off after a specified period
        of inactivity? (QINACTITV)
        What is the time interval?
        *System variable QINACTITV can be set from 5 to 300 minutes. It
        should be set to a reasonable level. Default is *NONE, no time out
        limit. In addition, the system variable QINACTMSGQ should be set to
        *ENDJOB. This will end inactive jobs as opposed to simply sending a
        message to the specified queue. Care should be taken in implement-
        ing this technique as it may terminate lengthy interactive jobs.*

COMMENTS

Audit Journals

10. Has the security audit function been activated?
    *This feature provides for logging of the following events in the secu-
    rity auditing journal: programs that use restricted instructions; all
    programs that access objects using unsupported interfaces; save and
    restore information; authorization failures; deleted objects; and secu-
    rity related functions. It is very easily enabled by setting system vari
    able QAUDLVL. Default is *NONE. (Reference AS/400 Security Con-
    cepts and Planning)   These security auditing records are assigned a*

A. INFORMATION SYSTEMS ADMINISTRATION (CONT'D)

two-character entry type identifying the nature of the event that was logged. Thus, query software can produce reports by type.

a. How long are the history logs and security auditing journal retained?

b. Are reports produced analyzing the security auditing journal?

Y/N   c. Does the security officer review the history log or the auditing journal on a regular basis for attempted sign-on violations and object access violations?

History log messages in the CPF2200 range indicate authorization failures. The security auditing journal (QAUDJRN), if option *AUTFAIL is elected, includes messages with type AF (authority failure) and PW (user ID and password errors).

COMMENTS

Y/N   11. Have the dedicated service tools (DST) passwords been modified since system installation?

Dedicated Service Tools (DST) is a group of service functions used to service the system when the operating system is not running. If these passwords are not changed, it may be possible to gain access to DST. Under DST, the security officer password can be reset to the default; therefore, it is desirable to limit the people who are capable of running DST by changing the DST passwords. DST can be brought up only with the keyswitch in the manual position, during an attended IPL.

COMMENTS

Y/N   12. Has the "operating system install security" been changed to a secure level?

Establishing this security prevents a user with basic authority for DST from installing the operating system. See Chapter 8 of *AS/400 Programming: Security Concepts and Planning.*

COMMENTS

Y/N   13. Do users signing on from a remote system go through the normal sign-on procedure? (QRMTSIGN)

COMMENTS

A. INFORMATION SYSTEMS ADMINISTRATION (CONT'D)

14. Are the following special authorities within the system restricted to appropriate personnel?

Y/N   a. All object (*ALLOBJ)

Y/N   b. Security Administrator (*SECADM): allows administration of user profiles

Y/N   c. Save System (*SAVSYS): allows a user to do save and restore operations for all resources on the system

Y/N   d. Job Control (*JOBCTL): allows manipulation of work queues

Y/N   e. Spool Control (*SPLCTL): allows control of spool functions

Y/N   f. Service (*SERVICE): allows the user to perform service functions such as storage display, alter, and dump; *SERVICE should be assigned very restrictively

      IBM publication AS/400 Security and Auditing Considerations contains a grid of special authorities that are automatically granted to each user class (if QSECURITY is set to 30). Accordingly, classification of terminal users according to this suggested grid can automatically confine these special authorities to logical groups of people. Also note that special authorities can be granted at the user profile level, implying that a user may have authorities beyond that of those implied by the user class.

COMMENTS

Y/N   15. Are objects used in a production mode required to include an object description?

COMMENTS

Y/N   16. Do naming conventions prohibit the naming of an object that begins with the letter Q?

      IBM supplied programs use the letter Q as a first character. A number of those properly are specified as adopting the authority of the security officer when they execute. If the shop prohibits creation of objects beginning with the letter Q, local programs that adopt security authority can be easily controlled.

COMMENTS

17. **Group Profile Considerations**

Y/N   a. Do naming conventions clearly distinguish between group and individual profiles?

A.   INFORMATION SYSTEMS ADMINISTRATION (CONT'D)

Y/N   b. Are users prohibited from signing on using a group profile?

COMMENTS

18. Adopt Authority and Public Authority

Y/N   a. Are all programs that adopt *ALLOBJ or *SERVICE authority reviewed by a security officer?

Y/N   b. Are programs that adopt the authority of a powerful user restricted to authorized personnel?

Y/N   c. Is public authority for source and object programs set to *EXCLUDE?

COMMENTS

19. Job Descriptions

Y/N   a. Are job descriptions with a public authority specified as USER(*RQD)?

Y/N   b. Do job descriptions that specify a user profile name have public authority *EXCLUDE?

COMMENTS

Y/N 20. Are encryption techniques in use?

COMMENTS—Please describe what they are being used for and why.

Y/N 21. Dial-up communication, if in use, should be controlled. Has this been done for your location?
Dial back, dynamic passwords, and encryption are three possible ways to do this.

COMMENTS

Y/N 22. Are there procedures ensuring that separated/terminated personnel are immediately removed from the system?

COMMENTS

A. **INFORMATION SYSTEMS ADMINISTRATION (CONT'D)**

D. **CHANGE MANAGEMENT**

1. **Project Request Procedures**

Y/N   a. Is there a standard form used to request additions and/or changes to systems?
Please attach one blank and one completed form.

Y/N   b. Are there procedures for using the standard form?
Please attach a copy or describe the procedures.

COMMENTS

Y/N 2. Is there evidence of authorization for program modifications?

Y/N   Does the evidence include a project request or other identification method?

COMMENTS

Y/N 3. Are changes to production source and executable programs monitored via reporting that is reviewed by a responsible person (with review evidenced by signature or initials)?

COMMENTS

Y/N 4. Are programmers limited to *USE (read-only) authority for source programs?

COMMENTS

5. **Library Management**

Y/N   a. Are sensitive libraries restricted to appropriate users?

Y/N   b. Are separate libraries being maintained for program development, testing, and production?

Y/N   c. Are source programs recompiled after being transferred into production?

Y/N   d. Are the application source, object, and data files stored in physically separate libraries?

Y/N   e. Are program owners and data owners separate group profiles? This approach can help to separate users and programmers from an access standpoint—users are kept out of software libraries and programmers are kept out of data libraries.

COMMENTS

A. INFORMATION SYSTEMS ADMINISTRATION (CONT'D)

Y/N 6. Is a log or standard form kept for all changes to the production environment?
Attach an example of a completed log sheet or form and describe any means to determine the actual detail changes to the program code.

COMMENTS

Y/N 7. Are there any programs for which the source code is not available? Please identify them below and comment on how they are maintained.

COMMENTS

Y/N 8. Are you current on all software releases?

COMMENTS

9. If application software is leased or purchased and vendor support is utilized:

Y/N a. Is there sufficient documentation of in-house changes to the software?

Y/N b. Is there a procedure for applying updates to the system?

COMMENTS

E. BACKUP, RECOVERY AND CONTINGENCY PLANNING

1. Please complete the following table concerning the backups you make.

Type of Backup	Frequency (daily, weekly, etc.)	Number of Generations Stored On-Site	Number of Generations Stored Off-Site
SAVSYS			
SAVLIB (*NONSYS)			
SAVLIB (*ALLUSR)			
SAVLIB (*IBM)			
SAVOBJ			
SAVCHGOBJ			
Other:			

A. INFORMATION SYSTEMS ADMINISTRATION (CONT'D)

Y/N 2.Are backup commands fully coded and compiled as control language programs, as opposed to being typed in at the system console when required?
Please provide a sample of backup instructions/commands, if they exist.

COMMENTS

Y/N 3. Are tapes and diskettes written on the AS/400 subject to controlled physical access?
IBM literature indicates that AS/400 produced magnetic media can be read on IBM equipment that has different architecture—implying that AS/400 produced media could be read on an IBM mainframe and potentially circumvent AS/400 security.

COMMENTS

Y/N 4. Do you have any applications that include a communications component? (Examples would include purchasing that had an EDI component and shop floor data collection utilizing store and forward logic.)
Identify fall-back alternatives and applications that incorporate communications in comments below.

COMMENTS

Y/N 5. Do you have a disaster recovery plan?
Does it address the following:
Y/N   a. Identification of vital records?
Y/N   b. Assignment of specific responsibilities during an emergency?
Y/N   c. Establishing an off-site agreement?
Y/N   d. Determining how long it will take to replace damaged equipment?
Y/N   e. Ranking jobs/systems in terms of criticality?
Y/N   f. Determining what processing power will be needed to support critical activities?
Y/N   g. Are involved employees familiar with emergency procedures?
Y/N   h. Do involved employees have a copy of the procedures, or their section, at an off-site location?
Y/N   i. How often is the plan updated?

COMMENTS

A. **INFORMATION SYSTEMS ADMINISTRATION (CONT'D)**

Y/N 6. Is a copy of the current systems/operations documentation kept either off-site or in a fireproof place?
Where is it kept?

COMMENTS

Y/N 7. Is the MULIC (Model Unique Licensed Install Code) tape on the same media as your system backup?

F. **OPERATIONS**

1. **Sensitive Information**
Y/N a. Are procedures in place to ensure that surplus output material is destroyed, and that sensitive information will be shredded or destroyed in some other manner which ensures security?
Y/N b. Is sensitive or confidential information secured before distribution?

COMMENTS

Y/N 2. Is anything done to monitor system utilization?
If so, describe what is done, how the data is used, and attach an example of one of the reports.

COMMENTS

Y/N 3. Do you keep a log book of problems?
Such a book would normally include the time when it was discovered and reported, what and where it happened, and when and how the situation was resolved.

COMMENTS

Y/N 4. Is the ability to perform backup and restore operations restricted to appropriate individuals?
(This can be achieved by restricting access to tape commands or to the tape drive itself.)

COMMENTS

A. INFORMATION SYSTEMS ADMINISTRATION (CONT'D)

5. Journaling

Y/N   a. Is journaling activated for key application files?

Y/N   b. Are the journaling commands restricted to appropriate parties?

Y/N   c. Are there compiled CL programs to process journals when a roll-forward is necessary?

Y/N   d. Have roll-forward capabilities, where needed, been tested?

Y/N   e. Are journals and data files physically resident on separate disks?

       Without specific action, the operating system may spread database and journal fragments to multiple disks, resulting in journals and the databases sharing a physical drive. This problem can be avoided using a technique called Auxiliary Storage Pools (ASPs). If journaling is used only to support commitment control, and roll-forward operations are not intended, this is not relevant.

COMMENTS

Y/N 6. Is commitment control activated for transactions having multiple updates to one or more master files?

       Commitment control allows the defining and processing of a number of changes to database files as a single "transaction group." This frequently occurs in a manufacturing database where item master records, manufacturing order records, and job requirements records can all be updated as a result of pressing the enter button once. Use of this technique will ensure that all changes within a "transaction group" are completed for all files affected. Under commitment control, if processing is interrupted before the "transaction group" is completed, any changes made to the database will be backed out.

COMMENTS

7. Physical Tape Management

Y/N   a. Are expiration dates specified for tapes?

Y/N   b. Are tapes checked electronically for the existence of unexpired files prior to reformatting?

Y/N   c. Are tapes periodically checked for wear?

Y/N   d. Are tapes periodically checked for errors?

Y/N   e. Are file inventories taken periodically to determine obsolete files?

COMMENTS

Section 14
Auditing the Network

The personal computer, originally know as the microcomputer, was the third generation of business computers. The original computers were driven by commands, and appeared to be operated just as the system operators ran the networks. The difference was that where the network could simultaneously support thousands of users, the microcomputer's resources were completely dedicated to one user, and for years only one application at a time.

Microcomputers only supported business needs in the beginning by doubling as a network or minicomputer terminal. Later, new technologies were developed that permitted microcomputers to be linked together, with the idea that their combined capabilities could offer an alternative to midrange computers, although they were not considered alternatives to networks until more recently.

A significant change from the midrange and network environment is that no effective security functionality has been available for the microcomputer because it continues to be designed to support the individual user, and the security of having a single power-up password was deemed to be sufficient for most cases. Network software providing the connectivity between microcomputers adds certain security functionality, helping to make the network an acceptable business tool.

The IT auditor has a less technical challenge when auditing the local area network and network software, although the development of alternatives for effective control mechanisms requires creativity and a complete understanding of compensating and mitigating controls in the end-user areas.

Change management becomes an even more critical control problem in a local area network setting. These environments are likely to have very small staffs, with an almost nonexistent segregation of duties, which can only be compensated for with proper end-user procedures.

The audit process follows the same three steps that were followed in both the network and midrange environments: planning, fieldwork, and finalization.

PLANNING THE AUDIT

The IT auditor should always begin with planning and should be careful to put the proper effort into planning every audit, even if the auditor has performed the same basic review many times in the past. Every audit may be different, and failing to allocate to each audit assignment the appropriate amount of planning time can lead to unreliable audit results.

Contacting the Auditee

The IT auditor should make initial contact with the auditee by phone if possible, because it is less formal than sending a letter or even a note by electronic mail. Once the audit timing or scope is committed to paper, even as a draft, it can create subsequent problems for the IT auditor. The auditor should begin by communicating the areas to be reviewed, which can include all or a portion of the following:

- IT administration
- Physical security
- Logical security
- Operations
- Backup and recovery
- Systems development

The auditor should contact the head of the IT department initially, unless it has previously been agreed to that contact at a lower level is more appropriate. In the latter instance, it is appropriate to copy the head IT person once the scope and schedule of the audit have been determined. The network environment is likely to require 3 to 10 days of effort, to a maximum that is only limited by the auditor's decision to discontinue detailed testing.

The network environment is not likely to have more than a single manager, so little time should be lost to coordination. The IT auditor should send a letter confirming the planning details. This letter should be made available to the field auditors at least two weeks in advance of fieldwork so that any questions or comments can be communicated, researched, and resolved before starting fieldwork.

Preliminary Office Planning Before Fieldwork

The auditor should complete the following procedures while still in the office before initiating fieldwork procedures:

- Prepare an audit planning memo, including these elements.
  —Location background
  —Prior audit scope and results
  —Detailed list of prior recommendations
  —Current planned scope and timing
  —Planned staffing
  —Time budgets

- Define the specific audit program based on the standard program, the intended objectives based on the audit department's planning and selection of the audit, and the planning conversations held with location personnel.
- Send out the Information Technology Internal Control Questionnaire (Workpaper III-14-1), specifying a date for its completion that will permit time for it to be returned and reviewed before fieldwork. (If there is a questionnaire from a previous audit, and if it is not materially different from the questionnaire currently in use, copy it and have the location personnel update the previous form.)
- Obtain prior audit reports related to this location and place a copy in the workpapers.
- Review past audit files for permanent and carry-forward information, and incorporate any previous findings into the current workpapers.
- Set up any necessary files on the personal computer or laptop that will facilitate the performance of fieldwork.

PERFORMING FIELDWORK PROCEDURES

Fieldwork will almost always be done at one time. The IT auditor must take the time to ensure that there is a workable schedule and that all involved parties are aware of it, particularly with the limited available time. The general items that should be completed in the field that do not relate to any of the specific areas are:

- Conduct an entrance conference and document the results of that meeting.
- Prepare a list of all issues from the prior audit and determine the current status of those items by contacting the appropriate personnel, performing detailed procedures if necessary. Document the current status of those items in the workpapers. The auditor's effort to complete this step is not related to the environment as much as it is to the nature and extent of prior audit recommendations.
- Take a plant tour, noting any unusual items or observations. This gives the IT auditor an opportunity to become acquainted with the business and to gain some indirect information about how that particular business or location is operating, which may be useful when the auditor is evaluating potential recommendations and their cost/benefit considerations. The tour, observations, and other items that the auditor deems important should be documented in the workpapers.

AUDITING SPECIFIC PROCEDURES BY AUDIT AREA

The IT auditor should be ready to begin specific detailed audit procedures once the planning and the general office procedures have been covered.

The audit tasks are discussed in the subsequent sections, followed by the estimated time to complete and additional comments if necessary.

IT Administration

The IT administration has eight tasks and should take between two and four hours to complete, exclusive of testing.

Task 1: Review Security and Control Questionnaire. The IT auditor should make a copy of the IT administration portion of the security and control questionnaire so that the original completed questionnaire can be kept whole in the carry-forward workpapers. The auditor should evaluate the questionnaire responses and document any items that required additional investigation or follow-up. The estimated time is one hour to complete this procedure. The network audit may be the least predictable in terms of which controls are possible, making general estimates of the potential effort equally unpredictable.

Task 2: Review the Organization Chart. The IT auditor should obtain a copy of the top-level organization chart and review the placement of IT in the organization in terms of its overall effectiveness. The estimated time to complete this task is 15 minutes.

Task 3: Evaluate the Long-Range IT Plan. The IT auditor should obtain the long-range IT plan and evaluate it in terms of supporting business objectives, its consistency with the business plan, the likelihood of meeting management's objectives, and its being properly developed in terms of scope, detail, quantitative analysis, and responsibility. The time estimate to complete this review is less than one hour.

Task 4: Audit Expense and Budget Statements. The IT auditor should obtain and review appropriate expense and budget statements, paying particular attention to significant fluctuations between periods or any unusual items. The time estimated to complete this area is less than two hours.

Task 5: Examine Job Descriptions. The IT auditor should obtain and evaluate the IT department's job descriptions based on the business structure and observed regular responsibilities. The time estimate for this is one hour or less.

Task 6: Review and Evaluate the IT Standards Manual. The IT auditor should obtain and evaluate the IT standards manual in terms of scope, timeliness, and general qualitative usefulness. The standards manual is less important in network environments because consistency across the staff is probably not an issue. Its importance in this setting lies in its ability to perpetuate approaches and standards. The estimated time to complete this portion of the review is less than two hours.

Task 7: Perform a Complete Inventory of All IT-Related Hardware. The IT auditor should obtain a complete inventory of all IT-related hardware used at the audited location and this inventory should be included in the permanent workpapers. This inventory should be tested based on a judgmental sample in both directions: from the inventory to the actual hardware and from selected hardware to the inventory. This procedure should take no more than one hour, including the preparation of the workpapers.

Task 8: Prepare a Summarization Memo. The IT auditor should prepare a memo summarizing the work performed in the IT Administration area, all potential findings, and any other information deemed important. This task should take less than one hour to complete, as will all of the remaining tasks, unless otherwise indicated.

Physical Security

The review of physical security has five tasks and should take less than one hour to complete.

Task 1: Review Security and Control Questionnaire. The IT auditor should make a copy of the physical security portion of the security and control questionnaire so that the original completed questionnaire can be kept whole in the carry-forward workpapers. The auditor should evaluate the questionnaire responses and document any items that required additional investigation or follow-up.

Task 2: Test to Ensure that All Security Features Are Operational. The IT auditor should test the procedures identified in task 1 to ensure that all of the appropriate security features are in place and functioning.

Task 3: Review Physical Security Layout of Data Center. The IT auditor should obtain a layout diagram of the data center, review it for completeness and accuracy, and ensure that it identifies all key security features.

Task 4: Determine any Additional Audit Procedures. The IT auditor should consider the need for additional procedures based on his or her judgment, observations made during fieldwork, and results of the other audit procedures performed. The time required for this task cannot be estimated until the auditor reviews his or her findings over the course of the fieldwork.

Task 5: Prepare a Summarization Memo. The IT auditor should prepare a memo summarizing the work performed in the physical security area,

including any potential findings and any other information deemed important.

Logical Security

The review of logical security has eight tasks.

Task 1: Review Security and Control Questionnaire. The IT auditor should
make a copy of the IT administration portion of the security and control
questionnaire so that the original completed questionnaire can be kept
whole in the carry-forward workpapers. The auditor should evaluate the
questionnaire responses and document any items that required additional
investigation or follow-up.

**Task 2: Audit the List of Logical Security Values Obtained from the System and
Security Software.** The IT auditor should, if possible, obtain the list of the
logical security values from the system and security software and trace the
values from the questionnaire to the list. Any differences should be noted
and followed up to determine what the correct value should be and why the
difference between the document and the list exists.

**Task 3: Identify All Standard Security Profiles Supplied with the System and
Security Package.** The IT auditor should determine if there are any standard
security profiles supplied with the system and security package. There is a
risk that, if these are not reset, anyone familiar with the system will be able
to use one of these standard profiles to access the system and potentially
perform unauthorized activities. The auditor should attempt to log onto the
system using the standard profiles to ensure that the profiles were reset.

Task 4: Test Password Controls. The IT auditor should also test other password controls to the extent possible to evaluate their functioning. The
results of these tests should be documented in the workpapers.

Task 5: Identify and Document Access Privileges. The IT auditor should
ascertain the details of how persons within the enterprise are granted
access to the system. That process should be documented if that information is not already documented. The process of granting access should then
be tested by selecting a judgmental sample of users from the system and a
similar sample of users from the files, and by confirming that the documents
authorizing their access are present and properly completed.

Task 6: Test User Profiles. The IT auditor should select a cross-sample of
user profiles on the system and review them for consistency in the way that
they are set up and authorized to use the system; any special capabilities

given; and exceptions to established password management rules. The results of this review should be documented in the workpapers.

Task 7: Determine Any Additional Audit Procedures. The IT auditor should consider the need for additional procedures based on his or her judgment, observations made during fieldwork, and results of the other audit procedures performed.

Task 8: Prepare a Summarization Memo. The IT auditor should prepare a memo summarizing the work performed in the logical security area, including any potential findings and any other information deemed important.

Change Management

The review of change management has five tasks.

Task 1: Review Security and Control Questionnaire. The IT auditor should make a copy of the change management and systems development portion of the security and control questionnaire so that the original completed questionnaire can be kept whole in the carry-forward workpapers. The auditor should evaluate the questionnaire responses and document any items that required additional investigation or follow up.

Task 2: Test to Ensure that All Change Control Features Are Operational. The IT auditor should test the procedures identified in task 1 to ensure that all of the appropriate control features are in place and functioning. This procedure should take between two and eight hours to complete, depending on the extent of the testing required.

Task 3: Test the Change Control Management Process. The IT auditor must determine the extent of testing that is desirable for the current audit, which is most likely based on the need to reach a conclusion on the reliability of the change management process. Once the extent of testing is determined, the auditor should perform the tests that address reviewing the changed code, evaluating the authorization process, and verifying the testing and documentation that was done.

Task 4: Review and Evaluate the Questionnaire Responses. The IT auditor should, before preparing the conclusion memo for this area, review the control questionnaire responses to determine if any of them have not been reviewed or tested in any way. Any items identified during this task should either be further evaluated or noted in the workpapers to indicate why no evaluation was needed.

Task 5: Prepare a Summarization Memo. The IT auditor should prepare a memo summarizing the work performed in the control change management area, including any potential findings and any other information deemed important

Backup, Recovery, and Contingency Planning

The review of backup, recovery, and contingency planning has five tasks.

Task 1: Review Security and Control Questionnaire. The IT auditor should make a copy of this portion of the security and control questionnaire so that the original completed questionnaire can be kept whole in the carry-forward workpapers. The auditor should evaluate the questionnaire responses and document any items that required additional investigation or follow-up.

Task 2: Identity, Test, and Document Backup Procedures. The IT auditor should identify the strategy for making periodic backups as it relates to the business conducted by the locations served by the installation. The results should be documented.

Task 3: Obtain and Evaluate the Corporate Business Continuity Plan. The IT auditor should obtain and evaluate the business continuity plan for the data center under review and for the business location by using the audit program included as Workpaper 11-1. If a plan is in place, even if the plan only covers the recovery of the data center, the estimated time to complete this task is between four and eight hours. A comprehensive business plan could add 10 to 15 hours to the review. As with other control areas, the final time required for this task is dependent on the level of testing desired and the results of those testing procedures.

Task 4: Review Questionnaire Responses. The IT auditor should, before preparing the conclusion memo for this area, review the questionnaire responses to determine if any of them have not been reviewed or tested in any way. Any items identified during this task should either be evaluated or noted in the workpapers to indicate why no further evaluation was needed.

Task 5: Prepare a Summarization Memo. The IT auditor should prepare a memo summarizing the work performed in the backup, recovery, and contingency planning area, including potential findings and any other information deemed important.

AUDIT FINALIZATION

The IT auditor should review the workpapers for clarity and completeness. The auditor should have the workpapers reviewed by a manager and clear all manager's review notes.

The auditor should perform the following tasks to issue the final report:

1. Prepare a draft report.
2. Have the draft reviewed, clearing all questions and comments.
3. Mail the draft to the auditee for review and response development.
4. If the responses are not received as scheduled, contact the auditee by telephone to determine when the responses can be expected.
5. Evaluate the responses for adequacy; add them to the draft report; and review them with Internal Audit management as needed.
6. Based on the preceding tasks, prepare a final report.

The auditor should complete the audit program and any other remaining pieces of the audit and submit the final workpapers for filing and appropriate retention.

Workpaper 14-1. Network Questionnaire (Novell)

GENERIC DOMESTIC COMPANY

Information Technology Internal Control Questionnaire

(Novell LAN Version)

SEGMENT   _____

DIVISION   _____

CITY/STATE   _____

PREPARED BY   DATE

_____   _____

_____   _____

_____   _____

_____   _____

INTRODUCTION

This questionnaire was developed to gather the basic data required to evaluate information technology internal controls. We appreciate your timely completion of this questionnaire. The time spent completing it will greatly reduce our onsite interview and documenting time.

ASSUMPTIONS

1.   A "No" or "NA" does not automatically identify a problem.
2.   The "comments" sections provided at the end of a question, or group of questions, can be used for comments, explanations, or even questions to be followed up when we are on site.
3.   **This is not a policy document.** You should not interpret the questions as requiring compliance, unless the question references established policies within Generic Domestic Company.

INSTRUCTIONS

This document is divided into several sections, each containing three types of questions. There are questions requiring a specific response, which have a space for the data. Other questions require a response of "Yes", "No", or "NA", and have a response block and space for your comments, explanations, or questions. There are also tables that should be self-explanatory. This document is set up in table format. All responses can be included in the document itself (with the exception of requested attachments).

GENERAL INFORMATION ITEMS

Please attach documents covering the following topics and check (√) the items that are attached.

_____ Computer and peripheral hardware listing

_____ Purchased and written software listing

_____ Organization chart and position descriptions

_____ Data center and department floor plan

_____ Network diagram

_____ Login Script(s), Mapping, File Server Directory Tree

TABLE OF CONTENTS

Logical security   C
Change management   D
Backup, recovery, and contingency planning   E
Operations   F

A. INFORMATION SYSTEMS ADMINISTRATION

Organization

1. <u>Personnel</u>   (If Part Time)
                                        <u>Number</u>   <u>Hours/Week</u>
   a. Managers
   b. Technical Support Programmers
   c. Systems Analysts
   d. Analyst/Programmers
   e. Programmers
   f. Computer Operators
   g. Other

Annual Budget or Estimated/Actual Expenditures

2. Hardware (CPU, printers, etc.)   <u>Budget or Actual</u>
                                                      <u>Dollars</u>
   a. Lease/Rental Expense
   b. Maintenance Fee/Charges
   c. Depreciation
   d. Other
3. Software (packages, support programs)
   a. License, Rent, Maintenance Fees
   b. Amortization of Purchased Package
   c. Other
4. Personnel (hourly/salary wages)
5. Supplies (paper, ribbons, etc.)
6. Total Budget or Approximate Expense for IT Department

Computer Hardware

7. Item   <u>Quantity</u>   <u>Model</u>   <u>Size</u>
   a. Processors
   b. Disk Units
   c. Tape Units
   d. Printers
   e. Other
8. Item   <u>Install Date</u>   <u>Acquisition</u>
   a. Processors   Buy or Lease
   b. Disk Units   Buy or Lease
   c. Tape Units   Buy or Lease
   d. Printers   Buy or Lease
   e. Other   Buy or Lease

Computer Software

	Purchase Price	Vendor Maintenance Cost/Year
9. System Support Software		

    a. Operating System(s)
    b. Telecommunications Access
    c. Database System(s)
    d. Decision Support System(s)
    e. Office System(s)
    f. System Development Aid(s)
    g. System Security Software
    h. Utilities
    i. Other

Application Software

	Purchase Price	Vendor Maintenance Cost/Year
10. Application		

_____

_____

_____

_____

_____

_____

_____

11. Planned Use of Staff   Staff Days
    a. New Systems Development and Training
    b. Maintain/Support Existing Systems

12. Computer Operations Schedule   Days/Week   Hours/Day
    a. Server is operational
    b. Server support is staffed

13. **IT Planning**

Y/N   a. Do you have a written short- or long-range plan for information technology activities?

Y/N   b. Is there a management steering committee that oversees information technology projects and priorities?
       If so, how often does the committee meet?

Y/N   c. Is there an annual plan for scheduled application projects? Please attach a copy.

COMMENTS

Y/N 14. Is departmental charge-back (or other allocation of information technology costs) used?
What is the basis for the charges?
Y/N   Is there a separate calculation for production usage versus development charges?

COMMENTS

Y/N 15. Do you have a written standards manual, or other document, that describes the normal practices for departmental employees to follow?
Please attach a copy (if small) or the table of contents.

COMMENTS

16. **Personnel Issues**
Y/N   a. Investigations have shown that the risk of loss is as great in the area of swindle and sabotage as it is for fire and water damage. In light of these facts, is the background of those who will be employed in **sensitive** positions carefully checked?
Y/N   b. Is continuing a requirement for information technology personnel?
What is the annual minimum hours of training?
Y/N   Is training information recorded anywhere?
Y/N   c. Is the IT staff cross-trained, and expected to cover other functions in the department?
Y/N   d. Have all employees taken at least five days of vacation in the past year?

COMMENTS

17. Are the following functions segregated from each other within the IT department? (Note that this may not be practical at smaller installations.)
Y/N   a. Systems analysis and design?
Y/N   b. Programming?
Y/N   c. Physical library of tapes and disks?
Y/N   d. Operating the computer?

COMMENTS

Y/N   18. Are any outside consultants or time-sharing services in use?
        If yes, please identify those in use, and provide an estimate of the
        total payments made to them in the past year.

COMMENTS

Y/N   19. Is there a practice of conducting post-implementation reviews for
        significant projects?
        Please describe the process (comments section), what deliver-
        ables it has, and what happens to the information. Also, provide
        one example of the report from such a review.

COMMENTS

B.   PHYSICAL SECURITY

LAN Equipment Room Access

        1.   How many entrances/exits are there?
Y/N   2.   Do all doors have locks?
Y/N   3.   Are the doors locked at all times the room is unattended?
        4.   What types of locks are used?
            a.   How often are they changed?
Y/N   b.   Are they changed automatically when someone leaves?
Y/N   5.   Is the LAN equipment room a separate fire zone (e.g., floor to ceil-
             ing walls, etc.)?
Y/N   6.   Does security patrol the IT area?

        COMMENTS

LAN Equipment Room Sensor/Alarm System

Please indicate which of the following are in place and functioning.

Y/N   7.   Smoke detectors
Y/N   8.   Heat sensors
Y/N   9.   Particle sensors
Y/N   10. Water detectors
Y/N   a.   Is water damage a risk in the data center?
Y/N   b.   Is there a raised floor?
                  If yes, how high is the floor from the subfloor?
Y/N   c.   Are under-floor sprinklers needed?
Y/N   Installed?
Y/N   d.   Does the data center have a drainage system?

Y/N   Is there any risk of flooding due to water rising out of the drainage system?

Y/N   Are automatic shut-off valves used?

Y/N   11. Are any or all of these sensors connected to the guard or other outside monitoring systems such that the triggering of any of these devices will require timely investigation?

Y/N   12. Are any or all of these systems tested regularly?

Y/N   How often is testing performed?

Y/N   Who does the testing?

Y/N   Are the results of the testing recorded?

COMMENTS

Fire Suppression Systems—Please note which of the following you have.

Y/N   13. Halon system

Y/N   Is there a prevent discharge button?

Y/N   Are there posted instructions by the prevent discharge button to ensure it is used properly?

Y/N   14. CO_2 system

Y/N   15. Sprinkler system

Wet   Is it a wet or dry pipe system?

Dry

      16. If you have a Halon system, is there a plan to replace it with a non-CFC chemical?

COMMENTS

Electrical Considerations

Y/N   17. Do you have an uninterruptible power source (UPS)?
         How many minutes of backup does it provide?
         What items are protected?

Y/N   Are the UPS and CPU logically linked to manage the power outage?

Y/N   18. Is the room air conditioned?

Y/N   Is it on a separate system or systems?

Y/N   Are air ducts closed automatically?

COMMENTS

Y/N   19. Is there an emergency power cutoff switch for the room?
         Where is it located?

Y/N   Is it protected from accidental contact?

COMMENTS

Y/N   20. Is the data center on a dedicated circuit breaker?
Y/N   Is the breaker protected from accidental shut-off?
Y/N   21. Is there battery powered lighting in place?

COMMENTS

Other Physical Security Considerations

22. Is the file server keyboard locked?
Y/N   23. Does the installation use System Fault Tolerance (SFT) technology
      to prevent system outages?

COMMENTS

Y/N   24. Is smoking permitted in the data center?
Y/N   25. Is trash removed promptly so that the risk of fire and accidents is
      minimized?
26. Who cleans the data center?
Y/N   If an outside cleaning service is used, are the employees supervised?
Y/N   27. Are cables and electrical wires either under a raised floor or covered
      to prevent accidents?

COMMENTS

Wiring Closet(s)

Y/N   28. Do all doors have locks?
Y/N   29. Are the doors locked at all times the closet is unattended?
Y/N   30. Exposed to fire from other equipment?
Y/N   31. Are the walls fire rated?

C.   LOGICAL SECURITY

Netware Security Administration

1. Security Administrator/Supervisor

Y/N   a. Has one individual been provided supervisor rights?
Y/N   b. Is a copy of the supervisor password written down and locked
          in a secure location?
Y/N   c. An alternate or backup supervisor established?
          d. How often are the SUPERVISOR's passwords changed?
Y/N   e. Are different passwords used on different file servers?
Y/N   f. Does each file server have different security administrators?
Y/N   g. Do security administrators have a separate login and a pass-
          word different to that of the SUPERVISOR account?

Y/N h. Are activities of supervisor user accounts monitored by an appropriate individual separate from the LAN administration group?

Y/N i. Are there accounts (other than the supervisor accounts) that have effective ownership to the SYS:SYSTEM directory?

Y/N j. Is there an adequate audit trail of activities performed in the SYS:SYSTEM directory?

Y/N k. Are SUPERVISOR accounts restricted to secure stations?

COMMENTS

Y/N 2. Have administrative procedures been developed and the approvals defined to manage user profiles?

Y/N a. Are user access request forms used to obtain approval from management for access to the system?

b. Describe the security policy.

COMMENTS

3. **User Profile Management**

Y/N a. Is each user assigned a unique profile?

Y/N b. Are passwords required for all users?

Y/N c. Do users establish their own passwords?

Y/N d. Are there accounts that do not require password to log on to the LAN?

Y/N e. Is a new user forced to change his or her password at first sign-on?

Y/N f. Do all users change their passwords at a regular interval?

g. What is the interval for changing passwords?

Y/N h. Are end users of the system confined to menu-driven capabilities?

Y/N i. Are system utilities restricted to LAN administration accounts?

Y/N j. Is there a limit on unsuccessful access attempts?

k. What is the limit?

Y/N l. Are workstation users notified of their last sign-on and the number of invalid sign-on attempts each time they access the system?

Y/N m. Are users restricted as to the times they can use the system?

Y/N n. Are users restricted to workstations they can use on the system?

Y/N o. Has accounting been installed?

Y/N p. Are system access security violations monitored?

Y/N   q. How often, and by whom, is the review performed?

COMMENTS

Y/N 4. Are inactive user profiles (i.e., has not signed on the network for XXX days) automatically revoked?

Y/N   a. Is the "SECURITY.EXE" or a similar report reviewed for accounts that have not been used for XXX days?

Y/N   b. Is the GUEST ID active?

COMMENTS

Y/N 5. Are accounts restricted from concurrent connections (limited to one connection at a time)?

COMMENTS

      6. **Password Syntax**: please indicate which of the following, if any, are in use.

Y/N   a. Password minimum length

Y/N   b. Character Restriction

Y/N   c. Consecutive digits

Y/N   d. Repeated characters

Y/N   e. Required digits

Y/N   f. Password re-use restricted

COMMENTS

      7. **Profile Considerations**

Y/N   a. Do naming conventions clearly distinguish between group and individual profiles?

Y/N   b. Have group profiles or authorization lists been set up to facilitate security administration?

Y/N   c. Does the user group EVERYONE have only R (read) and F (file scan) access in the public directories PUBLIC, LOGIN, and MAIL?

Y/N   d. Are there user profiles that are not restricted to R and F access in directories other than their own directory?

COMMENTS

Y/N 8. Have procedures been developed and the approvals defined to assign trustee rights to a group profile?

Y/N   a. Are request forms used to obtain approval from management for access to the profiles?

         b. Describe the security policy.

COMMENTS

Y/N   9. Are changes to trustee rights monitored and reviewed?

     10. Who is performing this review and how often?

COMMENTS

Y/N   11. Are directories logically structured (such as by application) to provide consistent protection requirements for each library?

Y/N   a. Are there users with excessive rights in critical system directories (SYS:, SYS:SYSTEM, and SYS:PUBLIC, for instance)?

Y/N   b. Is NET$ACCT.DAT protected from unauthorized access?

Y/N   c. Are all critical files stored in the SYS:SYSTEM directory that could cause system disruptions?

Y/N   d. Are all trustee rights assignments removed from the SYS:LOGIN directory for all users?

COMMENTS

Y/N   12. Is encryption software available or being used?

COMMENTS

Y/N   13. Are workstation users automatically signed off after a specified period of inactivity?

        Time interval:

COMMENTS

Y/N   14. Do users signing on from a remote system go through the normal sign-on procedure?

COMMENTS

DOS

Y/N   15. Are there any AUTOEXEC.BAT files and any other batch files that automatically log a workstation on the network?

COMMENTS

Y/N 16. Are time-out features available on the local microcomputer/work-
stations?

COMMENTS

Y/N 17. Has a security package been installed on local PCs to prevent unauthorized access by intruders?

COMMENTS

D. **CHANGE MANAGEMENT**

Project Request Procedures

Y/N 1. Is there a standard form used to request additions and/or changes
to application systems?

COMMENTS

Y/N 2. Is there evidence of authorization for program modifications?

COMMENTS

Y/N 3. Does the evidence include a service request, or some other identification method?

COMMENTS

Y/N 4. Are changes to production source and executable programs monitored via reporting that is reviewed by a responsible person (with
review evidenced by signature or initials)?

COMMENTS

Y/N 5. Are programmers limited to read-only authority for production
source programs?

COMMENTS

Y/N 6. Is a log or standard form kept for all additions and changes to the
production environment?

COMMENTS

Operating System

Y/N 7. Is there a written procedure for performing operating system updates?

Y/N 8. Are these updates performed as required to ensure that support for the changes is maintained?

COMMENTS

E. **BACKUP, RECOVERY AND CONTINGENCY PLANNING**

1. Please complete the following table concerning the backups you make.

Type of Backup	Frequency (daily, weekly, etc.)	Number of Generations Stored On-Site	Number of Generations Stored Off-Site
Full			
Selected			
Other:			

Y/N 2. Are backup commands fully coded and compiled as control language programs, as opposed to being typed in at the system console when required?
Please provide a sample of backup instructions/commands, if they exist.

COMMENTS

Y/N 3. Are tapes and diskettes written on the system subject to controlled physical access?

COMMENTS

Y/N 4. Do you have any applications that include a communications component? (Examples would include purchasing that had an EDI com-

ponent and shop floor data collection utilizing store and forward logic.)
Identify fall-back alternatives and applications that incorporate communications in comments below.

COMMENTS

Y/N   5. Do you have a disaster recovery plan?
          Does it address the following:
Y/N   a. Identification of vital records?
Y/N   b. Assignment of specific responsibilities during an emergency?
Y/N   c. Establishing an offsite agreement?
Y/N   d. Determining how long it will take to replace damaged equipment?
Y/N   e. Ranking jobs/systems in terms of criticality?
Y/N   f. Determining what processing power will be needed to support critical activities?
Y/N   g. Are involved employees familiar with emergency procedures?
Y/N   h. Do involved employees have a copy of the procedures, or their section, at an offsite location?
Y/N   i. How often is the plan updated?

     COMMENTS

Y/N   6. Is a copy of the current systems/operations documentation kept either offsite or in a fireproof place?
          Where is it kept?

     COMMENTS

F.   OPERATIONS

Y/N   1. Is system utilization monitored?

     COMMENTS

Y/N   2. Are system errors logged?

     COMMENTS

Y/N   3. Are magnetic tapes periodically checked for wear?

     COMMENTS

Y/N   4.   Are magnetic tapes periodically checked for errors?

<u>COMMENTS</u>

Y/N   5.   Are file inventories taken periodically to determine obsolete files?

<u>COMMENTS</u>

Part IV
Performing a Complete Evaluation

The IT Audit Professional is less likely to find an IT department utilizing the classical methodology today than in the past, but it is still in use in many of the larger IT departments, and contains all of the elements that are normally found in any of the other development methodologies.

Part IV is divided into the five phases of the systems life cycle: initiation, definition, system design, programming and training, and evaluation and acceptance. It prescribes audit coverage for consideration throughout the systems development life cycle. The audit approach and considerations for each phase, however, are presented as separate modules for use in review during the systems development phase or at the completion of a particular phase.

Section 15
Performing a Basic Evaluation

The IT Audit Professional, armed with an understanding of the general and specific control objectives and process participants, may choose to perform a basic evaluation of the systems development methodology in place. This review may even be done as a discovery effort, with the results used as the foundation to perform a more extensive review.

The Basic Evaluation Approach

The basic information can be gathered by obtaining answers to the following list of questions. A brief discussion of the significance of each question follows this list.

1. What methodology is in use?
2. Is it documented?
3. What are the phases?
4. Are there deliverables?
5. Are samples or examples provided?
6. What compliance or enforcement method is in place?
7. Does it include procedures for the following?
   a. Documenting the need or opportunity
   b. Authorizing or justifying the project
   c. Developing the application specifications
   d. Coding and testing the application
   e. Providing training and documentation
   f. Implementing the application
8. What change management processes have been established?
9. Are procedures in place for emergency maintenance?
10. Are post-implementation reviews conducted?
11. How are priorities established and changes accommodated?

What Methodology Is in Use?

The company should have a methodology to ensure that systems are implemented using techniques designed to provide effective systems without taking unacceptable risks with the enterprise's ability to do business. The IT

Auditor may be told that there is no methodology, but this cannot be the case.

The organization may choose to have a completely informal process that each systems developer may modify to suit his or her own preferences, and this would be their methodology. The IT Audit Professional might very well choose to make a number of comments on the risks associated with such an approach to systems development, but that would not change the reality of the development methodology in place.

The IT Auditor may know what methodology has been selected, but the auditor must still remain aware that the experienced professionals on the development staff are likely to have their own opinions about what constitutes an effective set of procedures. Even if they agree with the selected methodology, there may be performance pressures on the individual that are not easy to meet. If they are too difficult, it may lead the information systems professionals to take shortcuts, and to fail to comply with even their own set of best or proper procedures.

Is the Methodology Documented?

This is a very important follow-up question when the systems audit professional is told that a methodology is in place and followed. A documented methodology is available to all of the systems developers, and there is no need to interpret oral instructions. If the plan is not documented, the systems audit professional will not be able to rely on the methodology because compliance with it cannot be tested, measured, and quantitatively measured.

An undocumented methodology does not mean that the audit is over, only that there is almost no other circumstance for which the systems audit professional can come to a positive conclusion for the systems development area. The auditor still needs to discuss the answers to the remaining questions so that a preliminary opinion can be formed. This gives the auditor the opportunity to advise the information systems staff on whether formalizing their informal methodology will be sufficient, or whether they should consider changes or improvements before making the effort to formalize the existing procedures.

What Are the Stages in the Methodology?

The common elements discussed earlier will be present in some form in every development methodology unless someone in the enterprise has specifically decided to eliminate it for business or cultural reasons. Variations between projects are more likely, such as not comparing alternatives in a situation where a completely new idea is being pursued, and no one else is going to have a product that would be a competitor.

The phases will also differ based on the type of methodology in use by the enterprise. The methodology may have eight or more phases if it has its roots 10 to 15 years in the past when it was considered more important to have every activity and decision fully documented, reviewed, and formally approved by two or more persons. On the other hand, the entire process may only have three phases in today's environment of total quality, continuous improvement, and employee empowerment.

Either of these alternatives can be well controlled and completely appropriate for an enterprise, as well as a myriad of other alternatives in between. The number of people in the information systems department, and how many of them are assigned to systems development, is also likely to be significant. Until the number is large enough to reach critical mass, any formal methodology is likely to be unreliable due to a lack of segregation of duties through the program implementation/change control process.

The number of people required to reach critical mass is not a fixed value, so the systems audit professional will have to exercise judgment when forming an opinion on the development methodology, the adequacy of the development staff size, and what recommendations are appropriate for the circumstances.

Are There Deliverables?

Deliverables are important because they have the potential to provide substantial value to the enterprise. Each systems development life cycle phase represents a milestone in that certain objectives should have been met, decisions made, data gathered or analyzed, etc. The least deliverable may be a one- or two-paragraph memo that documents a judgmental decision made without any other support, but even that decision can now be evaluated, if needed.

The IT Audit Professional will have to evaluate the deliverables based on the situational considerations, although there are certain assumptions that can be made. The minimum deliverables should be defined in advance, and examples provided so the person preparing the deliverable has complete information and thus the best chance to efficiently develop an effective deliverable.

Are Samples or Examples Provided?

The presence of example documents has the primary benefit of working to ensure that project by project deliverables are of the appropriate quality. Another benefit is that the systems audit professional can review the sample deliverables and establish a benchmark for auditing the deliverables in specific systems development projects.

By reviewing the sample deliverables, the systems audit professional has the opportunity to form opinions and develop recommendations that could affect the deliverables on any active and all potential future projects. This may also support improved relations with the internal customers as the review of samples is very impersonal, while reviewing the deliverables in any particular project will have more of a direct impact on the involved information systems personnel.

What Compliance or Enforcement Method Is in Place?

Systems development life cycle deliverables, being closely associated with project milestones, are much more reliable when they are mandatory and not optional. It has not been considered unreasonable for many enterprises to require a completed deliverable including time for review and approval before any work on the next phase can begin. Without a requirement for production, there is a very clear risk that other priorities will displace the deliverable, or at least delay it such that it has little value other than for providing information about the phase long after it is over and the next phase begun.

What Procedures Have Been Established for Change Management?

Most IT Audit Professionals should be familiar with the phrase "program change controls" as the phrase that covers the identity of persons capable of moving programs into the production environment and the procedures that are supposed to be followed. Program change controls developed as having a very limited focus on one type of change within the Information Systems function.

Over time, this focus expanded to encompass all of the changes that could impact information systems, with an emphasis on the ones that could affect, or disrupt, the production environment on the system. This expanded focus is referred to as "change management." Change management should cover any change within the information systems function that has the potential, directly or indirectly, to have a negative impact on the operating environment.

The IT Auditor is most likely to be concerned about the environmental impacts that could cause system functioning to be unexpectedly disrupted; ones that could cause existing approved programs to function in unexpected and potentially unauthorized ways; and ones that result in unauthorized programs being introduced into the systems environment and then functioning in an unauthorized fashion.

Maintenance Procedures for Emergency Situations

In every situation, whether applications are completely custom coded or purchased and processed without any customization or changes, the IT Auditor should not forget to consider that applications can fail without warning and require immediate attention to resume normal processing. This attention, or maintenance, is therefore usually done on very little notice, done in isolation, and done while violating standards program change control procedures.

The IT Auditor should determine whether there are procedures for flagging emergency maintenance situations and requiring subsequent performance of at least the most critical control procedures. Requiring subsequent control procedures is an attempt to limit the organization's risk related to an unauthorized change made during emergency maintenance.

The risk is limited as the person making the change should be easily identified if there is a subsequent problem or unauthorized processing cycle in the system.

Are Post-implementation Reviews Conducted?

The post-implementation review can be a very effective technique with total quality and continuous improvement benefits if it is done in a positive way. Being done in a positive fashion protects individual personalities, and gives people a chance to get the information they need to do *better* during the next systems development life cycle project.

Better can be defined in several contexts, some of which are described in the following list, which is not meant to be all-inclusive.

- a more effective and efficient systems development life cycle project
- higher quality deliverables
- reduced development costs
- shorter total life cycle time

This is about the extent of the review that should be done as part of the initial assessment of general system controls. The next chapter goes into additional detail for an IT Auditor reviewing a classical systems development life cycle methodology, which is considered to be the most extensively controlled methodology currently in use.

GENERIC DOMESTIC COMPANY CAPITAL EXPENDITURE REQUEST			Office use only:
Requester	Department	Phone	Date
Change requested			
Reason/justification			
Approval		Date	
TECHNICAL EVALUATION			
Cost		Personnel	
Hours		Other	
Comments			
Approval		Date	
END USER ACCEPTANCE			
User		Date	
FINAL ACTUAL DATA			
Budget hours		Budget cost	
Actual hours		Actual cost	

Section 16
Performing
a Complete Evaluation

Controls over applications development should ensure that applications are only developed or acquired in ways that support the appropriate strategic or tactical interests of the organization. The IT Audit Professional will discover that there are a variety of ways a particular organization may choose to organize the development process, or development methodology.

It is possible to utilize a standard methodology for developing and maintaining applications because experience has shown that there are common activities to every development and maintenance effort. The common activities are described in the following list.

- Recognizing an opportunity or need.
- Identifying and evaluating alternatives.
- Making a decision to either implement one of the alternatives, defer it, or to discontinue any further consideration of it.
- Developing or acquiring the application code needed to realize the selected alternative. The IT Auditor should note that acquiring an application can be much less costly than developing one, if a purchased alternative can be found that is either able to fully meet the requirements or can be modified to do that with only a reasonable effort.
- Implementing the new application once the activities included in the prior step are complete.
- Correcting problems identified during implementation, and completing end-user and system documentation.
- Conducting a post-implementation review to evaluate the system as developed and implemented.

Each methodology encompassing these activities effectively guides the organization through the life of the development project. This led systems professionals to describe the development process as the Systems Development Life Cycle (SDLC). The SDLC in the organization under review should encompass the following general control objectives.

GENERAL CONTROL OBJECTIVES

The organization's SDLC should be able to address the following general control objectives, regardless of the size of the project. The size of the project could be defined using only cash expenditures, the number of full-time-equivalent (FTE) working days, or the total of tangible and intangible costs. The control objectives can be addressed in different ways, as it is unreasonable to expect that projects requiring 40 hours to complete can be easily compared to projects requiring 4000 hours to complete.

1. Development activities should always support either the strategic or tactical objectives of the enterprise.
2. Development projects requiring approval for funding and resources should include mechanisms to ensure that all costs are captured and monitored in a manner that is consistent with company guidelines.
3. Application security should complement the overall security approach taken within the enterprise.
4. Application design and testing should ensure that the application would be available and responsive to the needs of the application end users.

Specific Objectives

Each one of the systems development life cycle's common elements should meet specific objectives to increase the likelihood that the general objectives described above are met. The specific objectives described below are not meant to be all-inclusive, and can be modified or supplemented to better fit the specifics of the situation.

Recognizing Needs or Opportunities. The enterprise should develop mechanisms to promote this recognition so that problems are solved and opportunities are capitalized on in an effective manner. To make these mechanisms effective, company employees should receive specific training so they are better able to recognize these situations, as recognizing these situations can be advantageous to both the employee and to the enterprise.

Evaluating Alternatives and Details. The enterprise should have a policy that provides for assessing the proposed application, which includes general business issues, specific business issues, and the expected impact on revenues and expenses. This policy should include a form or at least a format for all of the appropriate information so that anyone looking at the proposed application can see that the homework has been done prior to submitting the request.

The IT Audit Professional should evaluate this form to ensure that it is not so complex that completing the form discourages company personnel from making the effort because they are unsure of the significance of their idea. The risk of never identifying an important opportunity can be more harmful to the organization than the resources spent on documenting applications the organization chooses not to pursue.

Making a Decision. There should be a place to record the authorization of the person or persons making the decision so there is later accountability in the event of a question. The authorization should be on the form or attached to the forms defining the application and work being requested to reduce the risk of misunderstanding or erroneous approval of the wrong specifications.

Develop or Acquire the Solution. Procedures should be in place to see that this is done on a timely basis. All costs should be in accordance with the approved request, and any potential overruns exceeding a predetermined threshold should go back to the persons authorizing the original activity so that any approval or denial of additional expenditures is consistent with the original decision.

Detailed specifications should be developed so that whether the application is acquired or developed, the information is available to make the application most effective in terms of meeting the needs as specified. These specifications should be the foundation for corresponding testing activities. Testing procedures should be included that test both individual programs and functions of the application but also the application taken as a whole, including the interfaces to other systems.

Implementing the New Application. When implementing any solution that includes data which already exists in the organization, care should be taken to ensure that the data is either converted or migrated in a way that ensures the integrity of that information and eliminates the risk of data loss to the enterprise.

Implementation procedures should also provide for making the actual change to the production environment either overnight, over a weekend, or during any other time when the production environment cannot be interrupted. This is one way to protect the continuity of business within the organization.

The implementation procedures should also include procedures for stopping the implementation, reversing the changes made through the stopping point, and falling back to the prior application. This backout procedure also protects the organization's continuity, like the timing of the implementation does.

Documenting the Application. The systems, operations, and end-user documentation being developed throughout the development project should be finalized once the application is fully implemented. Trying to complete the documentation before that time creates the risk that changes made late in the process will not be reflected in the documentation. Waiting to develop the final documentation also creates the opportunity to include all final changes and corrections as well as a complete understanding of the lessons learned through the final development and implementation activities.

Performing a Post-implementation Application Review. The IT Audit Professional may find that application developers and users believe that the principles of total quality management, continuous improvement, and the like are contradicted by a subsequent review. The IT auditor must find a way to convey the fact that this review is critical if enterprise personnel are to get a chance to learn to do future development activities more effectively.

There is a significant risk that a post-implementation review will become punitive rather than constructive, particularly in the case of an application that has been delivered late or is over budget. The goal of the review, whether done by the IT Audit Professional, someone else, or a team, should only be to determine whether project objectives were met and whether there are any lessons that should be applied in the next development effort.

Failing to keep these reviews both constructive and objective is likely to lead to an environment where no post-implementation reviews are conducted. This situation is clearly not in the best interests of the organization.

The IT Audit Professional should also obtain a clear understanding of the identity and interests of the participants in each development effort. The following sections describe many, if not most, of the potential participants.

PARTICIPANTS IN THE SYSTEMS DEVELOPMENT LIFE CYCLE

The IT Audit Professional is likely to find that every project may have a unique or unusual organization participant, although that is certainly not automatic. Several of the most common participants have been identified below. Along with each identified participant there is an analysis of what responsibilities that specific participant may have in significant stages of the project.

Senior Management. The organization's senior management will spend the least time involved in any development project, although their participation can easily be the most significant. Senior management is ultimately responsible for the success of the organization, making them responsible for all projects even if they have delegated the ability to make financial commitments such that entire projects are completed without the need for their approval or intervention.

One or more members of senior management may be involved at each stage of a project, if an approval from that level of signing authority is required. Otherwise, senior managers are more likely to be kept aware of the progress of important projects during staff meetings than any other direct participation.

Project Steering Committee. The existence of a steering committee is also likely to be contingent on the magnitude of the project, senior management's need or desire to delegate authority, and the nature of the project itself. The project steering committee, if it exists, will almost certainly represent the first formal approval of critical project deliverables. This approval may cover some or all of the following:

- Functional requirements deliverable document
- Components of the project plan such as validation, verification, and testing
- Key deliverables from other project stages

The IT Audit Professional should remember that these approvals almost always represent the final step in one of the stages of the systems development life cycle methodology the organization has chosen to follow.

Project Sponsor. The IT Audit Professional can find that the project is sponsored by an individual or a team. The magnitude of the project is likely to determine that nature of the project sponsorship. The project sponsor may be responsible for one or more of the following items:

- Identifies and validates the original need or opportunity
- Develops the needs statement
- Directs the feasibility study and risk analysis
- Prepares the cost/benefit analysis
- Selects a project manager.

The project sponsor will have certain additional responsibilities if some or all of the development project is handled by contractors. If all or part of the life cycle effort is contracted, the project sponsor, in coordination with the project manager, incorporates a preliminary assessment of the need for contracted services in the life cycle stages. The IT auditor should be aware that utilizing the services of a contractor can require a long lead time; thus, the impact on the project schedule must be recognized and understood.

Project Team. The IT Audit Professional will need to determine if there is a project team that is separate from the project sponsor. If there is an independent project team, the team's responsibilities may include one or more of the following:

- Updating the project plan
- Revising detailed subproject plans
- Developing end-user and other manuals
- Developing and maintaining the project plan and functional and data requirements documents

Information Technology Manager. The IT Audit Professional is not likely to find that the IT manager is a direct participant in every systems development project. The IT manager is too likely to have other commitments that would never permit direct participation in every project. When the IT Manager does participate in a specific project, that person is likely to have a more technical perspective on the related issues than the Project Steering Committee, although the basic responsibilities will be approximately the same.

Security Specialist. The security officer may have the role of security specialist in all projects, or may have designated agents drawn from the information systems or end-user populations. Further, the person or persons responsible for security may keep that responsibility directly, or may provide support so that other persons in the project handle the direct responsibilities.

Some of the possible responsibilities include the following:

- Consultations on security matters
- Reviews key deliverables
- Reviews system and subsystem components
- Evaluates database specifications
- Analyzes planned access controls
- Reviews test plans and related specifications

These reviews can be extended to encompass the end-user manual, operations manual, implementation plan, etc. All of these activities are likely to be focused on the security and internal control components of the items under review.

Internal Auditor. This is more likely to be an IT Audit Professional than a Financial Audit Professional or an Operational Audit Professional, although any of the above may satisfy these responsibilities. It is also possible the Internal Audit role may encompass the responsibilities that might be handled by the security specialist.

The IT Audit Professional should evaluate the need for independence and objectivity whenever there is a request that Internal Audit satisfy the responsibilities of the security specialist. Consistent with all professional activities, the line differentiating recommendations and decisions can become unclear, and responsibilities to the organization may compete with professional standards.

Any such conflicts can only be resolved at the time based on the specific context and issues of the situation. The IT Audit Professional can only be directed to consult with third parties as needed at the time.

Quality Assurance Specialist. The organization may have a separate quality assurance function with a different mission from either the security specialist or the IT auditor. Many of the responsibilities are the same, and the need for duplicate functions, if they exist, is one of the obligations of the IT auditor, even if the review is more operational than control oriented in nature.

The quality assurance specialist may review the project definition, the system design; validation, verification, and testing components and documentation; and the program definition, program code, documentation, and training to ensure compliance with the needs statement and IT standards.

Section 17
Initiation Phase Review

During the initiation phase, the need for an automated solution to a problem is identified, quantified, and confirmed. The person or team initiating a potential project should investigate alternative methods for satisfying the need and finally develop a recommendation for which alternative should be selected. The recommendation is presented to management, and if approved, the project continues through the remaining phases of systems development.

The IT auditor's primary objective during this phase is to ensure that the system need has been established and that the cost for satisfying that need is justified. The IT auditor reviews the initiation phase by examining the documents produced during that phase and by interviewing the initiation phase participants and other involved parties. The result of the audit review of this phase may become input to the appropriate parties for determining whether or not to approve the initiation phase recommendation, if the review is done on a realtime basis.

OVERVIEW

The initiation phase begins with the recognition of a problem and the identification of a need. During this phase, the need is validated and the exploration of alternative functional concepts to satisfy the need is recommended and approved. The decision to pursue a solution must be based on a clear understanding of the problem, a preliminary investigation of alternative solutions, and a comparison of the expected benefits versus costs (including design, construction, operation, and potential risks) of the solution. At this stage, the sensitivity of the data in the system should also be considered.

It is immaterial, during the initiation phase, whether the solution will be developed internally, contracted to be developed externally, or purchased from a software vendor. The objective of this phase is to consider alternative solutions that might satisfy the end user's need. This stage of the systems development life cycle methodology is not affected by the alternative approach chosen.

Likewise, the IT auditor should not vary the approach to the audit based on whether the application is purchase, developed internally, or developed externally.

INITIATION PHASE DELIVERABLES

The IT Audit Professional should now focus on the deliverable documents produced during the phase. Although the IT auditor will find that there are variations in the exact documents produced and their contents, it is possible to identify baseline examples. A number of these examples are described below.

The Needs Statement. This describes the deficiencies in existing capabilities, opportunities for increasing the effectiveness of existing capabilities, or describes completely new capabilities. The needs statement should also justify the exploration of alternative solutions.

The Feasibility Study. This provides an analysis of the objectives, requirements, and system concepts; an evaluation of alternative approaches, as identified in the needs statement, to achieve the objectives reasonably; and the recommendation of one of the alternatives.

This identifies the system's internal control and security vulnerabilities; determines the nature and magnitude of associated threats to data and assets; and provides managers, designers, systems security specialists, and auditors with recommended safeguards to be included during the design, development, installation, and operation phases of new or modified systems.

The Cost/Benefit Analysis. This deliverable is intended to provide managers, end users, application developers, security specialists, etc., with cost and benefit information for decision-making purposes. This information should include the impact of security, privacy, and internal control requirements on that information, enabling the decision makers and the IT auditor to analyze and evaluate alternative approaches to achieving the objectives.

AUDITING THE INITIATION PHASE

In preparing for the initiation phase review, the IT auditor must gain an understanding of the phase by gathering documentation and interviewing the appropriate personnel. Most of this can be done with the team established to implement the project. The tasks that must be completed during the audit survey are to study the initiation phase elements, review initiation phase plans, and other procedures as necessary.

Studying the Initiation Phase. The IT auditor should begin the review of the initiation phase by performing the following specific review tasks:

- Determining whether prior evaluations of this methodology have been made and, if so, how its effectiveness was evaluated.

- Determining whether the development team understands and supports the methodology.
- Evaluating the effectiveness of the methodology through inquiry and review of documentation.
- Comparing the methodology with that defined in this book and noting any differences, particularly where problems might occur because of development deficiencies.
- Identifying the documents produced by the methodology.
- Determining through interview whether the project team has been adequately trained in the use of the methodology.
- Becoming familiar with the organization's cost-justification process.
- Becoming familiar with the appropriate regulations and policies for the area being considered for automation.

Reviewing Initiation Phase Plans. The IT auditor must become familiar with the problem that has been recognized. The plan to initiate the system should be reviewed to ensure that it will result in the type of deliverable documents described earlier in this section.

Evaluating the Status of the Initiation Phase. The IT auditor must gather status information in three areas. First, the auditor must determine whether the five initiation phase documents have been prepared and, if so, whether they have been prepared in accordance with the life cycle methodology.

Second, the IT auditor must determine whether the project is on time and needed tasks have been completed and, if not, when completion is expected.

Third, the auditor should identify any changes in the problem or need, and ensure that those changes have been properly incorporated into the documents developed during this phase.

The IT auditor should very initiation phase information by reviewing the five documents mentioned earlier and interviewing the chief preparers about their exact role in preparing those deliverables. The project begins with the needs statement, which either includes or is supported by a needs validation and justification statement.

The project sponsor must in some manner be able to justify undertaking the initiation phase. The auditor must consider valid alternatives during this phase, even if they are not included in the deliverables.

The needs statement becomes the basis for a feasibility study and a risk analysis study. The objective of these parts of the initiation phase is to identify a proposed approach and its vulnerabilities. The risk analysis provides input to supplement the needs statement so that a cost/benefit analysis can be prepared. This document, in conjunction with the feasibility study document, provides the necessary information for management to decide either to initiate or continue the development or to take other appropriate actions.

Different life cycle methodologies produce slightly different documents. The information defined in these five documents can be consolidated into fewer documents or expanded into a greater number of documents. What is important to the IT auditor is that the information included in these five documents be developed during the initiation phase.

The auditor must ensure that all of the appropriate documents have been prepared and must determine the appropriate accumulation of information for the system decision paper to verify the correctness of that document. If the missing documents or document attributes are significant, recommend that the methodology be corrected to provide that missing information.

SETTING THE SCOPE FOR THE SDLC AUDIT

The IT auditor's coverage will be affected by the development methodology utilized by the organization. The chosen methodology will include processes and activities that may be easy, difficult, or impossible to audit. The IT Audit Professional will determine the appropriate audit scope during and after the preliminary review of the development methodology, based on the knowledge and understanding gained during that preliminary review.

The IT auditor will follow up setting the audit scope by allocating staff resources and deciding what the timing of the review will be.

The IT auditor's decisions will be impacted more by the perceived effectiveness of the development methodology than by its formality. While deliverables are significant and critical and necessary at certain points in the systems development life cycle, all of the deliverables in the world are made meaningless by tolerated noncompliance with the preparation and use of those deliverables.

The audit scope decision is also likely to be affected by the results of prior audits. For example, if the IT auditor has found that the development process has been well controlled in the past, the auditor may choose to limit the nature, timing, and extent of the current procedures.

The IT Audit Professional may even choose to conduct one review focused exclusively on the work done by the quality assurance personnel. An audit of their activities that support a conclusion of reasonable reliance on them could lead the IT auditor to conduct only those procedures needed to confirm that quality assurance activities are taking place as expected.

Assuming that the IT auditor will be reviewing the development methodology directly, the next audit step will be to interview the key participants in the initiation phase. The interviews will have two primary objectives: to determine whether the phase is ready to be audited, and to identify the specific contact personnel associated with particular audit steps.

The following list of interview questions and tasks may need to be adjusted by the IT auditor to meet the needs of a particular situation. This list is organized by project participant, and the questions related to that party.

Project Sponsor.

1. Has the needs statement been developed?
2. Has the project sponsor confirmed or validated the needs?
3. What direction did the sponsor provide to the personnel preparing the feasibility study, risk analysis, and cost/benefit analysis.
4. Has a project team been established?

Project Team.

1. Has the project team completed their development of the feasibility study, risk analysis, and cost/benefit analysis?

Information Technology Manager.

1. How has the IT manager or designee participated in the initiation phase of the project?

Security Specialist.

1. Has the security specialist been involved in the development of these deliverables on a continuing basis? Or reviewed them before they were considered final?
2. Were internal control considerations included in the security specialist's review?

Quality Assurance Specialist.

1. Has (or will) the quality assurance specialist reviewed the initiation phase deliverables before they are presented to the appropriate managers and other company personnel?

The IT auditor should provide either a report or brief memorandum summarizing the work done through this point, important observations made, and recommendations if they are appropriate. If the IT auditor fails to provide this information, there is a chance that a project will be accepted and implemented when it should not have been.

CUSTOMIZING THE AUDIT OBJECTIVES

The IT Audit Professional will not normally be able to utilize any preset approach without modification. Most organizations will find a reason to make their approach just a little different than the standard approach. The following sections describe some of the changes companies make and discusses how the audit might choose to adjust to that change.

The initiation phase is designed to fully develop the understanding of the problem or potential opportunity and to produce the data and information required to support effective decision-making within the organization. The decision to proceed with defining detailed requirements will based on the information gathered to date, along with a recommendation from the project sponsor, or project team, if one was assembled to support the development of the initiation documents.

Rather than produce two or three or four distinct documents that lead to an organizational decision, the organization may choose to present all of this information in a single document. The IT auditor should not be particularly concerned about the number of documents prepared, but should concentrate on the information in those documents to ensure that it contains the necessary information with consistent quality.

The IT Audit Professional will find that the information needed for decision support is not always fully documented. Some organizations may utilize presentations to initiate projects, with the decision support information documented only on visual aids. In those instances, the IT auditor should attempt to be invited to the participation.

A presentation is likely to include questions and other participation with the attendees, and the IT auditor will find that subsequent conversations trying to find out what happened in the meeting will almost never provide the nuances and other intangibles that come through when you are present.

The IT auditor should include a review of the formal initiation phase deliverable or deliverables with other initiation phase procedures. The auditor should include a specific evaluation of the established need and the cost-justification for implementing an application to address that need.

There are several external considerations that can affect the nature, timing, and extent of the audit procedures. Some of those considerations are included in the following list:

1. Laws, regulations, or other standards directing audit involvement in the computerized application
2. Requirements included in contractual provisions defining the internal audit role during systems development

3. The presence or absence of internal assessment groups (e.g., quality assurance or computer security officers) necessitating greater or lesser audit involvement
4. Computerized applications that are administratively sensitive within the organization
5. Resource constraints on the audit organization (e.g., the lack of budget, expertise, or tools to perform the function)

The Use of Contractors. Another discretionary factor is based on the potential use of contractors in the development effort. The difference the IT auditor must be most wary of in situations where the company utilizes contracted resources in the initiation phase is that the contractors may have a vested interest in reaching conclusions that will result in more work for the contractor.

A contractor may be responsible for supporting the project sponsor or the project team for all of their activities. Contractors may also consult with the Steering Committee or to support the IT auditor by reviewing or evaluating the feasibility study. In any case, the organization's interests can be protected by rigorously defining the contractor's role, responsibility, and authority.

The responsibility for using contractors can reside with the steering committee, project sponsor, or project steering committee. It will depend on the nature and extent of the proposed use of the contractor, and the signing authority of the internal personnel. The analysis to determine whether or not a contractor should be used is included in the alternatives analysis, feasibility study, risk analysis, and cost/benefit analysis.

DETAILED AUDIT TESTING

The IT auditor should select the deliverables, portions of deliverables, and other elements that appeared to make a significant contribution to the decision to either proceed with the project or to discontinue it. These items should be tested to the extent necessary for the IT auditor to form an opinion on the reasonableness of the decision taken related to the application under review.

The Audit Test. The IT auditor should develop an audit program that indicates the audit objectives and identifies the key controls to be evaluated in the initiation phase. For each audit objective and indicator, there are one or more audit tests to be performed. When appropriate, tools and techniques are listed to assist the auditor in performing these tests.

In some instances, the audit tool or technique consists of a general description; and in other instances, the program refers to a specific product or document containing a specific audit approach for the indicated test.

Verification. The IT auditor has two verification tasks to perform. The auditor should first determine which of the forms, worksheets, and documents specified by the life cycle methodology have been prepared. The auditor should then attempt to evaluate the accuracy of the information on the documents.

The extent of these tests depends on the specific audit objectives selected. The IT auditor should attempt to avoid being cast into the role of verifying the decision support information. The auditor's role is more appropriate if confirming that a verification was done by someone directly involved in the process, or in evaluating the veracity of the information.

The auditor may also evaluate the deliverables, and not just the information or message they contain. The auditor should not simply attempt to confirm that the deliverables have been prepared, as the deliverables alone have little value to the organization.

The Needs Statement. This deliverable should include an expression of the need in terms of a company mission, deficiencies in existing capabilities, new or changed program requirements, opportunities for increasing economy and efficiency of user operation, the internal control and security needed for the system, and alternative solutions for meeting the need.

The Feasibility Study. This should include an analysis of the objectives, requirements, and system concepts, an evaluation of alternative approaches for reasonably achieving the objectives, and a description of the proposed approach. This information should be sufficient to provide the decision-makers with the information required to make a decision.

The information provided should be adequate so that the decision-makers have at least two alternatives. There are always two alternatives: support the application or determine it is not needed. There may be additional alternatives, with a direct positive correlation between the number of alternatives and the quality and quantity of information required to support the decision.

The Risk Analysis. The IT auditor should find that this deliverable includes the identification of internal control and security vulnerabilities, the nature and magnitude of associated threats to data and assets covered by the proposed system, recommended safeguards to be included in the design to address the identified risks, and a detailed review of all data and assets to be processed or accessed by the system.

The Cost/Benefit Analysis. This deliverable should include the cost to build the system, the benefits to be derived from the system, an assessment of the impact of the system on security, privacy, and internal control requirements, an analysis and evaluation of alternative approaches proposed in meeting the mission deficiencies, and a detailed cost/benefit analysis of the proposed alternatives.

AUDIT RESULTS AND REPORTING

The IT Audit Professional should begin this activity by creating a list of all the potential errors or opportunities. The auditor should then evaluate the potential impact of the variance before deciding to propose a recommendation related to it. The items having sufficient potential impact should be included in draft recommendations.

The IT Audit Professional should review these draft recommendations with all of the appropriate personnel and require them to provide responses to be included in the audit report summarizing that particular review and findings. This step gives the auditor a chance to confirm the findings, as it is possible to make a mistake during an audit, or to have complete information, or to not have developed the best recommendation for change.

The IT Audit Professional should attempt to guarantee that either the report or its contents are available to the decision-makers prior to their deadline for making a decision. If this is not done, then one of the most important impacts of the audit may be lost.

The IT auditor should clearly state the objectives of the initiation phase review in the report. The following two objectives are normally included in almost every review: to identify errors or deficiencies, and to identify missed opportunities.

Any such items, assuming they have the requisite significance, should be included in the report, along with related recommendations. Although specific deficiencies will vary between situations, certain deficiencies are more common than others. The following list of problems can be used as a basis for comparison against deficiencies identified in the review.

- The needs statement is incomplete, and thus the possibility exists that the implemented system will not meet the true needs of the user.
- A reasonable set of alternatives has not been considered, and thus the alternative selected might not be the best alternative.
- The appropriate individuals from user or executive management did not become involved in the initiation phase, resulting in a potentially suboptimal decision. This is more likely to occur when two or more departments or locations are involved in the same application project.

- All vulnerabilities have not been identified, or the magnitude of those vulnerabilities has not been determined, which could result in extensive additional costs or significant failures of the application to meet the indicated need.
- The cost/benefit analysis did not identify all of the costs or benefits, or else misstated the costs and benefits that were included, which could call into question the decision taken.

The IT Audit Professional will have to modify the list above as needed to meet the needs of a particular application review. Once this portion of the work is complete, it is necessary to determine what the audit of the next phase will encompass.

Refining the Audit Approach. The initiation phase audit should conclude with a determination of the audit strategy for the remaining developmental phases that includes:

- The nature, timing, and extent of audit involvement in the remaining system development phases.
- Specific auditor assignments for the activities planned in the preceding step. If possible, the same staff members should be involved over the course of the review. If this is done, the advantage obtained will be fewer obstacles and learning curves to work through. Specific tasks where a specialist is required represent one of the few exceptions to this rule.
- The audit tools and techniques to be used. Some tools require unique skills and extended preparation time.

The IT auditor's analysis and conclusions related to the initiation phase will affect how the scope is set for the requirements definition phase of the project. The following list presents a sample of the conclusions the auditor might reach.

- That there are external considerations that should be reflected in the planned procedures
- That there are other internal groups like Quality Assurance whose competence affects the planned procedures
- That the initiation phase deliverable either support proceeding with the requirements phase or they do not
- Whether or not there is agreement within the organization as to the optimal course of action

Section 18
The Requirements Definition Phase Review

The IT Audit Professional should be careful when deciding how to allocate resources between the requirements definition phase and the remaining phases. Poorly defined requirements will almost certainly result in systems that do not meet the organization's objectives.

The IT auditor is likely to find that defining requirements is an iterative process. This is appropriate because most employees spend their time focused on how their work has to be done, and do not spend time considering new alternatives for that work. Their lack of experience with systems design makes it difficult to adequately define the requirements for an application.

Audit objectives: The audit objectives during the definition phase are to evaluate how well the end-user needs have been defined and translated into the requirements definition, and whether the appropriate internal controls have been included in the final requirements document.

These audit objectives are accomplished by participating in selected definition meetings and review draft and final requirements deliverables. In addition, the auditor may choose to look directly at the participants in the process and evaluate their individual performance.

OVERVIEW

The requirements definition phase refocuses the organizations attention from the needs and opportunities and on to the solutions. The systems analysts must identify the inputs, processes, and outputs that will meet the end-user needs as expressed in the initiation deliverables.

The analysts, or systems designers, usually spend most of the time in this activity involved with end users, other company personnel, and in certain cases third parties such as customers, attorneys, and the like. The IT auditor may be a direct party to the process, depending on the organization.

Once the requirements have been defined, there is another significant approval point, whether the magnitude of the project is great or small. The auditor should confirm what actions were approved as early as possible in the definition phase so that any deviations noted by the IT auditor that are not caught by the development process can be properly addressed.

The IT Audit Professional should find that the definition phase has another significant output: a much more specific plan for the remaining development effort. A preliminary plan had to be included in the initiation phase as part of the estimate of total project costs.

The final plan is dependent on the final requirements, as the definition process is likely to either have some changes or else just be better understood. It defines the goals and activities for all remaining project phases, including resource estimates, goals, and expected methods to the extent they are not identified in the standard systems development life cycle methodology.

The IT auditor is likely to find that there many more participants in the definition phase than in the initiation phase. Instead of a sample of end users all critical end users, should participate, along with all necessary systems analysts and other concerned parties.

Participants and Their Activities. The IT auditor is likely to find that the major participants and their activities are described in the paragraphs below.

Senior Management. If this is not done within the Project Steering Committee, then senior management will approve the initiation phase deliverable, consulting with other project participants as needed.

Project Steering Committee. This committee may approve the initiation phase deliverables if it is within their signing authority. This committee should also approve the project plan and requirements definition document.

Project Sponsor/Project Team. They will do the specific development of the project plans and provide the initial approval of the deliverable for the current phase.

Information Technology Manager. This person provides consultation and review of the project plan, functional requirements document, and data requirements document.

Security Specialist. This person selectively reviews project plan, functional requirements document, and the data requirements document.

Quality Assurance Specialist. This person reviews and evaluates the system decision paper, project plan, functional requirements document, and data requirements document, monitors compliance with the development methodology, and may even directly participate in the development of these items.

DELIVERABLES IN THE REQUIREMENTS DEFINITION PHASE

The IT Audit Professional may find the information and data most often included as deliverable information from this phase recorded on up to five different deliverable documents. Just as in the initiation phase, the number of deliverables is not significant provided the necessary information is present in the deliverables provided.

The IT auditor should also evaluate whether each phase includes a requirement that the original cost/benefit analysis be updated, and the updated information included in the deliverables. This is crucial if the organization is to have the opportunity to evaluate the reasonableness of proceeding with a particular project.

Most IT Audit Professionals are not accustomed to seeing this step in their organizations systems development methodology, because almost no company will discontinue a project once the initial approval has been given. The project scope may be altered, the timeline may be changed, but there are usually too many political considerations for a project to be stopped.

The IT auditor should consider challenging this situation, due to the increasing demand for development resources in a downsized and outsourced environment. The modern organization should be able to recognize an error and realize that scarce resources that could have more effect spent on another development project should be spent there.

One possible set of definition phase deliverables and the information they should most likely include are shown below.

The updated project plan: Any changes that were identified during the definition phase should be reflected in the original project plan, and the updated document should be sent to the original distribution so that those individuals have access to the updated information. As before, the updated project plan should outline the remainder of the development effort.

The Functional Requirements Document. This deliverable captures the detailed information that the systems developers will use as their guide for preparing input screens, coding the automated processes and interfaces, and defining required outputs.

The Security and Control Requirements Document. This deliverable identifies the specific security and control requirements for the application.

These need to be identified in the requirements phase so that the security and control procedures can be implemented along with the application.

The Data Requirements Document. This deliverable should provide a detailed description of the data the application will require as an input, along with a similar description of the data that will be generated by the application and thus be available to end users and other applications.

The data requirements document should also describe the potential threats related to this data for use in defining access security, in formal risk analyses, and other uses that may be identified later. This is a good example of information that could be part of another deliverable, such as being included as an appendix to the data requirements document.

THE INITIAL AUDIT EVALUATION

The IT Audit Professional's basic evaluation of the requirements definition phase will involve reviewing the previously developed deliverables along with the documents produced in the present phase. The IT auditor should also have the documented results of the initiation phase review available for reference.

The initial evaluation should bring the IT auditor up to speed with the status of the development project. If the phases are brief, the initial evaluation in this and later phases may not be necessary. It is more common for several weeks or months to elapse between the conclusion of one phase and the conclusion of the subsequent phase.

The IT auditor's initial evaluation involves four steps. First, the auditor must review the output documents produced in the previous phase in addition to the appropriate audit workpapers. Second, the auditor must review and become familiar with the plans to complete this phase.

The IT auditor continues by gathering the documentation produced during this phase and comparing the actual progress against the plan. Finally, the auditor must verify the documents produced during this phase by challenging and analyzing those documents as well as by interviewing the participants in the phase. The specific work within these four tasks depends on the customized audit objectives selected for this phase.

Reviewing Initiation Phase Output. The IT auditor should review all initiation phase deliverables. The key deliverable is the one used to support the decision to perform the project because it should include much of the information from all of the deliverables. The auditor should refer to the other documents, as appropriate, to get more detailed information.

The IT auditor should review the audit workpapers prepared during the initiation phase in order to become reacquainted with the deficiencies and recommendations from the initiation phase. The auditor should ensure that these items either have been, or are being, reasonably and adequately addressed during the definition phase.

One of the major audit tasks in each review phase is to evaluate the adequacy of the actions taken on the deficiencies and recommendations from the previous phase.

Reviewing Definition Phase Plans. The IT auditor should review the plans for the definition phase as part of the planning for the audit procedures in this phase. The auditor should be aware that the plans may be written or they may be maintained in automated scheduling and project management systems. The auditor may choose to have the plans printed or to review the plans online.

The IT Audit Professional will not compromise the audit by reviewing online information, although it will be necessary to print those items the auditor believes are necessary to provide the proper support in the workpapers for the conclusion reached.

Evaluating the Definition Phase Status. The IT auditor should monitor the project status to remain aware of developments in the project and to determine when reviews should occur. This can be done by contacting key participants, reviewing written status reports, or querying automated project status systems.

The IT auditor should consider which elements of the project need to be monitored. One project aspect is its administrative status, comprised of the budget and schedule. This is necessary to determine where the project stands and its availability for review.

Another aspect is the status of definition phase documentation. If schedule and budget are tight, the project team may decide to eliminate certain parts of documents in order to stay on schedule. If this is done, the auditor should note those missing items as project deficiencies. One last example is for the auditor to determine the status of any changes that have been approved through the point of the review.

Verifying the Status of the Definition Phase. The IT auditor procedures for this task will involve following up on key elements and observations from the prior step of determining the current status of the project. These procedures will mostly likely emphasize interviewing the personnel for developing the deliverable, or for providing the information that was included in it.

The document flow for the definition phase is determined by the development methodology. The project plan specifies the strategy for managing the software development process and indicates how the system will be certi-fied before installation and operation.

The project plan is used to develop the functional requirements docu-ment, the security and control requirements, and detailed data require-ments mentioned earlier in this section. The preparation of these documents is likely to require extensive interaction among the responsible participants, which is a significant portion of the value of the documents. The cooperation required to produce the documents is only a small portion of the cooperation required to make the project a success.

All documents developed during this phase, or some portion of them, should be used by appropriate members of the development team to update the overall project plan. The auditor should review the overall project plan to determine if it is current and complete.

Regardless of the IT auditor's interest in the updated project plan, it is more important for the project steering committee or senior management. At this point in the cycle, one of these parties should be deciding whether to continue the project through the next phase, cancel the project, or pro-pose modifications to the project. This decision process may cause part or all of the initiation and definition phases to be repeated.

The IT Audit Professional has two major concerns regarding the partici-pants responsible for the definition phase. First is that the appropriate indi-viduals participate, and second is that they participate effectively in the process. The auditor should address these concerns by identifying the par-ticipants and the roles and responsibilities of those individuals.

The IT auditor might consider the following descriptions of possible par-ticipants and questions the auditor might ask them.

Senior Management. If senior management approval was required, was it obtained before commencing the definition phase?

Project Steering Committee. The approval of the committee should have been obtained before commencing the definition phase.

Project Sponsor/Project Team. These are the participants responsible for either updating or preparing the definition phase deliverables.

Security Specialist. Has this specialist reviewed security and control com-ponents of the project plan, functional requirements document, or the data requirements document?

Quality Assurance Specialist. Has this specialist provided consultation and review of the systems security and internal control components of the project plan, functional requirements document, and data requirements document?

ADJUSTING AUDIT OBJECTIVES

IT Audit Professionals should attempt to identify specific user needs that can be traced to the functional definition, along with the security and control requirements. This involves the creation of a set of specific audit objectives for the definition phase. The auditor's involvement in the definition phase depends in part on a series of factors that can cause the system to have greater impact on the company.

The IT auditor will find that the better controlled the development methodology is, the less likely it is that the auditor will have to be involved in each project, or in each phase of each project. In addition, the greater the number of factors that can hinder the projects success, the greater the need for audit involvement during this phase. This involvement should be reflected in the customization of audit objectives.

DETAILED AUDIT TESTING

The IT auditor is responsible for two aspects of verifying documents. First, the auditor must ensure that the documents are prepared in accordance with the system development methodology. Second, the auditor should determine whether information transferred between documents is accurate.

The IT auditor is also responsible for obtaining an accurate and complete understanding of the project as well as the flow of documents and any other deliverables throughout the process.

Detailed Testing. The IT auditor should identify key control and process attributes of the definition phase and then test a sufficient number of those attributes to support the conclusions required to meet the audit objectives. The auditor should prepare a list of exceptions, deficiencies, and observations to provide to the appropriate project participants, along with any related recommendations for their consideration.

The auditor's testing should be performed using a definition phase audit program. This program includes a potential set of objectives, key indicators for each objective, along with specific audit procedures and with the tools and techniques to facilitate those tests.

The IT auditor can use the following paragraphs as a checklist for evaluating certain key elements of the development methodology.

The Project Plan. This should include a strategy for managing the software, goals, and activities for all phases and subphases, resource estimates for the duration of the system life cycle, intermediate goals, and methods for system development, documentation, problem reporting, and change control.

The Functional Requirements Document. This should include the proposed methods and procedures, a summary of improvements, a summary of security and control considerations, cost considerations, and alternatives. This document may also include qualitative and quantitative software functional requirements, the means by which the software functions satisfy performance objectives, what the performance requirements are, and an explanation of inputs and outputs.

The Security and Control Requirements Document. This should include the vulnerabilities identified during risk analysis, established internal control and application control requirements.

The Data Requirements Document. This should include data collection requirements, logical groupings of data, the characteristics of each data element, and procedures for data collection. This area also includes descriptions for sensitive and critical data, which should include sensitive and critical types of data along with the degree of that sensitivity.

AUDIT RESULTS AND REPORTING

The IT auditor should develop a list of findings and recommendations at the end of this phase, just as was done at the end of the initiation phase. It is possible for there to be many more findings than recommendations, as the auditor may conclude that some of the findings either are not material, or do not warrant a recommendation.

There are certain deficiencies that are common to many situations, some of which are presented below:

- Unrealistic estimates of the resources and time required to implement the system
- Poorly developed requirements that do not support a decision to move onto the next phase of systems development
- Incomplete input requirements that will make it difficult to properly develop the application
- Incomplete output requirements that can make system development impractical and uneconomical
- Incomplete processing specifications that do not clearly indicate how inputs should be converted into outputs
- Potential system failures and appropriate responses that are not well defined, and appropriate recovery techniques that are not properly developed

- Undefined service levels that could result in a system that does not have the necessary processing capacity to handle the system requirements
- Security and control requirements that have not been fully defined, which may lead to the application not including adequate security and controls

The IT Audit Professional is reminded that problems inadequately addressed in the definition phase can escalate costs throughout the remainder of the system development process. Implementing elements omitted from the requirements definition may cost between 10 and 100 times more than addressing the same problem in definition. This adds a responsibility for the auditor to not only identify the deficiencies but also to estimate the impact of those deficiencies on the organization. The impact of definition phase deficiencies can be estimated in two ways.

First, the IT auditor can estimate the actual cost of the deficiency itself. For example, the lack of controls can result in the loss of assets in the operational system. Second, the auditor can estimate the escalating cost of fixing definition problems. The informal rule is that for each unit of work estimated to need to be expended to fix a definition phase deficiency, it will require ten units of work to do during the test phase, and 100 units of work once the system is placed into operation.

CONFIRMING THE AUDIT STRATEGY

The IT Audit Professional should reassess the audit strategy for the rest of the project based on the findings and recommendations during the current phase. The IT auditor's plan should be based on one or more of the following objectives, which should confirm that systems and applications:

- Carry out the policies that management has prescribed for them
- Provide the controls and audit trails needed for management, auditor, and operational review
- Include the controls necessary to protect against loss or serious error
- Are efficient and economical in operation
- Conform to legal requirements
- Are documented in a manner that provides the understanding of the system required for appropriate maintenance and auditing

Section 19
Application Development Phase

The IT Audit Professional will find that this phase includes the procedures for developing and testing the new or modified application. The implemented programs should be based on the detailed design and program specifications prepared in the system design phase. If the design is done correctly, the development phase should not be difficult. If there are gaps in the specifications, they will have to be filled during the development phase.

The gaps have to be filled because programming is very detailed and requires that almost every design decision be made before the code can be written. In other words, the IT auditor should confirm that either the development methodology or the specific application fully comprehends the design specifications, and that documentation and training provide for a usable and maintainable system.

The IT Audit Professional accomplishes these objectives by evaluating programming phase documentation. To do this, the auditor must understand the system development methodology, the documents that are produced by that methodology, and the flow in which the documents are produced. The documents produced during this phase vary among methodologies. Even the same methodology can be implemented differently among two or more companies and thus produce different documents.

PROGRAMMING PHASE OVERVIEW

Programming is the process of implementing the detailed design specifications into program code. The process of converting specifications to executable code depends heavily on the quality of the program definition. If the application is well defined, programming is not technically complex.

Most system development methodologies clearly define how systems move from the definition phase to the programming phase. In fact, most IT professionals are well trained in programming, but few have extensive training in definition and design skills. Therefore, the IT auditor finds that programming is frequently the best specified and most mastered skill.

ASSESSING SYSTEMS DEVELOPMENT

The application developers may also begin to develop end-user and maintenance manuals during this phase, as is a preliminary installation plan. The preliminary installation plan specifies the approach and other details of the application installation.

Participants and Their Tasks

The IT auditor is likely to find that the programming phase includes the same participants that were in the definition phase. The responsible participants and their functions during this phase include the following:

Senior Management. Approves the updated project plan to advance to the programming phase, in consultation with the sponsor and other participants.

Project Steering Committee. Approves the updated project plan to advance to the programming phase, in consultation with the sponsor and other participants. Approves the revised project plan; revised validation, verification, and testing plan and specifications; user manual; operations and maintenance manual; and installation and conversion plan. The sponsor/user also updates the system decision paper and initiates user training.

Project Sponsor/Project Team. Updates the project plan; revises the validation, verification, and testing plan and specifications; develops the user manual, operations and maintenance manual and the installation and conversion plan. The project manager is also responsible for programming and testing.

Security Specialist. Reviews the user manual, operations and maintenance manual, installation and conversion plan, and revised validation, verification, and testing plan and specifications.

Quality Assurance Specialist. Reviews the program definition, program code, documentation, and training for compliance with design and DP standards.

PROGRAMMING PHASE DELIVERABLES

The IT auditor is likely to find three new deliverables developed by the end of this phase, along with one or more revisions to existing deliverable documents. The three new documents produced during this phase are:

- *The user manual:* This document describes the functions performed by the software in nontechnical terminology so that the user organization can determine its applicability as well as when and how to use it.

- *Operations and maintenance manual:* The operations manual provides system operations personnel with a description of the software and the operational environment so that the software can be run. The maintenance manual provides the maintenance programmer with the information and source code necessary to understand the programs, their operating environment, and their maintenance procedures and security requirements.
- *Installation and conversion plan:* This document directs the installation or implementation of the system at locations other than the test site and is used after testing of the systems, including security and internal control features, has been completed.

THE INITIAL AUDIT ASSESSMENT

The IT Audit Professional faces two challenges in the programming phase. The first is determining if the application as programmed is consistent with the definition. The second is to review the control over changes made to the definition or other changes made during the programming effort.

Reviewing Definition Phase Output. The IT Audit Professional will probably find that the size and detail of the deliverables increase as the project progresses. The definition document review is significantly more time-consuming than the initiation phase review.

The IT auditor must therefore focus on the most important elements of the security- and control-related specifications and the verification and testing specifications. The security and control review should emphasize the adequacy of those elements.

Evaluating Security and Control. The auditor should identify the nature and extent of the risks faced by the system, along with the compensating controls, and then attempt to evaluate the adequacy of those controls in terms of meeting their objectives. The auditor's opinion is based on this assessment.

The verification and testing plan provides the standards against which the IT Auditor evaluates the implementation and define the tests for evaluating controls. This document indicates how the project team plans to implement the application controls.

The IT Audit Professional has the information on controls as defined and programmed, which precisely defines how the controls should be implemented. This provides the information the auditor requires for conducting the programming review.

Reviewing Programming Phase Plans. The IT Auditor should review programming phase plans, paying particular attention to the flexibility in the planned deadlines. The programming phase is the one most likely to be beset by problems or unexpected situations that require additional time to resolve.

Project plans that include hard deadlines with little or no flexibility may have to be compromised to meet those dates. If the project is late going into the programming phase with hard deadlines, it becomes likely that one or more of these compromises will occur.

One of the frequently compromised areas is the programming of security and controls. Compromises in this particular area may not appear to directly affect the application's functionality, which is the basis of the compromise. The application may very well produce the desired reports, but not in a controlled manner.

The IT auditor should attempt to determine whether the project plans are sufficient to ensure that the appropriate security and control features are properly implemented. The project plan should indicate who is responsible for these controls, along with a description of how they are to be implemented.

Gathering information for the review. The IT auditor should attempt to gather the information that should be included in one or more of the following deliverables. As with the other stages, the existence and quality of the information is much more important than the names or number of deliverable documents:

- The updated project plan
- The verification and testing plan
- The user manual
- The operations and maintenance manual
- The implementation and conversion plan

Evaluating programming phase status. The IT Audit Professional should make this evaluation by examining the proper implementation of security and control features and that all of the design specifications are being realized in the final application.

The auditor should compare the work flow with the system development methodology in use. If other deliverables are produced, the auditor should include them as well. When documents are not produced or updated, it is normally indicative of a potential problem in the application design.

Verifying programming phase status. The IT Audit Professional should review the documents being produced to ensure that the appropriate information has been collected, recorded, and is consistent with previous documents. Verification is primarily a quality control responsibility and should normally be performed by the quality assurance specialist or other direct participant in the process.

During the programming and training phase, the auditor must verify new and updated documents. The verification questions that might be used are shown below.

User manual.

Does the user manual:

- Describe the functions sufficiently?
- Indicate when and how it is to be used?
- Explain how to prepare input data and parameters?
- Explain how to interpret output results?
- Provide a full description of the application?
- Explain all user operating procedures?
- Explain user responsibilities related to security, privacy, and internal controls?
- Describe how to correct errors?
- Describe how to recover operations?

Operations Manual.

Does the operations manual:

- Provide operations personnel with a description of the software?
- Provide operations personnel with the instructions necessary to operate the software?
- Provide operations personnel with sections on nonroutine procedures, remote operations, and security requirements?
- Provide operations personnel with error procedures?
- Provide operations personnel with recovery procedures?
- Provide maintenance programmers with the information and source code necessary to understand the programs?
- Provide maintenance programmers with an overview of the architecture and structure of the system?
- Provide maintenance programmers with maintenance guideline procedures?
- Provide maintenance programmers with the design of internal control and security procedures so that they can be individually maintained?

Installation and conversion plan.

Does the installation and conversion plan:

- Explain how to install the software?
- Explain how to activate security procedures?

- Explain how to interconnect the software with other software packages?
- Explain how to install the software onto the operating environment?
- Provide sections in nontechnical language that are directed toward staff personnel?
- Provide sections in suitable terminology that are directed toward operations personnel?

Updated project plan.

Does the project plan:

- Provide a strategy for managing the software?
- Contain goals and activities for all phases and subphases?
- Provide resource estimates that are stated for the duration of the system development process?
- Provide intermediate goals (e.g., management and technical reviews)?
- Contain methods for design, documentation, problem reporting, and change control?
- Contain supporting techniques and tools?
- Reflect changes in strategy occurring during this phase?
- Contain controls to determine whether goals have been accomplished?
- Provide appropriate actions to be taken if goals are not accomplished?

Verification and testing plan.

Does the verification and testing plan:

- Include a plan for testing the software?
- Include detailed specifications, descriptions, and procedures for all system tests?
- Include a test data reduction and evaluation criterion?
- Relate to the system plan?
- Provide assurance that the system plan drives the specifications?
- Include general project background and information on the proposed solution to any mission deficiencies?
- Include validation, verification, and testing requirements, measurement criteria, and constraints?
- Include procedures to be applied during development in general and in each phase?
- Include supporting information for validation, verification, and testing selections made?
- Include appendices that describe project and environmental considerations?
- Include tests of security and internal controls?
- Include appendices that define the testing technique and tool selection information?

- Reflect changes in strategy occurring during this phase?

User and operations manuals.

Do the user and operations manuals:

- Provide procedures to keep the training materials in the manuals up to date?
- Include controls to ensure that training materials based on the manuals are updated as associated information in the manuals is updated?

CONDUCTING INTERVIEWS

The next step is for the IT auditor to interview the programming phase participants. If there are too many participants, the auditor should interview only the individuals needed to ensure that the auditor can satisfy the audit objectives. The questions that the auditor should ask of the responsible participants are listed below.

Senior Management.

- Has the revised project plan been approved?
- Has the revised user manual been approved?
- Have the revised operations and maintenance manual and the installation and conversion plan been approved?
- Has the revised updated system decision paper been approved?
- Have the appropriate user training tasks been initiated?
- Have the validation, verification, and testing plan and specifications been approved?

Project Steering Committee.

- Has the revised project plan been approved?
- Has the revised user manual been approved?
- Have the revised operations and maintenance manual and the installation and conversion plan been approved?
- Has the revised updated system decision paper been approved?
- Have the appropriate user training tasks been initiated?
- Have the validation, verification, and testing plan and specifications been approved?

Project Sponsor/Project Team.

- Has the project plan been updated?
- Have the validation, verification, and testing plan and specifications been revised?
- Has the user manual been developed?

- Has an operations and maintenance manual been developed?
- Has the installation and conversion plan been developed?
- Has it been ensured that appropriate programming was performed?

Security Specialist.

- Has the user manual been reviewed?
- Has the operations and maintenance manual been reviewed?
- Have the installation and conversion plan and the validation, verification, and testing plan and specifications been reviewed?

Quality Assurance Specialist.

- Has the program definition been reviewed for compliance to design and DP standards?
- Has the program code been reviewed for compliance to design and DP standards?
- Has the documentation been reviewed for compliance to design and DP standards?
- Has the training been reviewed for compliance to design and DP standards?

SETTING THE AUDIT OBJECTIVES

The IT Audit Professional may need to make adjustments to the audit objectives, depending on the design methodology used or other issues that may have arisen during the procedures up to this point in the process.

Development Methodology Audit Considerations. The IT auditor may customize the two audit objectives for this phase based on one or more of the following factors.

First, the status of design up to this point must be considered. The fewer problems involved in this application, the less need there is for audit attention during this phase. Second, the design methodology used must be noted. Audit involvement changes significantly, depending on whether the software is developed in-house, contracted, or purchased, as follows:

- For software developed in-house, the audit involvement should be at critical management checkpoints, usually at the end of developmental phases.
- For contracted software, the audit involvement must either be specified in the contract or else be limited to the points in time when key deliverables prepared by the contractor are made available to the organization.

- For purchased applications, the only audit involvement is an assessment of the design methodology for determining whether adequate controls were incorporated to develop an effective application. This is done in preparation for a decision to purchase or contract.

Third, the IT Audit Professional should consider technology integration factors. During the implementation phase, the risk attributes of technology integration can be reassessed to evaluate the implementation risk. The greater the risk, the greater the need for audit attention in this phase. The technology integration attributes that must be considered in evaluating the scope and objectives of audit work include:

- The make-up of the project team in relation to the technology used (i.e., number, training, and experience)
- The applicability of the DP design methodologies and standards to the technology in use
- User knowledge of related technology
- The margin for error (i.e., is there reasonable time to make adjustments, corrections, or perform analyses before the transaction is completed?)
- The availability of automated error detection and correction procedures
- The degree of dependence on the system
- The criticality of interfaces with other systems and external organizations

DETAILED AUDIT TESTING

During detailed audit testing, the IT auditor should evaluate the adequacy of the programming effort by reviewing the test results. First, the auditor should evaluate the results of quality assurance reviews of testing efforts.

The results of this evaluation determine the effectiveness of the quality assurance department's reviews and thereby affect the nature and extent of audit procedures in this phase. If no effective quality assurance function exists, and there is no provision for another project participant to assume those responsibilities, then the IT auditor may be asked to evaluate the adequacy of testing efforts.

Second, the IT auditor may evaluate the adequacy of documentation-user, programming, maintenance, and installation manuals. Again, the auditor may review quality assurance efforts in these areas, yet try not to duplicate the work done by that function. If, however, there is no effective quality assurance function, and none of the other project participants assume those responsibilities, the auditor may be asked to substitute for the quality assurance specialist.

THE AUDIT TEST

The IT Audit Professional should also develop a standard audit test program for the programming phase. The test begins by outlining the more common audit objectives. For each objective, the IT auditor is given one or more tests to perform, and for each test, one or more tools and techniques are suggested.

AUDIT RESULTS AND REPORTING

The result of the programming phase review should be documented and given to project management. Deficiencies and their potential effect on meeting the system mission should be reported to project management on a timely basis. Delays in submitting review reports can significantly increase the cost of correcting deficiencies.

Common Deficiencies. In the programming and testing phase, some deficiencies occur more frequently than others. The following deficiencies are among the more common ones for this phase.

- Documents and tasks are not completed or are not completed on time (i.e., goals are met but documents and tasks are not completed).
- Goals are not met because of incomplete tasks.
- Applications are coded that could be done more economically through contracting or purchasing off-the-shelf software.
- Documentation for programming and training is not prepared in accordance with standards or is not prepared at all, resulting in additional maintenance and operational costs.
- The program documentation is not kept current; as programs are changed, the documentation is not updated and therefore is unusable for maintaining the system.
- No quality control is exercised over the documentation to ensure that it is complete and in compliance with standards.
- Programs are not fully tested, resulting in the operation of defective programs.
- Users are inadequately trained in the use of the application; thus, they either misuse the software or are unable to use the software features.
- User manuals are not prepared or are not prepared in accordance with standards, resulting in incorrectly entered or processed transactions and improper use of output.
- Audit and quality assurance tools and techniques are not included or are not properly implemented in the system.

Deficiencies in programming result in inaccurate or incomplete processing, which causes abnormal terminations in processing, resulting in reruns of processing and late delivery of output. Deficiencies not uncovered through operational controls result in improper processing by users.

In addition, deficiencies in documentation and training result in operational malfunctions and erroneous processing. These deficiencies can also result in uneconomical operations, because tasks must be performed several times to be performed correctly.

The IT Audit Professional should be able to quantify the impact of these potential deficiencies, and should demonstrate the potential adverse effects that can occur because of inadequate programming, documentation, and training.

In particular, the auditor should process test data to show that the system was not properly programmed to prevent erroneous processing, compare user and programmer documentation to identify discrepancies between these two critical documents, and compare user documentation with training documentation and instruction to identify inconsistencies.

EVALUATING THE AUDIT STRATEGY

The IT Audit Professional, at the end of the programming and training phase, should determine the nature and extent of the audit procedures to be performed. As with other phases, if only minimal problems are detected by the end of this phase, the auditor may not need to expend extensive effort in the evaluation and acceptance phase. Conversely, if the auditor suspects that there are potential weaknesses in the system, extensive audit involvement may be warranted during the next phase.

The IT auditor should also finalize any post-implementation audit programs, tools, and techniques during this phase. As the project sponsor is evaluating the system during the next phase, the auditor should be prepared to evaluate the audit program developed for use during operations. At a minimum, this audit program should include:

- A list of potential areas for audit investigation
- Tools for file analysis and software packages for use during operation for file analysis
- Step-by-step audit programs for the audit team to use in auditing the operational system
- A permanent working file on the system, including key aspects of documentation, with references to official systems documents

Section 20
The Evaluation and Acceptance Phase

The IT Audit Professional will review this phase to ensure that the system has been evaluated and that the end users have formally accepted the system before it has gone "live" in a production environment. During this phase, unit testing is completed, and integration and system testing are undertaken.

The results of these tests provide user management with the information it needs to decide whether to accept, modify, or reject the system. The total system and data must be validated and must fully meet all user requirements.

The IT auditor should continue to emphasize internal control requirements as an area requiring specific audit attention. The fulfillment of this objective can be done in conjunction with the validation, verification, and testing plan and specifications—or independently of that plan.

In any event, the IT auditor should review the work of the validation, verification, and testing team and conduct additional tests as appropriate. The actual performance of the task usually is too time-consuming for the auditor to perform. It has been estimated that this phase of the developmental process can consume as much as 30 percent of the developmental effort.

If testing is properly performed, a test plan, test results, and a test report should be available. The test plan should indicate the system's functions and then cross-reference them to the tests designed to validate the correct operation of those functions. Test results should be specifically documented and retained. The test report should indicate the results of those tests and relate the results to the function, indicating whether it performs correctly.

Once the test results have been completed and prepared for the test report, the IT auditor's role becomes much easier. In these instances, the auditor needs only to perform sufficient tests to ensure that the test results are correct. The auditor should then be able to draw the same conclusions from the test results as the test team drew.

OVERVIEW

The IT auditor should conduct this portion of the review in accordance with the revised validation, verification, and testing plan and specifications. Completed code is tested as described in the revised plan.

Three types of program testing are usually performed: unit, integration, and system. If performed properly, unit testing validates the functioning of the unit, integration testing validates the interfaces between the units and the operating environment, and system testing validates the interaction between the application system and the user area. Although it is often difficult to do, unit testing should be completed before integration testing commences, and integration testing before system testing commences.

Adequate time must be allocated to testing. Software testing is an underplanned and undermanaged facet of the developmental process because the previous phases are frequently completed late, although the installation date remains fixed.

After the review, analysis, and testing of the system, including execution of the programs on test data, the system should be field-tested in one or more representative operational sites. For particularly sensitive systems, disaster recovery and continuity of operations plans should be fully documented and operationally tested as well.

The IT auditor should also determine if the application or any of the data stored within it should be designated as sensitive. If this designation has been granted, then the security in the system should be comprehensively tested prior to implementation, and certified if the testing is successful.

Security evaluation should be part of the broader test results and test evaluation report. The accreditation statement—the last critical activity of the phase—is a statement from the responsible accrediting official (e.g., the sponsor/user or information resources management official) that the system is operating effectively and is ready to be installed. Any caveats or restrictions should be provided at this time.

Participants and Their Tasks

The IT Audit Professional should find that all or most of the participants responsible for the system play an active role in evaluation and acceptance. In the early phases, the responsible participants are frequently senior people. For example, the manager or assistant managers of the user area may be directly involved in the early developmental phases.

As the work becomes more technical, the responsibilities are frequently delegated downward to lower-level people in the operational areas. During the evaluation and acceptance phase, as critical decisions have to be made, the senior people should again be involved. The participants and their responsibilities in the evaluation and acceptance phase are:

Senior Management/Project Steering Committee: Approves the updated system decision paper to advance to the evaluation and acceptance phase, in consultation with the sponsor/user and the DP manager (this occurs between phases).

Project Sponsor: Approves the revised project plan and installation and conversion plan, updates system decision paper, oversees training, and accepts (accredits) system for operation.

Project Team: Updates the project plan, supports and oversees the test analysis and security evaluation report, and certifies system security. This person revises the user manual, operations and maintenance manual, and installation and conversion plan, based on test results.

Security Specialist: Reviews the test analysis and security evaluation report and security components of the installation and conversion plan.

Quality Assurance Specialist: Reviews the validation, verification, and testing results and advises responsible participants on system achievement of the needs statement.

Evaluation and Acceptance Phase Deliverables

The IT auditor evaluates the work performed in this phase by looking at the phase documentation. The phase produces one new document and updates of existing documents.

The new document is the test analysis and security evaluation report. This document details the test analysis results and findings; presents the demonstrated capabilities and deficiencies, including the security evaluation report needed for system certification; and provides a basis for preparing a statement of system and software readiness for implementation.

INITIAL ASSESSMENT OF THE ACCEPTANCE PHASE

The IT auditor's primary source of information for the procedures performed in this phase are the audit results and workpapers from previous phases. If the same individuals are involved in evaluation and acceptance as were involved in previous phases, background preparation work should be minimal.

The IT auditor, however, is still concerned with the flow of work, ensuring that the responsible participants have fulfilled their roles, and acquiring and reviewing the documentation produced during this phase.

Reviewing Programming Phase Output

At this point, the system is complete. The IT auditor's objective of this phase is to identify and remove significant defects from the system, if have not already been addressed by someone else. This can be accomplished through the creation of a series of test conditions that, when processed against the executable code, produce the proper results by which the system is judged.

The IT auditor may wish to review some of the documents from the earlier phases because they indicate what the system is supposed to do. The programming phase documents are oriented toward what the system does to meet its objectives, and the user manual is unique to the company for which it was developed, explaining how the system should be operated by the end users.

The auditor must understand both the "what" and the "how," in preparation for reviewing this final phase of the system development process. The auditor must also ensure that the test data and testing documentation is saved for use in validating subsequent changes to the system.

Reviewing Evaluation and Acceptance Phase Plans

The final phase is frequently between the point at which the programs are complete and the date when those programs must be placed into production. If the production date is firm, the time allocated to this phase may be insufficient.

Therefore, the IT auditor should determine that someone has determined that any critical systems have been tested and are functioning as expected. It is unrealistic to expect exhaustive testing to occur, although it is desirable. There are always compromises between budget and schedule, and complete testing.

Frequently, there are no options regarding when the system is placed into production, particularly when it is mandated by legislation. It is important to optimize the test time available.

GATHERING AND VERIFYING INFORMATION ON THE PHASE STATUS

The IT Audit Professional will look for the status testing reports that should have been developed and retained during the development process on the status of testing. The criteria for testing should be included in the verification and testing plan and specifications.

These criteria indicate which functions are to be tested and what conditions are to be used to test those functions. In the hierarchy of testing, the units or programs should be tested first. When these have been validated as performing correctly, the integration or interfaces among the units or programs are tested. Once those interfaces have been validated, the acceptance test, which validates the interfaces between the users and the system, is performed.

The test status reports should indicate which functions have been tested, which functions work, which functions are in the process of being corrected, and when those functions should be retested. At any point, the IT Audit Professional should be able to determine how many functions have been validated and how many remain invalid.

If this status information is not available, the IT auditor should be concerned over whether the end-product of testing will adequately indicate systems performance before the system is put into production. Without this information, management cannot make a knowledgeable decision regarding the installation and operation of the system.

By the time this phase commences, all of the work necessary to develop the system should be complete and the company should have an executable system. The company must be assured that the executable system meets the system requirements and specifications.

The IT Audit Professional will find that almost all of the development work that is performed in the evaluation and acceptance phase is testing. Once the modules are successfully tested, they can be assembled into programs. Some of the assembled programs involve utility programs and other aspects of the computer's operating software. These programs are then tested prior to assembling them into modules.

Finally, the modules are put together as a system. This new system is then tested and validated to determine that it works in the operating environment, when interfacing with other systems, and that it meets user requirements.

The IT auditor must become familiar with the flow of work during this phase. This includes becoming familiar with the various types of testing and the expectations from those tests. As in other aspects of system development, the exact flow of documents varies from methodology to methodology and among companies using the same methodology.

The validation and acceptance phase may produce one completely new deliverable, while all the other deliverables are updates of deliverables from other phases. The auditor should look at all of these documents, but should emphasize verifying that the test analysis and security evaluation report properly implements and accomplishes the test plan objective and that the test results are properly reflected in the evaluation report.

ASSESSING SYSTEMS DEVELOPMENT

The auditor must verify that all appropriate responsible participants are involved in this phase, that they have been assigned the appropriate role, and that they have correctly fulfilled that role. The auditor usually interviews the participants to verify their needed contribution. The desirable participants and the questions that the auditor must ask them follow.

Senior Management/Project Steering Committee.

- Have the appropriate updates to the project plan been made?
- Has the test analysis and security evaluation report been supported and overseen?
- Has the system security been certified?
- Has the user manual been revised, based on test results?
- Has the operations and maintenance manual been updated, based on test results?
- Has the installation and conversion plan been updated, based on test results?

Project Sponsor/Project Team.

- Have the test results been reviewed?
- Has the test analysis and security evaluation report been reviewed?
- Have the security components of the installation and conversion plan been reviewed?
- Has the revised project plan been approved?
- Has the revised installation and conversion plan been approved?
- Have the necessary updates been made in the system decision paper?
- Has the necessary training been overseen?
- Has the system been accepted for operation?

Security Specialist.

- Have the test results been reviewed?
- Has the test analysis and security evaluation report been reviewed?
- Do the updates to the user manual, operations and maintenance manual, and installation and conversion plan reflect any impact on the security documentation?

Quality Assurance Specialist.

- Have the validation, verification, and testing results been reviewed?
- Have responsible participants been advised on the system achievement of the needs statement?

SETTING OBJECTIVES FOR THE AUDIT

The IT auditor will find that the audit objectives to be accomplished during this phase vary with management's needs. If the project team does not have an adequate test plan, management may ask the auditor to play a more active role in testing. Sometimes, the auditor performs some of the testing that occurs during this phase. Although this is not recommended, it is sometimes a necessity because testing would not be performed otherwise.

The test program outlined here includes the more common audit objectives for this phase. It is these objectives that must be customized on the basis of the needs of management as well as the audit evaluation of previous phases. This phase is the auditor's last opportunity to evaluate the system before its placement into production. The greater the risks associated with the system or the greater the concerns uncovered in previous phases, the greater the need for audit involvement during this phase.

EVALUATION AND ACCEPTANCE PHASE CONSIDERATIONS

The IT auditor should pay particular attention to the adequacy of testing. If the testing is inadequate, or deficient, the organization runs the risk of serious problems or disruptions due to an unsafe system being implemented.

If the development methodology is deficient in the testing area, the IT Audit Professional may wish to suggest one of the previous references as a test strategy. The key aspects of testing for this phase are the development of an adequate test plan, the execution of the test plan, and the analysis and reporting of test results. The auditor should be particularly concerned with the test report. This report should not only indicate what works and does not work, but also include the test group's opinion on the adequacy of the system.

Companies can use one of two test approaches. First, they can use an independent test team (a group of people independent of the project users that are professional testers). Second, system users can create their own test conditions and determine whether the system is acceptable to them for use in production.

DETAILED AUDIT TESTING

The project sponsor relies on the test analysis and security evaluation report to determine whether to accept the system. The sponsor, however, is usually not technically oriented and does not have the necessary background to challenge the information included in the report. The independent opinion of the adequacy of that report, provided by the auditor, can be important in determining whether the application will be accepted or, if it is accepted, whether any counter-strategy must be put into place to compensate for potential weaknesses.

Testing is a critical phase of the life cycle. Programs and applications should pass system and acceptance tests before being implemented. These tests cover two different areas of concern, yet they have the same goal.

The system test provides an internal assessment of the correctness, performance, and reliability of the operational system, whereas the acceptance test determines user reaction to the product, its performance, installation procedure, documentation, and reliability.

Once these tests have been performed, the project team reviews the results to ensure that the system meets user requirements and is acceptable to the user. In addition, the auditor must ensure that testing is adequately planned and performed in compliance with approved standards and that the test results are properly evaluated and included in system documentation.

Evaluation and Acceptance Phase Audit Tests. Once again, the IT auditor should develop an audit program for this phase of the audit. The audit program should include secondary objectives for the audit, suggested tests to accomplish those objectives, and tools for conducting those tests. This program should increase the auditor's effectiveness in reviewing systems in the evaluation and acceptance phase.

AUDIT RESULTS AND REPORTING

If the IT Audit Professional identifies a problem or weakness in part of the application, management may desire to have assistance from the audit department in the form of recommendations about changes to make or courses of action to take.

The IT auditor should only propose recommendations that are appropriate based on the nature and extent of the problems. A minor variance may not warrant highlighting in an audit report or offering recommendations. Recommendations should be limited to those findings that have a significant impact on the company's mission.

Deficiencies identified in this phase most often represent operational deficiencies. If they are not corrected before the application is placed into production, they can cause or lead to a system failure. At this point in the development cycle, there is no time to compensate for deficiencies in future phases. The following deficiencies are common to the evaluation and acceptance phase:

- Testing does not include all tests contained in the test plan, which results in untested functions being placed into production.
- A test report is not prepared or, if prepared, does not adequately indicate which areas have been validated to function correctly; this can result in applications being placed in production without the user knowing what does and does not work.
- User management is not involved in the decision of whether to put the system into production; therefore, systems are placed into production that may have defects.
- The test plan, test results, and test reports either are not complete or are not prepared in a format that can be used as ongoing maintenance documentation, and maintenance personnel must therefore spend more time and money reproducing test conditions and test results.
- A parallel test is not conducted; when current capabilities are in existence, this leaves the user uncertain as to whether the new system can produce the same results as the old system.
- The system is not field-tested at selected locations and thus it may not work properly in the operational environment.
- Systems development documentation is not updated to reflect the changes and activities that occurred during development. The application may end up being maintained based on inaccurate documentation, with the potential of either increasing the defect rate or maintenance costs.
- A written installation and conversion plan is not prepared and followed; this results in the potential for increased conversion costs and inaccurately or incompletely performed conversion tasks.
- System security is not certified, causing potential security vulnerabilities in the operational system.

EVALUATING AUDIT RESULTS AND PLANS

The IT Auditor should complete the audit program once the system becomes operational. The insight gained during the developmental process should be passed on to the audit team reviewing the operational system in order to properly focus and maximize the audit effort. The insight to be included in the program is described in the previous phase.

The auditor must select the final operational audit tools during this phase. These tools should be tested (when the system is tested) to ensure that they work. Thus, the auditor undergoes an evaluation and acceptance of audit tools while user management undergoes an evaluation and acceptance of the system.

Part V
Assessing Implemented Systems

The IT Audit Professional is likely to find the most significant challenges when assessing automated application systems that are fully implemented when the audit is done. The sections included in Part V are designed to support effectively performing these reviews.

Section 21, "Initial Review Procedures," focuses on the IT auditor's understanding of the applications design and its control procedures.

Section 22, "Audit Evidence," focuses on the types of data and information the IT auditor will need to fully substantiate their conclusions and recommendations.

Section 23, "Identify Application Risks," details several alternative approaches the IT auditor can employ to determine where the most important potential reviews are that might be done.

Section 24, "Develop a Detailed Plan," presents both the components and a detailed process for developing plans that will ensure that the work performed meets the intended objectives.

Section 25, "Evaluate Internal Controls," is designed for the IT auditor to determine whether the controls in a particular application are adequate to reduce the potential risks to an acceptable level.

Section 26, "Test Data Integrity," takes the IT auditor through a range of techniques he or she might employ to determine whether the data within an application has integrity, which is one of the most crucial areas for the auditor in order to reach the proper conclusion.

Section 27, "Certify Computer Security," describes an optional step in an IT audit. It should be performed when security is important to the successful operation of the automated application system.

Section 28, "Analyze Audit Results," takes the IT auditor through a step-by-step process to analyze and use the information produced by the data tests.

Section 29, "Review and Report Findings," describes how the IT auditor develops the audit report, distributes it, and follows up on the recommendations. Good ideas are of little value unless they are accepted and implemented, and the value of the audit is frequently rated on acceptance of the audit report by both auditee and senior management.

Section 30, "Review Quality Control," defines a process for performing a self-assessment of the audit and the audit process followed while the audit was performed.

Section 31, "Workflow Diagramming," is intended to be a primer for IT auditors to be able to either review existing diagrams or develop their own.

Section 21
Initial Review Procedures

IT auditors should begin application reviews *after* the audit preplanning is concluded, but *before* the final audit plan is completed. The initial application review procedures focus on auditors gaining or confirming an understanding of the applications design and its control procedures.

INITIAL REVIEW PROCEDURES

The initial review procedures include reviewing permanent and carryforward workpapers, holding a planning meeting with selected users, reviewing existing documentation, and developing additional documentation, most often workflow diagrams.

REVIEW EXISTING AUDIT FILES

The IT auditor should review prior audit workpapers to identify one or more of the following items:

- Prior audit reports covering the same or related business areas
- Relevant permanent folder items

Carryforward workpapers covering the specific application or applications under review or the detailed workpapers from a prior review of the same or a similar area.

Prior Audit Reports. The IT auditor should locate any prior audit reports that could be related to the current area under review. From those past audit reports, the IT auditor should identify any significant issues along with management responses and, at least, the original disposition of any final audit recommendations. He or she should also determine whether the status of those recommendations agreed to by management was ever reported to the Internal Audit Department. If a status report is not available for that prior audit, the IT auditor should request one and place it in the current audit workpapers.

Permanent Files. IT auditors should review permanent audit files for the current area under review. They may find items in the permanent file that can further their understanding of the current area being audited. They may also find that permanent file items need to be updated, or that a permanent file is incomplete and should be updated during the current review.

Carryforward Files. IT auditors are likely to find that the carryforward files for an audit location either include documentation related to the current review or they do not. If the carryforward files include related information, that information should be duplicated. The copies are placed in the prior files and marked to indicate that the originals were carried forward, updated, and included in the current workpapers.

Prior Detailed Workpapers. IT auditors should have copies made of any detailed workpaper that might be directly relevant or useful for reference purposes. This retains the integrity of the prior workpapers, while making the information available for the current procedures. If no other use exists, this information may represent a baseline for evaluating test procedures later in the review.

THE PLANNING MEETING

IT auditors should initiate a planning meeting to explain the audit objectives, inform the internal customers of all appropriate information, and solicit their assistance in conducting the audit. The planning meeting also provides the auditee with the opportunity to express concerns or ask questions about the audit. The IT auditor may also choose to make at least initial inquiries about the status of prior audit recommendations.

IT auditors should attempt to ensure that the planning meeting memorandum is complete and accurate. *All* IT auditors in the meeting should read the memorandum and offer comments as needed. If any disagreement arises during the meeting or if the audit team cannot agree on a common conclusion or action, the auditor in charge should either make a decision or request further clarification from the auditee. The IT auditor should update the memorandum for all final changes or additions made.

Critical Success Factors. IT auditors should emphasize the following objectives for successful planning meetings.

- Invite all appropriate personnel to the planning meeting.
- Prepare as completely as is reasonable for the meeting.
- Give the auditees every reason to support the review.
- Follow through on any commitments made or issues arising during the planning meeting.

Section 22
Audit Evidence

Internal and external auditors reviewing manual applications have always been handicapped by control procedures that could be compromised at any time for a variety of different reasons. For the portion of an application's manual processes, any error, oversight, or negligent act could result in non-compliant processing for a single transaction. The auditors evaluating manual systems can ask only about procedures and attempt to infer conclusions about those procedures based on any tangible output from the procedures.

Both internal and external auditors realize that automated applications can significantly reduce, if not eliminate, this handicap. If the auditors can test the programs at a particular point in time and then identify and test program changes, it becomes easier to reach conclusions about the processing of every transaction based on testing a small sample of those transactions.

Auditors evaluating an automated application need to review many new items, including program listings, database structures, and system history logs, for example. Automated applications have provided the impetus for developing the data processing. Automated applications have provided the impetus for developing the data processing audit discipline. Until computers became an effective contributor to the business process, the audit community had little need to acquire computer-related skills.

INITIAL WORKPAPERS

IT auditors must understand the types of evidence normally available for applications and their characteristics or attributes. The information normally available for computerized applications includes narratives, flow diagrams, file and field descriptions and specifications, and output specifications and distribution. At this point in the review, IT auditors should find that the available background information is sufficient to meet the audit objectives. Several workpapers can be used to replace any missing documentation, or can be used as a baseline for evaluating the current information provided they relate to the application.

In most application reviews, IT auditors find a clear relationship between the quantity and quality of the application documentation and the time required to complete audit procedures. The auditor's time is also affected by the magnitude of the system and the volume and sensitivity of the data passing through the application.

Selecting the Sample. The IT auditor should begin by identifying all of the end users for the application he or she is reviewing. The IT auditor should work with management to identify any end users and strongly consider randomly selecting a similar number of end users.

Distributing the Survey. The IT auditor reproduces the required number of surveys and sends the questionnaire to the selected end users with an explanatory letter, visit, or telephone call. The questionnaires can be returned anonymously if appropriate.

Evaluating Survey Results. The IT auditor in this situation has an unusually difficult task. The completed surveys reflect end-user opinions, although each end user may believe that his or her responses are much closer to being facts than opinions. The IT auditor must form an independent conclusion, but be sensitive to any of the end users whose opinions or conclusions differ from his or hers. The IT auditor may consider conducting a survey optional and decide whether to use the survey based on the objectives of the audit he or she is performing.

Section 23
Identify Application Risks

Auditors of every discipline often rely on their experience and instincts to determine which audit areas to emphasize or exclude. Automated applications often include an increased level of risk and complexity. This increase makes it much more risky, if not impossible, for the IT auditor to rely strictly on judgment for final audit planning. This section presents a risk-based approach for the initial evaluation.

General Risk Assessment. IT auditors evaluate application risks to determine the level of resources to commit to the review and then to determine how to allocate the assigned resources.

Time Requirements. IT auditors preparing a risk/control matrix should plan to spend 20 to 80 hours preparing a matrix for all applications never before reviewed, and 8 to 24 hours to update an existing matrix.

Specific Procedures. The IT auditor will need to prepare a list of controls related to a particular application, along with a comparable list of potential risk exposures. The overall goal is to determine whether existing risk exposures are adequately addressed by existing controls. Application risks can be grouped into one or more of the following three areas:

1. *Inherent risk* is always part of a particular application.
2. *Technological risk* may be based on the use of unknown technology, the use of new technology by untrained personnel, or the risk that someone will use powerful new software against the company's interest.
3. *Situational risk* is based on the idea that additional risks may be created by the facts and circumstances surrounding a particular transaction.
4. *Volume risk* is founded on the idea that transaction volumes, average transaction value, and other similar items may reflect a higher level of risk.

THE MEANING OF RISK

IT auditors should adopt one of the possible meanings of risk and use it consistently within the enterprise. The two primary alternative definitions are differentiated by the consideration of controls. Risk can be defined as the potential for problems, errors, or unauthorized activity. Alternatively, risk can be defined as the residual potential after consideration of the existence and effectiveness of controls.

There is no single definition in use within the profession, and this author will not advocate one over the other. The former definition is used for the purposes of this publication.

The specific risks included in each risk area above are not meant to be all-inclusive. IT auditors should note that the author has assigned a risk level to each risk area as well as to each specific risk. This was done to reduce the chance that one area could inappropriately overshadow the others.

The IT auditor is expected to assign a numeric risk level to each specific risk item based on his or her review procedures for gathering background data and evaluating that data. The risk level (1–3) is multiplied by the estimated risk to get a weighted score, and the weighted scores are totaled to determine total risk.

IT auditors completing the initial risk assessment procedures will need to consider application risk in two contexts. First is stand-alone risk, while the second is relative risk.

STAND-ALONE RISK

IT auditors focusing on stand-alone risk will need to compare the risk between application elements to determine how audit resources should be allocated. This approach is most significant in situations where a more complex application is being reviewed, and there is a need to select which components will receive the most attention.

RELATIVE RISK

IT auditors focusing on relative risk are most likely to estimate the total risk per application so that comparison can be made. The simplest comparison is to take all of the application totals, sort them in descending order, and start by auditing the applications from the ones with the highest scores to the lowest.

IT auditors can use the risk score in two ways. They can evaluate a single application by comparing its risk score to the maximum possible score. They can also compare the scores of two or more applications in total or in detail. The auditors should be careful not to read too much into scores that are similar. They probably can make preliminary assessments based on significant differences of 15% or more.

ENSURING SUCCESS

IT auditors can increase the likelihood that these tasks will be completed successfully. They can consult external sources for traditional applications, provide the planning time and resources required to produce reliable results, and draw their opinions carefully from the data collected, among others. IT auditors should consider using a risk assessment work plan.

The IT auditor is likely to recognize that there are going to be situations where a new type of application requires a different approach. This enhanced approach is based on the work of a single, experienced individual who can take the application information and perform the same analysis that would otherwise be performed by the group. This individual would perform essentially the same activities as demonstrated below for the regular risk assessment process.

1. *Form risk assessment team.* The auditor in charge should probably be the risk assessment team coordinator. The coordinator's responsibilities include identifying the team members, outlining the proposed process, keeping the meeting(s) on track, and handling necessary administrative requirements.

    IT auditors should not need to include the entire audit team unless the team is limited to one or two individuals, or the risk assessment is so complex that it will be necessary to break into subteams. The IT auditor includes the entire audit team to ensure that every team has at least one audit representative. The auditor will have to see that the appropriate personnel from other business areas are included. The possible organizational participants were described in detail in Part VII, and included end-user management, end users, security personnel, and other IT personnel.

2. *The risk assessment approach.* The IT auditor in charge should work with select client personnel to determine whether a group meeting or one-on-one interviews would be more effective. The IT auditor then schedules the meeting or meetings as deemed necessary. The IT auditor should make theses arrangements to take place as quickly as possible as the results are needed to continue the overall review.

3. *Final meeting preparation.* The auditor in charge should ensure that the appropriate materials have been organized and copied well before the meeting. He or she is also responsible for ensuring that the meeting facilities are suitable to their intended purpose.

4. *Conduct the meeting or meetings.* The IT auditor has probably realized that these meetings probably need less structure than many other meetings. The meeting format needs to encourage creativity and brainstorming—an open exchange of ideas with no immediate recrim-

ination, ridicule, or retort. The following techniques often help ensure the meeting has a successful overtone.

   a. Team members should state their understanding of the meeting's objective(s). This can keep the meeting focused and provide a basis for subsequent brainstorming.

   b. Someone should record brainstorming sessions in some fashion from the team. The team leader might need to structure this activity, at least during the first time around to ensure that every participant has a chance to present his or her ideas and thoughts. There should also be at least one chance to comment on other's ideas.

   c. The IT auditor in charge should strongly encourage a requirement that the team(s) develop one or more specific solutions to the problem the team(s) is(are) addressing. A team may choose to record its version as an update of an existing diagram or narrative. Unless this existing item can be enlarged, IT auditors are strongly encouraged to provide flip charts or whiteboards so the entire group can see the same solution. This should help prevent confusion and inconsistency when a final draft is prepared.

5. *Completing the risk assessment.* IT auditors should ensure that the final opinions regarding potential and existing risks, along with existing or proposed solutions, are fully documented in an effective manner.

IDENTIFYING APPLICATION RISKS

IT auditors will find that an entire set of application-specific workpapers has been developed to comprehensively identify the risks that might be associated with that application. The risks are grouped by business cycle, allowing the IT auditor to identify relevant risks within the context of the business cycle being reviewed.

The IT auditor should use the comment column to provide additional information related to the risk as needed. This workpaper can be modified or supplemented with additional risks as needed.

OVERCOMING OBSTACLES TO SUCCESS

IT auditors will normally face only one obstacle as they attempt to meet their objectives in this area: getting complete and accurate information about all of the potential risks in an application setting. IT auditors can overcome this obstacle by including at least one highly experienced auditor as a team member or reviewer, referring to general reference sources such as the included workpapers, and conducting effective interviews with client personnel.

ASSIGNING MATERIALITY

IT auditors have only completed the first step where the relevant risks are identified. The IT auditor will need to determine the materiality, or relative significance, of each risk in relation to an established standard. For the purposes of this book, the following standard is used.

1. The realization or occurrence of this risk poses only minor consequences to the business.
1. The realization of this risk might be major or minor, depending on the specific event and functioning or failure of other controls.
3. The realization of this risk is likely to have a major effect on either the affected application or the business as a whole.

IT auditors will end up multiplying the original number value assigned to each risk by this materiality to provide the foundation for subsequent planning activities. These planning activities will result in the IT auditor's identification of the application or applications to be covered during the audit.

IT auditors have an assortment of alternative methods available to them for quantifying the potential risk in a particular application. Several of these alternatives are described in the following pages.

The time required to conduct this task varies with the approach taken. If the historical method is used to gather statistical information, the time can be quite extensive. If a structured approach is used to estimate the risk, the time required for this task is minimal—in most cases, less than that required to identify the risk. The historical and structured methods are compared in the following example.

Describing the Unfavorable Event. The IT auditor needs to describe application risks in sufficient detail to make the frequency and loss conditions apparent. For example, in a risk situation in which merchandise is shipped but not billed, the unfavorable event would be that the value of the products shipped to a customer but not billed represents a loss to the organization each time such a shipment occurs.

This particular loss of value has two components. First is the actual cost of the goods shipped, which is a sunk cost to the enterprise. Second is the gross margin associated with the particular sale, which should have provided the return on the cost of these goods. This becomes further complicated because even a simple delay in billing a shipment has a time value of money impact on the return realized from the shipment.

Calculating the Frequency and Loss for the Unfavorable Event. The historical method requires that the IT auditor analyze the risk situation and gather background information. The IT auditor can use financial analysis methods to identify inventory shortages. One assumption could be that all or part of this shortage is associated with unbilled shipments. The IT auditor might also look for missing shipping numbers or use other methods to attempt to estimate the frequency of the occurrence of this risk and the losses associated with it. This method provides data that is most easily accepted by most clients.

The IT auditor employing the structured method uses the calculation of frequency and loss as an audit assessment tool whose objective is to provide estimates rather than precise numbers. If estimates are acceptable, then the IT auditor can select frequency and loss estimates from a list of frequency and loss categories rather than making the effort to calculate precise frequency and loss valuation.

For example, frequency and loss can be estimated in multiples of five—loss would be estimated at $1, $5, $25, $125, and frequency would be estimated at once every five years, once every year, five times per year, 25 times per year. IT auditors should remember that this process is performed for the purpose of planning the audit, not to develop extremely precise numbers. It is therefore immaterial whether a risk produces an annual loss expectation of $1 million or $100 million, as long as it becomes one of the major risks for audit investigation.

While IT auditors may often express frequency as a number of times per year and losses in dollars and cents, they can also use high, medium, and low categories to quantify annual loss expectations (ALEs). The IT auditor should establish specific parameters based on the organization.

For example, the low category might include the range of numeric values from 1 to 10, while the medium category ranges from 11 to 40, and the high category ranges from 41 to 50. If the IT Auditors choose to utilize categories, then they should be consistent and continue to use categories in every situation.

COMPUTING A RISK SCORE

IT auditors should normally use the ALE quantification method as the direct basis for calculating the risk score. If they choose to make judgmental adjustments to the results, they can easily compromise not only the reliability of the results but also their own credibility. Client personnel can often be convinced of many ideas if they can accept the basis for those ideas; but if they begin to believe that the methods only provide cover for the IT auditor actually making personal or even biased selections or evaluations, then the credibility of the entire IT audit function can be called into question.

Section 24
Develop a Detailed Plan

It has always been recommended that audit objectives be written so that they are clearly measurable. The precision involved in a computer application requires that computer audit tests and procedures must also be precise and conducive to measurement. It is important to eliminate inconsistencies among the criteria on which the success of the audit will be judged and the risks evaluated. Reconciling these factors and developing measurable audit objectives from them may involve rewriting some of the success criteria or changing the risks to be investigated. Developing measurable audit objects is the basis of the detailed audit plan.

WRITING MEASURABLE AUDIT OBJECTIVES

Audit objectives should be written for each identified risk. A nonmeasurable objective might read "evaluate the adequacy of internal controls in the payroll application." Rewritten in measurable terms, the same objective might be stated "identify any vulnerability in the payroll system that has the probability of resulting in a loss of more than $1000."

VERIFYING THE COMPLETENESS OF MEASURABLE AUDIT OBJECTIVES

A detailed audit plan should not be developed until there is agreement that the measurable objectives will satisfy the success criteria, or that success criteria are changed to be compatible with the defined measurable audit objectives. If, in the opinion of the audit team, differences still remain between the measurable audit objectives and the previously determined success criteria, they should be reconciled with audit management. The IT Auditor must be sure that audit management wants specific objectives—generalized audit objectives (e.g., "probe x") should be avoided and an effort should be made to put difficult objectives into measurable terms.

A detailed audit plan delineating the execution of the audit should be developed for use during fieldwork. The plan is an extension of the individual audit plan developed during the planning process. A properly prepared plan can make the audit more effective by allocating audit resources to the areas that have the highest probability of problems. The planning process often consumes as much as one-third of the total audit effort. In addition, for a small audit, this task could replace the prefieldwork planning.

At this point, the basic components of the IT audit plan have been developed and the activities to be accomplished have been defined. Determining how to accomplish these goals must now be completed. This involves deciding:

- The sequence (if appropriate) in which the objectives must be accomplished
- The person to be assigned to complete each objective
- The resources to be allocated to each objective
- When the work on the objective is to begin and end
- How the objective is to be accomplished (if not through a standardized process)

In an IT audit, the sequencing of events may assume more importance than in a non-IT audit. Computer programs may have to be written, tested, and operated before a task or objective that uses the information produced by that program can be started. Putting the tasks on a Gantt chart can be a valuable step: it identifies any critical period in the audit when the work cannot be accomplished, it helps identify slack periods as well as critical paths through the audit process, and because the individual time commitments and scheduling are clearly documented, it aids in assigning staff.

The key to good planning is the development of realistic estimates. Organizations new to IT auditing frequently have difficulty in this area; as they become more proficient, their estimates improve. Some of the more sophisticated audit software packages include scheduling systems, and many IT departments have already acquired sophisticated scheduling systems. Because the audit process is similar in nature to the system development process and objectives can be equated with tasks in the development process, these scheduling packages often can, and should, be used for audit purposes. The main advantages of such packages include:

- What-if games that can be played to determine the optimum scheduling algorithm
- Critical paths that are easily identified
- Schedules that can be quickly changed when new variables are introduced

Under certain conditions, these objectives could be difficult to achieve. The shipped but not billed amount, for example, may be too small to detect, or it may be impossible to determine the cause of the shortage. Inventory shortages may be the result of theft or shipping the wrong product instead of shipping a product but not billing for it—the IT auditor must therefore examine all evidence carefully.

Section 25
Evaluate Internal Controls

Philosophies of control in automated computer systems (as in other areas) differ. One philosophy holds that computers make few mistakes and have never defrauded systems—people, on the other hand, do defraud and do make mistakes. Therefore, if duties are properly segregated, control can be assumed to be adequate. The other philosophy holds that transactions should be controlled: if transactions are adequately controlled; so are people. There is merit in both arguments.

This part of the audit process is designed to determine whether the controls are adequate to reduce the risks to an acceptable level. In the process of making this determination, the IT auditor will be able to identify potential vulnerabilities for closer examination later in the audit process.

Few organizations have established standards for the development of internal control. Without such standards, control activities frequently do not comply with the organization's developmental standards and requirements and become a cause for concern after a system has been operating for some time. In many instances, the extent of internal control depends on the individual experience and desires of the systems analyst or programmer.

DOCUMENT SEGREGATION OF RESPONSIBILITIES

This task examines the segregation of responsibilities within an automated application to identify areas in which one person performs two tasks and thus creates potential responsibility conflicts that can be considered control vulnerabilities. Areas to examine include:

- Organizational charts
- Job descriptions
- Department or function charters
- Procedural manuals
- System documentation

Identifying Actions. Each action that occurs during application processing should be identified. An application action usually involves one of the following functions:

- Originating a transaction
- Approving a transaction

- Entering a transaction into a computer system
- Communicating information
- Processing information
- Storing data
- Reporting data out of the computer system
- Using information

Identifying Personnel Responsible for the Actions. Everyone involved in the application processing should be listed, even if the system performs the action. If the application system is set up to approve credit automatically, for example, it is important to know which person in the organization was responsible for that process. The names of the personnel should be listed vertically on the workpaper in the order in which the actions are performed.

CONDUCT AN INTERNAL CONTROL REVIEW

The objective of this review is to identify the controls in place in the application system. Questionnaires are used to gather information about data origination, input, processing, and output. At the conclusion of this task, the IT auditor will be aware of the controls that have been established and where they are located. This information enables the IT auditor to conduct a vulnerability assessment, further investigating the identified control weaknesses to determine whether they have been converted into losses to the organization. The control review uses questionnaires that coincide with the major areas of an application system. Each questionnaire includes guidelines that explain its use and purpose. The questions indicate the items to be investigated and provide responses of yes, no, and not applicable. All responses should be indexed to the appropriate supporting documents or interview records. Positive answers represent good control practices—negative ones indicate potential control weaknesses or other vulnerabilities. A Comments column is used to explain all negative answers and identify alternative procedures. Negative answers are investigated further (in a later task) to determine the magnitude of the vulnerability.

The questionnaires are simply guides to use in identifying and documenting the existence of controls; they are not intended to be the sole investigative tool. The IT auditor should also investigate any areas that are inadequately addressed on the questionnaire, as well as those needing further study as indicated by the answers. Some questions may be repeated in two or more questionnaires because the type of control needed in processing, for example, could also be needed in storage and output. The IT auditor should remember that because the objective is to identify the totality of controls designed to reduce specific risks, implementation of the same control in more than one area of the application must be identified.

To complete this task successfully, the IT auditor must clearly understand all the questions. This understanding will help the respondent avoid misinterpreting the question and thus providing the wrong response. Although it is important that the questionnaire be complete, the IT auditor should not rely too heavily on it, thereby neglecting to do additional probing.

DEVELOP INTERNAL CONTROL DIAGRAMS

Although the information provided by the questionnaires in the previous task is valuable in assessing the adequacy of controls, it is rarely specific enough for a thorough control assessment. The objective of this task is to show where the internal control operates in the application. Entering the controls in a work flow diagram indicates whether the control over the flow of data is adequate to reduce the perceived risks. Selected key transactions should also be identified, their flow documented, and the appropriate controls indicated wherever they operate in the flow. Completing this task provides documentation on the system of controls that can be used as input to the control assessment.

Completing the Work Flow Control Diagram. This diagram is essentially a work flow diagram with controls superimposed on it. The following procedures should be used in completing work flow control diagrams:

- Every process, storage, and movement of data represents a point of risk; there should be at least one control at each of these points.
- Only the key controls—those that management relies on for the correctness of processing—should be indicated on the diagram.
- Controls should be summarized wherever practical. The phrase "data validation," for example, can be used to summarize the possibly hundreds of individual controls that check and evaluate data entering an automated system.
- The selected controls should be those identified on the questionnaires.

Documenting Transactions on Work Flow Diagrams. It may be necessary to indicate the different processing paths taken by the various parts of the transaction. For example, an invoice may contain both product and sales-tax information, which may enter different systems and thus be subject to different controls. Each action performed on a transaction represents a risk point. It is at those points that controls should occur. The workpaper should provide room to record the transaction and show the segments of an application system. The IT auditor should enter the name of the transaction and, in each of the system segments, indicate the control over that transaction at that point. For example, an authorization control in data origination would be documented in that column next to the transaction to which it applied. The following are guidelines for completing the diagram.

- At a minimum, one control should be located in each area of transaction processing.
- Business transactions rather than computer records should be used; this reduces the number of individual transactions shown.
- Only the most critical financial transactions should be selected.
- If transaction processing divides, only segments with significant financial implications should be followed.
- The controls identified should be the key controls—where practical, they should be consolidated.

Identifying Responsibility Vulnerabilities. To represent a vulnerability, two actions must permit a single individual to both perform and conceal an act. If the event cannot be concealed, it should not be considered a vulnerability. There is, in addition, no vulnerability in the presence of a compensating control (e.g., an independent bank reconciliation) that would otherwise detect any irregularity.

Identifying Transaction Vulnerabilities. A vulnerability can be detected in the following situations:

- An action without a control appears on the data flow diagram
- A transaction without a control appears on one of the application system segments
- Risks that have been identified for which there appear to be inadequate controls
- Questions on one of the questionnaires have received negative responses

The area in which the vulnerability is perceived should be indicated on the workpaper for the identified business transaction, preferably with a brief written explanation rather than a checkmark.

Selecting the Vulnerabilities to be Tested. Once all personnel- and transaction-related vulnerabilities have been identified, the IT auditor must determine which of these vulnerabilities to pursue during the test steps of the audit. This determination is based on the following criteria:

- The magnitude of the vulnerability
- The amount of audit resources available for testing
- The IT auditor's judgment regarding both the need for testing and the potential effect if the vulnerability is realized

To complete this task successfully, the IT auditor must ensure that all risks leading to vulnerabilities are identified. In addition, the IT auditor must have sufficient knowledge about the application to identify the significant vulnerabilities. It is equally important that even the most abstract vulnerability be able to be quantified.

TEST INTERNAL CONTROLS

The vulnerabilities that have been identified represent potential weaknesses in the internal control system. Vulnerabilities that have no controls need little testing; vulnerabilities with weak controls, on the other hand, should be tested. The IT auditor's concern is that the controls be in place, working, and effective; all three factors are tested. The IT auditor may also test a control for which no vulnerability is perceived but that is relied on to reduce some risk. The controls to be tested are based on the IT auditor's judgment, using the information collected in the previous steps.

The objective of this task is to develop a plan to test the internal controls selected in the previous step. It involves:

- Confirming the selection of controls to be tested
- Choosing the test method
- Determining who will be responsible for conducting the test
- Deciding when the test should be conducted
- Selecting the test process itself

Testing the control can be done in a static or dynamic mode. A static test usually involves evaluating a procedure or a program; depending on what the control is designed to do, the IT auditor will make an assessment as to whether the control achieves its desired objective. A dynamic test involves executing the control and examining the results. For a manual control, the transactions subject to that control must be examined; in an automated system, test data must be prepared or transactions found that are subject to the control.

The dynamic test is preferred if it can be easily arranged. Many situations are difficult to simulate; however, and these can be tested by a static evaluation. The IT auditor should be certain that the controls selected for testing are the key controls and that the correct type of test for the given control is selected. A static test involves a work program; a dynamic test involves either creating a test condition or finding a transaction that will test the control.

It is important that the limits of the control be tested. For example, if a control is designed to permit only codes A, B, and C to be entered, the test conditions must verify that all other codes are rejected. The IT auditor must therefore understand both the functioning of the control and the attributes of the data that needs controlling. The test should be designed to define the control objective being tested (there may be more than one test objective for a given control), define the test condition, and describe the expected results. In developing the tests, the IT auditor should ask the following questions about each control and develop conditions to answer them:

- Does the control reject values and codes that are not authorized?
- Is the control consistently applied?
- Does the control cover a wide range of conditions? Should each of those conditions be tested?
- Is this control related to another control? If so, should both be tested simultaneously?

The objectives of the control must be clearly understood, or the wrong test conditions will be prepared. In performing this task, the IT auditor also must ensure that test conditions are sufficient to test the control and that the right control is tested.

The IT auditor in charge should select the appropriate test program and assign it to an IT auditor who is responsible for its timely completion. Any special test preparation required should be indicated in the Comments column on the workpaper. When this task has been completed, the effectiveness or adequacy of the controls can be evaluated and the appropriate data tests performed. To complete this task successfully, the IT auditor must ensure that adequate computer time is available to conduct the tests and that the designed test works in production. The IT auditor must be alert to flaws in the test that produce correct results when, in fact, the control does not function properly.

EVALUATE INTERNAL CONTROL EFFECTIVENESS

Controls that are either not in place or not functioning can be identified by comparing the actual results with the expected results. When there is a discrepancy, the IT auditor should ascertain that the results are those of a valid test and that the expectation was correctly stated. Once the integrity of the test has been verified, the adequacy of the control can be evaluated.

Comparing Expected and Actual Results. If the expected and actual results of each test are the same and the IT auditor has a high degree of confidence in the reliability of the test, the control assessment can be developed and the next two parts of this task can be omitted. If the actual and expected results differ, however, the entire process should be performed.

Verifying Proper Test Functioning. If the expected and actual test results differ, it is important to confirm that the test was properly constructed and executed to avoid basing a recommendation on an invalid result. Unless fraud or a similar problem is suspected, the IT auditor may wish to ask user or IT personnel to confirm the proper functioning of the test.

Confirming Correctness of the Expected Result. An incorrect actual or expected result could lead to an improper finding. If the actual result is reasonable and has been so verified, the IT auditor should reconfirm the correctness of the expected result. The result can be checked with the user or IT person or by consulting the system documentation or company policies and procedures.

Developing a Control Assessment. When the actual and expected results differ and the actual result is incorrect, the control should be rated less than adequate. When the results agree, the assessment should be that the control is fully adequate. In some cases, there may be multiple conditions to test, in which all major conditions produce the expected results but have some minor conditions that present problems. Despite these problems, the IT auditor may decide to give an "adequate" assessment.

If the control is considered less than adequate, the IT auditor should recommend actions to be taken by the auditee. Even when a control has been given an assessment of adequate, the IT auditor may wish to make minor recommendations to strengthen the control; the IT auditor must be extremely careful that the information about the results expected from the execution of a control is accurate.

Section 26
Test Data Integrity

Testing the integrity of the computer-produced data is an important procedure. Such testing can be used to:

- Determine the magnitude of a potential system and control vulnerability
- Evaluate the functioning of the control
- Analyze transactions to identify potential problem conditions
- Substantiate the correctness of financial statements

Much of testing data integrity involves computer programs written and executed under the control of the IT auditor.

CONDUCT A DATA FILE SURVEY

Conducting a data file survey familiarizes the IT auditor with the types and attributes of data in a data file. Documentation of data file contents is not always up to date, and the IT auditor may encounter problems caused by misinterpretation of data content. The survey also provides the IT auditor with demographic statistics about the file that can be helpful in determining the sample size or the type of data to examine. Although the objectives are the same, the methods of conducting manual and computer file surveys differ. The IT auditor can examine the material in the manual file visually, whereas the computer file requires translation. Because of the time required to compile manual file statistics, IT auditors rarely accumulate statistics about the entire file. The manual file survey is therefore conducted primarily through interviews. The computer file survey is handled through program analysis of the file. Generalized audit software often includes such powerful survey facilities as stratification, automatic totaling, and automatic statistical analysis (e.g., producing mean, median, mode, and standard deviation). Information to be collected about a file includes:

- Organizational structure: the sequencing and retrieval methods for information.
- Record formats: the type and content of data in records (usually documented, in computer records).
- Size: the number of records and the amount of space allocated to the file.
- Distribution: an analysis of how the records are distributed (e.g., in an accounts receivable file, the number of records in different dollar values: $0 to $100, $101 to $200).

- Statistical analysis: an overview of demographic statistical information that aids in understanding file attributes.
- Dollar value analysis: information describing dollar characteristics of the population of records in the file.
- Suspense items: accounts or records in the file for which the proper distribution is unknown. It is helpful to know how long such records have been in the file.

Because statistical analysis is economical and usually easy to perform when records are in an electronic form, more statistical information can be acquired from the computer file than from a manual file. By the end of the file survey, the IT auditor often has already made some initial audit findings; for example:

- A large number of small values on the file (it may be uneconomical to carry small items)
- A large number of negative items on the file
- A large number of suspense items on the file
- Records on the file for long periods of time without appropriate action

The results of the survey are used for planning data tests, and the information can dictate the test approach. When the stratification of records in the file is known, for example, the IT auditor can develop a sampling program that will easily accommodate all the large values and provide a statistical sample of the smaller values. To complete this task successfully, the IT auditor must be prepared to deal with the possibility that the software to produce statistical information about the computer file may not be readily available or that the people maintaining a manual file might not know its characteristics. In addition, audit calendar time must be available to perform the survey.

CREATE DATA TEST PLAN

The IT auditor must identify and describe the data tests needed to accomplish the stated measurable audit objectives. The test plan should be based on the results of the file survey. The IT auditor is testing data to substantiate the financial values in the organization's financial statements, to determine (or estimate) the magnitude of a detected control vulnerability, or to accomplish one or more of the measurable audit objectives.

The test plan should clearly state the condition or objective the IT auditor hopes to accomplish by the test and how that objective is to be accomplished. The plan should indicate the type of evidence that will be examined, who is to be responsible for conducting the test, and the start and stop dates of the test. In developing the plan, the IT auditor must:

- Create a correctness proof for the data test: a hypothesis such that proving or disproving it accomplishes the audit objective. For example, if the audit objective is to confirm accounts receivable to prove correctness within 1%, the IT auditor could develop a correctness proof statement as follows: "The actual value of accounts receivable as of 9/30/xx is within 1% of $1,386,275." The dollar value from the organization's financial records as of that date is taken.
- Create a test that meets the following conditions:
  —It can be performed on the available audit evidence.
  —It can be performed using tools available to the IT auditor.
  —It can be performed within the skill level of the audit team.
  —It can be performed within the time available.
  —It will prove the integrity of the computer file.
  —It will produce reliable results for use in developing findings and recommendations.

DEVELOP TEST TOOLS

Testing a computer file requires developing an appropriate test tool; manual testing (using manual procedures) can usually omit this task, except when statistical samples or other sophisticated manual review processes are used. The objective of this task is to specify the data to be used, the processing to be performed on it, and the types of output reports to be produced. Completing the task should provide sufficient detail to develop or customize a tool (e.g., audit software) for performing the specified test. It is helpful for the IT auditor designing a test tool to know the tools already available and their capabilities and limitations. Although in most instances, the primary tool available is the audit software package, the IT auditor may also want to consider other utility programs that might be available in the IT department.

Test tool specifications should be developed from the perspective of the desired audit output. The IT auditor should first specify the information wanted for audit purposes, identify the available input, and then specify the processing; this is usually the fastest method of designing a computerized test tool. The output specification should include:

- The proposed name of the report
- The period the report will cover (this will determine the input to be used)
- All data elements to be included in the report
- Any editing to be performed on the data elements
- Totals and subtotals to be prepared
- Any special paper to be used
- The number of copies of the report to be produced

ASSESSING IMPLEMENTED SYSTEMS

- Any special security that must be observed during output production or distribution

After the output reports have been specified, the IT auditor documents the available input records or data elements, usually by acquiring a record format or file description of the data, but sometimes by obtaining the needed information from the data dictionary. The IT auditor needs the following information about the input:

- Data element definitions that will be used in processing
- Attributes of each data element; expected range of value and codes
- Any important file characteristic uncovered during the file survey
- Volume of records
- Time period covered by each file and the number of files to be analyzed

Once the input and output are known, the required processing can be determined. Cross-referencing input fields to output fields indicates one of the following processing conditions:

- There is no input field for a given output field; hence, the required information cannot be produced.
- There is a one-to-one relationship between input and output. In this case, data from an input record need only be moved to an output file so that processing is simply a matter of moving data.
- The desired information must be calculated from the input. Totaling, editing, calculations, or comparisons based on two or more input fields or records may be required.

The following factors must be taken into account during the development of the test tools.

- If the sequence of input is not the sequence desired for output, the file must be sorted.
- If the test tool cannot perform the desired processing, another test tool may be required, necessitating the specification of more than one test tool to accomplish one test condition. Other possibilities are to change the processing specifications or to perform the work formed in two or more audit analyses.
- If the data file is not in a format that can be read by the test tool, the data may have to be reformatted. Some audit software packages, for example, cannot read from database systems, and a special program must be written to convert these records into a sequential file that can be read by the audit software.

The successful completion of this task requires that the selected tool be able to meet the specifications. In addition, the IT auditor must check for errors in logic that would prevent producing the desired results and incomplete logic that would preclude creation of the test tool.

VERIFY FILE INTEGRITY

Because of the real risk of producing invalid conclusions, it is essential that the IT auditor not develop opinions or recommendations based on data analysis from a file whose integrity cannot be verified. The objective of this task is to prove the integrity of the file from which data is obtained, allowing its use as a basis for an opinion. (If the data is to be used for background purposes only, this task can be omitted.) Verifying the integrity of a computer file means proving that the totality of data on the file is correct. In an accounts receivable file, for example, this involves reconciling the totals of the records on the file with the amount of accounts receivable on the organization's financial statements. This is accomplished by adding all the open items on the accounts receivable file and comparing the total with that on the financial statement. If the two are equal or reconcilable, the integrity of the file is proved, and the file can then be used to extract or analyze data for audit purposes.

Key Field Proof. With this method, a field, usually the control field, is totaled and compared with an independent source. (The accounts receivable file verification example used the key field proof method.)

Completeness Proof. This method counts some item on the file and verifies it against a count of that field. A simplified example would be verifying the completeness of a customer file by counting the number of customers on the file and comparing it with the total number of customers the organization believes it has. Other completeness proof methods include:

- Proof of pointers. The completeness of pointers in a database or random-type file is verified.
- Check digits. These are used to verify that the arrangement of data within a field is correct (can also be used for data within the record).
- Hash total. Data not otherwise used for control purposes (e.g., part numbers or invoice numbers) is counted to verify that the data is complete (or not rearranged). For example, the accounts receivable file might be complete based on a key field, but a new customer's name might have been substituted. The hash total would disclose a change in the structure of the records and thus indicate a completeness problem.

Simple Accounting Proof. A simple accounting proof is a reconciliation of processing over a period of time. It involves starting with a verified previous balance and substantiating additions and deletions to the file. The balance produced by the simple accounting proof is then compared with the balance on the computer file to verify its accuracy. In completing this task, the

IT auditor must be careful not to lose control of the file after its integrity has been proved but before it has been analyzed. It is also possible that the total value of the file is correct but the information in the file is incorrect; the IT auditor must confirm that this is not the case.

EVALUATE THE CORRECTNESS OF THE TEST PROCESS

Almost all auditing standards include a statement like "the systems are to be properly supervised." This statement places the responsibility on the IT auditor or audit organization for ensuring that staff members receive effective on-the-job training and sufficient guidance to produce high-quality work. Assistants must understand their assigned tasks, conform to auditing standards, and follow the audit programs as appropriate. The objective of this task, therefore, is to exercise supervisory responsibility over and provide guidance to an assistant-the computer audit program. To do so, the IT auditor must review the program to confirm that it functions properly and will produce the desired results.

Each computer program should be tested in terms of both structure and function. Structural testing determines whether the program is structurally correct and can work in an operating environment; that is, it confirms that the tables are large enough, the instructions are used correctly, and the program has been configured for the hardware on which it will run. Functional testing is designed to ensure that the system does what it is supposed to do. Although structural problems affect function, they may not do so during the test, and the program may perform properly when processing only one or two records. When several thousand records are processed, however, the internal tables may not be large enough to accommodate the necessary volumes.

Both static and dynamic tests should be used to verify the structural and functional aspects of the program. In a static test, the IT auditor analyzes the program in a nonoperational mode to determine whether it is performing correctly. In a dynamic test, test transactions are prepared or a limited set of live transactions are used to verify that the program works in an operational mode. The static test should be performed first, followed by the dynamic test.

Although it is generally advisable to prepare special test transactions, it may be possible to use a subset of the production file to test the program. Some generalized audit software has the capability to select a predetermined number of live transactions from a production file for test purposes. When conducting these tests, the IT auditor must understand that an undetected bug or untested but important logic path could cause the program to function incorrectly in a production environment. The IT auditor must also be aware of the possibility that the program might reach an untested limit and either terminate abnormally or produce incorrect results.

CONDUCT DATA TEST

The data test program is executed after the validity of the test tool has been verified; it provides the information for use during the audit. The task includes steps to ensure that the operational aspect of the program is correct (the correctness of the test tool was verified in the previous task). In many organizations, conducting the data test merely involves preparing a run request; in online systems, the IT auditor may be able to do this through a terminal. In either case, the time required is minimal. This task involves gathering all the needed data before executing the audit program and then verifying that the program was executed correctly.

Procedures for executing an audit program vary from organization to organization, and the method of execution depends on the operational strategy and the type of equipment. Processing in a highly secure centralized computer complex, for example, is significantly different from activating programs from a remote terminal. The installation may require charge numbers and job request forms before executing the job. Work may need to be scheduled and operator instructions prepared, programs may have to be cataloged before execution, or passwords may be needed.

The IT auditor should consult the operations group as early in the audit as possible regarding the organization's procedural requirements. The IT auditor should also have reasonable confidence that the program and data will not be modified before, during, or after execution. If checking the operational controls does not provide such assurance, the IT auditor should arrange to run the program in another computer center. The IT auditor should ensure that neither the wrong program or version of the program nor the wrong file or version of the file is used. It is also important to ascertain that the output is completely and correctly printed and that the correct number of copies is produced.

REVIEW DATA TEST RESULTS

A computer can be considered an assistant to the IT auditor, and the computer program can be considered the instructions covering the work that assistant is to produce. As is true with the work of any subordinate, a supervisor should review the results. The IT auditor must review the results produced by the computer application. The IT auditor should examine this data with the following questions in mind:

- Is this the information wanted?
- Is it of the expected value, quantity, and format?
- Does it appear to be complete?

In conducting the review, the IT auditor should determine whether the output data appears to be logical on the basis of reasonable values for the printed fields. The IT auditor's familiarity with the data will aid in detecting obviously incorrect material, especially if the same IT auditor performed the data file survey. Results should also tally with expectations: if the IT auditor expected to confirm about 80% of a total value, the totals produced by the run should be approximately 80% of the value. If 500 confirmations are expected, the IT auditor should look for about that number of confirmations. If the actual results vary significantly from what is expected, the IT auditor should determine whether there was a misunderstanding about the data file or a problem in producing the report. To complete this task successfully, the IT auditor must ensure that serious flaws in a report, incomplete data, or incomplete reports are not overlooked. It is important that the results be evaluated for reasonableness to avoid missing potential audit findings or making findings that are incorrect.

Section 27
Certify Computer Security

Some computer security risks threaten the very existence of an organization. Critical decisions regarding the adequacy of security safeguards in sensitive applications must be made by managers and must be based on reliable technical information. Computer security certification gives managers such reliability. A major advantage of a security certification program is the increased security awareness created by the certification process.

This is an optional step in information systems audit. It should be performed when security is important to the successful operation of the system. To provide a certification (or opinion) on the adequacy of security controls, the IT auditor must examine the controls, identify security risks, and provide recommendations on how they can be reduced.

CERTIFICATION TASKS

Certification consists of a technical evaluation of a sensitive application to see how well it meets security requirements. The process is composed of five tasks:

- Planning. This involves performing a quick, high-level review of the entire system to understand the issues, placing boundaries on the effort, partitioning the work within those boundaries, identifying areas of emphasis, and drawing up the certification plan.
- Data collection. Critical information that needs to be collected includes system security requirements; risk analysis data showing threats and assets; system flow diagrams showing input, processing steps, and output, plus transaction flows for important transaction types; and a listing of application system controls. If this information is not available in documents, it should be obtained from application personnel by use of tutorial briefings and interviews.
- Basic evaluation. A basic evaluation is always performed in a certification. Its three subtasks are:
    - Security requirements evaluation. Are the security requirements documented and acceptable? If not, they must be formulated from requirements implied in the application, and compared with federal, state, organizational, and user requirements.
    - Control implementation determination. The IT auditor must verify that security functions have been implemented. Physical and admin-

istrative controls require visual inspection; controls internal to the computer require testing.

—Methodology review. The IT auditor must review the acceptability of the implementation method (e.g., documentation, project controls, development tools used, skills of personnel).

- Detailed evaluation. In application areas in which a basic evaluation does not provide enough evidence for a certification, the quality of the security safeguards is analyzed by using one or more of three points of view:

  —Functional operation. Do controls function properly (e.g., parameter checking, error monitoring)?

  —Performance. Do controls satisfy performance criteria (e.g., availability, survivability, accuracy)?

  —Resistance. Can controls be easily broken or circumvented? (This establishes confidence in safeguards.)

- Report of findings. This is the primary product of a certification. It contains both technical and management security recommendations. It should summarize applied security standards or policies, implemented controls, major vulnerabilities, corrective actions, operational restrictions, and the certification process used, and should include a proposed accreditation statement.

The basic evaluation is high level and is the minimum requirement for security certification. In general, a basic evaluation suffices for most aspects of an application under review. Most security tests, however, need detailed work in problem areas and therefore require a detailed evaluation as well.

The time and resources required to perform a security test vary widely from case to case. In all instances, however, potential security risks must be weighed against certification costs. If the risk is low, certification costs must also be kept low. Risk analysis can help decide the degree of certification review that should be performed on an application. Typical staff resources for security testing vary from several days to many months. Minimum products required from certification and accreditation are a security evaluation report and an accreditation statement.

The certification process described here identifies what must be done and presents a general functional view of how to accomplish it. It does not present a detailed step-by-step method for performing security evaluation. The specifics of security testing differ widely from case to case, and any evaluation method must be adapted to meet individual needs. There is no shortcut to avoid the analysis required for this situational adaptation. Detailed methods and aids (e.g., matrices, flowcharts, and checklists) are helpful in the adaptation process. This special test procedure organizes and focuses the test process. Because the security certification process described is at a functional level, it can be applied to both applications under development and those already operational. Functionally, the two situations are similar; both include a review of similar application documentation (e.g., functional requirements documents and test procedures and reports).

Nevertheless, the detailed evaluation methods used within the certification process differ for the two situations because of differences in the following areas:

- Available data. Certification performed in parallel with development is more apt to have available security-relevant products from the developers. Such products might include vulnerability analyses and security design tradeoff analyses. Certification performed on operational systems has such operational documents as problem reports, audit journal data, availability statistics, and violation reports that are not available during development. Applications under development might be reviewed for acceptability by several offices or by a project steering committee. These reviews can be used to gather evidence for certification. For operational applications, users can be interviewed and can provide unique forms of evidence based on their personal experience.
- Organization of work. Certification activity during development is event-driven, being interleaved with the development process and based primarily on the availability of application documentation. Interim certification findings can be used to influence the development process itself. Certification work assignments can thus have peaks and valleys of activity as the development process occurs. Evaluations of an operational application can follow a more circumscribed, project-oriented structure and rely on a skill-based partitioning of the application.

Security Safeguard Evaluation Versus IT Audit

With respect to the technical processes themselves, a security safeguard evaluation and an IT audit have many similarities. For example, both assess compliance with policies; both assess the adequacy of safeguards; and both include tests to verify the presence of controls. Because IT audits are generally broader in scope (e.g., part of a general internal review), however, they often address such issues as cost and efficiency in achieving mission objectives that are outside the purview of evaluations for certifications.

Beyond this difference, there are others of a more subtle nature. For example, IT audits in general place more emphasis on data reliability and validate the data processed by the application (i.e., substantive testing). In a security safeguard evaluation, file inconsistencies are of interest mainly to the extent that they reveal inadequacies in the safeguards. As another example, IT audits usually are concerned with threats anticipated by systems developers and therefore are tested for in the application and in audit journals. Security safeguard evaluations, although also concerned with anticipated threats, are often additionally concerned that safeguards counter threats in which the application is used in ways not anticipated or intended by its developers. Penetration of an application through a design flaw is an example of an unanticipated threat. Analyses of these two forms of threats require different skills.

As both security audits and security evaluations evolve, the differences are diminishing and more overlap is occurring. For example, the historical limitation of IT audits to financial concerns is diminishing, as is the historical limitation of security evaluations to violations associated with unauthorized disclosure. IT audits now consider the entire spectrum of computer applications that are being used to manage information resources, and security safeguard evaluations increasingly consider such exposures as public embarrassment or competitive disadvantage that were formerly primarily of concern to IT auditors.

Plan Security Tests

The planning process is, in itself, a mini basic evaluation, because it must anticipate problem areas, needs for specialized skills and support tools, and other issues that cannot be determined without insightful situation-specific analysis. Indeed, the planning process might even determine that further evaluation is not required. This might be the case, for example, if planning analysis were to reveal general controls to be so weak that further evaluation would be of little value. (In such instances, the application still requires a security evaluation report and an accreditation decision.) Planning thus requires expertise in and knowledge of the application and the testing process. The enlistment of external support might be required to assist in planning.

During this task, the IT auditor must determine the need for security certification, partition the application system, assess the importance of that partition for evaluation, determine how resources should be allocated, and develop a security certification plan.

Determine the Need for Certifying Security. The IT auditor must decide whether certification is necessary. In some cases, management dictates the need for certification; in others, the IT auditor must make that evaluation.

Determine the Need for Certifying Security. The IT auditor must establish boundaries for certification. The rule of thumb is that the boundaries of an application must be drawn to include all relevant facets of an application's environment, including the administrative, physical, and technical areas. Without this, certification gives an incomplete and perhaps misleading picture of application security. For example, technical controls might be excellent, but they are worthless if administrative security is not properly defined or if physical security is inadequate.

As boundaries are formulated, it is important to document security assumptions that are made about areas outside the boundaries. For example, if the operating system is excluded from the security review, documentation should note that the operating system is assumed to provide a sufficiently secure base with respect to process isolation, authentication, authorization, monitoring and maintaining the integrity of security labels, and enforcing security decisions. Once boundaries have been established, the IT auditor must decide how to partition the work within the boundaries. Sometimes, one person has the skills and experience to perform the full evaluation; more often, a team is required.

External reviews often suffice in some of the areas. For example, reviews of physical and personnel security might have been performed for the organization as a whole. An internal control review might exist for administrative and accounting controls. The operating system and hardware might have been audited regarding the adequacy of their security.

In partitioning the work, the IT auditor examines several characteristics of the application to estimate required number of personnel, skill levels of security evaluators, and evaluation time and activities. The following major characteristics are examined:

- Size. This is a critical planning factor. The larger the application or partition, the greater the required time and number of people.
- Complexity. This is based on such factors as the nature of the functions being performed, the extent to which operating system specifics need to be examined, and the clarity and level of abstraction of the languages used. Size and complexity are assessed not just for the application as a whole, but for each of its component parts.
- Documentation quality. This is an important consideration in planning the evaluation. There are several questions to ask in this area, including:
  —Does an application flow diagram exist?
  —Is a listing of controls available or must this information be gathered from application documentation?
  —Does documentation distinguish security controls from other functions?
  —Do functional requirements documents, system specifications, test documentation, procedure manuals, and other documents exist?

—Are they up to date, accurate and complete, understandable, and (especially for requirements documents) agreed on?

There may be other characteristics of the application that can affect the evaluation. Examples include a distribution of functions over physically separate sites and anticipated resistance from applications personnel.

Select Areas of Emphasis. An evaluation must encompass the entire application, not just its major security components, because it cannot be assumed that security-relevant areas have been correctly identified. The reason for this comprehensiveness is that security deficiencies, which can occur almost anywhere, sometimes arise in unlikely places. This must be balanced against the facts that evaluation resources are usually extremely limited and that some areas (e.g., functions applicable only to nonsensitive assets) warrant less detailed coverage than do others (e.g., password management). The plan must achieve the proper blend of completeness and focused emphasis. In general, the greatest emphasis is placed on those assets, exposures, threats, and controls associated with areas of greatest expected loss or harm. In addition, less emphasis is placed on areas in which flaws are believed to be well known and understood. (Nevertheless, the existence of these flaws is addressed in the evaluation findings.)

Besides the IT auditor's basic experience, many factors can influence the proper placement of emphasis. Problem areas might have been identified by prior certifications. Audit or evaluation findings, risk analysis findings, and violation reports can identify areas of weakness and help set priorities. Applications personnel themselves should point out weak areas.

Probably the single most difficult question during the performance of an evaluation is determining how much is enough. For most areas of an application, a basic (i.e., high-level, overview-type) evaluation is sufficient for an evaluation judgment. Some situations warrant detailed evaluations because of their sensitivity or because their fundamental security safeguards are beyond the range of a high-level review. Several criteria must be taken into consideration to determine the amount of detail needed in an evaluation. In most cases, the major criteria are application sensitivity, evaluation evidence, and control location. Other criteria are the amount of evidential detail, application size and complexity, and the amount of IT auditor experience.

Application Sensitivity. In general, the greater the sensitivity of an application or application component, the greater the desirable evaluation detail. Extremely sensitive applications, whose potential for loss is high, almost certainly require detailed evaluation. Similarly, basic evaluations should suffice for applications areas that are sensitive but not critically so and whose potential for loss is low. Between these extremes, there is great need for judgment.

Evaluation Evidence. This is a broad criterion. It includes prior evaluation findings, prior problem or violation reports (for operational reviews), and new evidence obtained during the evaluation (for both operational and developmental reviews). The first two indicate areas of past strength and weakness, suggesting the degree of evaluation detail currently needed. Evidence obtained during the evaluation might be the single most important criterion and also suggests the degree of detail. For example, the planning portion of an evaluation might reveal that the application has never addressed security and is therefore in a completely insecure state. In this case, the planning process itself could suffice for an evaluation, in which a basic evaluation is performed once the major problem areas have been resolved. A detailed evaluation is inappropriate in the face of gross or fundamental security inadequacies. A detailed evaluation could also be inappropriate if the planning process reveals application security safeguards to be highly effective and well managed. Judgment is needed here, but the objective is to minimize spending resources on applications with either highly effective or highly ineffective security safeguards. It is usually preferable to place more security testing attention on intermediate cases.

The detection of a potential problem area can necessitate an auditor's more detailed analysis. This might be the case if the software development method has not provided adequate procedures for preventing and detecting errors. Although the implemented security functions seem acceptable, there is a need for more detailed evaluation to provide confidence that the entire implementation can be relied on.

Control Location. The issue here is the extent to which application security safeguards are internal. Several factors influencing this area include the degree to which:

- The application relies on programmed, as opposed to user, control
- Transactions are initiated externally or internally
- Transaction records are kept externally or internally

Applications in which control is external are typically evaluated at the basic level. Examples include externally controlled accounts-receivable or inventory applications, message processing applications, and automated teller applications. Applications in which control is primarily internal require a detailed evaluation. Examples include fully automated funds-disbursement and accounting applications and real-time control applications (e.g., air traffic control and automated production).

Determine Resource Allocation. The IT auditor plans the resources needed to accomplish the task (e.g., time, staff, administrative support, and technical tools) on the basis of the analysis of what must be done in the evaluation. Time estimates include not only the time required to perform the tasks but also the time needed to acquire the resources. General administrative support needs and technical tools should be defined. Other related forms of general support include copies of documents (e.g., policies and checklists), training, personnel clearances, and travel scheduling. The most difficult resource to obtain is usually personnel. Required personnel include consultants, technical writers, and couriers, in addition to security evaluators. For all resource estimates, underlying assumptions should be listed. The assumptions consider contingencies that could affect the availability of people or other resources.

Develop an Application Certification Plan. Once the analysis and resource definition have been performed, a plan for certifying the application must be drawn up and documented. This plan is usually issued by the IT auditor, who coordinates its elements with the involved parties before it is issued. The document should not be long or complex. The plan should be followed closely unless unforeseen problems arise that indicate a need to revise or modify it. The plan should schedule opportunities for such revisions or modifications. As the audit team gains experience in planning evaluations, these revisions can become less frequent.

COLLECT DATA

Most of the work performed during an evaluation (including the planning phase) serves the purpose of data collection. Often, the techniques used to collect data represent building blocks in the construction of evaluation methods. The exact nature of the data to be collected depends on the evaluation methods and tools selected. This task covers the following common data collection techniques:

- Provision by management
- Document review
- Interviews

Provision by Management. With this method of data collection, systems management provides introductory and detailed briefings and tutorials on the application and its security safeguards. It also includes the provision of four critical documents. Ideally, these documents already exist; however, they usually must be developed.

Security Requirements. Security requirements are the fundamental baseline for security testing. If an acceptable requirements statement does not exist, it must be formulated during certification. This is best accomplished through a joint effort of audit and development personnel. Audit personnel are needed because systems developers do not usually have a thorough understanding of security, especially with respect to external policies. Systems developers, however, have a better understanding of the application, especially with respect to user needs.

Risk Analysis. The application risk analysis shows threats and assets. This is useful in validating the requirements and defining the underlying problem to be solved. Again, when this document does not exist, it is best prepared through a joint effort by audit and development personnel.

Application Flow Diagram. The application flow diagram shows input, processing steps, and output. Complete transaction flows must be included for important transaction types. This is critical to understanding the application.

List of Application Controls. Controls can be the most difficult part of the security picture to define. One common difficulty is the seemingly simple task of distinguishing controls (e.g., authorization mechanisms, sequence checking) from application activities subject to control (e.g., initiation, recording, transcription, calculation). A useful rule of thumb is that a control is any protective action, device, procedure, technique, or other measure that reduces exposure.

Provision of this information by systems personnel can have benefits beyond that of easing the burden of data collection. In particular, it can increase the security awareness of systems personnel and draw the attention of testing personnel to application areas that are not well understood and might warrant further analysis.

IT auditors should not accept documentation provided by systems management as absolutely accurate, because systems personnel might not be objective. Document reviews and interviews can help validate this information. Nevertheless, documentation provided by systems personnel often proves to be an excellent source of information and has the added advantage of making the certification process as a whole less expensive.

Document Review. Document review becomes increasingly important as evaluation attention focuses on more detailed issues. The potential set of documents to be reviewed varies substantially in each certification, depending on objectives and the availability and value of documentation.

Interviews. Interviews, although time-consuming, can sometimes produce information not available through other means.

Ensuring Accurate Information. One purpose of a certification program is to provide checks and balances. This purpose is not served if IT auditors simply report on the opinions of developers and users. Some interviewees may not know the facts, and others may misrepresent them. In addition, IT auditors may misinterpret the answers. Using interviews, instead of simply requiring subjects to complete questionnaires, improves information quality—personal interaction helps in interpreting meanings behind words, counteracting biases, and following leads.

CONDUCT BASIC EVALUATION

The basic evaluation typically suffices for most aspects of an application under review, although most applications also require some detailed evaluation work in problem areas. The general distinction between basic and detailed evaluation is primarily concerned with the overall functional security posture, not with the specific quality of individual controls. For example, basic evaluation is concerned with whether access authorization at the file level is sufficient or whether it might be required at the record level. As another example, evaluation might be concerned with whether authorization subjects must include terminals or individuals and processes. Basic evaluation is also concerned with verifying that security functions actually exist and that the implementation method is of sufficient, reliable quality. Detailed evaluation, on the other hand, is concerned with whether security functions work properly, satisfy performance criteria, and acceptably resist penetration.

There are three subtasks in a basic evaluation:

- Security requirements evaluation. Are applicable security requirements acceptable?
- Control existence determination. Do the security functions exist?
- Methodology review. Does the implementation method provide assurance that security functions are acceptably implemented?

Security Requirements Evaluation. The major purpose of certification is to determine whether system safeguards satisfy security requirements. This process is meaningful only if the system has well-defined security requirements; unfortunately, most do not. For certification to be useful, then, security requirements must be critically examined to determine whether they are reasonable and comply with IT, company, and user requirements. These requirements are usually documented in the project request form. When these requirements are not documented, they must be formulated. Accurate, complete, and understandable security requirements are fundamental to certification. To formulate and evaluate security requirements for a system, the IT auditor must consider two classes of needs—policy and situational.

Policy needs derive from principles and practices (e.g., laws, regulations, standards, and company policies) with which the system must comply. Situational needs derive from the system's characteristics and environment. To determine situational needs, four primary areas are considered:

- Assets. What should be protected?
- Threats. What are assets being protected against?
- Exposures. What could happen to assets if a threat is realized?
- Controls. How effective are security safeguards in reducing exposures?

Control Existence Determination. Because controls are described in a document or discussed in an interview does not prove that they have been implemented. Basic evaluations must ensure that security controls exist. The existence of most physical and administrative controls can be determined through inspection. For controls internal to the computer, testing is needed. Such testing does not gather significant evidence toward determining how well controls work (that is beyond the scope of a basic evaluation). The intent is simply to verify that the functions exist. On the other hand, quality must be kept in mind in case there are fundamental shortcomings that call into question the overall effectiveness of the functions. A particularly vulnerable area here is the susceptibility of procedural controls to human error.

Tests for control existence determination are straightforward. In many cases, a short operational demonstration suffices. For example, the existence of a password function can be determined by attempting to use the application and verifying that a valid password is required. The existence of an access function can be determined by verifying that access is not allowed unless explicitly granted (e.g., by the file owner). External testing is generally sufficient for control existence determination.

Methodology Review. Control existence determination verifies that controls exist; it says nothing about their quality. Although this is a high-level evaluation, it is still desirable to gain some assurance that controls are acceptably implemented. The best way to do this without becoming immersed in testing or detailed analysis is to examine the methodology used to develop the application. A methodology review can help determine the extent to which controls are reliably implemented and the susceptibility of the application to flaws. If review findings suggest that the implementation cannot be relied on, detailed evaluation is typically required to find specific flaws.

CONDUCT DETAILED EVALUATION

In many cases, a basic evaluation does not provide sufficient evidence for certification. Examples are cases in which the basic evaluation reveals problems that require further analysis, the application has a high degree of sensitivity, or primary security safeguards are embedded in detailed internal functions that are not able to be examined at the basic evaluation level. These situations require detailed evaluations to obtain additional evidence and increased confidence in evaluation judgments. Detailed evaluations involve analysis of the quality of security safeguards. Primary subtasks are examinations of the application in three areas:

- Review functional operation. Do controls function properly?
- Review performance. Do controls satisfy performance criteria?
- Review penetration resistance. How readily can controls be broken or circumvented?

It is rarely feasible or desirable, even in a detailed evaluation, to examine everything. Two strategies are presented for focusing on small portions of security. One is based on security-relevant components and the other on situational analysis.

Security Components. This strategy is based on four components relevant to IT security: assets, exposures, threats, and controls. All of the components have already been considered in the basic evaluation or in a risk analysis. The current activity involves a detailed view. It can use basic evaluation or risk analysis data when suitable and extensions of such data, as needed, for the analysis reports. The list of sample analysis reports discussed for each component can be expanded. It illustrates that a variety of reports may be needed. The questions of how many and which types depend on evaluation results.

Assets. Assets are the tangible and intangible resources of an organization. The evaluation issue here is to determine what should be protected. It might be useful to examine assets (e.g., data, files, physical resources) in detail, along with their relevant attributes (e.g., amount, value, use, and characteristics). A variety of specific tasks may be needed. For example, an asset value analysis determines how the value differs among users and potential attackers; an asset exploitation analysis examines different ways to use an asset for illicit gain.

Threats. Threats are possible events with the potential to cause loss or harm. It is important to distinguish among accidental, intentional, and natural threats. Intentional threats can be the most complex. An example of an analysis task for intentional threats is to identify perpetrator classes (e.g., programmers, operators, and users) on the basis of knowledge, skills, and access privileges. Another useful analysis examines the factors affecting threat frequency. Threat frequency depends on such factors as threat magnitudes, assets (and whether their loss is full or partial), relevant exposures, existing controls, and expected gain on the part of the perpetrator. The nature of the threats can influence evaluation methods used. For example, a standard evaluation technique is to review samples of source code to determine compliance with established programming practices and to look for security flaws. If the threat is a malicious programmer, however, the assembled object code rather than the source code or specifications is reviewed.

Exposures. Exposures are areas of susceptibility to loss or harm. The evaluation issue is to determine what might happen to assets if a threat (internal failure, human error, attack, or natural disaster) is realized. Examples of exposures are disclosure violations, erroneous decisions, and fraud. An example of an exposure analysis is the examination of the impact (e.g., greatly increased response time for a service) of a particular exposure. Much exposure analysis focuses on identifying areas in which exposures are the greatest. The question of which exposure types represent the areas of greatest loss or harm can have a major influence on detailed evaluation activities. For example, if integrity or accuracy is the primary concern, the evaluation focuses on the basic application processing; if disclosure is the primary concern, the evaluation focuses on those functions and interfaces associated with disclosure protection.

Controls. Controls are measures that protect against loss or harm. Evaluation tasks here often focus on controls embodied in specific application functions and procedures. Examples of evaluation tasks are control analysis (to examine a particular control in-depth and determine its vulnerabilities and severity), work-factor analysis (to determine actual difficulties in exploiting control weaknesses), and countermeasure tradeoff analysis (to examine alternative ways to implement a control; this is often necessary to recommend corrective action).

Situational Analysis. One forbidding aspect of computer security evaluation is the complexity of an application and its protective safeguards. This limits not only the percentage of the application that can be examined but also the degree of understanding attainable for those portions that are examined. A solution to this problem is the use of situational analysis. Two forms of situational analysis are discussed: the analysis of attack scenarios and the analysis of transaction flows. Each is used to complement the high-level completeness of a basic evaluation with detailed, well-understood examples and can focus on particular aspects of the application.

An attack scenario is a synopsis of a projected course of events associated with a threat. It encompasses the four security components—assets, threats, exposure, and controls—interwoven with the specific functions, procedures, and products of the application. An example of an attack scenario is a step-by-step description of a penetration, describing penetrator planning and activities, the vulnerability exploited, the asset involved, and the resulting exposure.

A transaction flow is a sequence of events involved in the processing of a transaction. If the application as a whole contains only a small set of transactions, transaction flow analysis might be a sufficient vehicle in itself for the detailed evaluation.

The idea underlying situational analysis is to focus attention on a manageable set of individual situations that can be carefully examined and thoroughly understood. This makes the resulting analysis more meaningful because, first, it places threats, controls, assets, and exposures in context with respect to each other and to application functions. This allows for the proper consideration of interdependencies and presents a balanced, realistic picture. If a detailed evaluation decomposes security components into constituent parts, a situational analysis pieces these components together again into a coherent whole. Second, it emphasizes the objectives being served by controls and allows safeguards to be evaluated on the basis of these objectives. The increased understanding that can result from the use of situational analysis, as well as its illustrative value, make it an important tool for conducting and presenting detailed evaluations.

Review Functional Operation. Functional operation is the area most often emphasized in detailed evaluation because it assesses protection against human errors and casual attempts to misuse the application. Evaluations of functional operation assess whether controls perform their required functions acceptably. Although testing is the primary technique used in evaluating functional operation, other validation and verification techniques must also be used, particularly to provide adequate analysis and review during early phases of the system life cycle. The routine testing often satisfies certification objectives and verification performed during development and operation, and it is not practical for the audit team to duplicate these activities. On the other hand, when routine testing and verification does not provide sufficient assurance for the desired level of security, additional testing that focuses on security control functional operation must be added to satisfy the desired level of security needs.

Besides testing, there are other security evaluation tools and techniques than can be used in examining functional operation. For example, software tools for program analysis can be helpful in documentation analysis. Matrices can suggest ideas for test cases and scenarios. Checklists provide quick training as well as suggest ideas for tests. Their value increases as more varied checklists become available to meet particular needs. For example, it can be useful to have checklists of assets, exposures, policies, policy alternatives and issues, environmental characteristics, threats, threat and asset characteristics, factors influencing threat frequency, controls, control interactions, flaw categories, and penetration approaches.

Review Performance. The quality of safeguards depends on much more than proper functional operation. Several qualitative factors are listed under the general heading of performance, which is the second area of concern in detailed evaluation. These are:

- Availability
- Survivability
- Response time
- Throughput

They can be applied to individual controls or to entire applications. Testing is the best way to evaluate performance and the specific tests needed for each of these factors. A useful technique here is stress testing. This can involve using large numbers of users and requests, large amounts of background activity, or maximum resources to attain conditions of operational stress. Functional operation might also be examined under these conditions because stress loading often interferes with regular processing. Stress testing is also used to attempt to exhaust quota limits for such specific resources as buffers, queues, tables, and ports. These resources might be external or internal to the application and might support such application functions as jobs, transactions, and sessions. This directed stress testing is especially useful in evaluating protection against denial-of-service threats.

Review Penetration Resistance. The final area of concern in detailed evaluation is penetration resistance. The task here is to assess resistance against the breaking or circumventing of controls. Cryptanalysis is an example of a technique for breaking a particular control—encryption. Creating and using a fraudulent logon utility to discover passwords is an example of control circumvention. The nature of the evaluation activity here differs widely, depending on whether the potential penetrators are users, operators, application programmers, system programmers, managers, or external personnel. In addition, the notion of penetration resistance applies not only to attacks against data but to physical assets and performance.

Assessment of penetration resistance can be the most technically complex of the detailed evaluation categories. It is best performed to establish confidence in security safeguards and to find and correct flaws. In both cases, it:

- Provides an assessment of an application's penetration resistance
- Helps determine the difficulties involved in actually exploiting flaws

- Provides a clear demonstration of flaw exploitability (e.g., it might not be clear from analysis whether an asynchronous timing flaw can be exploited)

PREPARE REPORT OF RESULTS

The security evaluation report is the primary product of certification. It contains technical security recommendations for the application and is the main basis for the decision on the adequacy of security. The evaluation work is partitioned into three areas:

- Application software and administrative and procedural safeguards
- Physical security
- Operating systems and hardware

Most of the internal work is in the area of application software and administrative and procedural safeguards. The results of detailed evaluations are combined with basic evaluation results; all of the results are then integrated into the security testing report. It is preferable to integrate results from different evaluation areas into one final report rather than deliver several reports to management; the safeguards in each area can have complex interrelationships that require a technical interpretation.

Report Preparation. The report is composed of these sections:

- Introduction and Summary. This section briefly describes the application and summarizes testing results and recommendations.
- Background. This section provides contextual information. One important item is the security standards or policies that were applied. Another is a list of the general functional characteristics of the application (e.g., the presence or absence of user programming). Application boundaries are defined, along with security assumptions about areas outside the boundaries.
- Major Results. The first portion of this section summarizes the controls that are in place and their general roles in protecting assets against threats and preventing exposures. This emphasizes those areas in which safeguards are acceptable. The second portion summarizes major vulnerabilities. Vulnerabilities are divided into two categories: proposed residual vulnerabilities and proposed vulnerabilities requiring correction. This format serves as both a summary of results and a recommendation of which vulnerabilities to accept and which to correct. Authority to approve the recommendations resides with management.

Recommended Corrective Actions. Corrective actions and their anticipated costs are recommended and ranked. Responsibility for making the corrections might be proposed. Criteria for evaluating the corrections must be established. This section must be sufficiently complete to give a clear understanding of the implications of either accepting or correcting vulnerabilities. Because sensitive applications are usually also important to the company's operations, most flaws are not severe enough to remove an operational application from service, although some restrictions may need to be implemented immediately. Other than removing an application from service or delaying its implementation, there are many intermediate options available, including:

- Adding procedural security controls and restricting use of the application to sites that have compensating controls
- Restricting the application to process only nonsensitive or minimally sensitive data
- Removing especially vulnerable application functions or components (e.g., in a network environment, a particularly weak node might be excluded)
- Restricting use of the application to noncritical situations in which errors or failures are less severe
- Removing dial-up access (relying more on physical security)

Certification Process. This section summarizes the work performed in the certification process to enable management to determine the confidence that can be placed in the findings. The section should have the following appended:

- Attachment A, Proposed Accreditation Statement. This is a critical part of the report; it summarizes recommended actions. Judgments and recommendations embodied in the statement are subject to approval by management.
- Attachment B, Detailed Evaluation Reports. These describe the full set of findings, not just major ones. It can be useful, especially if separate evaluation teams are participating, to use standard forms to present basic and detailed findings.

Section 28
Analyze Audit Results

The purpose of producing the computer reports is to provide audit information. In many instances, the computer program will perform analyses; in others, additional audit steps will be needed to verify or refute findings in the report. The objective of this step is to analyze and use the information produced by the data tests.

DOCUMENT FINDINGS

The concerns raised during the audit tests should be documented as potential findings; a finding is the discovery of a difference between actual and expected or prescribed procedures, operations, or results. It should be understood that documenting a finding at this point does not necessarily mean that the finding will be included in the audit report. In this task, findings are described as they occur during the audit process. These can be operational or financial findings that represent a variance from the organization's policies, procedures, and guidelines or from general good business practices.

The analyses of auditee controls and data performed during the audit may uncover deviations from what is expected. In most cases, the IT auditor discovers deviations from company policies or procedures (including established transaction processing procedures) in the functioning of a control or in the result produced. When a finding (i.e., a factual circumstance) is located, it should be documented; however, the IT auditor should judge which findings are worth documenting. It obviously would not be prudent for the IT auditor to document a calculation that was off by a penny. The following guidelines can help the IT auditor determine whether or not to document a particular deviation:

- The amount in question is significant for the organization.
- During an extended period of time, the loss resulting from the deviation could be significant.
- The problem caused by the deviation could affect the credibility of the department and organization. The deviation exemplifies the generally sloppy manner in which the business is conducted.

At this point, the IT auditor is asked not to draw conclusions but to merely document the finding. The audit objectives are those stated in the workpapers—the narrative should be kept brief, and all supporting workpapers should be referenced. The IT auditor should avoid the two extremes possible in documenting findings. Documenting insignificant findings causes the audit function to lose credibility with the auditee. On the other hand, if the IT auditor fails to recognize the potential effect of a deviation and therefore fails to document a critical finding, the organization could be adversely affected.

ANALYZE FINDINGS

The investigative work has now been completed, and the IT auditor must begin to turn the disparate audit results into an audit report. The initial effort is an in-depth analysis of the findings that will be helpful in presenting the findings to the auditee and management and in developing recommendations. Analyzing an audit finding involves answering the what, where, when, who, how, and why questions about that finding—the questions that both the auditee and management will ask. This task explains the background information needed concerning a finding and how to obtain it. Six categories of analysis should be performed about every finding, each involving the following process:

1. Ask a factual question.
2. Counter that factual question with an analytical question.
3. Analyze the answer to the second question to determine the basic cause of the problem.

Analysis 1: The Finding Event

Factual Question:

What was done?

The IT auditor must be able to state exactly what has happened that is a problem.

Analytical Question:

Why that?

The IT auditor must determine why the event happened, and whether it was caused by inadequate training, employee oversight, or other problem.

General Analysis:

When there is a problem as to why something was done, an analysis of the finding generally leads to the conclusion that the event was nonessential or redundant.

Analysis 2: Location of the Event

Factual Question:

Where was it done?

The IT auditor must determine which part of the process, which department, or which job is the source of the problem.

Analytical Question:

Why there?

The IT auditor must determine why the event was performed at that location and whether that was in fact the right place for the event.

General Analysis:

In most instances when there is a problem associated with location, the results of the analysis will reveal that the event was performed at an inconvenient location or segment of the application.

Analysis 3: Timing of the Event

Factual Question:

When was it done?

The IT auditor must determine the time of the event.

Analytical Question:

Why then?

The IT auditor must challenge the timing of the event; that is, whether it was performed in the wrong part of the application.

General Analysis:

Usually, when the IT auditor believes that the finding was caused by timing, the results of the analysis indicate that the process was in a poor or improper sequence.

Analysis 4: Responsibility for the Event

Factual Question:

Who did it?

The IT auditor must be able to determine who or what caused the problem (e.g., a manual process, a person, or a program or part of a program).

Analytical Question:

Why that person?

The IT auditor must judge whether the right person performed this event, program, or process.

General Analysis:

When the event was performed by the wrong program or person, the results of the analysis reveal that the process was fragmented, the individual performing it lacked the proper skill, or the program that performed it should not, in fact, have done so.

Analysis 5: Process that Produced the Event

Factual Question:

How was it done?

The IT auditor must be able to substantiate the process that produced the unfavorable event or finding.

Analytical Question:

Why that way?

The IT auditor must investigate the chosen process to determine whether it could produce the desired results.

General Analysis:

In most cases in which the process appears to be the cause of the problem, the conclusion is that the process was either too complicated or too costly.

Analysis 6: Reason for Performing the Event

Factual Question:

Why was it done?

The IT auditor must determine who authorized or approved the occurrence of the event (either manually or through a computer program).

Analytical Question:

Why was it permitted?

The IT auditor investigates and determines whether the event was or was not performed in accordance with management policies and intent. If it was not, the IT auditor must determine why not and how it was allowed to occur.

General Analysis:

When there is a problem of authority, the conclusion generally finds that the authorization procedures either were not followed or were inherently ineffective. The analysis will produce a series of conclusions about the finding that should be recorded on a workpaper. These results become the basis for developing the recommendations, supporting both the finding and the audit report. If the steps of the task are followed faithfully, there is little risk that the analysis will be incomplete or that it will result in insufficiently developed conclusions.

DEVELOP RECOMMENDATIONS

After the cause of a problem has been determined, the next question to be addressed must be how to correct it. The task now is to advise management and the auditee how, in the IT auditor's best judgment, the problem can be corrected. Any recommendation made should be both sound and workable. Frequently, however, IT auditors add recommendations as an afterthought. Poorly or hastily constructed recommendations seriously affect the credibility of the audit department. Because the same types of control weaknesses usually occur repeatedly, the same audit recommendations are often made repeatedly.

An IT audit recommendation should make its intent clear; it must be extremely specific rather than general. A recommendation that data validation and controls be improved is too general; the recommendation must state specifically which controls are weak or nonexistent. A good recommendation should demonstrate that it will provide a positive return on investment. (Whenever it is practical to do so, the economics of the recommendation should be included.) The recommendation should be clearly written in managerial terms. At the same time, it should provide sufficient technical information to be accepted (technical data can be appended as appropriate). Any good audit recommendation in the computer field must be logical as well as creative because it must fit into a structured application system. The recommendations should relate directly to the audit findings and should be similarly categorized. It is essential for the IT auditor to understand that some recommendations cannot be cost-justified and that the IT department's resources may be inadequate to implement the recommendation. It is also important that the recommendation be fully thought through; otherwise, its implementation will be impractical.

DOCUMENT RECOMMENDATIONS

Findings are factual and, when properly stated, inarguable. Recommendations, on the other hand, because they are opinions and suggestions, must be supported by solid information and then marketed to the auditee and management. The objective of this task is to help the IT auditor structure these recommendations, a difficult task for IT auditors without a strong enough IT background to develop easily implemented, cost-effective recommendations. Effective IT audit recommendations take the following factors into account:

- How the recommendation can be implemented in the affected application systems
- The impact on other application systems and on operating hardware and software
- The availability of the skills needed to implement the recommendation
- The effect on data (e.g., the need to expand the data attributes)
- The effect on the users of the proposed altered or added or deleted information

IT auditors with minimal IT experience may find it helpful to consult with the project team, the user, or an independent consultant while developing the recommendations. Their recommendations may be accepted more easily if a highly skilled person in IT can be cited as a co-developer or supporter of the recommendation.

Economics is a major cause for rejecting audit recommendations. IT personnel may agree that the recommendations are good but add that they are unacceptable because of the high cost of implementation. Although some IT auditors consider this a ploy to avoid accepting the recommendations, the position may be valid. Studies have indicated that the cost of implementing a change in an operational system is at least a hundred times more costly than implementing that same change in a system under development. The solution to the cost dilemma is to work out the economic factors, with some concurrence from the IT project team regarding their reasonableness, before making the recommendation. The arguments can then center on the merits of the recommendation, not its cost. In addition to the economic feasibility of the recommendation, the IT auditor should consider the possibility that the IT department will have neither adequate staff nor skills available to implement it. It is important to look for alternatives that could address the finding at lower cost or with greater ease of implementation.

Section 29
Review and Report Audit Findings

During this step, the IT auditor develops the audit report, distributes it, and follows up on the recommendations. Good ideas are of little value unless they are accepted and implemented, and the value of the audit is frequently rated on acceptance of the audit report by both auditee and senior management. The report must be comprehensive, identifying the scope of the audit, explaining the factual findings, and suggesting recommendations to overcome any weaknesses or problems discovered during the audit. The report must be written clearly and effectively enough to cause action to be taken and must therefore include all information necessary to attain that end.

CREATE THE AUDIT REPORT

This task describes how to write a report for an IT application audit. The general principles of writing any audit report apply to an IT audit report; however, the technology discussed in this report is different and may present the IT auditor with such problems as the following:

- If the report is written in the technical jargon of the IT department, it will be incomprehensible to audit and senior management.
- The report may not contain enough technical information or practical detail for the IT department to implement the recommendations.
- The IT department may not understand the magnitude of the audit findings and recommendations.

The audit department may not have the support of the IT department in making IT-oriented recommendations. Most of these problems can be easily resolved. The IT auditor should be able to keep IT-oriented language at a level that can be understood by management (readability will be specifically addressed later). Support for the audit, recognition of the importance of the audit findings and objectives, and the problem of insufficient technical information from an IT perspective can be handled by discussing and reviewing the initial reports by the IT project team.

Writing a successful audit report requires a clear understanding of both the report objectives (what the IT auditor hopes that the report will accomplish) and the desired action (what the IT auditor wants management to do after reading the report). A good audit report includes no more than three objectives and three actions. An audit report with too much data or too many requests overwhelms the reader. If several items need reporting to management, the objectives should be ranked according to priority, and only the three most important should be included in the report. Small items can be reported in an appendix or a supplemental letter to the auditee. The IT auditor must keep them clearly in mind because these objectives and actions help limit the scope of the audit report. The IT auditor will also be able to arrange exit conferences and management presentations around the critical pertinent points.

Finally, the IT auditor must ensure that adequate time is available to write the report in an appropriate manner, incorporating relevant evidence into the report to support the findings and recommendations. Failure to do so will adversely affect the credibility of the audit department, and auditee management will almost certainly disagree with the factual information in the report.

REVIEW REPORT REASONABLENESS

This task involves verifying that the audit workpapers adequately support the findings and recommendations in the audit report and reviewing the means by which that information is presented. Reviewing the workpapers and audit report is the responsibility of audit management. In smaller audit departments, the review is performed by the director of internal audit; in large organizations, audit managers or supervisors may perform this function. Evidence of the audit management review must be included in the workpapers.

The IT audit review is a special challenge for management. The assumption that audit management can effectively review the IT audit workpapers implies:

- An understanding of computer terminology
- An understanding of IT principles and concepts
- An understanding of how systems are structured, how they operate, and how they are controlled
- Sufficient knowledge to understand the effect of the audit findings and recommendations
- Sufficient background to recognize whether the procedures are adequate to identify significant control problems

It is important that audit management be qualified to review the reasonableness of the audit report. If audit management lacks some of these skills, an outside consultant may be needed to assist with some of the reviews; internal audit departments might wish to use the services of their independent public accountants. Larger internal audit departments normally have sufficient IT expertise to conduct both the audit and review. The IT auditor should be certain that the workpapers adequately support the audit findings and recommendations.

REVIEW READABILITY OF REPORT

The audit report is designed not only to convey information but also to change behavior. A good audit report has the objective of persuading management to take certain actions and must, in this context, be considered a marketing document. The objective of this task is to assess the impact of the audit report in terms of its appearance, wording, and effectiveness in changing managerial behavior. This task requires audit management to view the report from the perspective of the auditee and senior management. Audit management must assess the impression, on the basis of both appearance and content, that the audit report will make on these readers, asking such questions as the following:

- If I were to receive this report, would I judge it to have been developed by a professional and knowledgeable group?
- Is it clear what the report is trying to tell me?
- If I were the auditee, would I find the information in this audit report offensive or disparaging? If so, would I be more concerned with developing countermeasures than with implementing the recommendations?
- If I were the recipient of this report, would it adequately build a case for me to implement the recommendations?
- Does this report clearly differentiate between important items and those that are less critical?

It is important to remember that although the report contains valid findings and recommendations, the auditee will not accept it if it is poorly written. The recipient of the report must understand the information included in the report and must be able to distinguish between important and unimportant information.

PREPARE AND DISTRIBUTE REPORT

The result of a good audit report is the acceptance of the findings and implementation of the recommendations by the auditee—an audit report that elicits no action has not accomplished its mission. The audit is of little use if the audit team is told that it did a good job and that its findings and recommendations are sound but that, for whatever reason, the auditee is not going to accept the findings or implement the recommended actions.

The objective of this task is to ensure implementation of the audit recommendations. The IT auditor should first meet with auditee management to explain the audit report and to obtain their concurrence. The IT auditor then issues the final report to the appropriate parties, following up as appropriate to ensure that action is taken. This task deals with obtaining concurrence, marketing the report, and other steps needed to ensure that the report findings and recommendations are accepted. It involves the exit conference and report issuance and follow-up procedures.

The Exit Conference. The exit conference provides an opportunity for the auditee to review and react to the audit findings and recommendations. If the exit conference is the auditee's first chance to see a copy of the audit report, the IT auditor will be able to deal with any immediate reactions before a defensive posture can be developed.

Report Issuance and Follow-up. The IT auditor can ensure certain action by sending copies of the report to the appropriate people; this is a pressure tactic, however, and it should be used cautiously. Nevertheless, auditing standards obligate the IT auditor to follow up on the actions taken. If no action has been taken, the IT auditor must initiate whatever procedures are necessary to instigate action, including calling on senior management.

The successful completion of this task requires strict adherence to a timely follow-up schedule. If the IT auditor does not follow up at all, recommendations may not be implemented; if follow-up is delayed, the system may have so changed that the recommendation is no longer appropriate.

Section 30
Review Quality Control

The last audit step in any audit is to perform a self-assessment of the audit and the audit process. This is part of the quality assurance activity in auditing. Quality assurance means looking at the process to determine whether it worked. If the audit process failed to work or worked ineffectively, action should be taken to initiate changes to that process. A failure to perform this step may mean that flaws in the audit process will remain through future audits, causing it to remain ineffective or become extremely time-consuming.

Quality assurance activities are divided into two parts. First, IT auditors look at the products of the audit, which is called quality control. Quality control is partially performed by the audit staff and partially by audit management. In addition, IT auditors determine the effectiveness of the process, which is called quality assurance. Quality assurance uses the results of the quality control review to assess deficiencies in the audit process. Quality assurance also provides an opportunity for the audit team to comment on the effectiveness and efficiency of the audit process.

CONDUCT A QUALITY CONTROL REVIEW

This task involves reviewing the audit to ensure that all the steps and tasks specified for auditing computer applications have been performed properly. Quality control is similar to quality assurance (which involves the third-party review of the audit) except that with quality control, the audit team that conducted the audit performs the review. For most audits of automated applications, this task is performed throughout the audit process by the IT auditor in charge, typically at the completion of each step. Although each IT auditor assigned to an audit should be accountable for the quality of individual work, the IT auditor in charge has supervisory responsibility for overall audit quality.

Although quality assurance reviews are recommended for internal audit departments, only a small percentage of such departments actually use them. Most internal audits rely on quality control—a line management responsibility—to ensure the quality of the audit. Although quality control is usually the responsibility of line audit management, the quality control process must be integrated into the audit process if audit resources are to be used effectively.

CONDUCT A QUALITY ASSURANCE REVIEW

The audit team must evaluate the audit process that was used in conducting the audit. A member of audit management usually performs this quality assurance activity, although audit management can delegate the task to the audit team. This task identifies deficiencies and inefficiencies in the computer application audit process. Two activities are involved in this task. The first activity is to identify problems that have occurred during the audit. These problems should have been documented during the course of the audit. This activity recognizes that the problem occurred and records it for action purposes. The most common sources of problem identification are:

- Audit management workpaper review comments list
- Problems noted by the audit team in the workpapers (these may be a special audit section, or they might be identified as notes for future audits)
- IT auditor to-do lists (these indicate tasks that have not been performed correctly or work that needs to be performed again)
- Tasks that have not been completed because of difficulty in completing them (examples are questions on the checklist that the IT Auditor did not understand or task instructions that were not understandable)
- Problems noted on workpapers indicating difficulty in performing these steps

These problems should be recorded in a workpaper. This workpaper should include a number to identify the specific problem, the name of the audit problem, a brief description of the problem that should reference the location of the problem (i.e., a workpaper reference), and an estimation of the significance of the problem, with a potential solution to the problem if one can be determined at this time.

The second activity that must be performed is to interview the audit team members to assess problems perceived by them. Although this can be done either individually by the quality assurance manager or as a team activity, it is recommended that it be done as a team activity by the entire staff that participated in the audit if the individuals can be assembled for this purpose. It is recommended that this procedure be followed for team reviews:

- Schedule a conference room for two to four hours for the review.
- Explain that the purpose is to identify problems with the audit process and to improve the audit process.
- Explain the meaning of each item.
- Permit each member of the team to indicate problems relating to the item topic being discussed.
- Record each potential problem.

- Encourage group reactions to audit members' ideas, eliminating those they do not perceive as problems and consolidating those that are, when possible.

The major impediment to documenting audit problems is that people do not like to recognize that problems occur. In addition, many individuals feel that documenting problems is indicative of poor performance. It is important for audit management to emphasize the fact that the problems occur most frequently because of the process—not the individual. Until the audit staff accepts the concept that the process causes the problems, IT auditors will be reluctant to spend much effort documenting problems.

IMPROVE THE APPLICATION AUDIT PROCESS

This step is the responsibility of the quality assurance group in auditing. If there is no quality assurance group, audit management can perform this task or it could be delegated to the users of the process. The objective of the task is to improve the process for auditing computer applications. This task involves two activities. The first is to identify the cause of each audit problem, and the second is to develop and implement a process improvement. These two activities occur for each identified problem with the audit process. The task begins with a list of identified problems. In determining the cause of the problem, IT auditors should consider the following procedures.

Cluster Similar Audit Problems. All of the audit problems that appear to address the same area should be clustered into a single group. If the number of audit problems identified is small, this can be done mentally. As the number of audit problems increases, however, it may be more efficient to write each problem on a 3×5 card and then sort the cards into clusters. When this has been done, the similar audit problems should be recorded in the appropriate workpaper. It is not unrealistic to include the same audit problem in more than one cluster.

Determine How the Problem Was Identified. In looking for the cause of the problem, it is important to know how the IT auditors realized that a problem existed. Did they have problems following a procedure? Was there a column missing on the workpaper? Were they unable to find needed information from another workpaper? This section should be referenced to the workpaper in which the problem was identified or noted.

Indicate Which Audit Process and Workpapers Are Involved. This procedure involves determining what process the IT auditor was performing when the problem occurred and what workpapers were being used. This may be the same or different items than were used to identify the problem. For example, the problem may have occurred in completing the workpaper, but it was identified during the supervisory review. All of the information about the process and workpapers should be recorded in the appropriate workpaper.

Identify the Skills Necessary to Perform the Identified Process and the Skill Level of the IT Auditors Involved in the Problem. This information can be obtained from the IT auditor-in-charge or departmental documents. It must be determined which skills the IT auditor must possess to properly perform an audit and to complete appropriate workpapers. The skills actually possessed by the IT auditors who performed the question procedure or completed the question workpaper should also be documented.

Identify the Cause of the Problem. The most likely causes are improper process instructions, improper or improperly sequenced process, incomplete or confusing workpapers, or IT auditors' lack of skills. The quality assurance manager should study the information about the problem and then attempt to determine what part of the process broke down, including training and staffing of IT auditors for the assignment.

The next activity is to identify the improvement to the process that will eliminate the cause of the problem. The quality assurance manager should attempt to identify as many potential solutions as is reasonable to improve the process. The solutions identified should be realistic on the basis of the size and skill level of the audit staff. For each identified potential solution, the advantages as well as the disadvantages of implementing that solution should be determined. It may be advantageous to discuss the potential solutions with the audit staff and get their input on which solution they prefer. Having the audit staff accept the solution is helpful in having it implemented.

The implementation plan should include what needs to be changed in the audit process, including the documentation of the workpapers, when the change will occur, and how the audit staff will be notified and trained to properly execute the changed procedures.

Section 31
Workflow Diagramming

IT auditors should determine whether the narratives and diagrams provided by the internal customers (i.e., the auditees) are adequate to describe the application that they are reviewing. If these are adequate, the auditors probably have no reason to prepare their own documents. However, if the narratives and diagrams are inadequate, IT auditors should prepare new workflow diagrams.

Diagramming is a process used to develop a symbolic representation of a situation or activity. These symbolic representations were originally used to document the logic that underlay the processing within an application, and they later became part of the standard toolkit for the IT auditor. Because of technological advances, particularly in the personal computer arena, diagrams are a standard tool for anyone needing to document or demonstrate a situation or process.

The person coining the phrase that "a picture is worth a thousand words" would have been more accurate to say that a picture could be worth a thousand words if it were drawn correctly. A well-developed diagram emphasizes the critical elements and processes in an application, identifies the decision points and range of possible alternatives, and indicates the persons either responsible for or involved with the process.

The IT auditor should develop diagrams to meet one or more of the following objectives:

- To document his or her understanding of an application
- To present an application's key features, strengths, or weaknesses
- To provide high-quality workpapers, while consuming fewer resources than developing extensive narratives
- To depict the details of a proposed solution or the process for implementing such a solution
- To prepare strategic or tactical plans for Information Systems administrative or project-related activities

A flowchart can depict any process that is made up of a series of steps. The process being depicted does not have to be automated. For example, diagrams can be used to describe the process of managing an audit department, conducting an audit, writing an audit report, or traveling between the internal audit home offices and the location that is going to be audited. The

IT auditor often prepares diagrams that depict the way in which manual or automated processes work, which is the reason for referring to them as workflow diagrams.

The workflow diagram should symbolically depict all of the elements required to understand a particular situation or process. An IT auditor might wish to describe the process of performing an audit to the personnel in a location soon to be audited.

Clearly describing the audit process in advance may help to address any concerns of the auditees. For example, as shown in the workflow diagram in Exhibit 31-1 if the event to be diagrammed was how to conduct an audit, the first step might be initiating an audit assignment, setting the audit objectives, planning the fieldwork and staffing, etc., until the audit report is issued and the files closed, which would be a likely final step in the audit process.

The IT auditor should begin the workflow diagramming process by determining the exact boundaries of the process to be diagrammed. Without boundaries, a diagramming project can extend into many other areas that could prevent a timely conclusion of the assignment originally approved.

Having set the boundaries for the assignment, the IT auditor begins by identifying the high-level components or steps making up the process being reviewed. This step does not have to be documented by using a diagramming software tool. Some IT auditors find that drawing this top-level diagram, as in the workflow diagram show in Exhibit 31-2, by hand or by describing it in a brief narrative is just as effective.

The IT auditor can then begin to diagram each top-level component. Each component should be broken down into its direct and indirect components. The direct components of a process are most often either actions or decisions. An action involves the performance of an activity by one or more persons, one or more machines, or a combination of the two. Some examples of an activity include: receiving a document in the mail; or entering new or changed information into a system, or a program checking for logical flags on orders to identify any that are due for shipment. A decision point occurs whenever there is more than one possible processing path, and one of those paths is chosen based on a condition or a test. Most of these decision points have only two alternatives—true or false or greater than or less than a threshold value, for example. However, many other situations exist that have more than two alternatives. One example is a company with four levels of signing authority. The workflow diagrams shown in Exhibits 31-3 and 31-4 depict two different but both acceptable ways for diagramming the situations just described.

Exhibit 31-1. Basic Audit Process Workflow Diagram

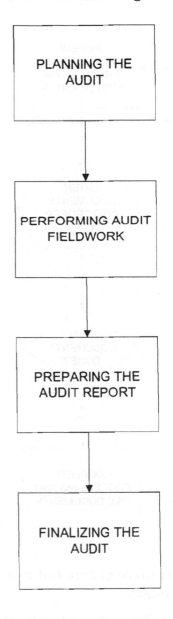

The IT auditor must select between alternatives, such as those based on personal preference along with any other diagramming considerations arising in that specific situation. The indirect components of the workflow diagram depict the inputs and outputs related to the activity being diagrammed. The inputs and outputs are often significant or necessary to the process being diagrammed, requiring their depiction in the diagram. Examples of indirect components include an order form sent in by a customer that someone takes and uses as the basis for entering a new order into the system. The order form is a trigger that initiates the entry process that may be followed by the issuance of an order confirmation. The confirmation

Exhibit 31-2. High-Level Flowchart Workflow Diagram

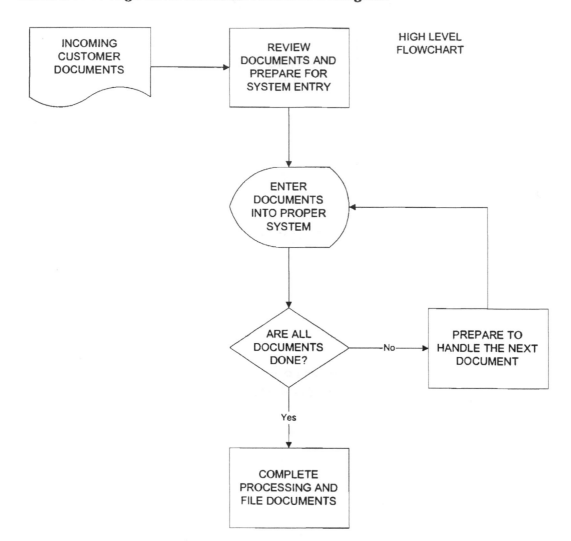

takes no action and makes no decision, but is an important element of the overall order handling process.

The IT auditor also must determine what level of sophistication is appropriate in any given situation. He or she can choose from a simple or limited set of shapes and increase the text portion of the diagram to present the information and specification the reader requires. A simple set of diagramming shapes, discussed in the following paragraphs, is depicted in Exhibit 31-5.

If the IT auditor chooses to omit the indirect elements of a situation or process, only two shapes may be required for the workflow diagram: a rectangle depicts an action and a diamond represents a decision. Exhibit 31-6 shows a diagram that uses only these two shapes to illustrate the complete process of auditing a computerized application.

Exhibit 31-3. Sample Workflow Diagram

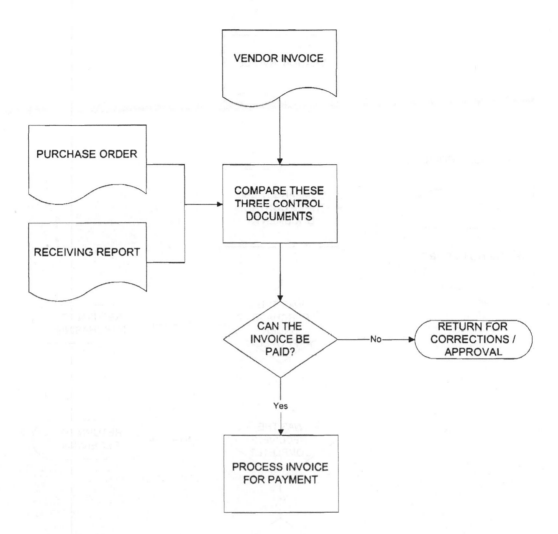

Alternatively, the IT auditor can select a set of shapes based on the idea that each shape will have a very specific meaning, so that anyone reviewing the diagram receives much of their information from just the shapes and the sequence in which they appear. One example of a more extensive set of diagramming shapes appears in Exhibit 31-7.

The IT auditor's selection of a set of diagramming shapes usually makes a significant difference in the diagram. In Exhibit 31-8, one portion of an application audit process can be diagrammed using only two shapes; that same process can be rediagrammed using a more extensive set of shapes. The contrast in terms of effect on the reader is clear: a more specific diagram communicates more information by using less text. Ultimately, the IT auditor must determine what is the appropriate type of diagram and what shapes should be used.

Exhibit 31-4. Sample Workflow Diagram

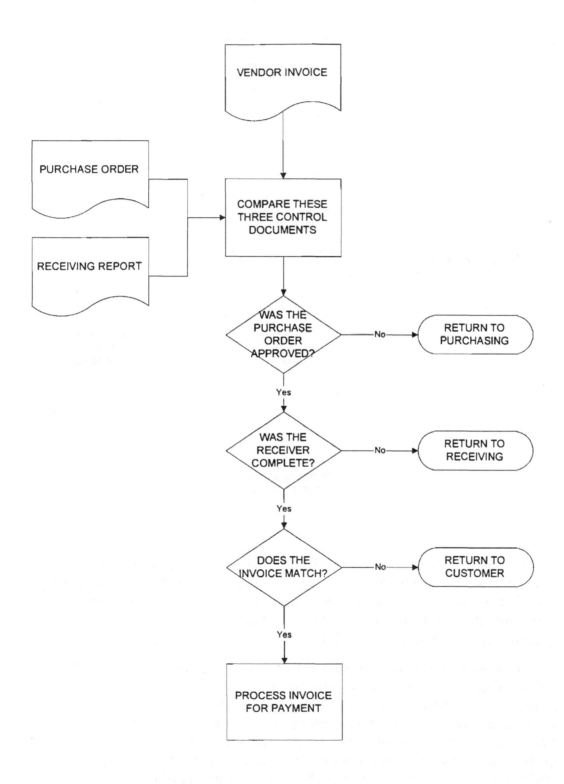

Exhibit 31-5. Simple Shape Set

The IT auditor should also consider adding narrative text directly onto the workflow diagrams or to draft separately, at least, a short narrative that can be easily related to the diagram. In the example workflow diagram depicting the process of conducting an audit, it is easier to understand the reasons or logic that support the actions if that information is presented in a complementary narrative, as shown in Exhibit 31-9, instead of being omitted from the diagram.

CREATING A WORKFLOW DIAGRAM

The IT auditor may develop workflow diagrams in a variety of situations, but it is likely that the majority of these situations will be either to document an existing or proposed system or to describe a new or alternative process that will be recommended as an available alternative to the audit customer. The workflow diagram can be used as a tool to document existing or proposed systems.

The IT auditor can use the following steps as an effective means for developing a workflow diagram.

- Determine the scope of the review.
- Work with the appropriate personnel to identify the major components of the process under review, along with key contacts for each component.

Exhibit 31-6. Audit Process Done with Limited Set of Shapes

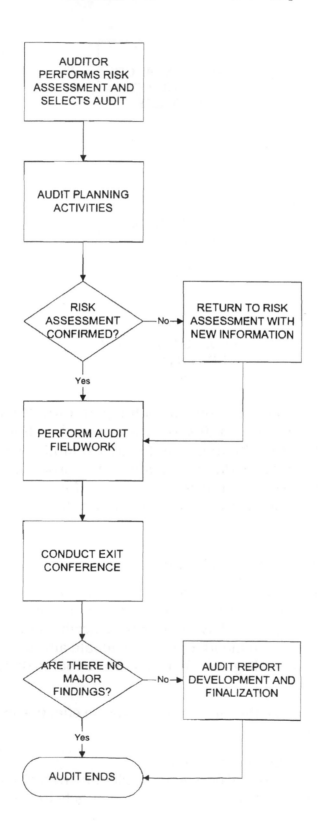

Exhibit 31-7. Audit Process Done with Limited Set of Shapes

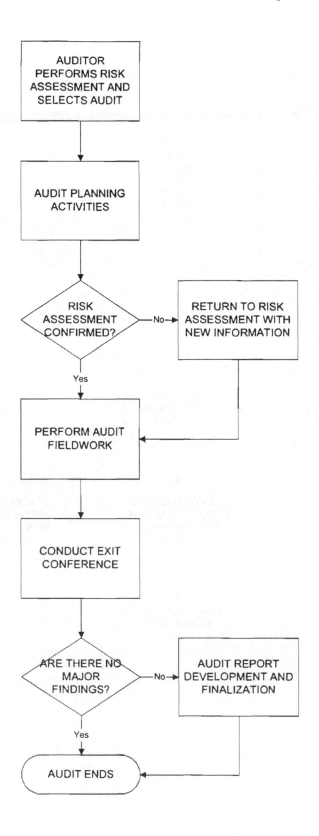

Exhibit 31-8. Audit Planning Activities

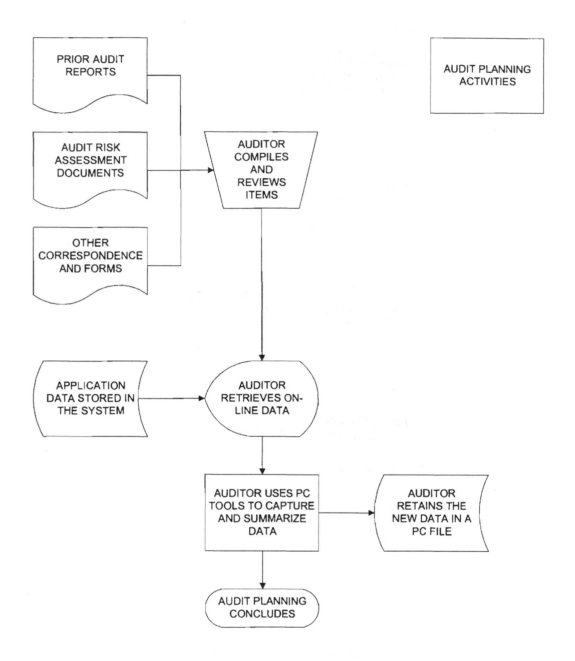

Exhibit 31-9. Workflow Diagram with Narrative Text

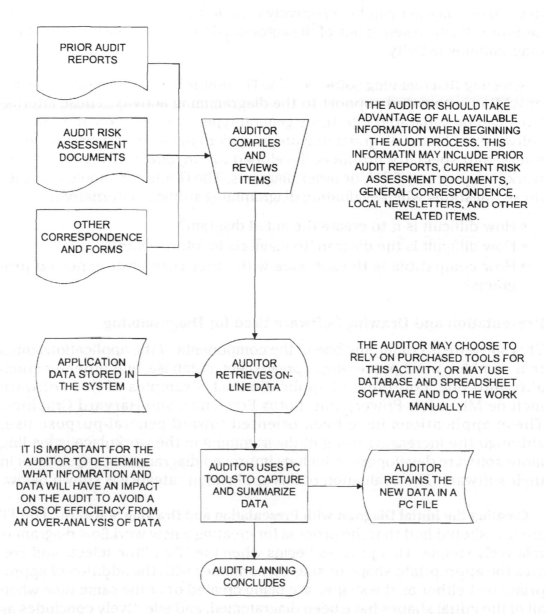

- Meet with these key contacts to obtain detailed information about the inputs, processes, and outputs that make up each major component.
- Create the first draft workflow diagram, manually or with diagramming software.
- Review the draft workflow diagram with the key contacts and make all appropriate additions and corrections based on their comments.
- Continue to develop the diagram until it is sufficiently correct to satisfy the objectives of the review.

The IT auditor should endeavor to set standards or minimum requirements for workflow diagramming within the audit department to ensure that any developed diagram can be effectively used in the future. Therefore, the IT auditor is likely to select one of the automated tools available to support the diagramming activity.

Selecting Diagramming Software. The IT auditor has many alternatives for providing automated support to the diagramming activity. These alternatives can be separated into three general types: presentation and drawing software; technical diagramming programs for engineers and system developers; and specialty products developed for anyone needing to prepare workflow, process, TQM, or other diagrams. The IT auditor should consider these questions when evaluating diagramming software alternatives:

- How difficult is it to create the initial diagram?
- How difficult is the diagram to maintain in future years?
- How compatible is the software with other current or expected programs?

Presentation and Drawing Software Used for Diagramming

This software is commonly one of the components of the application suites that combine word processing, spreadsheet, database, and other functionality into one, coordinated application set. Examples of this software include Microsoft Powerpoint, Lotus Freelance, and Harvard Graphics. These applications have been oriented toward general-purpose use, although the increasing using of diagramming in the workplace is leading more software developers to include improved diagramming capabilities in their software. The evaluation of this application category is shown below.

Creating the Initial Diagram with Presentation and Drawing Software. The IT auditor should find that the process for creating a new workflow diagram is relatively simple. This process begins when the IT auditor selects and creates the appropriate shape or shapes, continues with the addition of appropriate text either as the shapes are being created or at the same time when all of the initial shapes have been diagrammed, and effectively concludes as connectors and process flow lines are added. Then, the completed workflow diagram is printed or transmitted.

Creating Shapes. The IT auditor is likely to find that creating shapes with presentation software is relatively easy because there is a wide variety of shapes from which to choose. One difficulty that the IT auditor might experience in creating a complex workflow diagram by using very descriptive shapes is that the general shapes available in these applications do not provide the level of specificity that the he or she requires.

Adding Text. The IT auditor is likely to find that adding text within the shapes is difficult because the text and the shape represent two separate items within the diagram. The auditor may be required to indicate which should appear in front of the other (e.g., the text over the shape is most common). Then, he or she must join the two items into one, which must be done individually for each shape with text on the diagram. The IT auditor must also consider the amount of text to placed within the workflow diagram shapes. Presentation software is not likely to provide for automatic shape sizing or for text to wrap automatically at the edge of a shape. The lack of either or both of these features is likely to increase significantly the amount of time required to create the initial workflow diagram.

Connecting Diagram Shapes and Indicating Process Flow. The IT auditor must connect the shapes on the diagram to indicate the sequence of activities, to illustrate the possible outcomes at a branching or decision point, and to guide the users of the workflow diagram through the activities in which they are most interested. The lines should be straight whenever possible, or take the simplest path when straight lines cannot be used. Workflow diagram lines may cross each other, but there should be a break in one of the lines to indicate clearly that the process flows do not merge or overlap at the point of the crossover. Presentation software is likely to require that the IT Auditor plan the route of each connecting line, and either create the line following that path or create a line directly connecting the endpoints and then dragging the appropriate points of the line to move it into the correct position.

The IT auditor should be aware that most presentation software applications treat a connecting line as a separate item on the diagram, even if it is in contact with the edge of a shape on the diagram. Therefore, these lines must be joined if the auditor wants to be certain that the line will always be in contact with a particular shape.

Printing the Diagram. Presentation software should have standard printing capabilities, permitting the IT auditor to generate an output document for any workflow diagram that was created for audit or other purposes. The functions that presentation software is not likely to have include the automatic creation of off-page connectors for diagrams requiring more than one page to print, an advance preview of page breaks to identify potential disruptions to the diagram, and/or the ability to produce large diagrams in a format that makes them wall-mountable for team-based evaluation.

Maintaining an Existing Diagram. The IT auditor should plan to review draft workflow diagrams with the appropriate personnel to ensure their accuracy because what appears to be the correct understanding can be misinterpreted when translated onto a workflow diagram. This current review or the passage of time is almost guaranteed to create a need to change the diagram. The process of changing the workflow diagram is essentially the same, regardless of whether the change is being done to correct a draft diagram, to make the existing diagram clearer, or to reflect process changes that have occurred over time.

Editing and Adding Shapes. Presentation and drawing software is normally capable of accommodating changing a shape with little effort. Inserting additional shapes should also be handled efficiently because spaces can be created by blocking existing shapes, text, and connections and moving the blocked area to a new location.

Editing and Adding Text. The capability to add or edit text should not be any different from placing the original text on the workflow diagram. The IT auditor should expect that the text functionality of presentation and drawing software in a maintenance situation have the same advantages and disadvantages as in creating text.

Editing and Adding Connectors. It is likely that editing and adding connectors is the most significant weakness of presentation and drawing software. In situations in which the IT auditor has connected two shapes with a simple direct line, it is likely that moving one of the shapes leaves one end of the connecting line connected with nothing, or else connected with another item in the diagram. This situation is illustrated in Exhibit 31-10.

Compatibility with Other Software. The mainstream presentation and drawing software applications may have their own proprietary file formats for storing data in files, but they also have extensive import and export capabilities to facilitate an auditor's use with other industry standard formats. In a situation in which no export or import path exists to transfer diagrams, the IT auditor should be able to accomplish, at least, a basic transfer using clipboard functions in the appropriate personal computer operating system software. This capability represents a slight advantage for presentation and drawing software over its alternatives.

Technical Design Software

Technical design software is most often sold as an independent product that is directly marketed to the technical community. Examples of this software include AutoCAD and ProEngineer. These applications have been oriented toward very specialized use primarily for architects, engineers, and related fields in which it is critical to produce precise drawings for manufacturing, construction, or other similar purposes. Originally, it was unusual to find anyone using this type of software for diagramming, due to the complexity of the

Exhibit 31-10. Moving Shapes in a Workflow Diagram

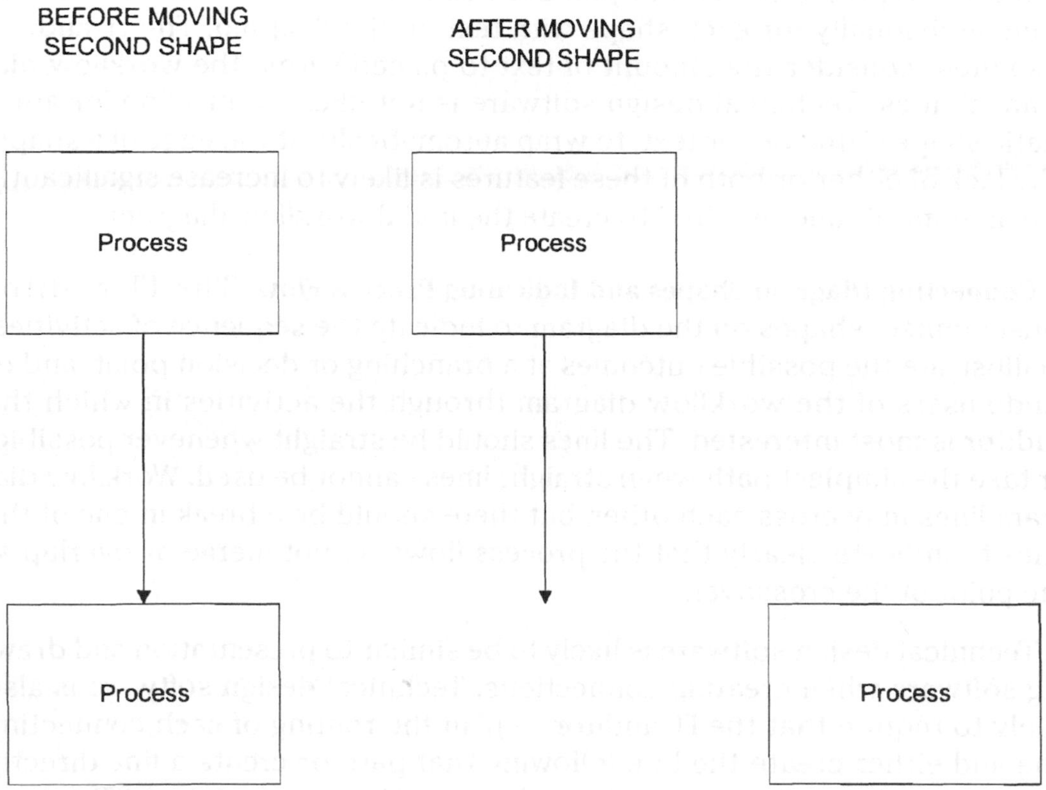

BEFORE MOVING
SECOND SHAPE

AFTER MOVING
SECOND SHAPE

```
┌─────────┐                    ┌─────────┐
│ Process │                    │ Process │
└────┬────┘                    └────┬────┘
     │                              │
     │                              │
     ▼                              ▼
┌─────────┐                              ┌─────────┐
│ Process │                              │ Process │
└─────────┘                              └─────────┘
```

product and its specialized focus. Over time, most of these applications have retained their function capabilities while becoming SACA much easier to use.

Creating the Initial Diagram with Technical Design Software. The process of creating a new workflow diagram is relatively simple. This process begins when the IT auditor selects and creates the appropriate shape or shapes, continues with the addition of appropriate text (either as the shapes are being created or all at once when all of the initial shapes have been diagrammed), and concludes as connectors and process flow lines are added. The final step occurs when the workflow diagram is printed or transmitted.

Creating Shapes. Creating shapes with technical design software is relatively easy because a wide variety of shapes are available from which to choose. It is also possible to find that basic technical design software may only include simple shapes, under the assumption that the designer will create whatever is needed based on lines and boxes.

Adding Text. Adding text within the shapes is difficult because the text and the shape represent two separate items within the diagram, similar to the same weakness in some presentation and drawing software applications. Adding text alongside a shape is likely to be easier, although the IT auditor will probably need to join the two items into one, which must be done individually for each shape with text on the diagram. The IT auditor also must consider the amount of text to placed within the workflow diagram shapes. Technical design software is not likely to provide for automatic shape sizing or, for text, to wrap automatically at the edge of a shape. The lack of either or both of these features is likely to increase significantly the amount of time required to create the initial workflow diagram.

Connecting Diagram Shapes and Indicating Process Flow. The IT auditor must connect shapes on the diagram to indicate the sequence of activities, to illustrate the possible outcomes at a branching or decision point, and to guide users of the workflow diagram through the activities in which the auditor is most interested. The lines should be straight whenever possible, or take the simplest path when straight lines cannot be used. Workflow diagram lines may cross each other, but there should be a break in one of the lines to indicate clearly that the process flows do not merge or overlap at the point of the crossover.

Technical design software is likely to be similar to presentation and drawing software when creating connections. Technical design software is also likely to require that the IT auditor to plan the routing of each connecting line and either create the line following that path or create a line directly connecting the endpoints and then dragging the appropriate milToints of the line to move it into the correct position. Unlike presentation and drawing software, technical design software is likely to recognize that a connecting line must remain connected to the shapes to which it is attached. Although this is an improvement, the software is not likely to have the capability to reroute a line after a change is made to the diagram, whether that change directly or indirectly affects the connecting line.

Printing the Diagram. Technical design software is likely to have advanced printing capabilities. This is based on the need for designers to produce blueprints and other high-quality documents. The most significant capability that is unlikely to exist in technical design software applications is the ability to create automatically connecting shapes with appropriate references at page breaks within a diagram.

Maintaining an Existing Diagram. The IT auditor should plan to review draft workflow diagrams with the appropriate personnel to ensure their accuracy. The current review, combined with the passage of time, is almost guaranteed to create a need to change the diagram. The process of changing the workflow diagram is essentially the same, regardless of whether the change is being done to correct a draft diagram, to make the diagram clear, or to reflect process changes that have taken place over time.

Editing and Adding Shapes. Technical design software is normally designed to accommodate changes, which are an expected element of the design process. Inserting additional shapes should also be handled efficiently because spaces can be created by blocking existing shapes, text, and connections and moving the blocked area to a new location.

Editing and Adding Text. The capability to add or edit text should not be any different from placing the original text on the workflow diagram. The IT auditor should expect that the text functionality of technical design software in a maintenance situation will have the same advantages and disadvantages as when creating text.

Editing and Adding Connectors. Technical design software is more efficient in this activity than presentation and drawing software. The IT auditor should expect that the text functionality of technical design software in a maintenance situation will have the same advantages and disadvantages when creating connections.

Compatibility with Other Software. The technical design software applications are likely to have their own proprietary file formats for storing data in files, but they will also have import and export capabilities to use other industry standard formats. In a situation in which no export or import path to transfer diagrams is available, the IT auditor should be able to, at least, make a basic transfer by using the clipboard functions in the appropriate personal computer operating system software.

Specialized Diagramming Software

Specialized diagramming software, like technical design software applications, is more often sold as an independent product and is directly marketed to the main professional communities responsible for developing diagrams. Examples of this software include Interactive Easyflow, Visio, Flowchart+, and ABC Flowcharter. These applications are directed toward a wide range of users with similar specialized needs. This software can be configured to the type of diagram being created. Its configuration is likely to feature the selection of a particular shape library or a shape and connector library. The differences are illustrated in Exhibit 31-11, which contains portions of three different shape libraries developed for different purposes.

Creating the Initial Diagram. The process to follow for creating a new workflow diagram is simple and represents a strength of this software. This process begins when the IT auditor selects and creates the appropriate

Exhibit 31-11. Comparing Various Shapes

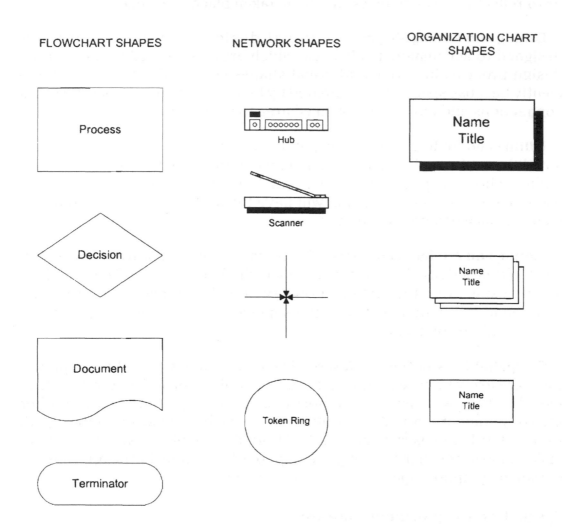

shape or shapes, continues with the addition of appropriate text (either as the shapes are being created or at one time when all initial shapes have been diagrammed), and concludes as connectors and process flow lines are added. The final step occurs when the workflow diagram is printed or transmitted.

Creating Shapes. Creating shapes with diagramming software is easy, usually selecting a shape with a mouse and dragging it onto the work surface.

Adding Text. Text management is an area in which specialized diagramming software excels. The IT auditor should confirm the text management capabilities of the packages being considered, if any from this category, to ensure that those capabilities meet the appropriate requirements. The IT auditor should not be overly concerned with the amount of text to be placed within shapes on the diagram. Specialized diagramming software is likely to provide for automatic text formatting, automatic shape resizing, and conditional text on lines, for example. These capabilities represent a significant advantage of diagramming software over the other diagramming software choices.

Connecting Diagram Shapes and Indicating Process Flow. This activity represents another significant advantage of specialized diagramming software over the other software choices. IT auditor must be able to connect diagram shapes and indicate the sequence of activities—to illustrate the possible outcomes at a branching or decision point and to guide the users of the workflow diagram through the activities in which they are interested. The difference with most specialized diagramming software is that connecting lines can be configured to find automatically an optimized path between the shapes that are supposed to be connected. The IT auditor may also be able to configure the lines to create breaks automatically where lines overlap but do not intersect. Last, most of the specialized diagramming software provide for lines to reroute automatically whenever there is a change to the diagram that affects the line or anything attached to it.

Printing the Diagram. Specialized diagramming software is also likely to have advanced printing capabilities. The most significant capability that is present in most of the diagramming software alternatives is the ability to create automatic off-page connectors. This is extremely important because planning for diagram pages can be particularly time-consuming, and not having to address this concern until the diagram is completed can reduce the time required to develop a diagram by 30 percent.

Maintaining an Existing Diagram. Maintaining a diagram may be less complex with the correct specialized diagramming software. Although the maintenance activities are approximately the same as for the other alternatives, the effort required may be different.

Editing and Adding Shapes. Specialized diagramming software is often able to support changing shapes by simply dropping a new shape onto an existing shape, and the related changes to text and lines are handled automatically.

Editing and Adding Text. Consistent with the other software choices, the capability of adding or editing text should not be any different from placing the original text on the workflow diagram.

Editing and Adding Connectors. Specialized diagramming software is the most efficient type of software for this activity. The reasons for this were previously discussed in the section describing the features that are often available when creating connectors.

Compatibility with Other Software. The specialized diagramming software applications are likely to have their own proprietary file formats for storing data in files, but will also have import and export capabilities for use with other industry standard formats. The IT auditor should evaluate the extent of these capabilities in terms of their most likely needs for transferring and exchanging workflow diagrams in their own environment.

Selecting the Most Appropriate Diagramming Software

The IT auditor should follow the basic development process that the company follows to select any business software application. The process begins with identifying the needs and alternatives, gaining approval for one of the alternatives, and implementing the approved solution. The IT auditor should consider soliciting the assistance of other members of the staff to perform the evaluation of alternatives, involving the personnel who are most likely to work with the selected application. A standard audit work program can be used for performing this evaluation, documenting the results of the evaluation, and reporting those results in a summarized fashion to the appropriate personnel or approving authority.

Using Workflow Diagrams Prepared by
Information Technology Professionals

When evaluating an automated system, IT auditors may have the option of using existing documentation that may include workflow diagrams or other similar devices prepared by either internal or external information technology professionals. This option has several distinct advantages and disadvantages.

The primary advantage of using an existing workflow diagram or flowchart is that it was probably developed by the persons involved in designing the application. These persons should have had the clearest understanding of the application, making it very likely that the diagrams are truly representative of the underlying manual and automated processes. The second advantage is simple: the IT auditor can virtually eliminate the time required to develop the diagram. Depending on the scarcity of resources, this could be a significant advantage.

There are two closely related disadvantages in relying on previously developed diagrams. First, no assurance exists that the diagrams are accurate. Any one of the following reasons could indicate that a previously developed diagram is inaccurate. The appropriate personnel were not involved in developing the diagrams.

The diagrams were developed quickly and are, therefore, not accurate. Subsequent applications changes are not reflected in the diagrams. Second, relying on existing workflow diagrams may not be prudent because such reliance should only be based on sufficient competent evidential matter to warrant the degree of reliance placed on that information. Not performing sufficient procedures creates a risk that the IT auditor will fail to comply with applicable auditing standards in reaching an audit conclusion. If this risk was realized and a false conclusion reached, several serious consequences would be possible. The consequences could affect the corporation in terms of creating a liability to shareholders or affect the IT auditor by causing a loss of his or her certification and license.

The IT auditor should consider following a four-step process as one way to acquire the ability to place appropriate reliance on the work of others, to gain the necessary level of understanding about the system, and to comply with professional standards related to the application under review:

- Step 1: Obtain existing workflow diagrams and supporting documentation.
- Step 2: Check the timeliness and completeness of the information.
- Step 3: Examine the workflow diagrams for errors or omissions.
- Step 4: Review the workflow diagrams with the appropriate client (i.e., auditees) or IT personnel.

Obtain Existing Workflow Diagrams and Supporting Documentation. The IT auditor should request all appropriate documentation required to support the workflow diagrams, which may include one or more from the following list of supporting items.

- A narrative description of the significant application processes and controls, if not for the entire system
- Documentation for user training and reference purposes
- Detailed program documentation
- Application backup and recovery procedures
- Record layouts
- Sample reports

The IT auditor should be aware that the preceding is not intended to be an all-inclusive list.

Check the Timeliness and Completeness of Information. The IT auditor should verify the completeness and timeliness of the documentation offered by answering these questions:

- Are all system changes reflected in the existing workflow diagrams?
- Do the workflow diagrams and narrative descriptions match?
- Were any proposed changes included in the diagrams that were never implemented in the system?
- Do the workflow diagrams and narrative description represent a system that meets the objectives of system users?

The answers to these questions should give the IT auditor a sense of the accuracy of the available documentation. The auditor generally should avoid using documentation that is out of date. In that case, the auditor should probably develop new workflow diagrams, unless, of course, the required changes are minor.

Examine the Workflow Diagrams for Possible Problems. The IT auditor should examine the workflow diagrams and supporting documentation, looking for the types of problems that could occur within the system. These problems can be summarized as minor errors, exclusion of elements that exist as part of the production activity, or inclusion of elements that are not actually part of the production activity or that are not being complied with by the involved personnel.

Review the Workflow Diagrams with End User or IT Personnel. During this step, the IT auditor should describe his or her understanding of the system to appropriate company personnel to obtain their feedback. The company personnel should then determine whether the IT auditor appears to have an adequate understanding of the system, while correcting any apparent misapprehensions.

RECOMMENDED PRACTICES FOR DEVELOPING WORKFLOW DIAGRAMS

The IT auditor has a single standard to establish a measurable compliance level within the terms of workflow diagramming technique. Although this is true, there are benefits to following certain basic principles for all workflow diagrams that are prepared:

- Use automated diagramming software if at all possible.
- Establish and use a single set (or limited number of sets) of diagramming shapes.
- Start the workflow diagram in the upper left-hand corner of the paper and work toward the lower right-hand corner.
- Use the connector symbol rather than drawing lines around or over parts of the diagram.
- Date the diagram and indicate who prepared it.
- Verify the correctness of the diagram with the individual or department responsible for the area under review.
- Indicate through a terminal symbol where processing starts and stops.
- Use text notes to clarify what the various processes mean.
- Use oversized symbols if the information will not fit within the standard-sized symbol.
- Divide the process into steps if possible and indicate those steps on the workflow diagram,

Problems to Avoid in Creating Workflow Diagrams

Although creating workflow diagrams offers the auditor many advantages, the following problems associated with this process must be taken into account.

- *Workflow diagrams do not inherently indicate the frequency of processing.* It is possible on the same diagram to have processing that occurs continuously (e.g., on an online terminal), daily, and monthly without clear differentiation. (This can be clarified either in a note or in the narrative description if necessary.)
- *Workflow diagrams can quickly become out of date.* If the auditor is using an existing diagram, it must be determined when it was developed and whether any changes have been made since.
- *Workflow diagrams may show inconsistent levels of detail.* Because the developer of the diagram uses it as a tool, processes that are well understood by the developer may appear as one or two process symbols, while less well-understood processes may be exploded into 30 or 40 shapes.

Part VI
Appendix

Workpaper A-1. Audit Assignment Interview Checklist

Assignment:		Assignment No.			
Person Interviewed:					
Interviewer:		**Date:**			

No.	Item	Yes	No	N/A
		Response		
1.	Are there senior management personnel who should be interviewed to obtain audit insight or other background data? *Comments:* _____ _____			
2.	Are there documents supplying background data that should be read? *Comments:* _____ _____			
3.	Does the audit area have a history of problems.? *Comments:* _____ _____			
4.	Have any major changes been made in this area since the last audit? *Comments:* _____ _____			
5.	Are any parts of the assignment unclear? *Comments:* _____ _____			
6.	How should the audit be conducted? *Comments:* _____ _____			
7.	How will the success of the audit be judged? (Document answer on Workpaper 1-1-2.) *Comments:* _____ _____			
8.	Are there computer tests that need to be prepared in advance? *Comments:* _____ _____			

Workpaper A-2. Audit Success Criteria Worksheet

Assignment:		Assignment No.
Criteria received from:		
No.	**Audit Objective/Task**	**Success Criteria**
Completed by:		**Date:**

Workpaper A-3. Preliminary Conference Background Information Checklist

Items to be Obtained	Workpaper Index (or location)
1. Last audit report	
2. Last audit workpapers	
3. Suggestions for next audit	
4. Permanent file about application	
5. DP short- and long-range plans for application area	
6. Application annual budget	
7. Customer complaints to third parties about application system	
8. Audit recommendations from management of related business area	
9. Recommendations from audits of applications supplying or receiving data from this application	

Some of this information may have been obtained and examined during the individual audit planning step.

Workpaper A-4. Conference Preparation Checklist

No.	Program Item	Assigned to	Completion Date
1.	Set time, date, location. *Comments:* _____ _____		
2.	Invite: Application user DP project personnel DP manager *Comments:* _____ _____		
3.	Develop conference agenda. *Comments:* _____ _____		
4.	Ask DP manager to request staff cooperation. *Comments:* _____ _____		
5.	Advise attendees of their conference roles. *Comments:* _____ _____		
6.	Assign auditor to record results of conference. *Comments:* _____ _____		
7.	Conduct conference. *Comments:* _____ _____		
8.	Debrief auditors on results immediately after conference. *Comments:* _____ _____		
9.	*Comments:* _____ _____		
10.	*Comments:* _____ _____		
11.	*Comments:* _____ _____		

Workpaper A-5. Post-Conference Background Information Checklist (page 1 of 2)

Items to be Obtained	Workpaper Index (or location)
1. Project request	
2. Feasibility study	
3. Cost/benefit analysis	
4. Functional requirements*	
5. Data requirements*	
6. System/subsystem specifications*	
7. Program specifications*	
8. Database specifications*	
9. User manuals*	
10. Operations manuals*	
11. Program maintenance manuals*	
12 Test plan*	
13. Test analysis report*	
14. Overview of computerized application system	
Highlights:	
System name and identification number	
Date of initial implementation	
Date of latest modification	
Number of modifications in the last two years	
Type of system (administrative, scientific, other [specify])	
Type of processing (batch or online)	
System flowchart and narrative description	

*See Appendix A for a detailed documentation checklist of these items.

Workpaper A-5. Post-Conference Background Information Checklist (page 2 of 2)

Items to be Obtained	Workpaper Index (or location)
Number of computer programs	
Size of largest computer program (in bytes of storage)	
Programming language(s) used	
Processing frequency	
Total processing hours per month	
Design of system (i.e., vendor-supplied or programmed in-house)	
System-testing method (i.e., with test or live data; if not done at all, mention this)	
Initial system	
Latest modification	
Availability of test results	
Initial system	
Latest modification	
Date of last audit or evaluation (obtain copy)	
Output distribution list	
Completed by:	**Date:**

Workpaper A-6. Input Transactions Worksheet

File Name	File Number	Type	Purpose	Name	Function
Input Transaction				Preparer	

File Name	File Number	Type	Purpose	Name	Function

Comments:_____
_____

Comments:_____
_____

Comments:_____
_____

Comments:_____
_____

Comments:_____
_____

Comments:_____
_____

Comments:_____
_____

Comments:

Comments:_____
_____

Prepared by:	Date:

APPENDICES

Workpaper A-7. Data File Worksheet

DP File Name	DP File Number	Contents of File (attach record formats)	File Structure	Record Volume	Frequency of Use	Length of Time Saved

Prepared by: | Date:

Worksheet A-8. Output Report and User Worksheet

Computer Product				User	
Report or Screen Name	**DP Report Number**	**Type and Medium**	**Purpose**	**Name**	**Function**
Comments: _____					
Comments: _____					
Comments: _____					
Comments: _____					
Comments: _____					
Comments: _____					
Comments: _____					
Comments:					
Comments: _____					
Prepared by:			**Date:**		

APPENDICES

Workpaper A-9. User Satisfaction Questionnaire (page 1 of 5)

Computer Output Report Identification (to be completed by auditor)

1. Title of report _____

2. DP identification number _____

3. Type of report _____

4. Part of report to be evaluated _____

   _____

   _____

5. Frequency of report_____

User Identification

6. Name _____

7. Date _____

8. Title _____

9. Organization _____

10. Phone number/address _____

11. Extent of knowledge about report _____

    _____

    _____

    _____

    _____

    _____

User Evaluation of Output Record

12. Check the purpose for which you use the report

    _____ Initiate transactions

    _____ Authorize changes to the system

    _____ Operate computer terminal

    _____ Maintain data controls

    _____ Design/program application

    _____ Other (explain)_____

Workpaper A-9. User Satisfaction Questionnaire (page 2 of 5)

13. Indicate (by circling the appropriate number) the importance of the report in relation to the work of your office or department.

Not at all important									**Very important**
1	2	3	4	5	6	7	8	9	10

14. Indicate (by circling the appropriate number) the comprehensibility of the report's contents.

Not at all important									**Very important**
1	2	3	4	5	6	7	8	9	10

                                                                        Yes   No

15. Could you effectively perform your duties:

    Without this report?   _____   _____

    If this report were produced less often?   _____   _____

                                                                        Yes   No

16. Can the report be used as is without correction, further

    identification, or analysis?   _____   _____

                                                                        Yes   No

17. In your judgment, is the report:

    Accurate and reliable?   _____   _____

    Available when needed?   _____   _____

    Up-to-date?   _____   _____

    Useful?   _____   _____

    Understandable?   _____   _____

    Please explain each No answer and provide examples.

    _____

    _____

    _____

    _____

    _____

Workpaper A-9. User Satisfaction Questionnaire (page 3 of 5)

	Yes	No
18. Check whether, in your opinion, the report should:		
Provide more data	_____	_____
Provide less data	_____	_____
Be combined with other output reports	_____	_____
Be considered obsolete	_____	_____
Be improved to make your job easier	_____	_____

Please explain each Yes answer.

_____

_____

_____

_____

_____

19. If you maintain manual records to supplement computer-processed information, briefly explain why.

_____

_____

_____

_____

_____

	Yes	No
20. Did you or anyone within your department help design the report?	_____	_____
21. Do you supply the raw data (input) for this report?	_____	_____
22. Does the report save you any clerical effort?	_____	_____

Explain.

_____

_____

_____

Workpaper A-9. User Satisfaction Questionnaire (page 4 of 5)

	Yes	No
23. Does the report duplicate other information you receive?	_____	_____

If Yes, explain briefly.

_____

_____

_____

	Yes	No
24. Can you readily obtain the information from other sources?	_____	_____

If Yes, list th other source(s).

_____

_____

_____

	Yes	No
25. Do you check the report for quality when you receive it?	_____	_____

If No, please identify the person or group performing this function. _____

	Yes	No
26. Is the report ever rerun by the data processing department?	_____	_____

If Yes

How frequently?_____

Why were reruns necessary? _____

_____

_____

How do you make sure that rerun material is correct? _____

_____

_____

_____

_____

_____

Workpaper A-9. User Satisfaction Questionnaire (page 5 of 5)

27. If you have problems with this report, with whom do you discuss them?

    _____

    _____

	Yes	No
Is this person authorized to make changes to the report?	_____	_____

28. Do you maintain correspondence with the data processing department

    or other user departments concerning the report? _____   _____

    If Yes, attach copies of recent corespondence.

29. Check how often you refer to this report

    _____ Daily

    _____ Weekly

    _____ Monthly

    _____ Annually

    _____ Never

    _____ Other (explain) _____

    _____

30. Indicate how long the report is kept after receipt

    _____ 1 day

    _____ 1 week

    _____ 1 month

    _____ 1 year

    _____ Other (explain) _____

    _____

    Where is it filed? _____

    _____

Workpaper A-10. Data Flow Diagram

Application System _____

Flow of Responsibility ⟶	
Flow of Data ↓	
Prepared by:	**Date:**

APPENDICES

Workpaper A-11. Structural Risk Assessment

Ratings:
L   Low
M   Medium
H   High
NA   Not Applicable

Risk		**Rating**	×	**Weight**	=	**Score**
1. Amount of time since last major change to existing automated system:		_____	×	3	=	_____
More than 2 years	L=1					
1 to 2 years; unknown	M=2					
Less than 1 year	H=3					
No automated system	H=3					
2. Frequency of change to proposed/existing system:		_____	×	3	=	_____
No existing automated system; or development effort insufficient for estimate	NA=0					
Fewer than 2 per year	L=1					
2 to 10 per year	M=2					
More than 20 per year	H=3					
3. Extent of total system changes in last year in percentage of programs affected:		_____	×	3	=	_____
No changes	NA=0					
Less than 10%	L=1					
10 to 25%	M=2					
More than 25%	H=3					
4. Magnitude of system change to be performed:		_____	×	3	=	_____
New development	NA=0					
Minor change(s)	L=1					
Significant but manageable change	M=2					
Major changes to system functionality and/or resource needs	H=4					
5. Project performance site:		_____	×	2	=	_____
Company facility	L=1					
Local non-company facility	M=2					
Not in local area	H=5					
6. Critical staffing of project:		_____	×	2	=	_____
In-house	L=1					
Contractor, sole-source	M=2					
Contractor, competitive-bid	H=6					

Workpaper A-11. Structural Risk Assessment

Risk		Rating	×	Weight	=	Score
7. Type of project:		_____	×	2	=	_____
Line and staff; project has total management control of personnel	L=1					
Mixture of line and staff with matrix-managed elements	M=2					
Matrix; no management control transferred to project	H=3					
8. Potential problems with subcontractor relationship:		_____	×	5	=	_____
Not applicable to this project	NA=0					
Subcontractor not assigned to isolated or critical task; prime contractor has previously managed subcontractor successfully	L=1					
Subcontractor assigned to all development tasks in subordinate role to prime contractor; company has favorable experience with subcontractor on other effort(s)	M=2					
Subcontractor has sole responsibility for critical task; subcontractor new to company	H=3					
9. Status of the ongoing project training:		_____	×	2	=	_____
No training plan required	NA=0					
Complete training plan in place	L=1					
Some training in place	M=2					
No training available	H=3					
10. Level of skilled personnel available to train project team:		_____	×	3	=	_____
No training plan required	NA=0					
Knowledgeable on all systems	L=1					
Knowledgeable on major components	M=2					
Few components understood	H=3					
11. Accessibility of supporting reference and/or compliance documents and other information on proposed/existing system:		_____	×	3	=	_____
Readily available	L=1					
Details available with some difficulty and delay	M=2					
Great difficulty in obtaining details, much delay	H=3					
12. Status of documentation for the current system:		_____	×	3	=	_____
Complete and current	L=1					
More than 75% complete and current	M=2					
Nonexistent or outdated	H=6					

APPENDICES

Workpaper A-11. Structural Risk Assessment

Risk		Rating	×	Weight	=	Score
13. Nature of periodic maintenance support with respect to updating project documentation:		_____	×	3	=	_____
New development project	NA=0					
Close coordination	L=1					
Significant but manageable changes with some coordination	M=2					
Major changes with poor coordination	H=5					
14. Degree to which documentation reflects specification/ program changes:		_____	×	3	=	_____
New development project	NA=0					
Excellent audit trail; good maintenance and availability of documentation	L=1					
Good audit trail; some problems with maintenance and availability	M=2					
Poor audit trail; inadequate for proper maintenance and availability	H=3					
15. Quality of documentation for the proposed/existing system:		_____	×	3	=	_____
Excellent standards; adherence and execution are integral parts of system and program development	L=1					
Adequate standards; adherence is not consistent	M=2					
Poor or no standards; adherence is minimal	H=3					
16. Quality of development and production library control:		_____	×	3	=	_____
Excellent standards; superior adherence and execution	L=1					
Adequate standards; adherence is not consistent	M=2					
Poor or no standards; adherence is minimal	H=3					
17. Availability of special test facilities for subsystem testing:		_____	×	2	=	_____
Complete or not required	L=1					
Limited	M=2					
None available	H=3					
18. Status of project maintenance planning:		_____	×	2	=	_____
Current and complete	L=1					
Under development	M=2					
Nonexistent	H=3					
19. Contingency plans in place to support operational mission should application fail:		_____	×	2	=	_____
None required	NA=0					
Complete plan	L=1					
Major subsystems addressed	M=2					
Nonexistent	H=3					

Workpaper A-11. Structural Risk Assessment

Risk		Rating	×	Weight	=	Score
20. User approval of maintenance/enhancement specifications:		_____	×	4	=	_____
Formal, written approval based on structured, detailed review processes	L=1					
Formal, written approval based on informal, unstructured, detailed review processes	M=2					
No formal approval; cursory review	H=3					
21. Effect of external systems on the system:		_____	×	5	=	_____
No external systems involved	NA=0					
Critical intersystem communications controlled through interface control documents; standard protocols utilized; stable interfaces	L=1					
Critical intersystem communications controlled through interface control documents; some nonstandard protocols; interfaces change infrequently	M=2					
Not all critical intersystem communications controlled through interface control documents; some nonstandard protocols; some interfaces change frequently	H=3					
22. Type and adequacy of configuration management planning:		_____	×	2	=	_____
Complete and functioning	L=1					
Undergoing revisions for inadequacies	M=2					
None available	H=3					
23. Type of standards and guidelines followed by system:		_____	×	4	=	_____
Standards use structured programming concepts, reflect current methodology, and permit tailoring to nature and scope of development project	L=1					
Standards require a top-down approach and offer some flexibility in application	M=2					
Standards are out of date and inflexible	H=3					
24. Degree to which maintenance/enhancement is based on well-specified requirements:		_____	×	5	=	_____
Detailed transaction and parametric data in requirements documentation	L=1					
Detailed transaction data in requirements documentation	M=2					
Vague requirements documentation	H=5					

APPENDICES

Workpaper A-11. Structural Risk Assessment

Risk	Rating	×	Weight	=	Score

25. Relationships with those who are involved with system (e.g., users, customers, sponsors, interfaces) or who must be dealt with during project efforts: _____ × 3 = _____
    No significant conflicting needs; system primarily serves one organizational unit — L=1
    System meets limited conflicting needs of cooperative organizational units — M=2
    System must meet important conflicting needs of several cooperative organizational units — H=3
    System must meet important conflicting needs of several uncooperative organizational units — H=4

26. Structural changes necessary to meet enhancement requirements: _____ × 3 = _____
    Not applicable — NA=0
    Minimal — L=1
    Somewhat — M=2
    Major — H=3

27. General user attitude: _____ × 5 = _____
    Good: values data processing solution — L=1
    Fair: some reluctance — M=2
    Poor: does not appreciate data processing solution — H=3

28. Status of people, procedures, knowledge, discipline, and division of details in offices using system: _____ × 4 = _____
    Situation good to excellent — L=1
    Situation satisfactory but could be improved — M=2
    Situation less than satisfactory — H=3

29. Commitment of senior user management to system: _____ × 3 = _____
    Extremely enthusiastic — L=1
    Adequate — M=2
    Some reluctance, or level of commitment unknown — H=5

30. Dependence of project on contributions of technical effort from other areas (e.g., database administration): _____ × 2 = _____
    None — L=1
    From within DP — M=2
    From outside DP — H=3

31. User's DP knowledge and experience: _____ × 2 = _____
    Highly capable — L=1
    Previous exposure but limited knowledge — M=2
    First exposure — H=3

Workpaper A-11. Structural Risk Assessment

Risk		Rating	×	Weight	=	Score

32. Knowledge and experience of user in application area: _____ × 2 = _____
    Previous experience   L=1
    Conceptual understanding   M=2
    Limited knowledge   H=3

33. Knowledge and experience of project team in application area: _____ × 3 = _____
    Previous experience   L=1
    Conceptual understanding   M=2
    Limited knowledge   H=3

34. Degree of control by project management: _____ × 2 = _____
    Formal authority commensurate with assigned responsibility   L=1
    Informal authority commensurate with assigned responsibility   M=2
    Responsibility but no authority   H=3

35. Effectiveness of project communications: _____ × 2 = _____
    Easy access to project manager(s); change information promptly transmitted upward and downward   L=1
    Limited access to project manager(s); downward communication limited   M=2
    Aloof project management; planning information closely held   H=3

36. Conformance of developed system to system specifications: _____ × 3 = _____
    New system   NA=0
    Operational tests indicate that procedures and operations produce desired results   L=1
    Limited tests indicate that procedures and operations differ from specifications in minor aspects only   M=2
    Procedures and operations differ from specifications in important aspects; specifications insufficient to use for testing   H=3

37. Sensitivity of information: _____ × 1 = _____
    None   L=0
    High   H=3

Total Score   _____
(enter here and on Workpaper A-14)

Prepared by: _____   Date_____

APPENDICES

Workpaper A-12. Technical Risk Assessment

Ratings:
L   Low
M   Medium
H   High
NA   Not Applicable

Risk		Rating	×	Weight	=	Score
1. Ability to fulfill mission during hardware or software failure:		_____	×	2	=	_____
Can be accomplished without system	L=1					
Can be accomplished without fully operational system, but some minimum capability required	M=2					
Cannot be accomplished without fully automated system	H=6					
2. Required system availability:		_____	×	2	=	_____
Periodic use (weekly or less frequently)	L=1					
Daily use (but not 24 hours per day)	M=2					
Constant use (24 hours per day)	H=5					
3. Degree to which system's ability to function relies on exchange of data with external systems:		_____	×	2	=	_____
Functions independently; sends no data required for the operation of other systems	L=0					
Must send and/or receive data to or from another system	M=2					
Must send and/or receive data to or from multiple systems	H=3					
4. Nature of system-to-system communications:		_____	×	1	=	_____
System has no external interfaces	L=0					
Automated communications link using standard protocols	M=2					
Automated communications link using nonstandard protocols	H=3					
5. System's program size limitations:		_____	×	2	=	_____
Substantial unused capacity	L=1					
Within capacity	M=2					
Near limits of capacity	H=3					
6. Degree of input data control procedures:		_____	×	3	=	_____
Detailed error checking	L=1					
General error checking	M=2					
No error checking	H=3					

Workpaper A-12. Technical Risk Assessment

Risk	**Rating**	×	**Weight**	=	**Score**
7. Type of system hardware installed:	_____	×	3	=	_____
No hardware needed NA=0					
Standard batch or online systems L=1					
Nonstandard peripherals M=2					
Nonstandard peripherals and mainframes H=3					
8. Basis for selection of programming and system software:	_____	×	3	=	_____
Architectural analysis of functional and performance requirements L=1					
Similar system development experience M=2					
Current inventory of system software and existing programming language skills H=3					
9. Complexity of projected system:	_____	×	2	=	_____
Single function (e.g., word processing only) L=1					
Multiple but related function (e.g., message generation, editing, and dissemination) M=2					
Multiple but not closely related functions (e.g., database query, statistical manipulation, graphics plotting, text editing) H=3					
10. Projected level of programming language:	_____	×	2	=	_____
High-level, widely used L=1					
Low-level or machine language, widely used M=2					
Special-purpose language, extremely limited use H=3					
11. Suitability of programming language to application(s):	_____	×	2	=	_____
All modules can be coded in straightforward manner in chosen language L=1					
All modules can be coded in a straightforward manner with a few exit routines, sophisticated techniques, etc. H=3					
Significant number of exit routines, sophisticated techniques, etc. are required to compensate for deficiencies in language selected H=3					
12. Familiarity of hardware architecture.	_____	×	2	=	_____
Mainframe and peripherals widely used L=1					
Peripherals unfamiliar M=2					
Mainframe unfamiliar H=4					

Workpaper A-12. Technical Risk Assessment

Risk		Rating	×	Weight	=	Score
13. Degree of pioneering (extent to which new, difficult, and unproven techniques are applied):		_____	×	5	=	_____
Conservative: no untried system components; no pioneering system objectives or techniques	L=1					
Moderate: few important system components and functions are untried; few pioneering system objectives and techniques	H=3					
Aggressively pioneering: more than a few unproven hardware or software components or system objectives	H=3					
14. Suitability of hardware to application environment:		_____	×	2	=	_____
Standard hardware	NA=0					
Architecture highly compatible with required functions	L=1					
Architecture sufficiently powerful but not particularly efficient	M=2					
Architecture dictates complex software routines	H=3					
15. Margin or error (need for perfect functioning, split-second timing, and significant cooperation and coordination):		_____	×	2	=	_____
Comfortable margin	L=1					
Realistically demanding	M=2					
Very demanding; unrealistic	H=3					
16. Familiarity of project team with application software:		_____	×	2	=	_____
Considerable experience	L=1					
Some experience or experience unknown	M=2					
Little or no experience	H=3					
17. Familiarity of project team with system environment supporting the application:		_____	×	2	=	_____
Considerable experience	L=1					
Some experience or experience unknown	M=2					
Little or no experience with:						
Operating system	H=3					
DBMS	H=3					
Data communications	H=3					
18. Knowledge of project team in the application area:		_____	×	2	=	_____
Previous experience	L=1					
Conceptual understanding	M=2					
Limited knowledge	H=3					

Workpaper A-12. Technical Risk Assessment

Risk		Rating	×	Weight	=	Score
19. Type of maintenance test tools used:		_____	×	5	=	_____
Comprehensive test/debug software, including path analyzers	L=1					
Formal, documented procedural tools only	M=2					
None	H=3					
20. Realism of test environment:		_____	×	4	=	_____
Tests performed on operational system; total database and communications environment	L=1					
Tests performed on separate development system; total database, limited communications	M=2					
Tests performed on dissimilar development system; limited database and limited communications	H=3					
21. Communications interface change testing:		_____	×	4	=	_____
No interfaces required	NA=0					
Live testing on actual line at operational transaction rates	L=1					
Loop testing on actual line; simulated transactions	M=2					
Line simulations within development system	H=3					
22. Importance of user training to the success of the system:		_____	×	1	=	_____
Little training needed to use or operate system; documentation is sufficient for training	L=1					
Users and/or operators need no formal training, but expertise is required in addition to documentation	M=2					
Users essentially unable to operate system without formal, hands-on training in addition to documentation	H=3					
23. Degree of system adaptability to change:		_____	×	3	=	_____
High; structured programming techniques used; relatively unpatched, well documented	L=1					
Moderate	M=2					
Low; monolithic program design, high degree of inter/intrasystem dependency, unstructured development, minimal documentation	H=4					

Total Score   _____
(enter here and on Workpaper 2-1-4)

Prepared by: _____   Date_____

Workpaper A-13. Size Risk Assessment

Ratings:

L   Low
M   Medium
H   High
NA Not Applicable

Risk		Rating	×	Weight	=	Score
1. Ranking of this project's total worker-hours within the limits established by the organization's smallest and largest system development projects (in number of worker-hours):		_____	×	2	=	_____
Lower third of systems development projects	L=1					
Middle third of systems development projects	M=2					
Upper third of systems development projects	H=3					
2. Project implementation time:		_____	×	1	=	_____
12 months or less	L=1					
13 months to 24 months	M=2					
More than 24 months, with phased implementation	H=3					
More than 24 months, no phasing	H=4					
3. Project adherence to schedule:		_____	×	1	=	_____
Ahead of schedule	L=1					
On schedule	M=2					
Behind schedule (by three months or less)	H=3					
Behind schedule (by more than three months)	H=4					
4. Number of systems interconnecting with the application:		_____	×	3	=	_____
1 to 2	L=1					
3 to 5	M=2					
More than 5	H=3					
5. Percentage of project resources allocated to system testing:		_____	×	2	=	_____
More than 40%	L=1					
20 to 40%	M=2					
Less than 20%	H=3					
6. Number of interrelated logical data groupings (estimate if unknown):		_____	×	1	=	_____
Fewer than 4	L=1					
4 to 6	M=2					
More than 6	H=3					

Workpaper A-13. Size Risk Assessment

Risk		**Rating**	$\times$	**Weight**	=	**Score**

7. Number of transaction types: _____ × 1 = _____
   Fewer than 6   L=1
   6 to 25   M=2
   More than 25   H=3

8. Number of output reports: _____ × 1 = _____
   Fewer than 10   L=1
   10 to 20   M=2
   More than 20   H=3

9. Ranking of this project's number of lines of program code
   to be maintained within the limits established by the
   organization's smallest and largest systems development
   projects (in number of lines of code):   _____ × 3 = _____
   Lower third of systems development projects   L=1
   Middle third of systems development projects   M=2
   Upper third of systems development projects   H=3

Total Score   _____
(enter here and on Workpaper 2-1-4)

Prepared by: _____   Date _____

Workpaper A-14. Risk Score Summary

Application System_____

Risk Area	Score	Comparative Rating with Company Applications		
		High	*Medium*	*Low*
Structure Comments: _____ _____				
Technology Comments: _____ _____				
Size Comments: _____ _____				
Total Risk Score Comments: _____ _____				

Prepared by:	Date:

Workpaper A-15. Risk Assessment Program

Application System _____

No.	Program Item	Assigned to	Completion Date
1.	Form risk assessment team and designate a facilitator. *Comments:* _____		
2.	Set date, time, and place for risk assessment exercise. *Comments:* _____		
3.	Gather the following materials for exercise: Application background data. Application Risk Worksheet (Workpaper 2.2.2). Industry risk experiences in: Application. Technology. *Comments:* _____		
4.	Conduct exercise. *Comments:* _____		
5.	Document identified application risks (use Workpaper 2.2.2).		

Workpaper A-16. Application Risk Worksheet

Application _____

Business Cycle	Application Risk	Applicable	
		Yes	*No*
Revenue	1. Cash receipts are lost. *Comments:* _____ _____		
	2. Recorded cash deposits are not credited by the bank. *Comments:* _____ _____		
	3. Cash whose source or application cannot be identified is lost. *Comments:* _____ _____		
	4. Receivables are accepted from unauthorized customers. *Comments:* _____ _____		
	5. Receivables are accepted from customers who have exceeded their limit. *Comments:* _____ _____		
	6. Receivables are billed to wrong customers. *Comments:* _____ _____		
	7. Overdue accounts are not followed up. *Comments:* _____ _____		
	8. Overdue charges are not assessed. *Comments:* _____ _____		
	9. The customer is improperly billed. *Comments:* _____ _____		
	10. The product is incorrectly priced. *Comments:* _____ _____		
	11. The terms of the sale are improperly stated. *Comments:* _____ _____		
	12. Unauthorized shipments are made. *Comments:* _____ _____		
	13. Back orders are lost. *Comments:* _____ _____		

Prepared by:	**Date:**

Workpaper A-16. Application Risk Worksheet (page 2 of 6)

Business Cycle	Application Risk	Applicable Yes	No
Revenue, cont.	14. Product is shipped but not billed. *Comments:* _____		
	15. The prices on the product master are wrong. *Comments:* _____		
	16. The effective date of the price is incorrect. *Comments:* _____		
	17. An improper reserve is established for bad debts. *Comments:* _____		
	18. Accounts receivable are written off without management approval. *Comments:* _____		
	19. Credit is not denied customers whose receivables are uncollectible. *Comments:* _____		
	20. Returned merchandise is not received or not returned to inventory. *Comments:* _____		
	21. The condition of the returned merchandise is not determined before credit is granted. *Comments:* _____		
	22. The amount of credit given the customer for the returned merchandise is wrong. *Comments:* _____		
	23. Customers are inaccurately charged for freight. *Comments:* _____		
	24. Incorrect rates are charged by common carriers. *Comments:* _____		
	25. The sales tax is inaccurate. *Comments:* _____		
	26. Billings are not made on at timely basis. *Comments:* _____		

Prepared by: **Date:**

Workpaper A-16. Application Risk Worksheet (page 3 of 6)

Business Cycle	Application Risk		Applicable	
			Yes	No
Revenue, cont.	27.	Billings are inaccurately recorded in receivables. Comments: _____		
	28.	Employees purchase items at prices for which they are not eligible. Comments: _____		
	29.	Merchandise on consignment or demonstration is lost. Comments: _____		
	30.	Other: Comments: _____		
	31.	Other: Comments: _____		
Expenditures	1.	Expenditures are not authorized. Comments: _____		
	2.	Expenditures are not recorded. Comments: _____		
	3.	Product or service is purchased but not received. Comments: _____		
	4.	Competitive bidding does not occur when applicable. Comments: _____		
	5.	Product or service ordered is not received. Comments: _____		
	6.	Product or service is not received when needed. Comments: _____		
	7.	The wrong quantity or product is received. Comments: _____		
	8.	An eligible discount is not taken. Comments: _____		
Prepared by:			**Date:**	

Workpaper A-16. Application Risk Worksheet (page 4 of 6)

Business Cycle		Application Risk	Applicable	
			Yes	No
Expenditures, cont.	9.	The item is paid for twice. *Comments:* _____		
	10.	Damaged, unordered, or unwanted merchandise is not returned. *Comments:* _____		
	11.	Credit for returned merchandise is not received from the vendor. *Comments:* _____		
	12.	Unapproved payments are made. *Comments:* _____		
	13.	Unauthorized employees are added to the payroll. *Comments:* _____		
	14.	Absences are not recorded. *Comments:* _____		
	15.	Terminated employees are not deleted from the payroll. *Comments:* _____		
	16.	Year-to-date information is not properly accumulated. *Comments:* _____		
	17.	Deductions are improperly calculated. *Comments:* _____		
	18.	Time worked is not properly recorded. *Comments:* _____		
	19.	Gross pay is incorrectly calculated. *Comments:* _____		
	20.	Net pay is incorrectly calculated. *Comments:* _____		
	21.	The system does not comply with government pay regulations. *Comments:* _____		

Prepared by: **Date:**

Workpaper A-16. Application Risk Worksheet (page 5 of 6)

Business Cycle	Application Risk	Applicable Yes	No
Expenditures, cont.	22. The existence of inventory is not verified. *Comments:* _____		
	23. Inventory or products are lost. *Comments:* _____		
	24. Other: *Comments:* _____		
	25. Other: *Comments:* _____		
	26. Other: *Comments:* _____		
Product/ Conversion	1. Production schedules are incorrect. *Comments:* _____		
	2. Inadequate materials are available for production. *Comments:* _____		
	3. Unneeded items are produced. *Comments:* _____		
	4. Needed items are not produced. *Comments:* _____		
	5. Produced items are lost or not billed. *Comments:* _____		
	6. Cost of products is incorrectly calculated. *Comments:* _____		
	7. Other: *Comments:* _____		
	8. Other: *Comments:* _____		
Prepared by:		**Date:**	

Workpaper A-16. Application Risk Worksheet (page 6 of 6)

Business Cycle	Application Risk	Applicable Yes	Applicable No
External Financial	1. Generally accepted accounting procedures are not followed. *Comments:* _____		
	2. Financial reports are inaccurate. *Comments:* _____		
	3. Needed financial information is not included in financial reports. *Comments:* _____		
	4. Government regulations are not compiled with. *Comments:* _____		
	5. Financial reserves are inadequately valued. *Comments:* _____		
	6. Other: *Comments:* _____		
	7. Other: *Comments:* _____		
	8. Other: *Comments:* _____		
Prepared by:		**Date:**	

Workpaper A-17. Application Risk Worksheet (blank)

Application _____

Business Cycle	Application Risk	Applicable	
		Yes	*No*
	1. *Comments:*_____ _____		
	2. *Comments:*_____ _____		
	3. *Comments:*_____ _____		
	4. *Comments:*_____ _____		
	5. *Comments:*_____ _____		
	6. *Comments:*_____ _____		
	7. *Comments:*_____ _____		
	8. *Comments:*_____ _____		
	9. *Comments:*_____ _____		
	10. *Comments:*_____ _____		
	11. *Comments:*_____ _____		
	12. *Comments:*_____ _____		
Prepared by:		**Date:**	

Workpaper A-18. Application Risk Ranking

Application _____

No.	Application Risk	Unfavorable Event	Annual Loss Expectancy		Risk Score (Rank)
			Frequency	*Loss*	

| Prepared by: | | Date: | |

APPENDICES

Workpaper A-19. File or Database Population Analysis

Name of File or Database _____

Type Characteristic \ Record/Transaction Type Code						Total for File
Number of Records						
Dollar Value by Type						
Total Negative Dollar Values						
Number of Dollar Value Fields with Negative Value						
High Value						
Low Value						
Mean Value						
Median Value						
Oldest Date						
Average Age						
Percentage over 90 Days Old						

Other Information Needed:

1) _____

2) _____

3) _____

Workpaper A-20. Measurable Application Audit Objectives

Name of File or Database_____

No.	Objectives (per audit assignment)	Audit Risks Affecting Objective	Measurable Audit Objective	Criteria to Measure Success

Prepared by: | **Date:**

Workpaper A-21. EDP Application Audit Plan

Application _____

No.	Detailed Audit Objective	Auditor Assigned	Hours Budgeted	Dates		Evidence Needed	Recommended Audit Process
				Start	Stop		
	Comments: _____						
	Comments: _____						
	Comments: _____						
	Comments: _____						
	Comments: _____						
	Comments: _____						
	Comments: _____						

Prepared by: Date:

Workpaper A-22. Responsibility Conflict Matrix

Application _____

	Actions							
People								

Flow of Work →

Movement of Responsibility ↓

Prepared by: **Date:**

WORKPAPER A-23. DATA ORIGINATION CONTROLS QUESTIONNAIRE

Data origination controls ensure the accuracy, completeness, and timeliness of data before it reaches the computer application. Controls over the data must be established as close to the point of its origination as possible and maintained throughout this manual process. The auditor should determine the adequacy of controls over the preparation, collection, and processing of source documents to make sure that no data is added, lost, or altered before it is entered into the computer system. Workpapers 3-2-1, 3-2-2, 3-2-3, and 3-2-4 are based on questionnaires from *Evaluating Internal Controls in Computer-Based Systems*, U.S. General Accounting Office, June 1981.

Workpaper A-23. Data Origination Controls Questionnaire

Application: _____ Completed by: _____ Date: _____

Item	Response		
	Yes	No	N/A
Source-Document Origination			
1. Do documented procedures explain the methods?			
Comments: _____			
_____			
2. Are duties separated to ensure that no individual performs more than one of the following operations:			
Data origination?			
Data input?			
Data processing?			
Output distribution?			
Comments: _____			
_____			
3. Are source documents designed to minimize errors and omissions? Specifically:			
Are special-purpose forms used to guide the initial recording of data in a consistent format?			
Are preprinted sequential numbers used to establish controls?			
Does each type of transaction have a unique identifier?			
Does each transaction have a cross-reference number that can be used to trace information to and from the source document?			
Comments: _____			
_____			
4. Is access to source documents and blank input forms restricted to authorized personnel?			

Workpaper A-23. Data Origination Controls Questionnaire

Application:_____ Completed by: _____ Date:_____

	Response		
Item	**Yes**	**No**	**N/A**
Comments: _____ _____			
5. Are source documents and blank input forms stored in a secure location?			
Comments: _____ _____			
6. Is authorization from two or more accountable individuals required before source documents and blank input forms are released from storage?			
Comments: _____ _____			

Source-Document Authorization

	Response		
7. Are authorizing signatures used for all types of transactions?			
Comments: _____ _____			
8. Is evidence of approval required for specific types of critical transactions (e.g., control bypassing, system overrides, manual adjustments)?			
Comments: _____ _____			
9. Are duties separated within the user department to ensure that one individual does not prepare more than one type of transaction (e.g., establishing new master records plus changing or updating master records)?			
Comments: _____ _____			
10. Are duties separated within the user department to ensure that no individual performs more than one of the following phases of data preparation:			
Originating the source document?			
Authorizing the source document?			
Controlling the source document?			
Comments: _____			

Workpaper A-23. Data Origination Controls Questionnaire

Application: _____ Completed by: _____ Date: _____

Item	Response		
	Yes	No	N/A
Source-Document Data Collection and Input Preparation			
11. Does the user department have a control group responsible for collecting and completing source documents? *Comments:* _____ _____			
12. Does the control group verify that source documents: Are accounted for? Are complete and accurate? Are appropriately authorized? Are transmitted in a timely manner? *Comments:* _____ _____			
13. Does the control group independently control data submitted for transmittal to the DP department for conversion or entry by using the following: Turnaround transmittal documents? Batching techniques? Record counts? Predetermined control totals? Logging techniques? Other? (specify) _____ *Comments:* _____ _____			
14. When the user department is responsible for its own data entry, does a separate group within that department perform this input function? *Comments:* _____ _____			
15. Are source documents that are transmitted for conversion transported in accordance with their security classifications? *Comments:* _____ _____			

Workpaper A-23. Data Origination Controls Questionnaire

Application:_____ Completed by: _____ Date:_____

Item	Response		
	Yes	**No**	**N/A**
Source-Document Error Handling			
16. Do documented procedures explain the methods for source-document error detection, correction, and reentry? *Comments:* _____ _____			
17. Do they include the following: Types of error conditions that can occur? Correction procedures to follow? Methods to be used for the reentry of source documents that have been corrected? *Comments:* _____ _____			
18. Does the control group identify errors to facilitate the correction of erroneous information? *Comments:* _____ _____			
19. Does the control group follow the same verification and control procedures described in Questions 12 and 13 when receiving corrected source documents? *Comments:* _____ _____			
20. Are error logs used to ensure timely follow-up and correction of unresolved errors? *Comments:* _____ _____			
21. Are source-document originators immediately notified by the control group of all errors? *Comments:* _____ _____			
Source-Document Retention			
22. Are source documents retained so that data lost or destroyed during subsequent processing can be recreated? *Comments:* _____ _____			

Workpaper A-23. Data Origination Controls Questionnaire

Application: _____ **Completed by:** _____ **Date:** _____

Item	Response		
	Yes	**No**	**N/A**
23. Does each type of source document have a specific retention period that is preprinted on the document? _Comments:_ _____			
24. Are source documents stored in a logical manner to facilitate retrieval? _Comments:_ _____			
25. Is a copy kept in the originating department whenever the source document leaves the department? _Comments:_ _____			
26. Is access to records in the originating department restricted to authorized personnel? _Comments:_ _____			
27. When source documents reach their expiration dates, are they removed from storage and destroyed in accordance with security classifications? _Comments:_ _____			

WORKPAPER A-24. DATA INPUT CONTROLS QUESTIONNAIRE

Data input controls ensure the accuracy, completeness, and timeliness of data during its conversion into machine-readable format and entry into the application. Data input can be batch or online. The auditor should determine the adequacy of both manual and automated controls over data input to ensure that data is input accurately with optimum use of computerized validation and editing and that error-handling procedures facilitate the timely and accurate resubmission of all corrected data.

Workpaper A-24. Data Input Controls Questionnaire

Application:_____ Completed by: _____ Date:_____

Item	Response		
	Yes	**No**	**N/A**
Batch: Data Conversion and Entry			
1. Do documented procedures explain the methods for data conversion and entry?			
Comments: _____			
2. Are duties separated to ensure that no one individual performs more than one of the following operations?			
Data origination?			
Data input?			
Data processing?			
Output distribution?			
Comments: _____			
3. Does the DP department have a control group responsible for data conversion and entry of all source documents received from user departments?			
Comments: _____			
4. Does the control group return all turnaround transmittal documents to the user department to ensure that no documents were added or lost?			
Comments: _____			
5. Does the control group account for all batches of source documents received from the user department to ensure that none were added or lost?			

Workpaper A-24. Data Input Controls Questionnaire

Application: _____ **Completed by:** _____ **Date:** _____

Item	Response		
	Yes	No	N/A
Comments: _____ _____			
6a. Does the control group independently develop record counts that are balanced with those of the user department control group? *Comments:* _____ _____			
6a. Are all discrepancies reconciled? *Comments:* _____ _____			
7a. Does the DP control group independently develop predetermined control totals that are balanced with those of the control group? *Comments:* _____ _____			
7b. Are all discrepancies reconciled? *Comments:* _____ _____			
8a. Does the DP control group keep a log or record showing the receipt of user department source documents and their actual disposition? *Comments:* _____ _____			
8b. Are there provisions to ensure that all documents are accounted for? *Comments:* _____ _____			
9. Does the control group independently control data submitted for conversion by using the following: Turnaround transmittal documents? Batching techniques? Record counts? Predetermined control totals? Logging techniques? Other? (specify)_____ *Comments:* _____ _____			
10. Are conversion operations established as close to the origination of the source documents as possible?			

Workpaper A-24. Data Input Controls Questionnaire

Application: _____ **Completed by:** _____ **Date:** _____

Item	Yes	No	N/A
Comments: _____			
11. Do conversion operations record document information directly onto machine-readable media (e.g., keypunch cards, key-to-tape, key-to-disk, key-to-terminal) rather than immediate media (e.g., coding documents)? *Comments:* _____			
12. Does the DP department have a schedule by application that shows when data requiring conversion will be received and must be completed? *Comments:* _____			
13. Are turnaround transmittal documents returned to the DP control group accounted for to ensure that no documents were added or lost during conversion? *Comments:* _____			
14. Are all batches of documents returned to the DP control group accounted for to ensure that none were added or lost during conversion? *Comments:* _____			
15a. Are all record counts developed during conversion balanced with those of the control group? *Comments:* _____			
15b. Are all discrepancies reconciled? *Comments:* _____			
16a. Are all predetermined control totals developed during conversion balanced with those of the control group? *Comments:* _____			
16b. Are all discrepancies reconciled? *Comments:* _____			

Workpaper A-24. Data Input Controls Questionnaire

Application: _____ Completed by: _____ Date: _____

Item	Response		
	Yes	No	N/A
17. Are all converted documents returned to the control group logged in and accounted for? *Comments:* _____ _____			
18. Does this group independently control data submitted for data entry by using the following: Turnaround transmittal documents? Batching techniques? Record counts? Predetermined control totals? Logging techniques? Other? (specify) _____ *Comments:* _____ _____			
19. Are data entry operations established as close as possible to the origination of the source data? *Comments:* _____ _____			
20. Does the DP department have a schedule by application showing when data requiring entry will be received and needs to be completed? *Comments:* _____ _____			
21. Must all documents entered into the application be signed or marked in some way to indicate that they were entered into the system, thereby preventing accidental duplication or reuse of the data? *Comments:* _____ _____			
22. Are turnaround transmittal documents returned to the DP control group accounted for to ensure that no documents were added or lost during data entry? *Comments:* _____ _____			
23. Are all batches of documents returned to the control group accounted for to ensure that none were added or lost during data entry?			

Workpaper A-24. Data Input Controls Questionnaire

Application: _____ **Completed by:** _____ **Date:** _____

	Response		
Item	**Yes**	**No**	**N/A**
Comments: _____			
24a. Are all record counts developed during data entry balanced with those of the control group? *Comments:* _____			
24b. Are all discrepancies reconciled? *Comments:* _____			
25a. Are all predetermined control totals developed during data entry balanced with those of the control group? *Comments:* _____			
25b. Are all discrepancies reconciled? *Comments:* _____			
26. Are all input documents returned to the control group logged in and accounted for? *Comments:* _____			
27. Are all input documents retained in a way that allows tracing them to related originating documents and output records? *Comments:* _____			
28. Is key verification used to check the accuracy of all keying operations? *Comments:* _____			
29. Are keying and verifying of a document done by different individuals? *Comments:* _____			
30. Are preprogrammed keying formats used to ensure that data is recorded in the proper field, format, etc.? *Comments:* _____			

APPENDICES

Workpaper A-24. Data Input Controls Questionnaire

Application: _____ Completed by: _____ Date: _____

Item	Response		
	Yes	No	N/A
31. Are data validation and editing performed as early as possible in the data flow to ensure that the application rejects any transaction before its entry into the system? Comments: _____			
32. Are data validation and editing performed for all input data fields even when an error is detected in an earlier field of the same transaction? Comments: _____			
33. Are the following checked for validity on all input transactions: Individual and supervisor authorization or approval codes? Check digits on all identification keys? Check digits at the end of a string of numeric data that is not subject to balancing? Codes? Characters? Fields? Combinations of fields? Transactions? Calculations? Missing data? Extraneous data? Amounts? Units? Composition? Logic decisions? Limit of reasonableness checks? Signs? Record matches? Record mismatches? Sequence? Balancing of quantitative data? Crossfooting of quantitative data?			

Workpaper A-24. Data Input Controls Questionnaire

Application:_____ **Completed by:** _____ **Date:**_____

	Response		
Item	**Yes**	**No**	**N/A**
Comments: _____ _____			
34. Are special routines used that automatically validate and edit input transaction dates against a table of cutoff dates? *Comments:* _____ _____			
35. Are all personnel prevented from overriding or bypassing data validation and editing problems? *Comments:* _____ _____			
36. If not, Is override capability restricted to supervisors only and in a limited number of acceptable circumstances? Is every system override automatically logged by the application so that these actions can be analyzed for appropriateness and correctness? *Comments:* _____ _____			
37. Are batch control totals submitted by the DP control group used to validate the completeness of batches received as input into the applications? *Comments:* _____ _____			
38. Are record counts submitted by the DP control group used to validate the completeness of data input into the application? *Comments:* _____ _____			
39. Are predetermined control totals submitted by the DP control group used to validate the completeness of data input into the application? *Comments:* _____ _____			
Batch: Data Input Error Handling			
40. Do documented procedures explain how to identify, correct, and reprocess data rejected by the application?			

Workpaper A-24. Data Input Controls Questionnaire

Application: _____ **Completed by:** _____ **Date:** _____

	Response		
Item	**Yes**	**No**	**N/A**
Comments: _____ _____			
41. Do error messages provide clear, understandable corrective actions for each type of error? *Comments:* _____ _____			
42. Are error messages produced for each transaction containing data that does not meet edit requirements? *Comments:* _____ _____			
43. Are error messages produced for each data field that does not meet edit requirements? *Comments:* _____ _____			
44. Is every data item that does not meet edit requirements rejected from further processing by the application? *Comments:* _____ _____			
45. Is every rejected data item automatically written on an automated suspense file? *Comments:* _____ _____			
46. Does the automated suspense file also include the following? Codes indicating error type? Data and time the transaction was entered? Identity of the user who originated the transaction? *Comments:* _____ _____			
47. Are record counts automatically created by suspense file processing to control these rejected transactions? *Comments:* _____ _____			
48. Are predetermined control totals automatically created by suspense file processing to control the rejected transactions? *Comments:* _____ _____			

Workpaper A-24. Data Input Controls Questionnaire

Application:_____ Completed by: _____ Date:_____

	Response		
Item	**Yes**	**No**	**N/A**
49. Are rejected transactions caused by data conversion or entry errors corrected by the DP department control group? *Comments:* _____ _____			
50. Does the DP control group independently control data rejected by the application by using the following: Turnaround transmittal documents? Batching techniques? Record counts? Predetermined control totals? Logging techniques? Other? (specify) _____ *Comments:* _____ _____			
51. Are transaction rejections not caused by data conversion or entry errors corrected by the user originating the transaction? *Comments:* _____ _____			
52. Does the user department control group independently control data rejected by the application by using the following: Turnaround transmittal documents? Batching techniques? Record counts? Predetermined control totals? Logging techniques? Other? (specify) _____ *Comments:* _____ _____			
53. Is the automated suspense file used to control follow-up, correction, and reentry of transactions rejected by the application? *Comments:* _____ _____			
54. Is the automated suspense file used to produce analysis of the following for management review:			

Workpaper A-24. Data Input Controls Questionnaire

Application: _____ Completed by: _____ Date: _____

		Response		
	Item	Yes	No	N/A
	Level of transaction errors?			
	Status of uncorrected transactions?			
	Comments: _____			
	_____			
55.	Are these analyses used by management to ensure that corrective action is taken when error levels become too high?			
	Comments: _____			
	_____			
56.	Are these analyses used by management to ensure that correction action is taken when uncorrected transactions remain on the suspense file too long?			
	Comments: _____			
	_____			
57.	Are reports made to progressively higher levels of management if these conditions worsen?			
	Comments: _____			
	_____			
58.	Are debit- and credit-type entries used instead of delete- or erase-type commands to correct rejected transactions on the automated suspense file?			
	Comments: _____			
	_____			
59.	Is the application designed to reject delete- or erase-type commands?			
	Comments: _____			
	_____			
60.	Do valid correction transactions purge the automated suspense file of corresponding rejected transactions?			
	Comments: _____			
	_____			
61.	Are invalid correction transactions added to the automated suspense file along with the corresponding rejected transactions?			
	Comments: _____			
	_____			
62.	Are record counts appropriately adjusted by correction transactions?			

Workpaper A-24. Data Input Controls Questionnaire

Application:_____ **Completed by:** _____ **Date:**_____

Item	Yes	No	N/A
Comments: _____ _____			
63. Are predetermined control totals appropriately adjusted by correction transactions? *Comments:* _____ _____			
64. Are all corrections reviewed and approved by supervisors before reentry? *Comments:* _____			
65. Are procedures for processing corrected transactions the same as those for processing original transactions, with the addition of supervisory review and approval before reentry? *Comments:* _____			
66. Does ultimate responsibility for the completeness and accuracy of all application processing remain with the user? *Comments:* _____ _____			
Online: Data Conversion and Entry			
1. Do documented procedures explain the methods for data conversion and entry? *Comments:* _____			
2. Are duties separated to ensure that no individual performs more than one of the following procedures: Data origination? Data input? Data processing? Output distribution? *Comments:* _____			
3. Is a separate group within the user department responsible for performing data entry operations?			

Workpaper A-24. Data Input Controls Questionnaire

Application: _____ Completed by: _____ Date: _____

	Item	Response		
		Yes	**No**	**N/A**
	Comments: _____ _____			
4.	Does the user department control group independently control data to be entered into the application by using the following:			
	Turnaround transmittal documents?			
	Batching techniques?			
	Record counts?			
	Predetermined control totals?			
	Logging techniques?			
	Other? (specify)? _____			
	Comments: _____ _____			
5.	If this control group does not control data entry, is at least simultaneous entry and recording of source data performed at the origination point?			
	Comments: _____ _____			
6.	Must all documents entered into the computer application be signed or marked to indicate that they were in fact entered into the system to protect against accidental duplication or reuse of the data?			
	Comments: _____ _____			
7.	Are data entry terminal devices locked in a physically secure room, with only query terminals located outside this room?			
	Comments: _____ _____			
8.	Must supervisors sign on each terminal to initialize it before operators can sign on?			
	Comments: _____ _____			
9.	Is the work that may be entered restricted by the authority level assigned to each terminal (data entry versus query)?			
	Comments: _____ _____			
10.	Is password control used to prevent unauthorized use of the terminals?			

Workpaper A-24. Data Input Controls Questionnaire

Application:_____ **Completed by:** _____ **Date:**_____

Item	Response		
	Yes	No	N/A
Comments: _____ _____			
11. Are nonprinting, nondisplaying, or obliteration facilities used when keying and acknowledging passwords and authorization codes? *Comments:* _____ _____			
12. Is a report produced immediately when unauthorized system accesses are attempted by way of terminal devices? *Comments:* _____ _____			
13. Does this report include the following: Location of the device? Date and time of the violation? Number of attempts? Identification of the operator at the time of the violation? *Comments:* _____ _____			
14. Is a terminal lockup used to prevent unauthorized access after a predetermined number of incorrect attempts to access the system have been made? *Comments:* _____ _____			
15. Does the system automatically shut down the terminal in question and allow intervention only by specially assigned DP department supervisors? *Comments:* _____ _____			
16. Is a data-access matrix used to restrict use or access levels by checking user identification and passwords? *Comments:* _____ _____			
17. Is each user of the online system limited to certain types of application transactions? *Comments:* _____ _____			

APPENDICES

Workpaper A-24. Data Input Controls Questionnaire

Application: _____ Completed by: _____ Date:_____

	Response		
Item	**Yes**	**No**	**N/A**
18. Are master commands controlling operation of the application restricted to a limited number of supervisory DP personnel and master command terminals? *Comments:* _____ _____			
19. Does senior management periodically review the propriety of the terminal authority levels? *Comments:* _____ _____			
20. Is senior management required to review the propriety of terminal authority levels in the event of a purported or real security violation? *Comments:* _____ _____			
21. Are passwords changed periodically? *Comments:* _____ _____			
22. Are passwords changed in the event of a purported or real security violation? *Comments:* _____ _____			
23. Are passwords deleted once an individual (a) changes job functions; (b) leaves; (c) no longer needs the same level of access; (d) no longer needs any access? *Comments:* _____ _____			
24. Is a log or data-access matrix that shows the purpose of user accesses reviewed by senior management to identify unauthorized use? *Comments:* _____ _____			
25. Has the security officer initiated an aggressive review program to ascertain that controls are fully operational? *Comments:* _____ _____			
26. Does terminal hardware include the following features: Built-in terminal identification that automatically validates proper terminal authorization?			

Workpaper A-24. Data Input Controls Questionnaire

Application:_____ **Completed by:** _____ **Date:**_____

Item	Response		
	Yes	**No**	**N/A**
Terminal logs that record all transactions processed?			
Messages that are automatically date- and time-stamped for logging purposes?			
Record counts that are automatically accumulated for logging purposes?			
Comments: _____			
27. Does each message contain an identifying message header that includes the following:			
Message number?			
Terminal and user identification?			
Date and time?			
Transaction code?			
Comments: _____			
28. Does each message contain the following indicators:			
End of message?			
End of transmission?			
Comments: _____			
29. Is parity checking used for each character?			
Comments: _____			
30. Is parity checking used for each message block?			
Comments: _____			
31. Is the message content checked for valid characters?			
Comments: _____			
Online: Data Validation and Editing			
32. Are preprogrammed keying formats used to ensure that data is recorded in the proper field, format, etc.?			
Comments: _____			

Workpaper A-24. Data Input Controls Questionnaire

Application: _____ Completed by: _____ Date:_____

Item	Response		
	Yes	No	N/A
33. Is an interactive display used to allow the terminal operator to interact with the system during data entry? *Comments:*_____ _____			
34. Are computer-aided instructions (e.g., prompting) used with online dialogue to reduce the number of operator errors? *Comments:*_____ _____			
35. Are intelligent terminals used to allow front-end validation, editing, and control? *Comments:*_____ _____			
36. Are data validation and editing performed as early as possible in the data flow to ensure that the application rejects any incorrect transaction before it can be entered into the system? *Comments:*_____ _____			
37. Are data validation and editing performed for all input data fields, even when an error is detected in an earlier field of the same transaction? *Comments:*_____ _____			
38. Are the following checked for validity on all input transactions? Individual and supervisor authorization or approval codes? Check digits at the end of a string of numeric data that is not subject to balancing? Codes? Characters? Fields? Combinations of fields? Transactions? Calculations? Missing data? Extraneous data? Amounts?			

Workpaper A-24. Data Input Controls Questionnaire

Application:________________ Completed by: ___________ Date:__________

	Item	Response Yes	No	N/A
	Units?			
	Composition?			
	Logic decisions?			
	Limit or reasonableness checks?			
	Signs?			
	Record matches?			
	Record mismatches?			
	Sequence?			
	Balancing of quantitative data?			
	Cross-footing of quantitative data?			
	Comments: ____________________			
39.	Are special routines used that automatically validate and edit input transaction dates against a table of cutoff dates?			
	Comments: ____________________			
40.	Are all personnel prevented from overriding or bypassing data validation and editing errors?			
	Comments: ____________________			
41.	If not,			
	Is override capability restricted to supervisors only and in a limited number of acceptable circumstances?			
	Are all system overrides automatically logged by the application so that these actions can be analyzed for appropriateness and correctness?			
	Comments: ____________________			
42.	Are batch control totals generated by the terminal, concentrator, or application used to validate the completeness of batches received as input data?			
	Comments: ____________________			
43.	Are record counts generated by the terminal, concentrator, or application used to validate the completeness of data input?			

Workpaper A-24. Data Input Controls Questionnaire

Application: _____ Completed by: _____ Date: _____

Item	Response		
	Yes	No	N/A
Comments: _____ _____			
44. Are predetermined control totals generated by the terminal, concentrator, or application used to validate the completeness of data input?			
Comments: _____ _____			
Online: Data Input Error Handling			
45. Do documented procedures explain how to identify, correct, and reprocess data rejected by the application?			
Comments: _____ _____			
46. Are errors displayed or printed immediately on detection for immediate correction by terminal operator?			
Comments: _____ _____			
47. Do error messages provide clear, understandable, cross-referenced corrective actions for each type of error?			
Comments: _____ _____			
48. Are error messages produced for each transaction containing data that does not meet edit requirements?			
Comments: _____ _____			
49. Are error messages produced for each input data field that does not meet edit requirements?			
Comments: _____ _____			
50. Is every data item that is rejected by the application automatically written on an automated suspense file?			
Comments: _____ _____			
51. Does the automated suspense file include the following:			
Codes indicating error type?			
Date and time the transaction was entered?			

Workpaper A-24. Data Input Controls Questionnaire

Application:_____ **Completed by:** _____ **Date:**_____

		Response		
	Item	**Yes**	**No**	**N/A**
	Identity of the user who originated the transaction?			
	Comments: _____			
	_____			
52.	Are record counts automatically created by suspense file processing to control these rejected transactions?			
	Comments: _____			
	_____			
53.	Are predetermined control totals automatically created by suspense file processing to control these rejected transactions?			
	Comments: _____			
	_____			
54.	Are transaction rejections caused by data entry errors corrected by the terminal group?			
	Comments: _____			
	_____			
55.	Are transaction rejections caused by data entry errors corrected by the terminal operator?			
	Comments: _____			
	_____			
56.	Does the user department control group independently control data rejected by the application by using the following:			
	Turnaround transmittal documents?			
	Batching techniques?			
	Record counts?			
	Predetermined control totals?			
	Logging techniques?			
	Other? (specify) _____			
	Comments: _____			
	_____			
57.	Is the automated suspense file used to control follow-up, correction, and reentry of transactions rejected by the application?			
	Comments: _____			
	_____			
58.	Is the automated suspense file used to produce analysis of the following for management review:			

Workpaper A-24. Data Input Controls Questionnaire

Application: _____ Completed by: _____ Date: _____

Item	Response		
	Yes	**No**	**N/A**
Level of transaction errors?			
Status of uncorrected transactions?			
Comments: _____ _____			
59. Are these analyses used by management to ensure that corrective action is taken when error levels become too high? *Comments:* _____ _____			
60. Are these analyses used by management to ensure that correction action is taken when uncorrected transactions remain on the suspense file too long? *Comments:* _____ _____			
61. Are reports made to progressively higher levels of management if these conditions worsen? *Comments:* _____ _____			
62. Are debit- and credit-type entries used instead of delete- or erase-type commands to correct rejected transaction on the automated suspense file? *Comments:* _____ _____			
63. Is the application designed to reject delete- or erase-type commands? *Comments:* _____ _____			
64. Do valid correction transactions purge the automated suspense file of corresponding rejected transactions? *Comments:* _____ _____			
65. Are invalid correction transactions added to the automated suspense file along with the corresponding rejected transactions? *Comments:* _____ _____			
66. Are record counts appropriately adjusted by correction transactions?			

Workpaper A-24. Data Input Controls Questionnaire

Application:_____ Completed by: _____ Date:_____

Item	Response		
	Yes	No	N/A
Comments: _____ _____			
67. Are predetermined control totals appropriately adjusted by correction transactions? *Comments:* _____ _____			
68. Are all corrections reviewed and approved by supervisors before reentry? *Comments:* _____			
69. Are the procedures for processing corrected transactions the same as those for processing original transactions, with the addition of supervisory review and approval before reentry? *Comments:* _____ _____			
70. Does ultimate responsibility for the completeness and accuracy of all application processing remain with the user? *Comments:* _____ _____			

APPENDICES

WORKPAPER A-25. DATA PROCESSING CONTROLS QUESTIONNAIRE

Data processing controls are used to ensure the accuracy, completeness, and timeliness of data during either batch or real-time processing by the computer. The auditor should determine the adequacy of controls over application programs and related computer operations to ensure that data is accurately processed through the application and that no data is added, lost, or altered during processing.

Workpaper A-25. Data Processing Controls Questionnaire

Application: _____ Completed by: _____ Date:_____

Item	Response		
	Yes	No	N/A
Batch: Data Processing Integrity			
1. Do documented procedures explain the methods for proper processing of each application program? *Comments:*_____			
2. Are duties separated to ensure that no individual performs more than one of the following operations: Data origination? Data input? Data processing? Output distribution? *Comments:*_____			
3. Do operator instructions include the following: System start-up procedures? Backup assignments? Emergency procedures? System shutdown procedures? Error message/debugging instructions? System and job status reporting instructions? *Comments:*_____			
4. Do computer program run books include the following: Definitions of input sources, input data, and data formats? Descriptions of setup procedures?			

Workpaper A-25. Data Processing Controls Questionnaire

Application: _____ Completed by: _____ Date: _____

Item	Response		
	Yes	No	N/A
Descriptions of all halt conditions?			
Descriptions of restart procedures and checkpoints?			
Descriptions of data storage requirements?			
Printer-carriage-control tapes?			
Descriptions of expected output data and formats?			
Descriptions of output and file dispositions on completion?			
Copies of normal console run sheets?			
Types of console message instructions?			
System flowcharts?			
Comments: _____			
5. Do computer program run books exclude the following:			
Program logic charts or block diagrams?			
Copies of program listings?			
Comments: _____			
6. Are application programs prevented from accepting data from computer consoles?			
Comments: _____			
7. Is a history log output on a line printer as well as displayed on a console?			
Comments: _____			
8. Does this log include the following:			
Hardware failure messages?			
Software failure messages?			
Processing halts?			
Abnormal terminations of jobs?			
Operator interventions?			
Error messages?			
Unusual occurrences?			
Comments: _____			

APPENDICES

Workpaper A-25. Data Processing Controls Questionnaire

Application: _____ **Completed by:** _____ **Date:** _____

	Item	Response		
		Yes	No	N/A
9.	Is the log routinely reviewed by supervisors to determine the causes of problems and the correctness of actions taken? *Comments:* _____			
10.	Does the DP department have a schedule, by application, that shows when each application program should be run and completed? *Comments:* _____			
11.	Does the DP department have a control group responsible for controlling all data processing operations? *Comments:* _____			
12.	Does this control group limit access to and use of job control cards so that unauthorized programs will not be executed? *Comments:* _____			
13.	Does the control group independently control data processing through the following: Ensuring that application schedules are met? Balancing batch counts of data submitted for processing? Balancing record counts of data submitted for processing? Balancing predetermined control totals of data submitted for processing? Maintaining accurate logs of input/output files used in computer processing? Ensuring that input/work/output files used in computer processing? Ensuring that restarts are performed properly? Other? (specify) _____ *Comments:* _____			
14.	Is there a means of verifying master file contents (e.g., drawing samples periodically from data files to review for accuracy)? *Comments:* _____			

Workpaper A-25. Data Processing Controls Questionnaire

Application: _____ Completed by:_____ Date:_____

Item	Response		
	Yes	No	N/A
15. Does each input transaction have a unique identifier (transaction code) that directs the transaction to the proper application program for processing? *Comments:* _____			
16. Do programs positively identify input data as to type? *Comments:* _____			
17. Are standardized default options built onto the computer program logic? *Comments:* _____			
18. Are computer-generated control totals (run-to-run totals) automatically reconciled between jobs to check for completeness of processing? *Comments:* _____			
19. Where computerized data is entered into the application, do controls verify that the proper data is used? *Comments:* _____			
20. Where computer files are entered into the application, do controls verify that the proper version (cycle) of the file is used? *Comments:* _____			
21. Do all programs include routines for checking internal file header labels before processing? *Comments:* _____			
22. Are there controls to prevent operators from circumventing file-checking routines? *Comments:* _____			
23. Are internal trailer labels containing control totals (e.g., record counts, predetermined control totals) generated for all computer files and tested by the application programs to determine that all records have been processed?			

Workpaper A-25. Data Processing Controls Questionnaire

Application: _____ **Completed by:** _____ **Date:**_____

Item	Response		
	Yes	**No**	**N/A**
*Comments:*_____			
24. Are file completion checks performed to make sure that application files have been completely processed, including both transaction and master files?			
*Comments:*_____			
25. Do data processing controls ensure that:			
Output counts from the system equal input counts to the system?			
Program interfaces require that the sending program output counts equal the receiving program input counts?			
System interfaces require:			
•The sending system's output counts equal the receiving system's input counts?			
•Shared files meet the control requirements of both the sending and receiving system?			
*Comments:*_____			
Batch: Data Processing Validation and Editing			
26. Are data validation and editing performed as early as possible in the data flow to ensure that the application rejects any incorrect transaction before master-file updating?			
*Comments:*_____			
27. Are data validation and editing performed for all data fields even when an error is detected in an earlier field of the transaction?			
*Comments:*_____			
28. Are the following checked for validity on all input transactions:			
Individual and supervisor authorization or approval codes?			
Check digits on all identification keys?			
Check digits at the end of a string of numeric data that is not subject to balancing?			
Codes?			

Workpaper A-25. Data Processing Controls Questionnaire

Application: _____ Completed by: _____ Date: _____

Item	Yes	No	N/A
Response			

Item	Yes	No	N/A
Characters?			
Fields?			
Combinations of fields?			
Transactions?			
Calculations?			
Missing data?			
Extraneous data?			
Amounts?			
Units?			
Composition?			
Logic decisions?			
Limit or reasonableness checks?			
Signs?			
Record matches?			
Record mismatches?			
Sequence?			
Balancing of quantitative data?			
Cross-footing of quantitative data?			
Comments: _____			
29. Is relationship editing performed between input transactions and master files to check for appropriateness and correctness before updating? *Comments:* _____			
30. Are special routines used that automatically validate and edit input transaction dates against a table of cutoff dates? *Comments:* _____			
31. Are full data validation and editing (see Questions 28 through 30) performed on all files interfacing with the application? *Comments:* _____			

Workpaper A-25. Data Processing Controls Questionnaire

Application: _____ Completed by: _____ Date:_____

	Response		
Item	**Yes**	**No**	**N/A**
32. Do programs that include a table of values have an associated control mechanism to ensure accuracy of the table values? *Comments:*_____			
33. Are all personnel prevented from overriding or bypassing data validation and editing problems? *Comments:*_____			
34. If not, Is override capability restricted to supervisory personnel only and in a limited number of acceptable circumstances? Are all system overrides automatically logged by the application so that these actions can be analyzed for appropriateness and correctness? *Comments:*_____			
35. Are record counts generated by the application used to validate the completeness of data processed by the system? *Comments:*_____			
36. Are predetermined control totals generated by the application used to validate the completeness of data processed by the system? *Comments:*_____			
37. Does a direct update to files cause the following to occur: A record is created and added to a backup file, containing a before-and-after picture of the record being altered? The transaction is recorded on the transaction history file, together with date and time of entry and the originator's identification? *Comments:*_____			
Batch: Data Processing Error Handling			
38. Do documented procedures explain how to identify, correct, and reprocess data rejected by the application?			

Workpaper A-25. Data Processing Controls Questionnaire

Application: _____ **Completed by:** _____ **Date:** _____

Item	Response		
	Yes	**No**	**N/A**
Comments: _____			
39. Do error messages provide clear, understandable corrective actions for each type of error?			
Comments: _____			
40. Are error messages produced for each transaction containing data that does not meet edit requirements?			
Comments: _____			
41. Are error messages produced for each data field that does not meet edit requirements?			
Comments: _____			
42. Is every data item that does not meet edit requirements rejected from further processing by the application?			
Comments: _____			
43. Is every data item that is rejected by the application automatically written on an automated suspense file?			
Comments: _____			
44. Does the automated suspense file also include the following:			
Codes indicating error type?			
Date and time the transaction was entered?			
Identity of the user who originated the transaction?			
Comments: _____			
45. Are record counts automatically created by suspense file processing to control these rejected transactions?			
Comments: _____			
46. Are predetermined control totals automatically created by suspense file processing to control the rejected transactions?			
Comments: _____			

APPENDICES

Workpaper A-25. Data Processing Controls Questionnaire

Application: _____ Completed by: _____ Date:_____

Item	Response		
	Yes	No	N/A
47. Are transactions rejections transmitted to the users originating them so that corrective action can be taken? *Comments:*_____			
48. Does the user department control group independently control data rejected by the application system with the following: Turnaround transmittal documents? Batching techniques? Record counts? Predetermined control totals? Logging techniques? Other? (specify) _____ *Comments:*_____			
49. Is the automated suspense file used to control follow-up, correction, and reentry of transactions rejected by the application? *Comments:*_____			
50. Is the automated suspense file used to produce an analysis of the following for management review: Level of transaction errors? Status of uncorrected transactions? *Comments:*_____			
51. Are these analyses used by management to ensure that corrective action is taken when error levels become too high? *Comments:*_____			
52. Are these analyses used by management to ensure that corrective action is taken when uncorrected transactions remain on the suspense file too long? *Comments:*_____			
53. Are reports made to progressively higher levels of management if these conditions worsen?			

Workpaper A-25. Data Processing Controls Questionnaire

Application: _____ **Completed by:** _____ **Date:** _____

	Response		
Item	**Yes**	**No**	**N/A**
Comments: _____ _____			
54. Are debit- and credit-type entries used instead of delete- or erase-type commands to correct rejected transactions on the automated suspense file? *Comments:* _____ _____			
55. Is the application designed to reject delete- or erase-type commands? *Comments:* _____ _____			
56. Do valid correction transactions purge the automated suspense file of corresponding rejected transactions? *Comments:* _____ _____			
57. Are invalid correction transactions added to the automated suspense file along with the corresponding rejected transactions? *Comments:* _____ _____			
58. Are record counts appropriately adjusted by correction transactions? *Comments:* _____ _____			
59. Are predetermined control totals appropriately adjusted by correction transactions? *Comments:* _____ _____			
60. Are all corrections subject to supervisory review and approval before reentry? *Comments:* _____ _____			
61. Does ultimate responsibility for the completeness and accuracy of all application processing remain with the user? *Comments:* _____ _____			

APPENDICES

Workpaper A-25. Data Processing Controls Questionnaire

Application: _____ Completed by: _____ Date: _____

Item	Response		
	Yes	No	N/A
Real-Time: Data Processing Integrity			
1. Do documented procedures explain the methods for proper data processing of every application program? *Comments:* _____			
2. Are duties separated to ensure that no individual performs more than one of the following operations: Data origination? Data input? Data processing? Output distribution? *Comments:* _____			
3. Is there a logging-type facility (audit trail) in the application to assist in reconstructing data files? *Comments:* _____			
4. Can messages and data be traced back to the user or point of origin? *Comments:* _____			
5. Does the application protect against concurrent file updates (i.e., does initial access of a record lock out that record so that additional access attempts cannot be made until the initial processing has been completed)? *Comments:* _____			
6. Are transactions date- and time-stamped for logging purposes? *Comments:* _____			
7. Are application programs prevented from accepting data from computer consoles? *Comments:* _____			
8. Is a history log output on a line printer as well as displayed on a console?			

Workpaper A-25. Data Processing Controls Questionnaire

Application: _____ **Completed by:** _____ **Date:** _____

Item	Response		
	Yes	**No**	**N/A**
Comments: _____			
_____			
9. Does this log include the following:			
Hardware failure messages?			
Software failure messages?			
Processing halts?			
Abnormal terminations of jobs?			
Operator interventions?			
Error messages?			
Unusual occurrences?			
Terminal failure messages?			
Terminal startup?			
Terminal shutdown?			
All input communications messages?			
All output communications messages?			
Comments: _____			
_____			
10. Is the log routinely reviewed by supervisors to determine the causes of problems and the correctness of actions taken?			
Comments: _____			
_____			
11. Does the DP department have a control group that is responsible for controlling all data processing operations?			
Comments: _____			
_____			
12. Does this control group independently control data processing by doing the following:			
Monitoring terminal activity?			
Investigating and correcting any terminal problems that cannot be resolved at the sources?			
Investigating and correcting terminal imbalances or failures?			
Investigating operator interventions?			
Investigating operator deviations from rules?			
Ensuring that restarts are performed properly?			

Workpaper A-25. Data Processing Controls Questionnaire

Application: _____ **Completed by:** _____ **Date:** _____

Item	Response		
	Yes	**No**	**N/A**
Balancing batch counts of processed data (developed during offline operations)?			
Balancing record counts of processed data (developed during offline operations)?			
Balancing predetermined control totals of data processed (developed during offline operations)?			
Other? (specify) _____			
Comments: _____			
13. Are periodic balances made at short intervals to ensure that data is being processed accurately?			
Comments: _____			
14. Is offline file balancing performed on the following:			
Batch counts?			
Record counts?			
Predetermined control totals?			
Other? (specify) _____			
Comments: _____			
15. Is there a means of verifying master file contents (e.g., samples are periodically drawn from data files and reviewed for accuracy)?			
Comments: _____			
16. Does each input transaction have a unique identifier (transaction code) directing it to the proper application program for processing?			
Comments: _____			
17. Do programs positively identify input data as to type?			
Comments: _____			
18. Are standardized default options built into computer program logic?			
Comments: _____			

Workpaper A-25. Data Processing Controls Questionnaire

Application: _____ Completed by: _____ Date: _____

	Response		
Item	**Yes**	**No**	**N/A**
19. Are computer-generated control totals (run-to-run totals) automatically reconciled between jobs to check for completeness of processing? *Comments:* _____ _____			
20. Where computerized data is entered into the computer, do controls verify that the proper data is used? *Comments:* _____ _____			
21. Where computerized files are entered into the computer, do controls verify that the proper version (cycle) of the file is used? *Comments:* _____ _____			
22. Do all programs include routines for checking internal file header labels before processing? *Comments:* _____ _____			
23. Are there controls to prevent operators from circumventing file checking routines? *Comments:* _____ _____			
24. Are internal trailer labels containing control totals (e.g., record counts, predetermined control totals) generated for all computer files and tested by the application programs to determine that all records have been processed? *Comments:* _____ _____			
25. Are file completion checks performed to make sure that application files have been completely processed, including both transaction and master files? *Comments:* _____ _____			
26. Do data processing controls ensure that: Output counts from the system equal input counts to the system? Program interfaces require that the sending program output counts equal the receiving program input counts?			

APPENDICES

Workpaper A-25. Data Processing Controls Questionnaire

Application: _____ Completed by: _____ Date:_____

Item	Yes	No	N/A
System interfaces require:			
•The sending system's output counts equal the receiving system's input counts?			
•Shared files meet the control requirements of both the sending and receiving system?			
*Comments:*_____			
Real-Time: Data Processing Validation and Editing			
27. Are data validation and editing performed as early as possible in the data flow to ensure that the application rejects any incorrect transaction before master-file updating?			
*Comments:*_____			
28. Are data validation and editing performed for all data fields even when an error is detected in an earlier field of the same transaction?			
*Comments:*_____			
29. Are the following checked for validity on all input transactions:			
Individual and supervisor authorization or approval codes?			
Check digits on all identification keys?			
Check digits at the end of a string of numeric data that is not subject to balancing?			
Codes?			
Characters?			
Fields?			
Combinations of fields?			
Transactions?			
Calculations?			
Missing data?			
Extraneous data?			
Amounts?			
Units?			

Workpaper A-25. Data Processing Controls Questionnaire

Application: _____ Completed by: _____ Date: _____

Item	Yes	No	N/A
Composition?			
Logic decisions?			
Limit or reasonableness checks?			
Signs?			
Record matches?			
Record mismatches?			
Sequence?			
Balancing of quantitative data?			
Crossfooting of quantitative data?			
Comments: _____			
30. Is relationship editing performed between input transactions and master files to check for appropriateness and correctness prior to updating? *Comments:* _____			
31. Are special routines used that automatically validate and edit input transaction dates against a table of cutoff dates? *Comments:* _____			
32. Are full data validation and editing (see Questions 29 through 31) performed on all files interfacing with the application? *Comments:* _____			
33. Do the programs that include a table of values have a control mechanism to ensure accuracy of the table values? *Comments:* _____			
34. Are all personnel prevented from overriding or bypassing data validation and editing problems? *Comments:* _____			
35. If not, Is override capability restricted to supervisors only and in a limited number of acceptable circumstances?			

APPENDICES

Workpaper A-25. Data Processing Controls Questionnaire

Application: _____ **Completed by:** _____ **Date:** _____

Item	Response		
	Yes	No	N/A
Are all system overrides automatically logged by the application so that these actions can be analyzed for appropriateness and correctness? Comments: _____			
36. Are record counts generated by the terminal, concentrator, or application used to validate the completeness of data input? Comments: _____			
37. Are predetermined control totals generated by the application used to validate the completeness of data processed by the system? Comments: _____			
38. Does a direct update to files cause the following to occur: A record is created and added to a backup file, containing a before-and-after picture of the record being altered? The transaction is recorded on the transaction history file together with the date and time of the entry and the originator's identification? Comments: _____			
Real-Time: Data Processing Error Handling			
39. Do documented procedures explain how to identify, correct, and reprocess data rejected by the application? Comments: _____			
40. Do error messages display clear, understandable, corrective actions for each type of error? Comments: _____			
41. Are error messages produced for each transaction containing data that does not meet edit requirements? Comments: _____			

Workpaper A-25. Data Processing Controls Questionnaire

Application: _____ Completed by: _____ Date: _____

Item	Response		
	Yes	No	N/A
42. Are error messages produced for each data field that does not meet edit requirements? *Comments:* _____ _____			
43. Is every data item that does not meet edit requirements rejected from further processing by the application? *Comments:* _____ _____			
44. Is every data item that is rejected by the application automatically written on an automated suspense file? *Comments:* _____ _____			
45. Does the automated suspense file include the following: Codes indicating error type? Date and time the transaction was entered? Identity of the user who originated the transaction? *Comments:* _____ _____			
46. Are record counts automatically created by suspense file processing to control these rejected transactions? *Comments:* _____ _____			
47. Are predetermined control totals automatically created by suspense file processing to control these rejected transactions? *Comments:* _____ _____			
48. Are transaction rejections transmitted to the users originating them so that corrective action can be taken? *Comments:* _____ _____			
49. Does the user department control group independently control data rejected by the application system, using the following: Turnaround transmittal documents? Batching techniques? Record counts?			

Workpaper A-25. Data Processing Controls Questionnaire

Application: _____ Completed by: _____ Date:_____

	Response		
Item	Yes	No	N/A
Predetermined control totals?			
Logging techniques?			
Other? (specify) _____			
*Comments:*_____			
50. Is the automated suspense file used to control follow-up, correction, and reentry of transactions rejected by the application?			
*Comments:*_____			
51. Is the automated suspense file used to produce analysis of the following for management review:			
Level of transaction errors?			
Status of uncorrected transactions?			
*Comments:*_____			
52. Are these analyses used by management to ensure that corrective action is taken when error levels become too high?			
*Comments:*_____			
53. Are these analyses used by management to ensure that correction action is taken when uncorrected transactions remain on the suspense file too long?			
*Comments:*_____			
54. Are reports made to progressively higher levels of management if these conditions worsen?			
*Comments:*_____			
55. Are debit- and credit-type entries used instead of delete- or erase-type commands to correct rejected transactions on the automated suspense file?			
*Comments:*_____			
56. Is the application designed to reject delete- or erase-type commands?			

Workpaper A-25. Data Processing Controls Questionnaire

Application: _____ **Completed by:** _____ **Date:** _____

Item	Response		
	Yes	**No**	**N/A**
Comments: _____			
57. Do valid correction transactions purge the automated suspense file of corresponding rejected transactions? *Comments:* _____			
58. Are invalid correction transactions added to the automated suspense file along with the corresponding rejected transactions? *Comments:* _____			
59. Are record counts appropriately adjusted by correction transactions? *Comments:* _____			
60. Are predetermined control totals appropriately adjusted by correction transactions? *Comments:* _____			
61. Are all corrections subject to supervisory review and approval before reentry? *Comments:* _____			
62. Are the procedures for processing corrected transactions the same as those for processing original transactions, with the addition of supervisory review and approval before reentry? *Comments:* _____			
63. Does ultimate responsibility for the completeness and accuracy of all application processing remain with the user? *Comments:* _____			

WORKPAPER A-26. DATA OUTPUT CONTROLS QUESTIONNAIRE

Data output controls are used to ensure the integrity of output and the correct and timely distribution of output produced. Not only must output be accurate, but it must also be received by users in a timely and consistent manner. Output production can be either batch or online. The interface between the data processing department and the user department is of critical importance. The auditor should evaluate the adequacy of controls over output to ensure that data processing results are reliable, output control totals are accurate, and reports are distributed in a timely manner to users.

Workpaper A-26. Data Output Controls Questionnaire

Application: _____ Completed by: _____ _____ Date: _____

Item	Response		
	Yes	No	N/A
Batch: Output Balancing and Reconciliation			
1. Do documented procedures explain the methods for the proper balancing and reconciliation of output products? Comments: _____			
2. Does the data processing department have a control group responsible for reviewing all output produced by the application? Comments: _____			
3. Does this control group monitor the processing flow to ensure that application programs are being processed according to schedule? Comments: _____			
4. Does the control group review output products for general acceptability and completeness? Comments: _____			
5. Does the control group reconcile output batch totals with input batch totals before the release of any reports, to ensure that no data was added or lost during processing? Comments: _____			
6. Does the control group reconcile output record counts with input record counts before the release of any reports, to ensure that no data was added or lost during processing?			

Workpaper A-26. Data Output Controls Questionnaire

Application:_____ Completed by: _____ Date:_____

	Response		
Item	**Yes**	**No**	**N/A**
Comments: _____			
7. Does the control group reconcile predetermined output control totals with predetermined input control totals before the release of any reports, to ensure that no data was added or lost during processing? *Comments:* _____			
8. Does the control group keep a log that summarizes the following: Number of application reports generated? Number of pages per report? Number of lines per report? Number of copies of each report? Recipient(s) of each report? *Comments:* _____			
9. Are system output logs kept to provide an output audit trail? *Comments:* _____			
10. Are output logs reviewed by supervisors to determine the correctness of output production? *Comments:* _____			
11. Is a transaction log kept by the application to provide a transaction audit trail? *Comments:* _____			
12. Is a transaction log kept at each output device to provide a transaction audit trail? *Comments:* _____			
13. Is the transaction log kept by the application compared regularly with the transaction log at each output device to ensure that all transactions have been properly processed to the final output steps?			

APPENDICES

Workpaper A-26. Data Output Controls Questionnaire

Application: _____ Completed by: _____ Date: _____

Item	Yes	No	N/A
*Comments:*_____			
14. Can transactions be traced forward to the final output? *Comments:*_____			
15. Can transactions be traced backward to the original source documents? *Comments:*_____			
16. On each output product, does the application identify the following: Title or name of product? Processing program name or number? Date and time prepared? Processing period covered? User name and location? Counts developed during processing? End-of-job/file/report indication? Security classification, if any? *Comments:*_____			
17. Does the user department have a control group responsible for reviewing all output received from the data processing department? *Comments:*_____			
18. Is this control group given lists of all changes to the application master file data or programmed data? *Comments:*_____			
19. Is the control group given lists of all internally generated transactions produced by the application? *Comments:*_____			
20. Is the control group given lists of all interface transactions processed by the application?			

Workpaper A-26. Data Output Controls Questionnaire

Application:_____ Completed by: _____ Date:_____

Item	Yes	No	N/A
Comments: _____ _____			
21. Is the control group given a list of all transactions entered into the application? *Comments:* _____			
22. Are all listings (see Questions 18 through 21) reviewed by the control group to ensure completeness of data processed by the application? *Comments:* _____			
23. Is the control group furnished with reports produced by the application that show the following: Batch totals? Record counts? Predetermined control totals? *Comments:* _____			
24. Does the control group verify all computer-generated batch totals with its manually developed batch counts? *Comments:* _____			
25. Does the control group verify all computer-generated record counts with its manually developed record counts? *Comments:* _____			
26. Does the control group verify all computer-generated predetermined control totals with its manually developed predetermined control totals? *Comments:* _____			
27. Does the control group verify the accuracy and completeness of all output? *Comments:* _____			
28. Does the user department retain ultimate responsibility for the accuracy of all output?			

APPENDICES

Workpaper A-26. Data Output Controls Questionnaire

Application: _____ **Completed by:** _____ **Date:** _____

Item	Yes	No	N/A
Response			
Comments: _____ _____			
Batch: Output Distribution			
29. Do documented procedures explain the methods for proper handling and distribution of output products? *Comments:* _____			
30. Are duties separated to ensure that no individual performs more than one of the following operations: Data origination? Data input? Data processing? Output distribution? *Comments:* _____			
31. Are users questioned periodically to determine their continued need for the product and the number of copies received? *Comments:* _____			
32. Does the cover sheet of every report clearly identify the recipient's name and location? *Comments:* _____			
33. Does the DP department have a control group responsible for distributing all output produced by the computer application? *Comments:* _____			
34. Does the DP control group have a schedule, by application, that shows when output processing will be completed and when output products must be distributed? *Comments:* _____			
35. Has a priority system been established so that critical output can be produced by the system?			

Workpaper A-26. Data Output Controls Questionnaire

Application:_____ **Completed by:** _____ **Date:**_____

Item	Response		
	Yes	**No**	**N/A**
Comments: _____ _____			
36. Does the DP control group keep a log, by application, of all output produced by the system? *Comments:* _____ _____			
37. Does this log identify the following for each output product: Job name? Time and date of production? Product name? Time and date of distribution? Name(s) of recipient(s)? Quantity distributed to each recipient Security status, if any? *Comments:* _____ _____			
38. Is each entry in the DP department control group's log signed by supervisors to indicate that the reports were in fact produced and transmitted to recipients? *Comments:* _____ _____			
39. Does this log include notes on problems that arose with processing (e.g., reruns, data checks)? *Comments:* _____ _____			
40. Does the DP department control group maintain a formalized output distribution checklist to show the disposition of each output product? *Comments:* _____ _____			
41. Are turnaround transmittal documents used to verify that the output product has been received by the authorized recipient? *Comments:* _____ _____			

Workpaper A-26. Data Output Controls Questionnaire

Application: _____ Completed by: _____ Date: _____

Item	Response		
	Yes	No	N/A
42. Is the output distribution checklist used to verify the acknowledgment of all turnaround transmittal documents from recipients of output? *Comments:*_____			
43. Does the DP department control group verify that only authorized numbers of copies of outputs are produced? *Comments:*_____			
Batch: Output Error Handling			
44. Do documented procedures explain the DP department's methods for reporting, correcting, and reprocessing output products with errors? *Comments:*_____			
45. Is the user department control group notified immediately by the DP control group of problems in output products? *Comments:*_____			
46. Does the DP control group keep a control log of output product errors? *Comments:*_____			
47. Is this log used to perform the following: Identify the problem? Note corrective action taken? Record date and time of resubmission? Record date and time of transmission to users? *Comments:*_____			
48. Do supervisors use this log to ensure that timely resubmissions of jobs are accomplished and that corrected reports are expeditiously transmitted to the users? *Comments:*_____			

Workpaper A-26. Data Output Controls Questionnaire

Application:_____ Completed by: _____ Date:_____

Item	Response		
	Yes	No	N/A
49. Does the DP control group develop an independent history file of output products with errors? *Comments:* _____ _____			
50. Is this file reviewed periodically by supervisors to identify causes of and trends in output product errors? *Comments:* _____ _____			
51. Are users apprised of progress being made to correct problems that cause output product errors? *Comments:* _____ _____			
52. Is the output from rerun jobs subjected to the same quality review as were the original erroneous output products? *Comments:* _____ _____			
53. Do documented procedures explain user department methods for reporting and control of output product errors? *Comments:* _____ _____			
54. Is the user notified immediately by the user department control group of problems in output products? *Comments:* _____ _____			
55. Does the user department control group keep a control log of output product errors? *Comments:* _____ _____			
56. Is this log used to perform the following: Identify the problem? Identify DP personnel contacted? Record date and time of contact? Record corrective action taken by DP department? Record date and time of receipt of corrected output product? Identify causes and trends of output product errors?			

APPENDICES

Workpaper A-26. Data Output Controls Questionnaire

Application: _____ Completed by: _____ Date:_____

Item	Response		
	Yes	No	N/A
Ensure the timely correction of output product errors?			
Comments: _____			
_____			
Batch: Handling and Retention of Output Records and Accountable Documents			
57. Have record and document retention periods been established?			
Comments: _____			
_____			
58. Are the periods reasonable for backup and audit purposes?			
Comments: _____			
_____			
59. Are appropriate methods (e.g., degaussing, shredding) used to dispose of unneeded records and documents?			
Comments: _____			
_____			
60. Is access to records and documents restricted to authorized individuals?			
Comments: _____			
_____			
61. Are periodic reviews made to determine whether output products are still needed by the user?			
Comments: _____			
_____			
62. Is the dual-custody technique used to control accountable documents (e.g., check, bond, identification card stock) during the following periods:			
In storage?			
In transit?			
Waiting to be used by the application?			
Being used by the application?			
Waiting for distribution?			
Waiting for destruction?			
Waiting for transit back to storage?			

Workpaper A-26. Data Output Controls Questionnaire

Application:_____ **Completed by:** _____ **Date:**_____

Item	Yes	No	N/A
	Response		

Comments: _____
_____

63. Is access to accountable documents restricted to authorized personnel?

Comments: _____
_____

Online: Output Balancing and Reconciliation

1. Do documented procedures explain the methods for the proper balancing and reconciliation of output products?

Comments: _____
_____

2. Does the DP department have a control group responsible for ensuring that output products are accurately processed and correctly transmitted?

Comments: _____
_____

3. Does this control group have a schedule, by application, that shows when pre-output processing ends and output processing begins?

Comments: _____
_____

4. Does the control group monitor the processing flow to ensure that application programs are being processed according to schedule?

Comments: _____
_____

5. Does the control group reconcile output batch totals with input batch totals before the transmission of output, to ensure that no data was added or lost during processing?

Comments: _____
_____

6. Does the control group reconcile output record counts with input record counts before the transmission of output, to ensure that no data was added or lost during processing?

Comments: _____
_____

Workpaper A-26. Data Output Controls Questionnaire

Application: _____ **Completed by:** _____ **Date:**_____

	Response		
Item	**Yes**	**No**	**N/A**
7. Does the control group reconcile predetermined output control totals with predetermined input control totals before the transmission of output, to ensure that no data was added or lost during processing? *Comments:* _____ _____			
8. Is a log kept by the application to provide an audit trail for transactions being processed? *Comments:* _____ _____			
9. Is a log kept at each output transmission device to provide an audit trail for output transmitted to user terminal devices? *Comments:* _____ _____			
10. Is the transaction log kept by the application compared regularly with the transmission log kept at each output transmission device to ensure that all output has been properly transmitted to the final users? *Comments:* _____ _____			
11. On each output product, does the application system identify the following: Title or name of product? Processing program name or number? Date and time prepared? Processing period covered? User name and location? Counts developed during processing? End-of-job/file/report indication? Security classification, if any? *Comments:* _____ _____			
12. Do terminal devices automatically disconnect from the computer-based system if they are unused for a certain amount of time? *Comments:* _____ _____			

Workpaper A-26. Data Output Controls Questionnaire

Application:_____ **Completed by:** _____ **Date:**_____

		Response		
	Item	**Yes**	**No**	**N/A**
13.	Do terminal devices need to be logged off at the end of the day so that they will be disconnected from the computer-based system? *Comments:* _____ _____			
14.	Are output devices located in secure facilities at all times to prevent unauthorized access? *Comments:* _____ _____			
15.	Do terminal devices need to be logged off at the end of the day so that they will be disconnected from the computer-based system? *Comments:* _____ _____			
16.	Is all output waiting for transmission entered on a backup log before being put into the transmission queue? *Comments:* _____ _____			
17.	As output products are transmitted and received, does the output device send a reply that they have been correctly received? *Comments:* _____ _____			
18.	Is the backup log purged when the reply has been received? *Comments:* _____ _____			
19.	Does the computer-based system automatically check an output message before displaying, writing, or printing it to ensure that it has not reached the wrong device? *Comments:* _____ _____			
20.	Is message content validated before it is displayed, written, or printed on the output device? *Comments:* _____ _____			
21.	Can transactions be traced forward to the final output products? *Comments:* _____ _____			
22.	Can transactions be traced backward to the original source documents?			

Workpaper A-26. Data Output Controls Questionnaire

Application: _____ Completed by: _____ Date: _____

	Response		
Item	**Yes**	**No**	**N/A**
Comments: _____ _____			
23. Are all activities of the day summarized and printed for each terminal device? *Comments:* _____ _____			
24. Are these activity reports used to provide an audit trail for the output products? *Comments:* _____ _____			
25. Are these reports reviewed by supervisors to determine the correctness of output production? *Comments:* _____ _____			
26. Does the user department have a control group responsible for reviewing all output produced by the computer application? *Comments:* _____ _____			
27. Does this control group reconcile output batch totals with input batch totals before the release of any reports, to ensure that no data was added or lost during processing? *Comments:* _____ _____			
28. Does the control group reconcile output record counts with input record counts before the release of any reports, to ensure that no data was added or lost during processing? *Comments:* _____ _____			
29. Does the control group reconcile output predetermined control totals with input predetermined control totals before the release of any reports, to ensure that no data was added or lost during processing? *Comments:* _____ _____			
30. Is this control group given lists of all changes to application system master-file or programmed data?			

Workpaper A-26. Data Output Controls Questionnaire

Application:_____ Completed by: _____ Date:_____

Item	Yes	No	N/A
Comments: _____			
31. Is the control group given lists of all internally generated transactions produced by the application? *Comments:* _____			
32. Is the control group given lists of all interface transactions processed by the application? *Comments:* _____			
33. Is the control group given a list of all transactions entered into the system? *Comments:* _____			
34. Are all listings (see Questions 31 through 33) reviewed by the user department control group to ensure completeness of data processed by the system? *Comments:* _____			
35. Does the control group verify the accuracy and completeness of all output? *Comments:* _____			
36. Is the user department ultimately responsible for the accuracy of all output? *Comments:* _____			
Online: Output Distribution			
37. Do documented procedures exist that explain the methods for proper handling and distribution of output products? *Comments:* _____			
38. Are duties separated to ensure that no individual performs more than one of the following operations: Data origination?			

Workpaper A-26. Data Output Controls Questionnaire

Application: _____ Completed by: _____ Date: _____

Item	Response		
	Yes	No	N/A
Data input?			
Data processing?			
Output distribution?			
Comments: _____ _____			
39. Are users questioned periodically to determine their continued need for the product and the number of copies received? Comments: _____ _____			
40. Does the user department have a control group responsible for distributing all output products produced by the application? Comments: _____ _____			
41. Does this control group have a schedule, by application, that shows when output processing will be completed and when output products must be distributed? Comments: _____ _____			
42. Does the control group monitor system output to ensure that application programs are being processed according to schedule? Comments: _____ _____			
43. Does the control group maintain a formalized output distribution checklist to show the disposition of each output product? Comments: _____ _____			
44. Are turnaround transmittal documents used by the DP department control group to verify that the output product has been received by the authorized recipient? Comments: _____ _____			
45. Is the distribution checklist used to verify the acknowledgment of all turnaround transmittal documents from output recipients? Comments: _____ _____			

Workpaper A-26. Data Output Controls Questionnaire

Application:_____ Completed by: _____ Date:_____

Item	Yes	No	N/A
Online: Data Output Error Handling			
46. Do documented procedures explain the methods for user department reporting and control of output errors? *Comments:* _____			
47. Is the user notified immediately by the user department control group of output problems? *Comments:* _____			
48. Does the user department control group keep a control log of output product errors? *Comments:* _____			
49. Is this log used to perform the following: Identify the problem? Note DP personnel contacted? Record date and time of contact? Record corrective action taken by DP department? Record date and time of receipt of corrected output product? Identify causes and trends of output product errors? Ensure timely error corrections of the output product? *Comments:* _____			
50. Are the output products from rerun jobs subject to the same quality review as were the original erroneous products? *Comments:* _____			
Online: Handling and Retention of Output Records and Accountable Documents			
51. Have record and document retention periods been established? *Comments:* _____			
52. Are the periods reasonable for backup and audit purposes?			

APPENDICES

Workpaper A-26. Data Output Controls Questionnaire

Application: _____ Completed by: _____ Date: _____

Item	Response		
	Yes	No	N/A
Comments: _____ _____			
53. Are appropriate methods (e.g., degaussing, shredding) used to dispose of unneeded records and documents? Comments: _____ _____			
54. Is access to records and documents restricted to authorized individuals? Comments: _____ _____			
55. Are periodic reviews made to determine whether output products are still needed by the user? Comments: _____ _____			
56. Is the dual-custody technique used to control accountable documents (e.g., check, bond, identification card stock) during the following periods: In storage? In transit? Waiting to be used by the application? Being used by the application? Waiting for distribution? Waiting for destruction? Waiting for transit back to storage? Comments: _____ _____			
57. Is access to accountable documents restricted to authorized personnel? Comments: _____ _____			

Workpaper A-27. Data Flow Control Diagram

Application System _____

	Flow of Responsibility ⟶
Flow of Data ↓	
Prepared by:	**Date:**

Workpaper A-28. Transaction Flow Control Diagram

Application _____ Prepared by: _____ Date: _____

Control Point / Transaction	Data Origination	Data Input		Process			Storage	Process		Use
		Batch	Online	Batch	Real-Time			Batch	Online	

Workpaper A-29. Responsibility Vulnerability Worksheet

Application System _____

No.	Vulnerability	Individual	Possible Performance	
			Action	**Concealment**
Comments: _____				
_____				
Comments: _____				
_____				
Comments: _____				
_____				
Comments: _____				
_____				
Comments: _____				
_____				
Comments: _____				
_____				
Comments: _____				
_____				
Comments: _____				
_____				
Comments: _____				
_____				
Comments: _____				
_____				
Prepared by:			**Date:**	

Workpaper A-30. Transaction Vulnerability Worksheet (page 1 of 4)

Application _____ Prepared by: _____ Date: _____

Control Point / Business Transaction	Data Origination Controls				
	Source-Document Origination	Source-Document Authorization	Source-Document Data Correction and Input Preparation	Source-Document Error Handling	Source-Document Retention

Workpaper A-30. Transaction Vulnerability Worksheet (page 2 of 4)

Application _____ Prepared by: _____ Date: _____

	Data Input Controls					
Control Point / Business Transaction	Batch: Data Conversion and Entry	Batch: Data Validation and Editing	Batch: Data Input Error Handling	Online: Data Error Handling	Online: Data Validation and Editing	Online: Data Input Error Editing

Workpaper A-30. Transaction Vulnerability Worksheet (page 3 of 4)

Application _____ Prepared by: _____ Date: _____

Control Point / Business Transaction	Data Processing Controls					
	Batch: Data Processing Integrity	Batch: Data Processing Validation and Editing	Batch: Data Processing Error Handling	Real-Time: Data Processing Integrity	Real-Time: Data Processing Validation and Editing	Real-Time: Data Processing Error Handling

Workpaper A-30. Transaction Vulnerability Worksheet (page 4 of 4)

Application _____ Prepared by: _____ Date: _____

Data Origination Controls

Control Point / Business Transaction	Batch: Output Balancing and Reconciliation	Batch: Output Distribution	Batch: Output Error Handling	Batch: Handling and Retention of Output Records and Accountable Documents	Online: Output Balancing and Reconciliation	Online: Output Distribution	Online: Output Error Handling	Online: Handling and Retention of Output Records and Accountable Documents

Workpaper A-31. Application Control Test Plan

Application _____   Prepared by: _____   Date: _____

No.	Control to Test	Control Type		Test Type		Auditor Responsible	Dates	
		Automated	Manual	Static	Dynamic		Start	Stop
	Comments:							
	Comments:							
	Comments:							
	Comments:							
	Comments:							
	Comments:							
	Comments:							

Workpaper A-31. Application Control Test Plan

Application _____ Prepared by: _____ Date: _____

| No. | Control to Test | Control Type | | Test Type | | Auditor Responsible | Dates | |
		Automated	Manual	Static	Dynamic		Start	Stop

Comments: _____

Workpaper A-33. Testing Controls (page 1 of 2)

Manual Controls

No.	Program Item	Assigned to	Completion Date
	Dynamic Test		
1.	Select evidence needed to verify functioning of control.		
	*Comments:*_____ _____		
2.	Request needed evidence from auditee responsible for control.		
	*Comments:*_____ _____		
3.	Evaluate functioning of control by examining the selected evidence.		
	*Comments:*_____ _____		
	Static Test		
1.	Identify procedure to be followed to exercise the desired control.		
	*Comments:*_____ _____		
2.	Create one or two test conditions typical of regular transactions.		
	*Comments:*_____ _____		
3.	Walk through the procedure to ensure that following the process accomplishes the desired result.		
	*Comments:*_____ _____		

Workpaper A-33. Testing Controls (page 2 of 2)

Automatic Controls

No.	Program Item	Assigned to	Completion Date
	Dynamic Test		
1.	Obtain computer record formats. *Comments:* _____ _____		
2.	Create batch or online test transaction. *Comments:* _____ _____		
3.	Determine from DP project personnel best method to run test condition. *Comments:* _____ _____		
4.	Arrange for test time. *Comments:* _____ _____		
5.	Execute computer test and obtain results. *Comments:* _____ _____		
	Static Test		
1.	Obtain computer programs in which the control resides. *Comments:* _____ _____		
2.	Create same type of test situations that would be used for dynamic testing. *Comments:* _____ _____		
3.	Walk through computer instructions to determine whether they achieve the desired result. *Comments:* _____ _____		

Workpaper A-34. Evaluation of Tested Controls

Application _____ Prepared by: _____ Date: _____

No.	Control to Test	Expected Result	Actual Result	Assessment			Recommended Action
				Fully Adequate	Adequate	Less than Adequate	

Workpaper A-35. Computer File Survey (page 1 of 3)

A. Name of File _____

B. Organizational Structure _____

C. Record Formats

   Name _____   Number _____

   _____   _____

   _____   _____

   _____   _____

   _____   _____

D. Size of File

   Number of Records _____

   Space Allocation _____

E. Distribution of File

	Stratum	Number of Records	Amount
1.			
2.			
3.			
4.			
5.			
6.			
7.			
8.			
9.			
10.			

F. Statistical Analysis

   Largest Value _____

   Mean Value _____

   Median Value _____

   Mode Value _____

   Smallest Value_____

APPENDICES

Workpaper A-35. Computer File Survey (page 2 of 3)

Statistical Analysis (cont'd)

Skewness _____

_____

_____

Clusters of Records _____

_____

_____

G. Dollar-Value Analysis

Dollars controlled by file _____

Positive dollar values _____

Negative dollar values _____

Zero dollar values _____

Number of negative value records _____

H. Suspense Items

Suspense account number(s) or name(s)

1. _____

2. _____

3. _____

4. _____

5. _____

6. _____

Values in Suspense Accounts

Age of Items:

Newest _____

Average _____

Oldest _____

I. Age of Transactions on File

Newest _____

Average _____

Oldest _____

Workpaper A-35. Computer File Survey (page 3 of 3)

J.   Unusual Condition(s) to Look for

Condition Examined	**Result**
1. _____	_____
2. _____	_____
3. _____	_____
4. _____	_____
5. _____	_____
6. _____	_____
7. _____	_____
8. _____	_____
9. _____	_____
10. _____	_____

K.   Dump Analysis

Condition Examined	**Result**
1. Codes not documented	_____
2. Data in blank fields	_____
3. Fields in incorrect location	_____
4. Values not in required fields	_____
5. Special codes in numeric fields	_____
6. Special codes in alphabetic fields	_____
7. _____	_____
8. _____	_____
9. _____	_____
10. _____	_____
11. _____	_____
12. _____	_____
13. _____	_____
14. _____	_____
15. _____	_____

Prepared by: _____   **Date:** _____

APPENDICES

Workpaper A-36. Manual File Survey

A. Name of File _____

B. Location of File _____

C. Contents of File _____

     1. _____

     2. _____

     3. _____

     4. _____

     5. _____

D. Sequence of File _____

E. Number of Records in File _____

F. Individual Responsible for File _____

G. Unusual Conditions to Look for _____

     1. _____

     2. _____

     3. _____

     4. _____

     5. _____

     6. _____

Prepared by: _____   **Date:** _____

Workpaper A-37. Data Audit Objective Test

Audit Objective						

No.	Test Condition	Audit Evidence Needed	Test Approach	Auditor Responsible	Dates	
					Start	Complete

Prepared by:				Date:		

Workpaper A-38. Test Tool Worksheet (page 1 of 3)

Test Condition		No.

Audit Evidence

File No.	File Name	Record No.	Record Name

Input Fields to Examine

File No.	File Name	Field Name

Workpaper A-38. Test Tool Worksheet (page 2 of 3)

Field Processing

Field No.	Field Name	Record Name

Output Report No. 1

Field No.	Field Name	Field Format	Totalling Information

Workpaper A-38. Test Tool Worksheet (page 3 of 3)

Output Report No. 2			
Field No.	Field Name	Field Format	Totalling Information

Processing Comments

Prepared by:	Date:

Workpaper A-39. File Integrity Program

File Name _____ **File No.** _____

No.	Program Item
1.	Select evidence method for proving filing integrity.
2.	Acquire copy of file.
3.	Obtain independent balance for reconciliation purposes.
4.	Develop/obtain method for obtaining file integrity count/balance.
5.	Prove method works.
6.	Run file integrity test independently.
7.	Verify integrity and/or investigate differences.

Prepared by:	Date:

Workpaper A-40. File Integrity Proof Sheet

File Name	File No.
Key Field Proof	
Key Field Name	
Key Field Total	
Verified to	
Verification Method	
Completeness Proof	
Item for Count	
Total Count	
Verified to	
Verification Method	
Simple Accounting Proof	
Previously Verified Total $	
Additions to File +	
Deletions from File −	
New Total = $	
Verification Method	
Prepared by:	**Date:**

Workpaper A-41. Structural Test Program

Test Program _____ Program No. _____

No.	Program Item	Assigned to	Completion Date
1.	Verify that all compiler errors are corrected. *Comments:* _____ _____		
2.	Verify that the language syntax is correct. *Comments:* _____ _____		
3.	Ascertain that all program limits are identified and properly addressed by the program. *Comments:* _____ _____		
4.	Verify that the program is executable. *Comments:* _____ _____		
5.	Verify that any needed job control language (JCL) works. *Comments:* _____ _____		
6.	Verify that sufficient space has been allocated to the program/file. *Comments:* _____ _____		
Prepared by:		**Date:**	

APPENDICES

Workpaper A-42. Functional Test Program

Test Program _____ **Program No.** _____

No.	Program Item	Assigned to	Completion Date
1.	Verify that expected input produces the expected output. *Comments:*_____		
2.	Verify that improper codes, values, dates, amount, and so forth are identified and properly addressed. *Comments:*_____		
3.	Verify that any expected output file is produced. *Comments:*_____		
4.	Verify the correctness of program logic. *Comments:*_____		
5.	Ensure that all significant program paths and instructions have been exercised by the test process. *Comments:*_____		
6.	Verify the accuracy and completeness of the program documentation. *Comments:*_____		
Prepared by:		**Date:**	

Workpaper A-43. Data Test Program

Test Condition _____ Test Name _____

No.	Program Item	Assigned to	Completion Date
1.	Collect the needed evidence and test tools for the test. *Comments:* _____		
2.	Arrange for computer time if needed. *Comments:* _____		
3.	Ensure that data files have appropriate backup (or have them duplicated). *Comments:* _____		
4.	Verify the integrity of the operating environment. *Comments:* _____		
5.	Execute the test. *Comments:* _____		
6.	Obtain the computer-produced output. *Comments:* _____		
Prepared by:		**Date:**	

APPENDICES

Workpaper A-44. Data Test Checklist

Test Condition _____ Test Name_____

No.	Item	Response		
		Yes	No	N/A
1.	Have all needed input files been obtained? *Comments:* _____ _____			
2.	Has the correct version of the test program been cataloged into the program library? *Comments:* _____ _____			
3.	Do the computer operators have the operator instructions? *Comments:* _____ _____			
4.	Have the needed printer forms/paper been obtained? *Comments:* _____ _____			
5.	Has a copy of the test program been filed in the workpapers? *Comments:* _____ _____			
6.	Has the proof that the program works been filed in the workpapers? *Comments:* _____ _____			
Prepared by:		**Date:**		

Workpaper A-45. Test Results Review

No.	Program Item	Assigned to	Completion Date
1.	Verify that the proper program was used. *Comments:* _____		
2.	Verify that the proper printer paper was used. *Comments:* _____		
3.	Determine whether the output results appear reasonable. *Comments:* _____		
4.	Check to determine whether there has been any printer or other obvious hardware and/or operator failure. *Comments:* _____		
5.	Are the results what were expected? If not, investigate the reasonableness of the results. *Comments:* _____		
6.	Verify that all reports were prepared. *Comments:* _____		
7.	Verify that the data in the reports represents the entire audit period. *Comments:* _____		
8.	Verify that the reports contain all the printed pages. *Comments:* _____		
9.	Verify the report results against an independent total/count. *Comments:* _____		
Prepared by:		**Date:**	

APPENDICES

Workpaper A-46. Key Security Planning Questions

No.	Question	Response
1.	Does organizational policy, or applicable regulation require certification to be performed?	
2.	What is the application involved?	
3.	How sensitive is it?	
4.	What are its major boundaries?	
5.	What are the major anticipated problem areas?	
6.	Was security a major developmental objective?	
7.	What major technological specialties are relevant?	
8.	How much money and time are available and appropriate for the certification?	
9.	Does an application risk analysis exist to help in determining appropriate certification costs?	
10.	Who are the responsible personnel?	
11.	What are their roles?	
12.	Are there major special objectives or concerns that influence the desired quality or level of detail of the certification work?	
13.	Are there any special restrictions that might constrain the work?	
14.	Is accurate, current, and complete documentation available that describes the application and its controls?	
15.	Does prior review evidence exist?	

Workpaper A-47. Partition of Applications

No.	Partition	Security Assumptions and Concerns	Importance of Partition	Extent of Evaluation	Resource Allocation
1.	Administrative security				
2.	Computer operation				
3.	Contingency planning				
4.	Change control				
5.	Data entry and output				
6.	Operating system				
7.	Communication security				
8.	Personnel security				
9.	Physical security				
10.	Environmental controls				
11.	Development method				
12.	Application software controls				
13.	Database management system				
14.	Hardware				

APPENDICES

Workpaper A-48. Security Requirements

No.	Partition	Security Requirement for Partition Area
1.	Administrative security	
2.	Computer operation	
3.	Contingency planning	
4.	Change control	
5.	Data entry and output	
6.	Operating system	
7.	Communications security	
8.	Personnel security	
9.	Physical security	
10.	Environmental controls	
11.	Development method	
12.	Application software controls	
13.	Database management system	
14.	Hardware	

Workpaper A-49. Risk Analysis

No.	Asset Controlled by Application	Threats to Asset	Magnitude of Threat

APPENDICES

Workpaper A-50. Document Review Guide (page 1 of 5)

Purpose Code	Area/Title	Reviewed Yes	Reviewed No
	Administrative		
R	Organization charts *Comments:* _____ _____		
R	Phone book *Comments:* _____ _____		
R, C	Position descriptions *Comments:* _____ _____		
	Operational		
R, C	Application run book *Comments:* _____ _____		
R, C	Application flowchart *Comments:* _____ _____		
R	Violation reports *Comments:* _____ _____		
R, C	Audit journals *Comments:* _____ _____		
R, C	Audit or evaluation findings *Comments:* _____ _____		
R	Problem reports *Comments:* _____ _____		
R	Operational statistics *Comments:* _____ _____		
R	Billing data *Comments:* _____ _____		
R, C	Application-specific documents (e.g., input and output) *Comments:* _____ _____		

Workpaper A-50. Document Review Guide (page 2 of 5)

Purpose Code	Area/Title	Reviewed	
		Yes	No
	Requirements		
C	Project request		
	Comments: _____		
	_____		
R	Feasibility study		
	Comments: _____		
	_____		
R	Risk analysis		
	Comments: _____		
	_____		
R	Cost/benefit analysis		
	Comments: _____		
	_____		
C	Functional requirements document		
	Comments: _____		
	_____		
R	Data requirements document		
	Comments: _____		
	_____		
R	Requirements traceability matrix (if applicable)		
	Comments: _____		
	_____		
	Plans		
R	Project management plan		
	Comments: _____		
	_____		
C	Contingency plan		
	Comments: _____		
	_____		
C	Software development/conversion plan		
	Comments: _____		
	_____		
C	Security development plan		
	Comments: _____		
	_____		
C	Configuration management plan		
	Comments: _____		
	_____		

APPENDICES

Workpaper A-50. Document Review Guide (page 3 of 5)

Purpose Code	Area/Title	Reviewed Yes	No
	Plans, cont'd.		
C	General test plan		
	Comments: _____		
R	System integration plan		
	Comments: _____		
R	Maintenance plan		
	Comments: _____		
R	Database management system plan		
	Comments: _____		
R	Integrated logistic support plan		
	Comments: _____		
R	System engineering facilities plan		
	Comments: _____		
	Specifications		
C, R	System/subsystem specifications		
	Comments: _____		
C, R	Program specifications		
	Comments: _____		
C, R	Database specifications		
	Comments: _____		
C, R	Interface specifications		
	Comments: _____		
C, R	Formal specifications		
	Comments: _____		
R	Engineering drawings		
	Comments: _____		

Workpaper A-50. Document Review Guide (page 4 of 5)

Purpose Code	Area/Title	Reviewed Yes	Reviewed No
	Specifications, cont'd.		
R, C	Human engineering design approach document Comments: _____		
R	Engineering change proposals, requests for deviations/waivers, and specification change notices Comments: _____		
C, R	Source listing Comments: _____		
R	Equipment lists Comments: _____		
R	Floor plan Comments: _____		
	Manuals		
C, R	User manual Comments: _____		
C, R	System security manual Comments: _____		
C, R	Computer operators manual Comments: _____		
R, C	Program maintenance manual Comments: _____		
R	System manuals Comments: _____		
	Technical Analysis Documents		
R	Security evaluation reports (from prior certifications) Comments: _____		

Workpaper A-50. Document Review Guide (page 5 of 5)

Purpose Code	Area/Title	Reviewed Yes	No
	Technical Analysis Documents, cont'd.		
R	Risk analysis Comments: _____ _____		
C	Test procedures Comments: _____ _____		
C	Test analysis reports Comments: _____ _____		
R, C	Security analysis reports Comments: _____ _____		
C	Formal verification reports Comments: _____ _____		
R	Design analysis reports Comments: _____ _____		
R	Failure mode and effect analysis report Comments: _____ _____		
R	Reliability and maintainability analysis report Comments: _____ _____		

Key:

C = Critical review. Area should be analyzed for security deficiencies, whether technical, procedural, or organizational.

R = Research and reference review. Are should be reviewed to understand application functions and characteristics or reported shortcomings for auditor to better perform critical reviews; use for reference purposes.

The role listed first is the highest priority role.

Workpaper A-51. Planning the Interviews

No.	Steps to Be Performed	Reviewed Yes	No	Results
1.	Determine which people should be interviewed (e.g., managers, users, developers, people from outside the organization).			
2.	Clarify the subject and purpose of each interview, and identify what expertise is required of the interviewer.			
3.	List when, where, and under what conditions (e.g., people in attendance) the interviews take place.			
4.	Determine what preparatory activities and materials (e.g., questionnaires, cameras) are needed.			
5.	Identify what interview documentation is required.			
6.	Outline the coordination needed to arrange the interviews.			
7.	Identify which interviews depend on findings from others.			

APPENDICES

Workpaper A-52. Interview Results

Interviewer_____ Date_____

Subject to Be Discussed _____

Results of Interview _____

_____

_____

_____

	Procedure to Ensure Accurate Data			
		colspan-Performed		
No.	Steps to Be Performed	Yes	No	Results
1.	Assess subject competence and bias. The subject might not be qualified to discuss certain topics. The subject might also have opinions or vested interests that bias responses.			
2.	Independently verify and document important facts.			
3.	Repeat answers to important questions so mutual understanding is ensured. Record key facts immediately, rather than entrust them to memory. Two interviewers are needed to help ensure accuracy and reduce misinterpretations of answers.			
4.	Determine facts upon which subject opinions are based. The interviewer might form different conclusions.			
5.	Tell subjects what will be done with the information. They might be more open as a result.			
6.	Allow subjects to remain anonymous. They might provide more information as a result.			
7.	Do not place great reliance on the confidence subjects associate with their own estimates.			
8.	If the subject's judgment appears faulty (e.g., on threat likelihood or impact), request the subject to construct most-likely, extreme, most-costly, or other scenarios. This can change and improve the subject's opinion. The interviewer should have at hand as many examples of realistic scenarios as possible to counter subject bias, because subjects sometimes form judgments based on the ease with which they can fabricate plausible scenarios. Suggest ranges, whether numeric (e.g., 0-10, 11-50) or verbal (e.g., low, medium, high), to prevent the subject from having to formulate precise numbers (e.g., for threat frequency, losses, error rates).			
9.	Return draft write-up to subjects so that they can correct any errors or misinterpretations by evaluators or change anything they have said and subsequently learned to be in error.			

Workpaper A-53. Security Requirements Evaluation

No.	Security Requirement	Assets Affected	Threat	Exposure	Controls	Effective		Evaluation
						Yes	*No*	

Workpaper A-54. Methodology Review

Methodology Used _____

Did methodology include security considerations?	☐ Yes ☐ No
Was methodology followed?	☐ Yes ☐ No

No.	Area of Methodology	Evaluation
1.	Documentation—Does current, compete, and accurate documentation exist? This applies to both development and operational documentation.	
2.	Objectives—Was security explicitly stated and treated as an objective, with an appropriate amount of emphasis for the situation? Were security requirements defined?	
3.	Project Control—Was development well controlled? Were independent reviews and testing performed and did they consider security? Was an effective change control program used?	
4.	Tools and Techniques—Were structured design techniques used (e.g., modular design, formal specifications)? Were established programming practices and standards used (e.g., high-level languages, structured walkthroughs)?	
5.	Resources—How experienced in security were the people who developed the application? What were the sensitivity levels or clearances associated with their positions?	

Workpaper A-55. Detailed Review of Security Safeguards (page 1 of 3)

Security Requirement _____

Security Safeguard/Control Subject to Detailed Review _____

		Performed		
No.	**Tests to Perform**	**Yes**	**No**	**Test Results**
Subtask 1: Review Functional Operation				
1.	Control operation (e.g., do controls work?).			
2.	Parameter checking (e.g., are invalid or improbable parameters detected and properly handled?).			
3.	Common error conditions (e.g., are invalid or out-of-sequence commands detected and properly handled?).			
4.	Control monitoring (e.g., are security events such as errors and file accesses properly recorded; are performance measurements of characteristics such as resource use and response time properly recorded?).			
5.	Control management (e.g., do procedures for changing security tables work?).			
6.	Access control (e.g., is access without a password not allowed?).			
7.	Password control (e.g., are valid passwords accepted and invalid passwords rejected?).			
8.	The interface between the password function and the access authorization (e.g., do valid passwords allow proper access and not allow improper access, and do invalid passwords result in proper access restriction?).			
9.	Invalid password response (e.g., does the system respond correctly to multiple invalid passwords?).			
10.	Reauthentication procedures (e.g., does system-initiated reauthentication function correctly?).			
11.	Interface security (i.e., connections prone to error) for: Human–human (i.e., operator messages) Human–system (e.g., commands, procedures) System–system (e.g., intersystem dialogue) Process–system (e.g., calls) Process–process (e.g., interprocess calls)			

APPENDICES

Workpaper A-55. Detailed Review of Security Safeguards (page 2 of 3)

		Subtask 2: Review Performance	
No.	Quantitative Factor	Question	Response
1.	Availability	What proportion of time is the application or control available to perform critical or full services? Availability incorporates many aspects of reliability, redundancy, and maintainability. It is often more important than accuracy. It is especially relevant to applications with denial-of-service exposures as primary concerns (e.g., air traffic control, automatic funds disbursement, production control). Security controls usually require higher availability than other portions of an application.	
2.	Survivability	How well does the application or control withstand major failures or natural disasters? This includes the support of emergency operations during the failure, backup operations afterward, and recovery actions to return to regular operation. Survivability and availability overlap where failures are irreparable.	
3.	Accuracy	How accurate is the application or control? Accuracy encompasses the number, frequency, and significance of errors. Controls for which accuracy measures are especially applicable are identity verification techniques (e.g., signature, voice) and communications-line error-handling techniques.	
4.	Response time	Are response times acceptable? Slow control response time can entice users to bypass controls. Examples of controls for which response time is critical are passwords (especially in distributed networks) and identity verification techniques. Response time can also be critical for control management, as in the dynamic modification of security tables. It is useful in evaluating response time to assess the impact of varying levels of degradation.	
5.	Throughput	Does the application or control support required use capacities? Capacity includes the peak and average loading of such things as users and service request. This can involve the analysis of such performance ratios as total users versus response time.	

Workpaper A-55. Detailed Review of Security Safeguards (page 3 of 3)

Subtask 1: Review Functional Operation		
No.	**Externally Exploitable Area**	**Assessment of Exploitability**
1.	Complex interfaces	
2.	Change control process	
3.	Limits and prohibitions	
4.	Error handling	
5.	Side effects	
6.	Dependencies	
7.	Design modifications/extensions	
8.	Control of security descriptors	
9.	Execution chain of security services	
10.	Access to residual information	

APPENDICES

Workpaper A-56. Security Certification Statement

Subject: Certification of[1] _____ .

Reference computer security policies[2] _____ .

This Certification has been performed because[3] _____ .

Attached are findings from security certification evaluation of[1] _____ .

The security evaluation report summarizes findings and presents recommendations. Attached to the report is a proposed accreditation statement for your review and signature.

Based on the report and my judgement, I hereby certify (with the exceptions or clarifications noted below[4]) that[1] _____ meets documented and approved security specifications, meets all applicable policies, regulations, and standards, and that the results of [testing] demonstrate that the security provisions are adequate.

(exceptions or clarifications)

In addition, weighing the remaining residual risks against operational requirements, I recommend that you authorize (continued) operation of[1] _____ (under the following restrictions):

(restrictions)

(I further recommend that you authorize initiation of the following corrective actions.)

(corrective actions)

_____

Signature and Date

---

[1] Name of the application being certified.
[2] Applicable policies.
[3] Reasons include the following:
  • Initial development has been completed
  • Changes have been made
  • Requirements have changed
  • A required threshold of time has been reached
  • A major violation has occurred
  • Audit or evaluation findings question a previous certification
[4] Parentheses indicate portions of the letter that are not required in some situations.

Workpaper A-57. Detailed Evaluation Report

Activity	Description of Threats or Flaws	Threat Classification[1]	Level of Risk					Countermeasures	Type			Protection Failure	Requirement
			Probability of Threat[2]	Statement of Impact					Prevent	Detect	Correct		
				Compromise	Data Integrity	Denial of Service							

[1] Hy = Hypothetical
R = Real

[2] VH = Very High   I = Intermediate
H = High   L = Low
M = Moderate   VL = Very Low

Workpaper A-58. Audit Finding Documentation

Related Audit Objective
Brief description of finding
Description of what condition should be
Description of what is wrong
Impact of problem
Cause of problem
Standard, guideline, policy, or regulation violated
Workpaper reference(s)

Prepared by:	**Date:**

Workpaper A-59. Analysis of Finding (page 1 of 2)

Finding _____

Factual Questions	Responses	Analytical Questions	Responses	General Analysis	Actual Analysis
What was done?		Why that?		Nonessential or redundant	
Where was it done?		Why there?		Inconvenient location	
When was it done?		Why then?		Poor sequence	

Workpaper A-59. Analysis of Finding (page 2 of 2)

Factual Questions	Responses	Analytical Questions	Responses	General Analysis	Actual Analysis
Who did it?		Why that person?		Fragmented or improper skill	
How was it done?		Why that way?		Complicated or costly	
Why was it done?		Why permitted?		Noncompliance or ineffective	

Workpaper A-60. Developing Recommendations (page 1 of 2)

Finding

Area	Analysis	General Principle Violated	General Action Recommended	Audit Recommendation
What		Productivity or need	Eliminate	
Where		Smooth flow	Rearrange	
When		Smooth flow	Rearrange	

Workpaper A-60. Developing Recommendations (page 2 of 2)

Area	Analysis	General Principle Violated	General Action Recommended	Audit Recommendation
Who		Productivity flow	Change or combine	
How		Simplicity	Improve	
Why		Compliance	Comply or revise	

Prepared by: **Date:**

Workpaper A-61. Effective Data Processing Control Practices

No.	Description of Effective Control Practice
	CONTROL AREA: DESIGN PRINCIPLES
1.	**Concentrate Change Activity.** When a data record is being updated during a file processing application, the application code should be locally structured so that it does not make any changes to the record until all tests have been passed and the transaction can be posted. Therefore, in the event that an error prohibits an update, the original record need not be reconstructed. This technique also minimizes the probability that an abort would leave the database in an inconsistent status.
2.	**Improve Data Quality.** Although item counts and hash totals are effective controls, the primary controls over a database should be selected from fields that are totaled and presented on the system's major reports; that is, the totals should be meaningful numbers used by the system's human monitors for work load, trend, financial, or value analysis.
3.	**Use Standard Data Elements and Codes.** Once the database concept is understood and integrated files are contemplated, MIS management usually appoints a database administrator. Typically, some responsibilities are transferred from the programming and operations departments to the new database administrator.
	Shortly after the appointment, the database administrator establishes procedures for the data file design and definition process, followed by standard file formats, record formats, data element formats, and local standards for encoding some data element values.
	These local standard encodings eventually give rise to common tables of values shared among application systems. A single common utility program under the control of the database administrator maintains these tables of standard values.
4.	**Perform Context Edits.** Edits on individual fields in isolation are less powerful than edits on fields in combination, because the latter are performed using recent history from fields and records already processed on the current computer run. For complex edits dealing with a sequence of input, as in an online dialogue, a structured edit tree should be built and specific tests should be made dependent on what has gone before. Strings of fields containing a structure can therefore be verified for reasonableness using an edit structure.
	For example, the response to the question "How many persons in your immediate family?" could be edited in isolation only as numeric, between 1 to 20. A follow-up question, "What are the names of the persons in your immediate family?" allows the two responses to be processed in combination. A programmer might be uncertain whether a response of "one" to the first question included the person being interviewed. A higher confidence level is achieved if the number of names matches the population count.
	If default options are used in conjunction with a complex context edit, the defaults inserted can be conditioned by the point in the edit tree at which the default is invoked. For example, a blank field could receive different default values based on different contexts.

APPENDICES

Workpaper A-61. Effective Data Processing Control Practices

No.	Description of Effective Control Practice
5.	**Perform Staged Edits.** This can be illustrated by the following example. The design for a large system that involved a high volume of complex high-value input included minicomputers controlling clusters of keyboards and batches of transactions being sent online to the central data processing system. The edit concept called for four discrete stages of editing: • The first edit was a field edit. This was performed online in real time. Following each end-of-field delimiter, the field was checked against the field specification for length, character set, and value range. • Following the last field in a record, the record was checked against the record specification to determine whether the fields existed in legal combinations for the record type and, when possible, whether the collection of fields in the record was a legal set of fields containing individually legal field values that constituted a legal value set. • After a group of records was completed by an individual operator, the batch was checked for batch consistency against a batch specification using the background partition of the minicomputer (operating under the control of the keyboard supervisor) before the batch was released for central processing. • Finally, when received by the central computer, the batch was edited for format, content, and context, and all encoded variables were verified with the appropriate authority list. Incorrect or questionable records were flagged to inhibit further processing, passed through the system, and eventually printed for final resolution. All of the errors found on the batch were kept together as an error batch and printed on error worksheets in the same sequence as they were received (to assist in matching errors and original documents during the resolution process).
6.	**Use Restart Logs.** It is a common practice to log input transactions during a database update. With the advent of inexpensive file storage, the logs have been specified to contain the "before" image of the data fields destined for change, and the "after" image of those same fields. It is therefore possible to rapidly recover the modified files by loading the data set produced during the last checkpoint dump and avoiding the cost and time penalties of reprocessing by simply replacing all before images with their companion set of after images from the log. In addition, if a sequence of transactions ends in failure and leaves the database in an unusable state, it is possible to reverse the effect of processing and replace all after images with before images back to the point of the first transaction in the erroneous sequence. If input transactions are sequentially numbered and logged on the same log with the before and after images, and if the sequence numbers appear in the before and after records logged as a byproduct of the update process, it is possible to tie a transaction to its related updates and therefore recover from a failure with transactions in process. (Such recovery requires a selective backout of changes to all records affected by the transaction in process at the time of failure.)

Workpaper A-61. Effective Data Processing Control Practices

No.	Description of Effective Control Practice
7.	**Use Default Options.** Default options are a reasonable way to fill in missing data elements or to correct erroneous element values where the processing context allows the correct value to be known to the program. When life or severe catastrophe is at risk, however, default values should not be used. If the critical process is online, safety considerations should require that the terminal keyboard be locked and that the computer insist on perfect data with all exceptions positively acknowledged (i.e., no assumed or default data values).
8.	**Take Equipment and Screen Design into Consideration.** The design of applications involving keyboard entry requires a careful appreciation of the human factors involved. The system designer must be familiar with the data and its various formats, the equipment to be used, and the environment (including workstations, lighting, and sound conditioning). Properly supervised professional data entry personnel may use heavy abbreviating to cut the keystrokes required. If the volume of input for a specific application is not sufficient to provide full-time employment for several operators, however, the designers should be wary of excessive abbreviations and any form of code compression at the input stations. Instead, the designer should provide alternative input sequences and varying codes for different levels of training, experience, and skill. These must be combined with a set of supervisory statistics that allow each operator's throughput to be measured against an appropriate skill classification. (The designer should beware of simple statistical averages because these push unskilled operators beyond their capability, resulting in error cycles.)
	CONTROL AREA: FILE STRUCTURE
9.	**Add Quality Flags.** Data quality flags can be added to files, records, groups of fields, or individual fields in a database and can be used to condition processing to avoid a mismatch between the quality of the data and its intended use. Every record can carry a quality flag. The flag indicates to each processing program which format and content checks the record has successfully passed. The quality flag should be the first field read by an application program and the last field written by an update program.
10.	**Use Activity Dates.** If each input transaction carries a date-of-event and each record in the file carries a date-of-last-transaction-processed, these two dates allow processing to be performed in the proper sequence (or manual intervention to be requested) in case of transportation or processing delays.
11.	**Ensure Reliability Through Batch Redundancy.** Hash totals and item counts ensure that batches retain their integrity through multiple transformations (i.e., editing, sorting, updating, and printing). Item counts should be carried completely through the process to ensure that every item is processed. This has long been a common practice in some industries.

APPENDICES

Workpaper A-61. Effective Data Processing Control Practices

No.	Description of Effective Control Practice
	The primary key used in file maintenance should be a unique numeric identifier carrying a check digit. When this is not possible, partial protection can be achieved by check summing (hash totaling) numeric key fields so that a batch of data maintains its initial integrity through all processing. It should be noted that check digits on ID fields and check sums on both records and batches constitute specific practical examples of added redundancy in the input stream. They increase the character count to achieve improved data reliability.
12.	**Ensure Reliability Through File Redundancy.** Some file systems carry check sums into the database to ensure that data quality does not deteriorate over time. More advanced systems carry separate check sums—one for the control information and the other for the data values.
13.	**Ensure Reliability Through Input Redundancy.** Additional redundancy can be built into input messages (at the cost of increasing the input character count) to provide context information for edit programs and to facilitate meaningful correction and operator dialogues. This redundant information takes several forms: check words, double entries, check digits, and batch totals.
14.	**Provide Redundancy for Audit.** Within the database, additional information can be carried in the record header to provide the basic parameters for certain types of integrity audits. Specifically, a record header could contain the identifier associated with the last program to update the record, the date of that last update, the time of the update, and the transaction sequence number causing the update.
15.	**Use Date Checks in Sequence.** During input processing, the effective date of the transaction can be processed as well. This allows the control group to identify old transactions and can inhibit their processing. When the effective date of the transaction is compared with the effective date of the last to update a data record, out-of-sequence transactions can be recognized and manual intervention can be requested.
16.	**Design Self-Defining Files for Integrity.** One technique for handling very large files (e.g., those taking at least a dozen full tape reels at 1600 bpi) involves designing files with directories on the front of every individual record. The directory describes the structure of the record and contains pointers to every data element contained in the record. Not only does this record format make files independent of the application programs (and therefore insensitive to changes on these programs), it provides extensive redundancy and allows the integrity of the large files to be audited and maintained.
	Key features of these techniques are:
	• A master dictionary defining all data elements in the system and awarding each data element a unique ID number.
	• A record format that provides for a directory on the front of every data record. (The directory should be of variable length and contain one four-byte entry for each data element in the record. The first two bytes are the data element ID number, the third byte is a pointer to the beginning of the related data value in the record, and the fourth byte is the length of the value field in the record.)

Workpaper A-61. Effective Data Processing Control Practices

No.	Description of Effective Control Practice
	As each program is loaded, it references the dictionary and provides the names of the data elements it plans to process; in return, it receives current descriptions, edit specifications, and ID numbers for those data elements. Then, when each individual record is read for processing, the data element ID from the directory is used to locate that data element and invoke the correct edit specification.
	A variation of this scheme provides a structure in which records always grow through the addition of new information and no information is ever deleted; only the pointers change. If correction is ever required, the old pointers are retrieved from the log and restored to their previous values (the data still exists in the records). This technique is most appropriate for standing master files of data with low rates of change.
17.	**Use Variable Names to Enhance Edit Logic.** One set of data management software stores the variable name adjacent to each occurrence of the variable. Although the storage space is increased, the name/value pair provides helpful redundancy for editing and lays the foundation for two stages of table-driven editing: one as the data is received, and the second immediately before the update. The update edits are used to test the validity of an input variable; compare it with other input values, stored values, or literals; and derive a replacement, 'sake appropriate cancellation action, or accept the value as input.
	If variable names appear in the input stream or are appended during input processing, they can be carried with the variable throughout the system. Then whenever a variable reference is required, the names are matched and the machine address of the adjacent data value is computed at the instant of reference. This provides a degree of independence between the program and its data. Furthermore, if the names do not match, an error routine can be called before erroneous data is introduced for processing.
	Although the permanent storage of named variables may increase file sizes disproportionately and therefore may not be able to be used in the database proper, the use of named variables on input and during preliminary processing provides a degree of flexibility in free-form input coupled with important editing enhancements for the price of a few additional characters in the input stream. This scheme can be contrasted with a highly efficient but unforgiving input format in which variable recognition in the input stream is based solely on its position.
18.	**Use Software with Restore and Reprocess Functions.** Some data management software has before and after images stored on the log tape. In addition, a RESTORE verb allows applications programs to request that the files be restored to a previous checkpoint. A REPROCESS verb allows application programs to request that a limited sequence of transactions be reflected in the file to a transaction previously found to be in error.
19.	**Provide Self-Defining Files for Audit.** An advantage of a file design that has a directory on the front of every record is the ability to validate the record after the update by using the transaction type code from the input and the database description, including the data element dictionary and the resulting record structure. It can then be determined whether all required data elements are present and all present data elements are permitted.

Workpaper A-61. Effective Data Processing Control Practices

No.	Description of Effective Control Practice
	Whenever a group of input fields routinely appears together, the group can be given a single identifier or transaction type code. This code may explicitly appear in the input record along with the group of fields that it names. This group name can be used to enter the database description so that the data editing specification can be obtained for the group. The desired structure of the input record can then be verified against the specification and the following determined:
	• Does each data element meet its specification?
	• Does the record match its structure?
	• Are all the required data elements present?
	• Are all present data elements permitted?
	In a similar way, the file can be verified at the time of the update or any later time. The file record would have a type code, and the record specification could be obtained from the database description. Each record could be individually verified and the collection of data elements in the record could be checked for presence and structure.
	CONTROL AREA: FILE CONTROLS
20.	**Program Read-Only Status.** When the correctness of basic records on master files of essentially static data has been established, a flag bit should be set in the record header to inhibit further update without special privilege. If an installation-standard file access method is used, this bit inhibits unauthorized updates and maintains the integrity of the basic data.
21.	**Build in Redundancy for Post-Audit.** After a database has been designed, the design should be reviewed and, when necessary, redundancy should be added to allow an audit program to verify the integrity of the file set. The audit program can then be run to prevent the data in the files from deteriorating unobserved.
	For example, the first level of detail in a payroll file provides a record on each employee. A second level summary record is provided for each department and the summary record contains a count of the total number of employees assigned to the department (item count), the total of the base salaries for all employees assigned to that department (control total), and an arithmetic total of all employee telephone numbers (hash total). Whenever the condition of the file is suspect, an audit program could verify that the detailed records summarize to the department totals. Just these few redundant control fields provide a fair level of confidence in the integrity of the file. Additional control fields of redundant information can be added to increase the degree of confidence.
22.	**Use Segmented Controls for Efficiency.** Most databases have two or more processing patterns over a full processing cycle. All database programs should maintain control totals although they may process transactions in random sequence. Any sequential processes should perform a complete verification of the parts of the file they process. The file controls should be segmented so that any sequential process handling part of the file can have access to control totals for just the part of the file routinely processed.

Workpaper A-61. Effective Data Processing Control Practices

No.	Description of Effective Control Practice
	In the payroll file example given in Item 21, in a disk-oriented database system, the department summary records would be kept in a file separate from the detailed data. When the pay file was referenced during an update, the appropriate department summary could also be updated. If the database design allowed individual summary records to be referenced, the maintenance of summary records would be inexpensive, yet they would provide necessary redundancy; an audit program could be called at any time to verify the file. The summary records should also be designed to provide statistical data useful for management reports.
	CONTROL AREA: PROCESSING SEQUENCE
23.	**Provide Operator Feedback.** For online systems, the computer should positively acknowledge each transaction by assigning sequential message numbers to the transactions emanating from each individual terminal. A new message is awarded the next consecutive number and a positive confirmation of receipt displays that same number to the terminal operator. This number provides transaction accountability, and in the event of restart, the operator can use numbered transactions to determine which transactions to reenter.
	Ideally, messages should be hash totaled by an intelligent terminal before transmission. If the terminal does not have this capability, the hash total can be appended by the first intelligent machine-controller, multiplexer, or host that handles the message.
	If messages originating in the host computer and directed to individual terminals are also numbered, the operator can ensure that no messages were lost in the communications network.
	Similarly, if the host develops a hash total for the outbound message and if that hash total is verified by an intelligent terminal as the message is displayed, the system can assure the operator that the messages are delivered with the content unchanged.
24.	**Use an Immediate Edit, Deferred Update Procedure.** One large database system collects input transactions during the day, edits them, stores them in a batch, and reflects the entire batch of transactions in the file during one massive overnight processing run. The system attempts to guarantee that transactions entered during the day will be reflected in the file that night by thoroughly editing each transaction online before accepting it for the overnight queue. Unless the transaction is incompatible with the database (e.g., attempts to change a master record that does not exist), the overnight processing will be successful.
25.	**Concentrate Update Activity.** With a database containing redundant information in several files or an integrated database that has redundant information in secondary indexes, multiple accesses are required to complete a single transaction. It is useful to establish a programming standard to minimize the risk of creating an incompatible file set as the result of an abort during update processing. At the risk of adding a few file accesses, all reading of all files can be accomplished before processing and all changes to all files can be collected into a single compact write sequence following processing (i.e., reads and writes should not be distributed uniformly across the processes). Concentrating the writes reduces the probability that a processing failure will prohibit the sequence of writes from being completed and leave the file set in an incompatible state.

APPENDICES

Workpaper A-61. Effective Data Processing Control Practices

No.	Description of Effective Control Practice
	CONTROL AREA: PROGRAM STRUCTURE
26.	**Avoid Interpretive Change.** Some programs unintentionally modify more data than they should; in an integrated database, storing a field one byte too long destroys the adjacent field. A table-driven interface module can be appended to the record fetch routine supplied by the database management system. A program can obtain any data needed but can return only the data that it is authorized to change. Furthermore, the data being placed in the record is edited to ensure that it matches the data element specification for the element addressed.
	CONTROL AREA: PROGRAMMING TECHNIQUE
27.	**Ensure Work Space Integrity.** The unused space in a data record and the unused space in a main storage allocation should be filled with a known pattern of bits. Some programs fill such spaces with a supervisor call to an error routine. Checking the pattern can determine whether the unused space is in fact unused and stays that way.
28.	**Use Space Erase.** After each input transaction has been processed, some large systems obliterate residual data to prevent previous values from being accidentally used in subsequent processing. The pattern used to obliterate data should not be a legal combination of characters (i.e., blanks, zeros, nines) because a program that fails to initialize its work space could still run properly under some circumstances. This is one of a set of techniques designed to keep a program within its allocated data and instruction space and to ensure that the program controls its entire environment but uses only data that it controls.
	One efficient way to set unused space to null values is to obtain the actual length of the record just read and store null values in any allocated but unused space set aside for the record. The original record length should continue to describe the length of the occupied space, unless it is consciously adjusted by a program adding a field, deleting a field, or extending an existing field. After all processing is complete, the updated record length can be used for two purposes: to write the modified record, and to check that any residual unused space is still filled by the null values stored after the read but before the processing sequence.
	CONTROL AREA: EDITING
29.	**Establish Classes in Edit Specification.** Many financial systems have established credit classifications and adjust a credit rating dynamically based on the customer's basic rating and the current status of the account. After the adjusted rating is established, the editing system invokes dollar limits appropriate to the customer's adjusted rating.
	Similarly, inventory systems establish classes for customers and edit order quantities for reasonableness against those customer classes.
	For example, a utility might establish four classes of subscriber service: apartment, single-family residence, large residence or light industry, and heavy industry. As meter readings are processed, edit criteria appropriate to the service classification would be invoked. Erroneous readings, overdue bills, or unusual use would all be recognized because use and edit criteria would be related according to the gradations established by the classification system.

Workpaper A-61. Effective Data Processing Control Practices

No.	Description of Effective Control Practice
30.	**Provide Classes of Limits.** Many database systems keep an order quantity limit on the master file along with the product description and status. If a quantity requested exceeds this limit, manual confirmation of the order is requested. In more sophisticated systems, a series of limits are stored by customer class so a small customer is protected against overordering by a low limit.
31.	**Define Normal Limits.** When many independent transactions are received related to members of a homogeneous group (e.g., customers, individuals, parts, or accounts), an aggregate average across all members of the group allows the system to determine whether any individual member of the group deviates significantly from the average. In addition, if the group average deviates unpredictably from its previous average for this same group, the entire batch of transactions can be held until the deviation is explained.
32.	**Set Trend Limits.** The behavior of an individual input transaction can be compared with the aggregate behavior of all individuals within its population or with its own previous behavior. The latter requires that a behavior history be maintained for each account so that account activity is retained for future comparison.
33.	**Establish Error Suspense Files.** When input transactions are lengthy and error corrections usually affect only a small portion of the original record, suspense files containing original records (complete with errors) are frequently maintained. The correction process then consists of reentering identifying information plus the fields in error. The computer updates the queue of incorrect transactions, usually by simple field replacement, and then passes the modified transaction back to the main input editing module. It is important that the entire corrected transaction be passed through all of the editing procedures and that it is not assumed that what was valid before is still valid.
	When systems are designed to maintain queues of transactions pending correction, an effective way to uniquely identify the error to be corrected is to cause the erroneous data to be reentered along with the transaction ID and the replacement data.
34.	**Maintain Limits.** Several editing schemes require data stored on a file to establish the editing limits and to adjust them based on seasonal, -6me, activity, or cyclic factors. These systems require edit, update, and reporting modules to maintain the file of edit limits. Furthermore, such systems require special data or additional programming to initialize the system at start-up before any real history is available.
	CONTROL AREA: POSTPROCESSING VERIFICATION
35.	**Use Dummy Processing.** A frequently used practice places dummy master records on the file and routinely processes fictional transactions against those dummy master records to produce predictable output. The results of processing are forwarded to the control group, which routinely confirms that the item counts for all input items were processed and verifies the control totals for those items. The results from the processing of fictional data against the dummy accounts are also verified to ensure that the actual detailed processing was correctly performed. In the case of a payables run, the check written for the dummy account must be captured and destroyed.

APPENDICES

Workpaper A-61. Effective Data Processing Control Practices

No.	Description of Effective Control Practice
	This technique works on many types of files. For example, a record can be established for a dummy part number in an inventory file, and fictitious receipt and withdrawal transactions can be processed against that part number. If the inventory algorithm embedded in the processing program is understood, input data can be prepared to test limit checks and a variety of transaction processes. The resulting inventory on hand is predictable and the processing procedures can be checked by verifying the computer-produced results against the predicted values. Sets of dummy records and dummy transactions can exercise a computer program and provide confidence that typical transactions are being processed correctly.
	CONTROL AREA: TROUBLE SYMPTOMS
36.	**Analyze Exception Reports.** A computer system can be designed to reject obvious mistakes and to process suspicious transactions while listing their occurrence on an exception report for manual review. The very quantity of items requiring review is an excellent indicator of the general condition of the system. In addition, the exception reports provide an indication of whether the trouble is consistent or, in the absence of a pattern, merely related to individual transactions. Examples of what exception reports might cover are: high-priced items only; all subscribers residing in California; items manufactured by the XYZ Co.; or only items input on December 15.
37.	**Monitor Performance Changes.** Performance changes are an indication of general systems condition, provided the programs have not been modified since the previous run. The operations staff should be notified whenever a program is changed. Furthermore, the operations staff should be provided with an indication of the processing pattern so that staff members can sense performance changes during lengthy runs. For example, the staff can be provided with an audio amplifier for CPU activity, a CPU activity meter, a hardware measurement box, or a printout of the CPU time used per transaction.
38.	**Inform Operator of Performance Anomalies.** In some cases, the estimated run time can be predicted by an equation based on a simple count of the input transactions. In other cases, run time must be estimated by a more complex equation that operates on the number of transactions in each of several transaction classes. In still other cases, the transaction run time varies unpredictably based on the parameters in the transaction and the constitution of the values contained in the files. Commands that select records from a database can cause varying parts of the entire database to be read in response to an inquiry. In these cases, operators should be provided with in-process progress reports (percentage of the transactions processed or percentage of the database read) so that they can confirm that an unpredictable process is progressing satisfactorily.
	The purpose of informing the operators of unpredictable transactions that are being processed is to confirm, by implication, that the remainder of the processes are predictable and that therefore performance should conform to historical expectations.

Workpaper A-61. Effective Data Processing Control Practices

No.	Description of Effective Control Practice
	A large file system should provide a communications path from the computer operator back to the system manager so that unexpected activities can be reported for review.
39.	**Analyze Adjustments.** The system can be programmed to recognize unusual transactions. For example, utility companies traditionally keep historical records of customer use, adjust them for seasonal and temperature variations, and use this data to screen each customer's current use for reasonableness. After all the out-of-character transactions are posted to an exception list, they must be manually reviewed to determine whether or not they are errors. The volume, magnitude, and sense of required adjustments provide an indication of problems in the flow of data through the system. Adjustment analysis can pinpoint the areas that need to be reviewed for correctness.
40.	**Analyze Error Logs.** All errors should be logged. In addition to recording the error and storing a unique error code, an error log should contain enough information to identify the discrete data path from the originator to the computer (e.g., source, observer, keyboard operator, batch, dates). The error log must contain the information necessary to identify the input transaction in its own local processing sequence. It should present the customer classification awarded by the input screening process, any classification associated with the master file, and the type of error discovered.
	The log should aggregate statistics on error trends during that processing run, day, week, and month; the entire context must be logged with the error.
	Careful analysis of such an error log can pinpoint error-prone processes or deficiencies in the system design that can be improved for economy and efficiency. Systematic improvements usually yield additional benefits in personnel efficiency: a high volume of routine errors often causes personnel to assume that errors are to be expected and to be less cautious in their own activities. When corrections that dramatically decrease the number of errors are made, personnel become more careful.
	CONTROL AREA: OPTIONAL CHECKING
41.	**Establish Adaptive Checking.** Computer operators learn the processing rhythm of a large job even when multiprocessing. Some systems have been constructed with optional checking features that can be invoked either by internal checks or by operator action. One system had a series of expensive checks designed to guarantee the continuing integrity of the database; they were inhibited during regular operations but invoked whenever the operator desired confidence that a suspicious processing pattern was not destroying the integrity of the database.
42.	**Ensure Program Integrity.** Some program designers structure their object program modules into read-only (reentrant) areas and into read-write (serially reusable) areas. A simple checksum on the read-only areas provides an initial value; subsequent checks at break points in the process can ensure that the program and its tables remain as loaded and unmodified.

APPENDICES

Workpaper A-61. Effective Data Processing Control Practices

No.	Description of Effective Control Practice
	More sophisticated checks are required to verify the patterns in the read-write areas. If these are performed at major break points in the process, the parameters and most work space use can be verified, proving the program is performing correctly to the extent that the output areas are properly configured and formatted.
43.	**Provide Automatic Error Analysis.** One leading manufacturer enhanced its operating system software to provide increased availability. It determined that system crashes were accompanied by incorrect modifications to the control blocks or parameter strings that dynamically controlled the operating system. To minimize the effects of an error and allow the system to be restarted with the greatest portion of the work load surviving, a series of optional programs called checker/fixers were provided. When called during the restart process, each checker verifies the format and contents of a control block. If the block is incorrect, the checker optionally calls the fixer to rebuild the control block from other available information stored redundantly within the system.
	Many commercial applications operate on several separate strings of data simultaneously and can benefit from an adaptation of the same technique. The extent of the error must first be determined and operations restored as soon as possible for the healthy parts of the system. Massive system restarts provide opportunity for compound failures: restarts frequently violate system controls and usually cause all operational personnel to follow unfamiliar and sometimes untested procedures.
44.	**Verify Duplication.** Every database has some built-in redundancy; in a well-designed database, redundancy may be considerable. A separate audit program can be created to check redundancy and verify the integrity of the file set. If properly programmed, some sections of the audit routine can be embedded in a file duplicate program so that the process of creating a backup file also checks that file for correctness.
	A simple utility program copies records from one file to another, treating each record only as a string of bits. A more sophisticated utility program first obtains the file description from the database dictionary. As each record is copied, the program verifies the specification for data elements, detail records, summary records, and the file structure. Because 100 percent of the file is handled every time the file is duplicated, a merger of the audit program and the file duplicate utility produces a major benefit at a small extra cost. If the file is self-defining, the audit/duplicate program need not reference the database description. This procedure works equally well on current files and archival files, although the file definitions may have changed over time.
45.	**CONTROL AREA: MATHEMATICAL COMPUTATIONS**
	Identify Arithmetic Representations. Every computer treats certain arithmetic points in a unique way. Before performing extensive math on an unfamiliar computer, each programmer should discover the arithmetic singular points in the system to determine whether these idiosyncrasies will affect the planned calculations. For example, if a negative number is subtracted from its equal (e.g., $-5 - [-51]$), some machines yield a zero with negative sign. If this result is then presented as an argument to a subroutine that accepts only positive arguments, it will be rejected.

Workpaper A-61. Effective Data Processing Control Practices

No.	Description of Effective Control Practice
46.	**Check Finite Arithmetic.** Arithmetic operations using the full range of a computer's arithmetic registers emphasize the importance of round-off, truncation, and the residue following arithmetic manipulations. Although programmed double-precision operations may not be contemplated, each programmer should discover how arithmetical calculations are treated at the extremes of the numeric ranges and whether the residual values are reliable or not. Because some systems behave differently when performing fixed-point, complement, and floating-point arithmetic, the results from each of these types of computation should be reviewed.
47.	**Beware of Numerical Hazards.** Programmers should beware of the singular points that are created by performing arithmetic on nearly equal floating-point numbers in the middle of a complex expression, the possibility of floating-point underflow and overflow, and the risks of division by zero.
48.	**Calibrate Numerical Approximations.** Many manufacturers offer subroutine libraries and, in some cases, built-in transcendental functions. Frequently, these are represented as primitive computer operations and treated routinely as an extension of the order list. Each user should calibrate the subroutine library to be used and enter the accuracy achieved by the algorithms it contains into the programming manual. Considerable effort is required to validate a library of subroutine approximations.
49.	**Perform Parallel Check Calculations.** In many scientific calculations, two different sets of equations often produce the same result, or in some cases, an additional equation can be introduced that exploits another physical property and provides a check calculation. When such redundant calculations are performed, the correct operation of the system can be verified. As a byproduct, the accuracy of the computer solution can sometimes be estimated. For example, an energy balance equation can be integrated with the equations of motion for a missile. The continuity of mass in the energy equation guarantees that no gross errors have been made as the set of differential equations are integrated.
50.	**Detect Errors with Numerical Aggregates.** In repetitive scientific calculations dealing with many observations of well-behaved data, standard statistical techniques (e.g., mean, variance, skewness, kurtosis) detect gross errors in the observations or subsequent processing. An example outside the field of science is the use of statistical measure to verify that stock market transactions were properly reported and processed.
	CONTROL AREA: DEVELOPMENT METHODS
51.	**Pilot Test Input.** When designing a larger high-volume system, the input system should be programmed first and pilot tested under actual or simulated conditions while the rest of the system is being completed. The results of these pilot tests should be used to verify the design, documentation, and planned training and, most important, to check the assumptions on which the input system design was based.

APPENDICES

Workpaper A-61. Effective Data Processing Control Practices

No.	Description of Effective Control Practice
52.	**Manage Keyboarding Errors.** In large shops with a high volume of similar keyboarding, error statistics should be kept by machine and by employee. Through the use of various employee–machine combinations, the error statistics can isolate employees with the best and worst records. These statistics should be analyzed so that the techniques of the superior employees can be shared and the habits of the inferior employees can be modified.
	CONTROL AREA: SYSTEM TESTING
53.	**Create Data for Test.** To provide a test environment without the risk of allowing an unchecked program to access real files, a set of test files should be maintained whose structure is identical to the structure in the live database. The operating system should select test or real files according to a control parameter that designates whether the run is test or production. Satisfactory runs on the test file should be mandatory before a modified system is allowed to run in production.
54.	**Build in Verification Tests.** When many data cases are run through a complex calculation, a standard case should be run routinely before, during, and after the massive set of live data. This verifies that the program and the computer system were operating correctly (at least for the paths exercised by the standard case) throughout the production run.
55.	**Build in Exercisers.** In an interactive system, a standard demonstration program should be cataloged and each remote terminal operator should be provided with a script that accesses standard data, exercises the system, and produces predictable results. The remote operator can then be assured of an operational terminal, communications network, central computer, operating system, and at least one operational path through the applications system and the DBMS. With experience, the remote operator can also determine whether the system response time is within normal limits.
56.	**Build in Diagnostics.** In the event that a remote terminal operator invokes the standard exercise package and receives unexpected results, a separate input diagnostic package can be invoked so the operator can follow a predetermined input script and the input diagnostic package can determine whether the character strings received are exactly those expected.
	Similarly, a file of predetermined output can be stored and an output diagnostic program can be invoked to display the output to the remote operator. The operator can then determine whether the standard output is being received and properly displayed or printed. The canned output stored for such a diagnostic program is usually geometric in nature. Patterns are displayed or printed to place known characters in the first and last display position of each and every line, cover the display field with a readily recognized pattern, and display every graphic character to ensure the character generation circuitry is properly functioning. All electromechanical functions of a printer are similarly exercised.
	Given the results of the input and the output diagnostics, the remote operator can intelligently call for assistance and indicate what seems to be the problem.

Workpaper A-61. Effective Data Processing Control Practices

No.	Description of Effective Control Practice
57.	**Perform Communications Exercises.** Communications lines that interconnect intelligent devices to computers and computers to intelligent multiplexers can be directed to repeatedly exchange standard messages to calibrate the line. If the measured error rates are excessive, the line can be scheduled for repair. In the interim, the line speed can be changed, alternative network paths can be used, or line capacity can be exchanged for optional checking.
58.	**Perform Online Testing.** In any system that involves elaborate error checking, provision must be made for declaring entry into a test mode so that the fault detection logic can be exercised by introducing faults into the system. The purpose of the test mode is to inhibit the sounding of alarms, the printing of error messages, and the logging of test events as actual errors, thereby destroying the integrity of the error statistics.

CONTROL AREA: ORGANIZATION

No.	Description of Effective Control Practice
59.	**Establish Database Administrator Position.** Even if all the files are related to a single system of application programs and no third party uses the data being created, a database administration function can facilitate systems management. As systems get larger, database administration is often separated from development programming, maintenance, and production operation. This pares the jobs down to a reasonable size and concentrates a series of similar functions under one administrator.

The database administrator and staff should address:

- Definition
- Data elements
- Controls
- Formats
- Procedures
- Records
- Backup
- Files
- Transitions
- File sets

In addition, the data base administrator should be solely responsible for the use of file utility programs to:

- Audit
- Reconstruct
- Verify
- Initialize
- Duplicate
- Reorganize

No.	Description of Effective Control Practice
60.	**Organize for Integrity.** Organizational responsibilities need to be reviewed, programming standards need modification, and the work force needs discipline to ensure that changes to a production system are controlled and loss of data integrity is avoided.

Data stored and untouched in a perfect world does not deteriorate. Machines, operators, and programmers, however, make mistakes. These are not always detected; even when they are, the correction of mistakes sometimes introduces other errors. Data can therefore deteriorate over time even when no transactions that update specific individual records are processed against the master file. Changes must be controlled and files must be audited to maintain data integrity over long periods. To ensure this, the organizational responsibilities must be properly defined and the files properly designed.

APPENDICES

Workpaper A-61. Effective Data Processing Control Practices

No.	Description of Effective Control Practice
61.	**Implement Quality Control.** Most DP shops have a control group, a team through which all computer input and output must pass. The control group checks the control totals on input batches and reconciles totals on output reports against the most recent input and the current file statistics. Report control totals must be reviewed before reports of other computer-produced documents are distributed. In addition to checking 1/0 totals, the OA group uses statistics to check file integrity and histograms of the input transaction mix so that deviations from the norm are caught before erroneous information is distributed. (Unfortunately, this control group must work when the production is being run, and that usually implies second and weekend shifts).
62.	**Use Master File Verification.** A properly designed database contains sufficient redundancy to ensure that its integrity can be independently verified without reference to other files, indexes, or supplementary information. An audit program is used to perform this verification. Typically, the file structure is explicit and additional redundant data elements are included that contain item counts, numerical sums, or hash totals. For more complex files, truth tables describing the logic and record sequencing are placed in a descriptive record at the beginning of the file. The database administrator should own the database audit program and run it for the benefit of all users sharing data. If running the program is expensive, samples of the files can be checked on consecutive runs. Runs can also be triggered by certain performance problems.
	The database administrator and the data librarian must coordinate their efforts to ensure that the release of grandparent files depends on both age and proven data integrity. Whenever a 100 percent sample of any file within a file set is checked, the audit program should verify all file controls and totals. Any errors should be resolved by the control group so that the baseline totals for the next set of production runs are automatically adjusted.
	The relationship between audit activities and the file retention plan deserves further comment. When a computer center deals with a master file that is cyclically updated, a retention plan is usually established that defines how many consecutive obsolescent versions of the master file should be retained. In batch operations with weekly updates, the current file plus the master files of last week and two weeks ago (i.e., child, parent, and grandparent versions) are usually saved.
	If the audit program is run every two weeks to verify the integrity of the master files, a retention plan providing for three cycles is sufficient. The file set, however, may be massive; the audit program may be long-running; or the audit program may be set up to perform a 100 percent verification of only a portion of the file. In these cases, the audit cycles must be considered when the retention plan is being prepared; it may be desirable to retain additional cycles of the obsolete master files to accommodate the audit cycle (i.e., the audit cycle and the retention plan cannot be independent of each other).

Workpaper A-61. Effective Data Processing Control Practices

No.	Description of Effective Control Practice
63.	**Build Local Expertise.** User-oriented programming packages provide risks as well as advantages. These packages are often bought under the assumption that little or no programming is required for their installation and use. When these packages are used for the main production flow or to summarize important data needed for decision-making, however, they introduce some risks.
	Users of these packages can be successful without having copies of the source programs, without knowing the details of the file layout, and without understanding the intricacies of restart and reload procedures. With luck, they never need expertise on the internals of the database package; however, power failures do occur in the middle of updates, computer circuits sometimes fail, and programs stored in a library can deteriorate or become incompatible with the operating system over time. These systems can fail at critical times, and although the vendor may assist in diagnosis, long-distance problem solving is difficult and the quality of service received when the package is new often deteriorates over time.
	If a programming package is used for critical work that must be completed on schedule, the manager should build some level of local expertise as insurance that the skills to deal with an emergency exist. This does not mean that every installation needs a seasoned programmer who is thoroughly conversant with every package. Instead, each manager should assess the organization's risks and develop the level of expertise necessary to hold those risks to a reasonable level.
	CONTROL AREA: COMPUTER OPERATIONS
64.	**Use Pilot Production Batches.** On large production runs, a small but representative sample of data should be routinely run as a pilot production. The control group can then check the output of this pilot run as the main run is processing. (Sometimes this technique requires minor changes to the system design to be feasible.)
65.	**Ensure Integrity in Names.** Check digits on procedure, job, and program names can be used to prevent calls for incorrect procedures or jobs. Although such incorrect requests are likely to abort, some may partially execute; they can destroy a portion of any database designated for output before the error is recognized.
66.	**Establish Online Controls.** Although many information systems accept input in random sequence and process the input stream in an as-required order, some installations have found that controls, restart, and error resolution are greatly simplified if the input transactions are sorted onto ascending sequence on the primary file key before the main update run is scheduled.
	Many systems are running with online update from remote terminals because an adequate system of controls has been satisfactorily automated. In some large and very complicated systems, however, online controls at the transaction level have proved difficult to achieve, and these systems must batch online transactions, sort them into a sequence, and supply a more traditional form of batch control procedure before the transactions are allowed to update the file.

Workpaper A-61. Effective Data Processing Control Practices

No.	Description of Effective Control Practice
67.	**Use Remote Backup.** If continuing operation from an online system is absolutely necessary, and if two separate remote systems are justified, a duplicate file set and duplicate control tables should be maintained on both systems so that the basic data and the network context are available whenever the terminals are switched from the primary to the backup system. Some systems also require the log file with its before and after images to be maintained dynamically at both sites.

Workpaper A-62. Audit Recommendation Worksheet

Audit Finding
Recommendation
Economics of recommendation
Individual/area responsible
Reaction of responsible individual/area
Effect on people
Effect on system
Effect if no action taken

Prepared by:	Date:

Workpaper A-63. Report Objectives Worksheet

Audit
Report Name
Report Objective No. 1
Report Objective No. 2
Report Objective No. 3
Desired Action No. 1
Desired Action No. 2
Desired Action No. 3

Prepared by:	Date:

Workpaper A-64. Audit-Report-Writing Program

Audit _____

No.	Program Item	Assigned to	Completion Date
1.	Establish audit objectives and desired management actions (Workpaper 8-7-1). *Comments:* _____ _____		
2.	Gather audit findings (Workpaper 7-1-1), audit recommendations (Workpaper 7-4-1), and audit objectives (Workpaper 2-5-1), plus any other appropriate audit documentation. *Comments:* _____ _____		
3.	Develop report outline. *Comments:* _____ _____		
4.	Write a draft report. *Comments:* _____ _____		
5.	Have draft reviewed by others. *Comments:* _____ _____		
6.	Rewrite report. *Comments:* _____ _____		
7.	Have report properly edited. *Comments:* _____ _____		
8.	Have audit management review report correctness and readability (Workpaper 8-2-1 and 8-3-1). *Comments:* _____ _____		
9.	Make necessary corrections clear with management. *Comments:* _____ _____		
10.	Review report with auditee (Workpaper 8-4-1). *Comments:* _____ _____		
11.	Issue final report, follow up as necessary (Workpaper 8-4-2). *Comments:* _____ _____		

APPENDICES

Workpaper A-65. Report Reasonableness Checklist[1] (page 1 of 3)

Report: _____

No.	Item	Response		
		Yes	No	N/A
1.	Has the primary audience for the report been identified? *Comments/Actions to Take:* _____			
2.	Has the report been written for that audience? *Comments/Actions to Take:* _____			
3.	Has the accuracy of the findings been reviewed with the area affected? *Comments/Actions to Take:* _____			
4.	Have the recommendations been reviewed with the affected area to determine whether they agree with the recommendations and, if not, why not? *Comments/Actions to Take:* _____			
5.	Are findings and recommendations stated in enough detail for the affected areas to take action? *Comments/Actions to Take:* _____			
6.	Is there sufficient supporting evidence to substantiate findings and recommendations? *Comments/Actions to Take:* _____			
7.	Have report recommendations been evaluated in sufficient detail to determine the cost-effectiveness of implementation? *Comments/Actions to Take:* _____			
8.	Will the report be issued on a timely basis so that the maximum benefit from the identified findings and recommendations can be realized? *Comments/Actions to Take:* _____			
9.	Does the report either eliminate or explain technical jargon? *Comments/Actions to Take:* _____			
10.	Does the report follow good writing practices? *Comments/Actions to Take:* _____			

Workpaper A-65. Report Reasonableness Checklist (page 2 of 3)

Report: _____

No.	Item	Yes	No	N/A
		Response		
11.	Has the significance of report findings and recommendations for the application/area under review been determined? *Comments/Actions to Take:* _____			
12.	Has the source of the findings and recommendations been identified (if other than the auditor)? *Comments/Actions to Take:* _____			
13.	Has the individual responsible for responding to findings and recommendations been identified, and will the report be directed to that person? *Comments/Actions to Take:* _____			
14.	Is the scope of the report delineated? *Comments/Actions to Take:* _____			
15.	Is sufficient background material available so that the reader can put the findings and recommendations into the proper perspective? *Comments/Actions to Take:* _____			
16.	If findings or recommendations relate to vendor products, are the vendors identified? *Comments/Actions to Take:* _____			
17.	Does the report create a positive visual impression? *Comments/Actions to Take:* _____			
18.	Is the structure of the report appropriate for its scope, findings, and recommendations? *Comments/Actions to Take:* _____			
19.	Does the body of the report build a case for and support the recommendations? *Comments/Actions to Take:* _____			

Workpaper A-65. Report Reasonableness Checklist (page 3 of 3)

Report: _____

No.	Item	Response		
		Yes	No	N/A
20.	Has a marketing plan for the report been devised? *Comments/Actions to Take:* _____ _____			
21.	Is the length of the report reasonable, based on the scope, findings, and recommendations? *Comments/Actions to Take:* _____ _____			
22.	Has valuable but peripheral information been placed in the appendices instead of the body of the report? *Comments/Actions to Take:* _____ _____			
23.	Has an executive summary been prepared and, if so, is it marketing oriented? *Comments/Actions to Take:* _____ _____			
24.	Have follow-up dates for further action been determined in the event the affected areas fail to act promptly on report findings and recommendations? *Comments/Actions to Take:* _____ _____			
25.	Has the report gone through the proper review process? *Comments/Actions to Take:* _____ _____			
26.	Has the report been subjected to editing and formatting? *Comments/Actions to Take:* _____ _____			
27.	Has the final report version been proofread? *Comments/Actions to Take:* _____ _____			

[1] From Report Writing for EDP Auditors by William E. Perry, © 1982 William E. Perry Enterprises. Reprinted with permission.

Workpaper A-66. Report Readability Checklist[1] (page 1 of 3)

Report: _____

No.	Item	Response		
		Yes	**No**	**N/A**
1.	Is the tone of the report informative and courteous? *Comments/Actions to Take:*_____ _____			
2.	Are the findings easy to understand? *Comments/Actions to Take:*_____ _____			
3.	Are the recommendations easy to understand? *Comments/Actions to Take:*_____ _____			
4.	Has the accuracy of all the factual information in the report been verified? *Comments/Actions to Take:*_____ _____			
5.	Is the report concise and to the point? *Comments/Actions to Take:*_____ _____			
6.	Is the report written in a way that would provoke resentment on the part of the reader? *Comments/Actions to Take:*_____ _____			
7.	Does the report use positive words rather than negative words? *Comments/Actions to Take:*_____ _____			
8.	Has nonessential or lengthy information been moved to appendices? *Comments/Actions to Take:*_____ _____			
9.	Is the report written in the same manner in which someone would present the information orally? *Comments/Actions to Take:*_____ _____			
10.	**Is the report written using the active voice?** *Comments/Actions to Take:*_____ _____			
11.	**Do any of the sentences contain unnecessary words?** *Comments/Actions to Take:*_____ _____			

Workpaper A-66. Report Readability Checklist (page 2 of 3)

Report: _____

No.	Item	Yes	No	N/A
		Response		
12.	Does the report avoid long sentences when possible? *Comments/Actions to Take:* _____			
13.	Is each sentence as specific as possible? *Comments/Actions to Take:* _____			
14.	Does the report use action words that express the intent of the report? *Comments/Actions to Take:* _____			
15.	Are words grammatically arranged in their best order? *Comments/Actions to Take:* _____			
16.	Does the report use balanced or parallel construction where appropriate? *Comments/Actions to Take:* _____			
17.	Has repetition been avoided in the report? *Comments/Actions to Take:* _____			
18.	Are the tenses of verbs consistent? *Comments/Actions to Take:* _____			
19.	Are singular and plural forms mixed? *Comments/Actions to Take:* _____			
20.	Have ambiguous pronouns and antecedents been avoided? *Comments/Actions to Take:* _____			
21.	Have ambiguous modifying words been avoided? *Comments/Actions to Take:* _____			
22.	Have parenthetic expressions been avoided? *Comments/Actions to Take:* _____			
23.	Did the report stop when it had accomplished its mission? *Comments/Actions to Take:* _____			

Workpaper A-66. Report Readability Checklist (page 3 of 3)

Report: _____

No.	Item	Response		
		Yes	No	N/A
24.	Does the report avoid using the same word twice in a single sentence when each use of the word has a different meaning? *Comments/Actions to Take:*_____ _____			
25.	Has the report avoided using "it" when possible? *Comments/Actions to Take:*_____ _____			
26.	Has jargon been removed from the report? *Comments/Actions to Take:*_____ _____			
27.	Are uncommon words and showy language avoided? *Comments/Actions to Take:*_____ _____			
28.	Have people's names been deleted from the report except where essential to make a point? *Comments/Actions to Take:*_____ _____			
29.	Are the auditor's opinions clearly identified? *Comments/Actions to Take:*_____ _____			
30.	Has the report avoided unverified hearsay evidence? *Comments/Actions to Take:*_____ _____			
31.	If corrective action has been taken by the area under review, has that been noted in the report? *Comments/Actions to Take:*_____ _____			
32.	Have significant digits been rounded? *Comments/Actions to Take:*_____ _____			
33.	**Will the report be issued on a timely basis?** *Comments/Actions to Take:*_____ _____			
34.	Have the editorial comments been reviewed with the originator? *Comments/Actions to Take:*_____ _____			

¹ From Report Writing for EDP Auditors by William E. Perry, © 1982 William E. Perry Enterprises. Reprinted with permission.

Workpaper A-67. Exit Conference Program

Audit _____

No.	Program Item	Assigned to	Completion Date
1.	Arrange for room, date, and time. *Comments:* _____ _____		
2.	Invite appropriate personnel: auditee, DP, user. *Comments:* _____ _____		
3.	Prepare agenda. *Comments:* _____ _____		
4.	Prepare sufficient copies of report to distribute at meeting. *Comments:* _____ _____		
5.	Assign member of auditing staff to record minutes of meeting. *Comments:* _____ _____		
6.	Conduct conference. *Comments:* _____ _____		
7.	Debrief audit staff attending meeting. *Comments:* _____ _____		
8.	Make appropriate changes. *Comments:* _____ _____		

Workpaper A-68. Report Issuance and Follow-Up Program

Audit _____

No.	Program Item	Assigned to	Completion Date
1.	Prepare report distribution list. *Comments:* _____ _____		
2.	Prepare final report, including changes agreed to at conference. *Comments:* _____ _____		
3.	Proofread final report. *Comments:* _____ _____		
4.	Disseminate final report. *Comments:* _____ _____		
5.	Establish follow-up schedule. *Comments:* _____ _____		
6.	Document auditee action and/or follow-up to ensure that action is taken. *Comments:* _____ _____		
7.	Prepare list of audit suggestions for future audits, based on information obtained during this audit. *Comments:* _____ _____		

Workpaper A-69. Computer Application Audit Quality Control Checklist

Application: _____ **Completed by:** _____ **Date:**_____

Item	Response		
	Yes	**No**	**N/A**
Batch: Data Processing Integrity			
1. Has an audit assignment sheet been issued?			
*Comments:*_____ _____			
2. Does the project team fully understand the audit assignment tasks?			
*Comments:*_____ _____			
3. Is the time allocated reasonable for the tasks to be performed?			
*Comments:*_____ _____			
4. Have appropriate senior management personnel been interviewed to obtain any audit insight or background data they can supply?			
*Comments:*_____ _____			
5. Has the audit team discussed the audit with the director of the internal audit?			
*Comments:*_____ _____			
6. Has the audit team obtained and read all appropriate background documents?			
*Comments:*_____ _____			
7. Has the audit team determined whether the audit area has a history of problems?			
*Comments:*_____ _____			
8. Has the audit team determined whether any significant changes have been made in the audit area since the previous audit?			
*Comments:*_____ _____			
9. Has the auditor in charge provided guidance regarding how the audit should be conducted?			
*Comments:*_____ _____			
10. Have criteria been established to evaluate the audit's performance?			

Workpaper A-69. Computer Application Audit Quality Control Checklist

Application:_____ **Completed by:** _____ **Date:**_____

Item	Response		
	Yes	**No**	**N/A**
Comments: _____ _____			
11. Has the audit team identified any computer tests or programs that require advance preparation? *Comments:* _____			
12. Has Workpaper 1 -1 -1 *(Audit Assignment Interview Checklist)* been completed? *Comments:* _____			
13. Has Workpaper 1-1-2 *(Audit Success Criteria Worksheet)* been completed? *Comments:* _____			
14. Have the previous audit reports been obtained and reviewed? *Comments:* _____			
15. Have the previous audit workpapers been obtained and reviewed? *Comments:* _____			
16. Has the permanent file for this audit area been obtained and reviewed? *Comments:* _____			
17. Is the audit team familiar with short- and long-term DP plans? *Comments:* _____			
18. Does the audit team have access to the audit area's annual budget? *Comments:* _____			
19. Does the audit team have access to all third-party correspondence or memos regarding the application under review? *Comments:* _____			
20. Has the audit team determined whether previous audit findings and recommendations have been addressed adequately?			

Workpaper A-69. Computer Application Audit Quality Control Checklist

Application: _____ Completed by: _____ Date:_____

Item	Response		
	Yes	No	N/A
*Comments:*_____ _____			
21. Has the audit team gathered and reviewed all appropriate application system documentation? *Comments:*_____			
22. Did the audit team properly prepare for the entrance conference? *Comments:*_____			
23. Were the appropriate individuals invited to the entrance conference? *Comments:*_____			
24. Did the audit team document any problems or requests that were raised during the entrance conference? *Comments:*_____			
25. Were those items incorporated into the audit work plan when appropriate? *Comments:*_____			
26. Did the audit team perform a debriefing at the end of the entrance conference to ensure that all comments were documented? *Comments:*_____			
27. Has Workpaper 1-2-1 *(Preliminary Conference Background Information Checklist)* been completed? *Comments:*_____			
28. Has Workpaper 1-2-2 *(Conference Preparation Checklist)* been completed? *Comments:*_____			
29. Has Workpaper 1-2-3 *(Post-Conference Background Information Checklist)* been completed? *Comments:*_____			

Workpaper A-69. Computer Application Audit Quality Control Checklist

Application:_____ **Completed by:** _____ **Date:**_____

	Response		
Item	**Yes**	**No**	**N/A**
30. Have the appropriate data elements been identified and studied? Comments: _____			
31. Have all applicable file definitions and documentation been obtained and reviewed? Comments: _____			
32. Does the system documentation apply to the audit objectives identified? Comments: _____			
33. Has the audit team identified all the input transactions that apply to the audit objective? Comments: _____			
34. Has Workpaper 1-3-1 *(Input Transactions Worksheet)* been completed? Comments: _____			
35. Has Workpaper 1-3-2 *(Data File Worksheet)* been completed? Comments: _____			
36. Has Workpaper 1-3-3 *(Output Report and User Worksheet)* been completed? Comments: _____			
37. Have user opinions of computer reports been collected? Comments: _____			
38. Has Worksheet 1-3-4 *(User Satisfaction Questionnaire)* been completed? Comments: _____			
39. Has a data flow diagram been developed? Comments: _____			

Workpaper A-69. Computer Application Audit Quality Control Checklist

Application: _____ **Completed by:** _____ **Date:** _____

Item	Response		
	Yes	No	N/A
40. Does the data flow diagram show audit evidence? *Comments:*_____ _____			
41. Does the data flow diagram identify the responsible parties associated with each major application task? *Comments:*_____ _____			
Identifying Application Risks			
1. Have application system operating statistics been obtained? *Comments:*_____ _____			
2. Has the audit team obtained all application system documentation and status reports? *Comments:*_____ _____			
3. Has the audit team interviewed key application personnel to collect information about potential system risks? *Comments:*_____ _____			
4. Has the audit team identified the structural risk attributes associated with the application? *Comments:*_____ _____			
5. Has the audit team identified the technological risk characteristics associated with the application? *Comments:*_____ _____			
6. Has the audit team identified the size risk characteristics of the application? *Comments:*_____ _____			
7. Has Workpaper 2-1-1 *(Structural Risk Assessment)* been completed? *Comments:*_____ _____			
8. Has Workpaper 2-1-2 *(Technical Risk Assessment)* been completed?			

Workpaper A-69. Computer Application Audit Quality Control Checklist

Application:_____ Completed by: _____ Date:_____

Item	Response		
	Yes	No	N/A
Comments: _____			
9. Has the audit team assessed the magnitude of risk in the application?			
Comments: _____			
10. Has the audit work program been adjusted based on the magnitude of the identified risk?			
Comments: _____			
11. Has the audit team collected data concerning the business transactions processed by the application?			
Comments: _____			
12. Has a risk-assessment team been formed to evaluate specific application risks?			
Comments: _____			
13. Has a coordinator been named for the risk-assessment team?			
Comments: _____			
14. Does the risk-assessment team have access to the appropriate material?			
Comments: _____			
15. Has the risk-assessment team identified specific application risks?			
Comments: _____			
16. Has Workpaper 2-2-1 *(Risk Assessment Program)* been completed?			
Comments: _____			
17. Has Workpaper 2-2-2 *(Application Risk Worksheet)* been completed?			
Comments: _____			
18. Have the significant risks identified by the risk-assessment team been documented?			

Workpaper A-69. Computer Application Audit Quality Control Checklist

Application: _____ Completed by: _____ Date:_____

	Item	Response		
		Yes	No	N/A
	*Comments:*_____ _____			
19.	Has the audit program been adjusted according to the identified application risks? *Comments:*_____ _____			
20.	Have the application risks been ranked according to a reasonable ranking method? *Comments:*_____ _____			
21.	Has Workpaper 2-3-1 *(Application Risk Ranking)* been completed? *Comments:*_____ _____			
22.	Are the final audit objectives based on the risk associated with the application? *Comments:*_____ _____			
23.	Have measurable audit objectives been developed? *Comments:*_____ _____			
24.	Are the audit objectives consistent with the criteria that the director of internal audit uses to evaluate the success of the audit? *Comments:*_____ _____			
25.	Has Workpaper 2-5-1 *(Measurable Application Audit Objectives)* been completed? *Comments:*_____ _____			
26.	Does the audit team believe that the audit objectives are attainable with the allocated budget, schedule, and personnel? *Comments:*_____ _____			
27.	Has a formal audit plan been developed? *Comments:*_____ _____			
28.	Is the audit plan consistent with the audit assignment objectives?			

Workpaper A-69. Computer Application Audit Quality Control Checklist

Application:_____ **Completed by:** _____ **Date:**_____

Item	Yes	No	N/A
Comments: _____ _____			
29. Has Workpaper 2-6-1 *(EDP Application Audit Plan)* been completed? *Comments:* _____ _____			
30. Does the internal audit director agree with the audit plan? *Comments:* _____ _____			
31. Have audit resources been reallocated (if appropriate) to ensure that the audit plan can be accomplished? *Comments:* _____ _____			
Evaluating Internal Control			
1. Has the audit team obtained organizational charts for all involved areas? *Comments:* _____ _____			
2. Have appropriate individual job descriptions been obtained? *Comments:* _____ _____			
3. Has the audit team obtained the charter or mission for all areas under audit? *Comments:* _____ _____			
4. Have appropriate procedure manuals been obtained? *Comments:* _____ _____			
5. Has the audit team interviewed appropriate employees to clarify roles and responsibilities within the audited areas? *Comments:* _____ _____			
6. Has the audit team interviewed appropriate members of the DP project team to clarify their roles and responsibilities? *Comments:* _____			

Workpaper A-69. Computer Application Audit Quality Control Checklist

Application: _____ **Completed by:** _____ **Date:** _____

Item	Response		
	Yes	No	N/A
7. Have all the individuals involved in the application system been identified? *Comments:*_____			
8. Have all the appropriate actions in the application system been identified? *Comments:*_____			
9. Has Workpaper 3-1-1 *(Responsibility Conflict Matrix)* been completed? *Comments:*_____			
10. Have potential responsibility conflicts been identified on the conflict matrix? *Comments:*_____			
11. Have potential responsibility conflicts been identified for additional investigation and tests? *Comments:*_____			
12. Has Workpaper 3-2-1 *(Data Origination Controls Questionnaire)* been completed? *Comments:*_____			
13. Has Workpaper 3-2-2 *(Data Input Controls Questionnaire)* been completed? *Comments:*_____			
14. Has Workpaper 3-2-3 *(Data Processing Controls Questionnaire)* been completed? *Comments:*_____			
15. Has Workpaper 3-2-4 *(Data Output Controls Questionnaire)* been completed? *Comments:*_____			

Workpaper A-69. Computer Application Audit Quality Control Checklist

Application:_____ **Completed by:** _____ **Date:**_____

Item	Response		
	Yes	**No**	**N/A**
16. Have the questionnaires been customized for specific applications as appropriate? *Comments:* _____			
17. Have potential control vulnerabilities been identified? *Comments:* _____			
18. Has the audit team obtained and reviewed application control documentation? *Comments:* _____			
19. Has the audit team interviewed project and audit area personnel regarding control as appropriate? *Comments:* _____			
20. Has Workpaper 3-3-1 *(Data Flow Control Diagram)* been completed? *Comments:* _____			
21. Has Workpaper 3-3-2 *(Transaction Flow Control Diagram)* been completed? *Comments:* _____			
22. If potential control weaknesses have been noted, has the audit team attempted to identify whether compensating controls exist? *Comments:* _____			
23. Have all potential vulnerabilities been identified? *Comments:* _____			
24. Has the magnitude of each vulnerability been specified? *Comments:* _____			
25. Has Workpaper 3-4-1 *(Responsibility Vulnerability Worksheet)* been completed? *Comments:* _____			

Workpaper A-69. Computer Application Audit Quality Control Checklist

Application: _____ Completed by: _____ Date: _____

Item	Response		
	Yes	No	N/A
26. Has Workpaper 3-4-2 *(Transaction Vulnerability Worksheet)* been completed? *Comments:*_____ _____			
27. Has the audit work program been adjusted to take into account the tests needed to evaluate the identified control vulnerabilities? *Comments:*_____ _____			
28. If the vulnerabilities are of great magnitude, has the director of internal audit been notified?			
Testing Internal Control			
1. Has the auditor in charge confirmed the controls to be tested? *Comments:*_____ _____			
2. Has the method to test the controls been determined? *Comments:*_____ _____			
3. Has the responsibility for conducting the control tests been established? *Comments:*_____ _____			
4. Does the individual conducting the test know which test methods will be used? *Comments:*_____ _____			
5. Does the individual conducting the test have the necessary skills to perform the test? *Comments:*_____ _____			
6. Is appropriate system documentation available to assist in control testing? *Comments:*_____ _____			
7. Has Workpaper 4-1-1 *(Application Control Test Plan)* been completed?			

Workpaper A-69. Computer Application Audit Quality Control Checklist

Application:_____ **Completed by:** _____ **Date:**_____

		Response		
	Item	**Yes**	**No**	**N/A**
	Comments: _____ _____			
8.	Has each test condition been evaluated to determine whether it should be tested in a static or dynamic mode? *Comments:* _____ _____			
9.	Do the tests demonstrate that existing controls reject unauthorized values, codes, etc.? *Comments:* _____ _____			
10.	Do the tests show that controls are applied consistently? *Comments:* _____ _____			
11.	Do the tests cover the important conditions covered by the control? *Comments:* _____ _____			
12.	If the control tested depends on another control, have they been tested simultaneously? *Comments:* _____ _____			
13.	Has Workpaper 4-2-1 *(Designing the Control Test)* been completed? *Comments:* _____			
14.	Has the audit team taken sufficient time to ensure that the test process is correct? *Comments:* _____ _____			
15.	Has the audit team verified that the results from the tests are accurate and complete? *Comments:* _____ _____			
16.	Do the test results appear reasonable? *Comments:* _____ _____			
17.	Has Workpaper 4-3-1 *(Testing Controls)* been completed?			

Workpaper A-69. Computer Application Audit Quality Control Checklist

Application: _____Completed by: _____Date:_____

Item	Response		
	Yes	No	N/A
Comments:_____ _____			
18. Did the audit team identify the expected test results before conducting the test? Comments:_____ _____			
19. Have the test results been documented? Comments:_____ _____			
20. Has Workpaper 4-4-1 *(Evaluation of Tested Controls)* been completed? Comments:_____ _____			
21. Has the audit team compared the projected test results with the actual results? Comments:_____ _____			
22. Has the audit team verified the proper functioning of the test? Comments:_____ _____			
23. Has the audit team confirmed the correctness of the projected results? Comments:_____ _____			
24. Has the audit team made a general determination as to whether existing controls are adequate? Comments:_____ _____			
Testing Data Integrity			
1. Has the audit team identified the computer files on which findings and recommendations will be based? Comments:_____ _____			
2. Has the audit team identified the organizational structure of these files?			

Workpaper A-69. Computer Application Audit Quality Control Checklist

Application:_____ **Completed by:** _____ **Date:**_____

Item	Response		
	Yes	**No**	**N/A**
Comments: _____ _____			
3. Has the audit team identified the record formats for these records? *Comments:* _____ _____			
4. Has the size of the files been identified? *Comments:* _____ _____			
5. Has the statistical description of the file (e.g., mean, median, mode, standard deviation) been identified? *Comments:* _____ _____			
6. Has the audit team completed a statistical analysis showing the shape (e.g., skewness, kurtosis) of the file population? *Comments:* _____ _____			
7. Has the audit team completed a dollar-value analysis of a population of records in the file? *Comments:* _____ _____			
8. Has the content of any suspense items in the file been determined? *Comments:* _____ _____			
9. Has Workpaper 5-1-1 *(Computer File Survey)* been completed? *Comments:* _____			
10. Has the audit team evaluated the statistical analysis of the file to determine whether there are any findings? *Comments:* _____ _____			
11. Has a correctness proof been created for the test data? *Comments:* _____ _____			
12. Has the audit team established data tests in order to accomplish the stated measurable audit objectives?			

APPENDICES

Workpaper A-69. Computer Application Audit Quality Control Checklist

Application: _____ Completed by: _____ Date:_____

Item	Response		
	Yes	No	N/A
Comments:_____			
13. Has Workpaper 5-2-1 *(Data Audit Objective Test)* been completed? Comments:_____			
14. Has the audit team selected test tools that will operate on the available audit evidence? Comments:_____			
15. Does the audit team have the necessary skills to use the audit tools selected? Comments:_____			
16. Can the audit tools produce the needed results in accordance with the time allocated by the audit schedule? Comments:_____			
17. Have computerized test tools been used whenever appropriate? Comments:_____			
18. Has Workpaper 5-3-1 *(Test Tool Worksheet)* been completed? Comments:_____			
19. Have all output reports produced by the software been properly identified? Comments:_____			
20. Is there a way to verify that the test tool has performed correctly? Comments:_____			
21. Has the audit team verified the integrity of the computer files used for test purposes? Comments:_____			
22. Is the verification process reasonable, based on the content of the computer file?			

VI-200

Workpaper A-69. Computer Application Audit Quality Control Checklist

Application:_____ Completed by: _____ Date:_____

Item	Response		
	Yes	**No**	**N/A**
Comments: _____ _____			
23. Has Workpaper 5-4-1 (*File Integrity Program*) been completed? *Comments:* _____			
24. Has Workpaper 5-4-2 (*File Integrity Proof Sheet*) been completed? *Comments:* _____			
25. Have procedures been implemented to ensure that the tests perform correctly? *Comments:* _____			
26. Has each computer program been tested? *Comments:* _____			
27. Have the tests of the computer programs included verification of the functional logic? *Comments:* _____			
28. Have the tests of the computer programs evaluated the correctness of the structural logic? *Comments:* _____			
29. Has Workpaper 5-5-1 (*Structural Test Program*) been completed? *Comments:* _____			
30. Has Workpaper 5-5-2 (*Functional Test Program*) been completed? *Comments:* _____			
31. Have the tests been executed in accordance with the test plan? *Comments:* _____			
32. Have the results been evaluated for reasonableness? *Comments:* _____			

Workpaper A-69. Computer Application Audit Quality Control Checklist

Application: _____Completed by: _____ Date:_____

Item	Response		
	Yes	**No**	**N/A**
33. Do the results approximate what the audit team expected, and if not, have variances been investigated? *Comments:*_____			
34. Are the test results complete? *Comments:*_____			
35. Has Workpaper 5-6-1 *(Data Test Program)* been completed? *Comments:*_____			
36. Has Workpaper 5-6-2 *(Data Test Checklist)* been completed? *Comments:*_____			
37. Was the output in the expected format? *Comments:*_____			
38. Have all potential problems been noted in the workpaper documentation? *Comments:*_____			
39. Do the workpapers include the results of testing the software tools? *Comments:*_____			
40. Has Workpaper 5-7-1 *(Test Results Review)* been completed? *Comments:*_____			
Analyzing Audit Results			
1. Have all the audit findings been documented? *Comments:*_____			
2. Do the findings indicate the extent of control problems? *Comments:*_____			
3. Do the findings include the cause of any problems?			

Workpaper A-69. Computer Application Audit Quality Control Checklist

Application:_____ **Completed by:** _____ **Date:**_____

		Response		
	Item	**Yes**	**No**	**N/A**
	Comments: _____ _____			
4.	Has the audit team made recommendations for each finding? *Comments:* _____ _____			
5.	Is there a finding for each measurable audit objective? *Comments:* _____ _____			
6.	Has Workpaper 7-1 -1 *(Audit Finding Documentation)* been completed? *Comments:* _____ _____			
7.	Has Workpaper 7-2-1 *(Analysis of Finding)* been completed? *Comments:* _____ _____			
8.	Do personnel in the audited areas agree with the findings? *Comments:* _____ _____			
9.	Do the workpapers substantiate the findings? *Comments:* _____ _____			
10.	Have auditee personnel been given the opportunity to respond formally to the findings? *Comments:* _____ _____			
11.	Has Workpaper 7-3-1 *(Developing Recommendations)* been completed? *Comments:* _____ _____			
12.	Has Workpaper 7-4-1 *(Audit Recommendation Worksheet)* been completed? *Comments:* _____ _____			
13.	Are the economics of the recommendation included? *Comments:* _____ _____			

APPENDICES

Workpaper A-69. Computer Application Audit Quality Control Checklist

Application: _____ Completed by: _____ Date:_____

Item	Yes	No	N/A
14. Do the recommendations indicate who is responsible for implementing them? *Comments:*_____			
15. Do the recommendations indicate the responsible individual's reaction to the recommendation? *Comments:*_____			
16. Do the recommendations indicate their effect on personnel? *Comments:*_____			
17. Do the recommendations indicate their effect on systems? *Comments:*_____			
18. Has the audit team determined how the organization will be affected if no action is taken on the recommendations? *Comments:*_____			
19. If the findings or recommendations represent significant items, have the appropriate people been notified? *Comments:*_____			
20. Have relatively minor findings and recommendations been handled in a manner other than through a formal report? *Comments:*_____			
Reviewing and Reporting Findings			
1. Have the report objectives been clearly defined? *Comments:*_____			
2. Do the report objectives represent significant objectives? *Comments:*_____			
3. Do the report objectives encompass the stated audit objectives as defined in the audit assignment and audit program?			

Workpaper A-69. Computer Application Audit Quality Control Checklist

Application:_____ Completed by: _____ Date:_____

	Item	Response		
		Yes	**No**	**N/A**
	Comments: _____ _____			
4.	Has Workpaper 8-1-1 *(Report Objectives Worksheet)* been completed? *Comments:* _____ _____			
5.	Has Workpaper 8-1-2 *(Audit-Report-Writing Program)* been completed? *Comments:* _____ _____			
6.	Have the objectives been limited in number (preferably to three or fewer)? *Comments:* _____ _____			
7.	Has Workpaper 8-2-1 *(Report Reasonableness Checklist)* been completed? *Comments:* _____ _____			
8.	Has audit supervision reviewed the audit report? *Comments:* _____ _____			
9.	Has Workpaper 8-3-1 *(Report Readability Checklist)* been completed? *Comments:* _____ _____			
10.	Do auditee personnel have the opportunity to review the audit report before it is issued to senior management? *Comments:* _____ _____			
11.	Are auditee personnel's comments incorporated in or appended to the report before it is submitted to senior management? *Comments:* _____ _____			
12.	Has the report been prepared in a professional manner? *Comments:* _____ _____			

Workpaper A-69. Computer Application Audit Quality Control Checklist

Application: _____ Completed by: _____ Date:_____

	Item	Response		
		Yes	No	N/A
13.	Has the report been distributed to the appropriate personnel?			
	Comments:_____			
14.	Has an exit conference been scheduled or conducted before the report's issuance?			
	Comments:_____			
15.	Is there a reasonable follow-up program to ensure that findings and recommendations are acted on as stated?			
	Comments:_____			
16.	If findings and recommendations are not acted on promptly, is there a program to enforce action?			
	Comments:_____			
17.	Has Workpaper 8-4-1 *(Exit Conference Program)* been completed?			
	Comments:_____			
18.	Has Workpaper 8-4-2 *(Report Issuance and Follow-Up Program)* been completed?			
	Comments:_____			
19.	Has the audit been critiqued to identify how it might be improved in the future?			
	Comments:_____			
20.	Have recommendations and comments regarding future audits been documented and filed so that the next audit team can retrieve and use them?			
	Comments:_____			

Workpaper A-70. Audit Performance Problem Worksheet (Blank)

Audit_____

No.	Audit Problem	Description of Problem	Significance of Problem/ Potential Solution

Workpaper A-71. Audit Performance Problem Worksheet

Audit _____

	Improvement Needed			Problems Identified by the Audit Team
Item	Yes	No	N/A	
1. Did you understand the steps/tasks that needed to be performed to execute the audit?				
2. Did you understand how to complete the workpapers associated with the individual audit tasks?				
3. Do you believe the steps and tasks were executed in a logical sequence?				
4. Do you believe that the workpapers were constructed in a format that made it easy to complete the workpapers? (Note: This may have to be done workpaper by workpaper.)				
5. Do you believe that two or more of the workpapers, or parts of various workpapers, could be combined to make the completion of the workpapers more effective?				
6. Do you believe other questions need to be added to the checklists included with the workpapers?				
7. Do you believe there are steps in the audit process that do not need to be performed, or parts of steps or tasks that do not need to be performed?				
8. Do you believe there are tasks that should be performed which are not included in the audit process?				
9. Do you believe there are better ways to perform some of the tasks included in the audit process?				
10. Do you believe you were properly trained or prepared to perform the audit before it started?				
11. What was the most difficult task that you had to perform during the audit?				
12. What task or activity caused you to make the most errors or waste the most time during the conduct of the audit?				
13. Do you believe you had the proper tools and workpapers to perform the audit most effectively and efficiently?				

Workpaper A-72. Audit Process Problem Cause Identification Worksheet

<u>**Similar Audit Problem**</u>

<u>**How Problems Identified (Reference)**</u>

<u>**Process/Workpapers Involved**</u>

<u>**Skills Needed/Existing**</u>

<u>**Root Cause of Problem**</u>

Workpaper A-73. Audit Process Improvement Recommendation Worksheet

Root Cause of Problem		
Potential Solution	**Advantages**	**Disadvantages**
Solution Selected		
Implementation Plan		
Date Implemented		

T - #0349 - 101024 - C0 - 279/216/39 [41] - CB - 9781138436930 - Gloss Lamination